BREAKING IN®

OVER 130 ADVERTISING INSIDERS REVEAL HOW TO BUILD
A PORTFOLIO THAT WILL GET YOU HIRED

Interviews by
William Burks Spencer

TUK TUK PRESS

Breaking In® Over 130 Advertising Insiders Reveal How to Build a Portfolio That Will Get You Hired

Second Edition

Interviews by William Burks Spencer

Bulk purchases: This book may be available at a discount for large quantities for educational use. Please email bulk@tuktukpress.com

Permissions: To contact the publisher regarding permission to re-publish portions of this book, please email permissions@tuktukpress.com

To contact the publisher for any other reason, please email hello@tuktukpress.com

ISBN Number: 978-0-615-41219-1

TABLE OF CONTENTS

INTRODUCTION
WILLIAM BURKS SPENCER
INTERVIEWER
BREAKING IN® ADVERTISING

What's this all about?

This book uses original interviews with the top people in advertising to teach you how to build a great advertising portfolio. Over one hundred insiders explain what they look for in a portfolio and provide practical advice that will help you get noticed and land your ideal job. The interviewees are industry professionals with experience hiring people for creative positions within advertising agencies. From agency founders and global chief creative officers to copywriters and art directors to creative recruiters, working for a variety of different types of agencies: big, small, digital, traditional, and the full range in between. Some experienced and brilliant freelancers, film directors, and ad school presidents have been included for good measure. Read this if you are serious about getting a creative job in advertising.

And who are you exactly?

I am a copywriter. I have worked for agencies including Wieden+Kennedy, Portland, London & Shanghai; Crispin Porter + Bogusky, Boulder & Miami; BBDO, New York & London; Mother, London; BBH, New York; JWT, New York & London; Leo Burnett, Chicago; La Comunidad, Miami; MTV, New York; Y&R, New York; TBWA, New York and others on brands such as Nike, Google, Powerade, Target, Nokia, Starbucks, and Virgin. I have also taught advertising at Miami Ad School in London and Pratt Institute in New York and given talks on advertising at Princeton University, Columbia Business School, and Miami Ad School in Hamburg. I have degrees from Princeton University and VCU Brandcenter.

Why did you decide to do this?

The advertising industry has gone through enormous changes in the past decade. Those changes continue today. The result is turmoil, uncertainty, experimentation, and opportunity—both in the industry in general and in the process of demonstrating skills and getting hired. There is a growing diversity of opinion about what makes a good portfolio, even as some things remain consistent. This book captures those different viewpoints and provides a direct line of communication from the people in a position to hire to those trying to get jobs. This book is something I wish I'd had when I was building my own portfolio. After knocking on a few doors and explaining the idea for the project, I was blown away by how nice, helpful, and eager to contribute everyone was. Every interview provided more encouragement that this would become an amazing resource for people interested in getting into advertising. Now in its second edition, the book contains more wisdom from more fantastic people than I ever could have imagined.

Who is this book for?

Anyone who wants to put together a portfolio (often called a "book") and get into advertising. If you are considering advertising as a career path, this will give you a better idea of what it's all about and what it takes to get in. For people currently working on their books, either in an ad school or independently, this will provide practical advice, lessons to live by and inspiration to go further.

Do you have any advice about reading this advice?

If you are new to advertising, you might want to just flip through and learn about the business and whether or not it is for you by reading different perspectives. If you are in ad school, recently graduated, or working in advertising already, you may know more about what agencies or people you want to work for. In that case, you may want to make friends with the table of contents and flip around to people and agencies you know and admire.

What's new in this updated version?

I added 29 new interviews with Creative Directors from all over the world. The collection is now more global and will help more students in more places get the job they want.

If I find a typo do I win anything?

Yes, our sincere thanks and appreciation. Please email us at: updates@breaking.in

Anything else?

Thank you for reading. Let's get started. BI

What do you look for in a student book? And what impresses you?

I look for intelligence, I think. It's not so much the packaging, or the choice of media, or necessarily how finished something is, but I look for something that makes me think, "I bet that the person who made that is a smart guy or a smart girl and I just want to learn more about that person." And I know that's a bit vague, but I think you have to look at something and go, "Did it take a little bit of wit, or insight, or knowledge of some sort to come up with that solution?" And then I think it's good. That gets me interested in seeing more.

You said you're not that concerned about the finish necessarily; do you think sketches can be enough these days, or not?

It's kind of a sliding scale. I think that I'd be lying if I said that I would prefer something that was unfinished. I think that we all pride ourselves on saying we're looking for something smart and it doesn't matter what form it takes. That said, polish can't hurt. It's just the old "polishing a turd" cliché that I think is absolutely true—it's not going to help if the idea's not there.

But what I wouldn't suggest is poking at something. I think we do this, whether it's a student book or an actual commercial you're working on. It's like poking at a dead thing on the road: the more you poke at the dead frog, it's going to start to fall apart. You've got that stick and you're just trying to tweak this, and push that. At best, no one's going to notice and it won't really matter. You're just wasting your time. At worst, you're actually going to make it worse and it's going to start to fall apart. So I think that you have to use trusted opinions around you because sometimes you get so close to something that you're not sure when to say, "Okay, pencils down. This is good enough to communicate the idea—that's all I need to do."

Now, there's lots of different jobs out there. If you're more design heavy or if you're hoping to get a studio job [it's different]. Certainly a lot of art directors would probably have a different answer. They are going to be looking for execution. But as far as I'm concerned, if a sketch can deliver that little flash of genius, or intelligence, then you're done—time to move to the next thing.

Are there other common mistakes or traps that you think people can fall into?

The big one is the desire to have something that ran—that was produced. I definitely think that that's not of value to someone. To a creative director, we know that lots of the worst ideas are the ones that get produced. So there's really no qualitative difference there. It's not some sort of "star" that the thing was produced. It doesn't make the idea suddenly better. It just means that some client bought it. And as creative directors, we should know well enough to make our own decisions about what's good or bad. So I wouldn't substitute out that thing that you think is great but wasn't produced for that kind of bullshit, throwaway, mediocre thing that some client was willing to run in the back of a magazine just because they did.

Do you think it's important to have a long copy campaign in your book?

Actually, I don't think print is even a factor anymore. Long copy, short copy, or no copy.

Really? So you don't want to see any print at all?

Right. To us, print is a dead medium.

Can you evaluate craft and campaign ideas when they are so intertwined with ideas that are more about how to use technology?

Yeah, I think that's the challenge. But great ideas done in new media should still be able to demonstrate the same intelligence and ability.

So then is writing important in digital media and do you want to see people demonstrate that in their work?

Yes, exactly. At least for copywriters, there's no reason why the ability to write can't come through. Whether it's literally the copy on a website or their social-media posts or even the way the individual writes about the application or stunt or mobile piece that they've chosen to include in their portfolio. Anything you write is an opportunity to demonstrate your writing ability. So it should be used that way.

What do you think about putting things in a book that aren't ads?

As an addendum I think it's great. It's all about self-editing and being really, really hard on yourself to say, "Yeah, this thing is great." Don't just pile it on for the sake of volume. But if you have a short story or a web application that was lauded and you think it's some of the best work you've ever done, put it in there. The thing is…it's slightly different for something like short stories and photography for art directors because it's all about holding attention span. And so if your short story's competing with a bunch of other quick stuff, it's a lot easier for me to flip the pages through the ads than to actually sit and get comfy in my chair and put my feet up and spend 10 minutes reading a story. So I am absolutely guilty of passing over short stories that may have potentially been the greatest thing since Mark Twain, but I didn't read them. So what I would suggest is that, if there's some fun or funny way of flagging the short story to say, "If you look at nothing else in this book, at least read this story." Put yourself out there. Commit to it, because otherwise, I would give short stories probably an 80 percent pass-over rate. And I'd hate to think that the aspiring copywriter felt like that was the best thing in their book and it never got read. So, like any other human being, a creative director is going to absorb the things that are quickest and easiest to absorb. And for art directors, photography's certainly easy—just takes a look. So you just have to keep that in mind.

Do you have any tips for someone who's trying to get into the business? Either on how to put a book together or how to improve?

I think constant exposure to really good work is absolutely a surefire way of doing it. And I think it's not just being aware of what's out there but figuring out little mental exercises for yourself on analyzing why they're great. So one drill I think is good—it's actually good for writing in general, and it came to me after doing this as a writer. There is an author that I love,

Philip Dick, who is a great short story writer. He's got a very unique style. So, just as a writing exercise, I tried to start writing Philip Dick short stories. So I'd come up with a concept of the story, the plotline, but then I would try and write it exactly like he would've written it. Just to understand how his brain worked. And I think you can do the same thing with ads. I think you can, if you see a spot on television that you love, you can go home and write the script yourself, and look at it and go, "What is it that worked? How did it change from script to execution? What role did the execution play?" But also I think looking at the script is a better way of saying, "What is it about that thing that really struck me?" So it's not just being exposed to great work and saying, "Yeah I like that" or, "I don't like that," but really analyzing it and deconstructing it.

> *"THERE HAS NEVER BEEN A TIME LIKE THIS, I DON'T THINK, FOR JUNIOR FOLKS TO BE NEEDED FOR SOMETHING THAT THEY CAN DO, THAT MORE SENIOR PEOPLE JUST CAN'T. THAT IS AN AWESOME OPPORTUNITY. SO USE IT."*

And then, as far as kind of getting a leg up, or making a go of it, I think new technology raises the expectations of juniors these days. As the "media landscape" shifts, the old-timers and the more senior people are going to be looking for people who bring expertise that they don't have. So being willing—not only being willing, but eager—to take, to tackle the assignments that you know somewhere in the agency people are not capable of doing. There has never been a time like this, I don't think, for junior folks to be needed for something that they can do, that more senior people just can't. That is an awesome opportunity. So use it. [BI]

To see Mark Fitzloff's work, please visit http://breaking.in

ANT KEOGH
EXECUTIVE CREATIVE DIRECTOR
CLEMENGER BBDO
MELBOURNE

What do you look for in a student portfolio? And what impresses you?

I suppose it's looking at things in a different way. Solving a problem with a different angle than most people would come up with and yet one that's still somewhat practical. An imaginative approach is what you're initially looking for, although if you get completely crazy ideas without any sense of practicality then that's too easy. Because advertising is that mix of lateral and logical thinking. Worse though is if it's too buttoned down, because it's easier to teach that than to teach raw creative instinct. You want to turn each page and say, "Great idea, great idea, great idea." And it doesn't matter if they are pencil drawings or the most simple version of an idea, if that idea shines through. But you just want to see a succession of them so you get a sense for their "strike rate" in problem solving.

My next question was going to be about finish and polish.

My initial reaction is, "No, I don't want to see that." But if it's great finish then it's okay, especially for art directors. The danger is in being halfway. It's either got to be a sketch or it's got to be really beautifully designed. I wouldn't say that about writers, but, for art directors, it will count against them if the finish is only halfway there.

And what about writing? For writers do you like to see evidence of writing ability, or is it all about thinking?

Maybe a little evidence of writing. Maybe one thing. But it's more about ideas. Although now we're looking for more people to write in the digital space and then the writing becomes much more paramount. And I'm really looking for style there. We were looking for someone to essentially write the blogs for a client the other day, and it's completely about great writing and not so much ideas, though that would be good too.

What about showing work that is not advertising?

I love to see that. But it's more a back-of-the-book kind of thing. I'm looking for how you solve a particular kind of problem that is much more defined. So the other stuff is a bonus I guess. You need to have some sort of commercial sense.

Do you think print is still important, or is it dead and it shouldn't go in a book?

I guess I wouldn't distinguish it that way. Print is often a great medium to put in a folio. Television (in storyboard form) is usually a really bad medium in a folio. It might not be true to what the actual job is but in some ways a folio is its own medium. And in some ways you've got to play to that. And if you're flipping through or clicking through, print works really well. It used to be the case that you'd want a lot of posters so you could flip through and do that thing of "Idea, idea, idea, great, great, great." It's the most immediate space for an idea in a two-dimensional medium. These days I'm looking at a lot of folios on the web and maybe it's not so true.

How do you prefer to see work?

I probably see more folios online now. What do I prefer? I think it's more effective if someone comes in. Because it's so much about whether they fit into the team. On the other hand it's much more efficient online. So I quite like it if someone sends me a link. I have a folder on my computer where I put people's PDFs.

Can you think of any remarkable portfolios that you've seen?

No. I can't recall any incredible portfolios, apart from the senior people. At the junior end they all have a mixture of good work, okay work, and often some bad work. The people we've employed have had, in comparison to all the others, pretty good folios. And then it also does come down to the person. If their work is pretty damn good then we take a chance on them if they just feel like they have what it takes and will be able to do it. I hope that's not discouraging. It probably should be encouraging because it shows that a folio doesn't have to be perfect, it just has to show a lot of promise.

Are there common mistakes that you see?

The mistake I see the most is not one that is so easy to fix, which is that the tone is often just a little off. It just doesn't show an understanding of human psychology and it's just off the mark. And I guess that's something that comes with experience or innate ability. But that's the talent: to do something that's appealing on a human level.

"AT LEAST IF YOU KNOW IT'S BORING, THAT'S A START."

It's like they are not emotionally mature enough to see that or something. Or they've gotten too caught up in the brief. Or it's boring. That's the big one, but then everyone has that problem. We all fight that day to day. But it's being able to see that, it's the difference between someone who's a professional and someone who's not. At least if you know it's boring, that's a start.

Do you have any other advice for students or juniors?

One trick is to ask the person you're seeing to give you recommendations for other people to see, if you sense that they like you or they think you have potential. And it depends on your own feeling about doing this, but it might be worth offering to work for free for a month or something. My first work was through just asking for some briefs. I can't remember if we asked for just some old briefs or a live brief but we were given a live brief. I teamed up with a guy from AWARD School and we went to Y&R and did what I'm saying. And they ended up running the work that we did. And they offered us a job after the work we did won an award. But it was too late because we were already working somewhere else. But doing that shows enthusiasm, and you also might get to make some work. And the other thing is to just focus on the work and make something great. Focus on that and make something that people love. And everything else will follow. ▣

To see Ant Keogh's work, please visit http://breaking.in

**MARK WAITES
CREATIVE PARTNER
MOTHER
LONDON**

What do you look for in a student book? And what impresses you?

Just great thinking. The quality of the thinking has to be fantastic. It has to be great, great solutions. I understand that the person in front of me might not be the finished article, but I have to see something, some base metal, that I know I can work with. Yes, if I'm looking at an art director, I want to see great design—really, really competent and professional and original stuff. And if I'm looking at a writer, I want to see somebody who's a great writer, but that is not the most important thing. The most important thing is that they have that spark.

What do you not like to see?

Well, dullness. One of the problems is—and anybody who's worked in this industry knows—that the really bad and the really good are dead easy to spot because they occupy the bottom and top two percent. And what we do really is we just sort of swim around in this gray world most of the time with some things being a little bit grayer than others. And that's a lot of what we see when we look at students' work is a lot of that grayness, you know? One thing I find myself saying to students a lot is, "I can see that you now know the construction of an advertising campaign, or about being single-minded and finding a tone of voice and all that good stuff, but now you've just got to concentrate on making the work better." They've found a look, a font, or a style of photography, or whatever, and they've stuck with that over the length of a campaign, whatever form that'll take, and they've found a particular tone of voice and they have a strategy and they tick all the boxes except, "Is it good?" And I think that's one thing I'm not looking for, but one thing we see more often than not is that: normality, I suppose.

What about sketches, or do you like to see finished, polished work?

I don't mind, however people want to do it. One of the problems is…don't be too precious about it. I've seen students before who have had their work laminated and they have taken work to a level where I wonder if I offer my advice, whether they're going to listen to me because I'm suggesting they go back and redo all this beautiful work. Sometimes I think a student might be a bit reluctant to do that, particularly if they've had it beautifully printed or bound into a book. But I don't mind. Some degree of finish is good, particularly for a designer, because this person is going to have to work with us. So if they have no Mac skills, I know they're going to be a drain on somebody else. It just shows that you can do the job. It just shows that you can be immediately employable. And I think that's something that I'm looking for and I think other creative directors would be looking for, is just somebody that can contribute immediately.

Do you like to see a long copy campaign in the book?

Not necessarily. I've never written one and I don't expect someone to do something that I've never done. But that's not to say a student shouldn't show long copy—just make sure it's great. But it's not something I'm particularly looking for. Truth be told, if a kid came in here with just a half-hour of the best stand-up [comedy] I've ever seen, that's as good a book as you're going to get. It's quality. But the fact that it hasn't been translated into an advertising campaign is neither here nor there. Because I think I can teach them to write an advertising campaign. To sort of harness their thinking and have it play out in that arena. But I don't think you can really teach people how to be extremely funny or have a different take on the world. Or just see things differently. That comes from somewhere else.

And that's starting to get into my next question which is, do you like to see things other than ads in a book?

Yes. But you must understand there are no rules as to what makes up a great book—they are only guidelines. I've seen books that have just been anything but an ad and that's a little frustrating because there is a discipline at work with an ad. It's a bit like how great screenplays are all about economy, and it's because

there's a discipline—taking your story and making it work. And I think taking all your mad thinking and making it work in a campaign, or in 30 seconds even, that's a good thing.

"…THERE ARE NO RULES AS TO WHAT MAKES UP A GREAT BOOK—THEY ARE ONLY GUIDELINES."

It's a discipline and it's a good discipline. And again, it points at a willingness to work and get involved, and it points at the fact that, yeah, we can probably use them…this person can contribute immediately because they've applied their thinking. It shows a willingness to apply a discipline, because I think anyone can sit down and do crazy cartoons like David Shrigley—perhaps not as good as David Shrigley—but it takes another kind of person to apply themselves to one discipline.

So ideally you'd like to see both?

Yeah, I've just used the example of, "if a kid came in here with the most amazing stand-up routine," I'd love to employ that person, but they'd have to be exceptional. This is the thing, unless you're going to be absolutely exceptional, then you're going to have to knuckle down and do a bit of the discipline because…I use the example of the art director—someone who has no Mac skills. Well, they're going to be a drain on someone else. But if they've managed to convey that unbelievable creativity, the type of creativity that you would be an idiot to pass up an opportunity to work with that person [then it's a different story]. Some students don't have a lot of Mac skills but [I say], "Commit to learning that when you come in, I want you to do all the training, all the tutorials, and all that kind of stuff. Get involved." Because they've been really exceptional, creative individuals, so I'm willing to overlook a weakness.

But it doesn't have to be [all ads]. For a student to come in and have a book full of billboards and 30-second TV ads shows that they're not really living in the real world. This is some kind of advertising heaven as it was. I'm 45 years old, and I'm looking for kids to teach me things. Because I know there's a whole bunch of really exciting things happening out there that I'm not invited into. And they don't happen on billboards and TV commercials like they used to. They happen on websites, and in discussion groups, and on the Internet. I'm looking for work that could live in the real world, and that, I think, will contribute and will make a difference to a piece of business. I think that's one thing: everything we do, as well researched as it is, and as much research and development that clients have done with their new products, it's always only ever going to be a shot in the dark.

So what we do is—and we'd like to think we've become pretty good at it—looking at something and going, "I'm going to guess that that's going to work. I'm going to guess that that's what the audience wants to hear about a product that they want to buy. And that's playing out in an environment or in a way that I think they're going to really like and engage with." And we apply that as well when we're looking at student books. And it's the same when we judge advertising and marketing awards. We don't know anything about that brief, we don't know anything about that product, and we don't know anything about that market, but I'm guessing that that idea will sell. We do it a lot. Right or wrong, and that will be employed when we're judging a book.

But then again, you know what? If a kid came in here...and it would be to their detriment if it was all 30-second ads and billboards, but if every billboard looked brilliant and every ad was brilliant and it was like Cliff Freeman on his best day, you're not going to overlook that talent. Because, and that's the other thing I think, is something that I've said a couple of times: we're never looking for the finished product. But there has to be enough of that special thing there—the basic substance, whatever it is—to work with.

And last question, do you have any tips for someone who's just starting out?

Just be great. And work really hard. I say this to kids all the time: "Look around your group. There's

20 or so other students in your year...that's your competition. But then there are 40 other classes like this meeting at this moment in England, that's your competition. And in Sweden, France, America, Brazil, and they all want to work at the same few agencies. They're all going to New York and want to work for the same few agencies. They're coming here and wanting to work for the same few agencies. And they're going to Amsterdam, and wanting to work for the same few." It's a really, really crowded market. And they need to understand that in order to understand just how hard they've got to work to get in any of those shops. Very few people are going to be so smart that they don't have to work at getting a job. Everyone else is going to have to put in lots and lots of energy, just working to get a start.

Do you think it's getting harder and harder?

Yeah. Maybe it's always been hard. But from where I am it just looks like it's so much hard work. I think the world's opened up now. I think that, to my last point, kids from over the world will now compete for jobs here, whereas at one time it was kids from all over the UK, and maybe one or two...some bizarre waifs and strays who just landed from Australia or Singapore. Now I think that, with the Internet, it's really opened up. But then I think there are opportunities. I think there's an opportunity now for kids to come in and tell a couple of old farts like me and him what it's like out there. Just how people are consuming messages and advertising and where one thing ends and the other starts as well...it's a whole new world out there. Nowadays you need an online product, don't you? Some people say, "Oh, we're going to have a game." And then Nike came along and said, "Actually we're going to do Nike+." And that's an online version of Nike and it's a contribution to that environment. And it's not like, "We've got cool jeans, and we've got a 10 million dollar budget, we're going to do some cool ads." It's just not that easy anymore. So I think there's an opportunity for people to come in and tell us how it is because I don't think we know. Well, we don't know enough. That's what I think. BI

To see Mark Waites's work, please visit http://breaking.in

What do you look for in a student book? And what impresses you?

Whenever we've hired people, it's always—and it's probably a cliché—but it's always the things they bring alongside the book. So sometimes, for example, we hired a young Scottish writer here a year ago, I think. I had seen his portfolio. He sent a PDF and there were all these odd mock-ups he made in London, and [for] another agency here. There were ads, and they were quite nice but it wasn't really showing any of his personality. And then he came again. I read his portfolio, then we chatted, and it was the same work—another couple of odd campaigns he made, produced while working his first job—and then he had a little bag with him. He was too shy to take it out, and he was probably thinking, "I don't have enough time." So I asked what was in there. He showed me, it was filled with his writing and it was great. I mean it was laugh-out-loud funny and he made his own illustrations which were good—really nice quality and very expressive and they told a lot more than the ads. We hired him on that basis. It's good to know that you can make an ad, but in the end we always hire people based on their free work.

The other thing we hire them on is just their personality. I mean, there's 35 people here and you're on top of each other all the time. There are no departments, so you kind of overlap with everyone and you can get in each other's way, so you have to be a pretty nice person to be able to deal with that without turning into an asshole.

And I remember Johan and Erik, the founders [Johan Kramer and Erik Kessels]. They hired creatives here and they didn't see their book at all. I think they hired one creative because he was a nice guy and he used to play professional football and they're both really big football fans. They knew there was a connection and he turned out to be a really, really good writer. So I

think for us these are the two things. The second one you can't get by email.

Nowadays everyone is too busy. You get emails of PDFs of books and you kind of flip through them really quickly and it's a little bit of a shame, but I would say to present your work in such a way that maybe…the best ones I've seen are the ones who have their own website where their free work is also there and I usually go straight to that and it says something about their personality without seeing them.

As far as the ads go, do you think sketches are okay or do you like to see finished work?

Sketches are fine. But it's good to see that somebody knows their way around a Mac because, especially here, we don't have a studio so everyone finishes their own work. And we're happy to present with mock-ups—just sketches, and we're happy to see sketches—but in the end it's good to know because you need to do it all yourself. Everyone is responsible for their own presentations and we don't have a DTP studio or anything like that to do that for you, so if you can't do it yourself, you have to find a way. And I don't think it's the basis of the job but it does help.

"STRIKE UP A RELATIONSHIP WITH SOMEONE YOU CLICK WITH."

So for art directors, it's nice to see design skills.

A little bit, yeah…

For writers, do you want to see copy?

Yeah, for sure. But I don't know the last time I really wrote a piece of copy in an ad. I'd like to see that for sure, if it's very quick, of course. The way it is here, as I said, things overlap. The writers do a lot of the strategy, and strategy helps the writer, and the two work very closely together. So you end up writing a presentation with strategies. So you need to be able to write…I'd rather see a good presentation than a funny piece of advertising copy or I'd rather see a short story.

We hired a writer from Kentucky here. He had a book and a website called "Very, very short stories." I think they were about three lines long but he had hundreds of them, and you could flip through them and see how good a writer he is with these stories. But for a writer, design skills are not necessary. There's much more multidiscipline students now than when I was a student. There were no computers, which was not so long ago but it feels like a long time ago in terms of where students are now. When I went to college it was just, "You're a writer, you are an art director, you're a designer." It was much more separate. Now it's a bit mixed up, I think. I hope.

So, I was gonna ask you if you like to see things that aren't ads in a book, but you already answered it right away.

I think a lot of agencies don't have time for it but then it depends on what you want as a student. If they don't have time for it then maybe they're not the right place for you. If you're more into the crafting of the ads then show them the ads, and they're really the right place for you. In a way, it's a two-way interview. You need to know it's the right agency for you, and they need to know that you're right for their agency.

What would be one piece of advice for students that are trying to improve or trying to get jobs?

I'd give you the one that Steve Henry gave me. I went to college in London. I had a kind of outside ambassador: Steve Henry from Howell Henry. He was a very nice, very smart guy and he told me to do what I didn't do and I wish I had: to find somebody—an ambassador—and keep seeing them. And don't go there once to show your book and never go back again. Just go there every week. And you're not hassling them, and they help you grow. And I saw Steve Henry twice a year in the year I had him as an ambassador and that was a waste. So if you find someone you click with, keep seeing them and it will sharpen everything. And not even to get a job, but eventually, something will come of it for sure. Strike up a relationship with someone you click with. BI

To see Dave Bell's work, please visit http://breaking.in

CC TANG
CHIEF CREATIVE OFFICER FOR GREATER CHINA
HAVAS WORLDWIDE
HONG KONG

What do you look for in a student portfolio? And what impresses you?

That's a really difficult question to answer. I taught in the university in 2005, and the way I would look at a student's portfolio was to see whether they knew how to see life. And organized it so they didn't show you everything they had done since primary school. People are not interested in how you learned to draw, how you learned Photoshop, how you learned to do a layout. But I really want to know how you look at things. How you communicate a message which can persuade people or connect with people.

So, first: are they being selective about what they put in their portfolio and how they organize it? And that applies to people in the industry. And, quite surprisingly, you'll see a copywriter or art director or ACD come to you with everything they've done from their first job to their latest work. Second, I like students to be able to articulate the reason behind the work. Because usually the work will not be D&AD quality—you don't expect that. But you expect it to be insightful. They look at something from their perspective and come up with a communication idea. Whether it's perfectly art-directed or perfectly written is not relevant. We're not looking for that. We're looking for people who bring a fresh perspective. That's what I'm looking for.

I still remember the website for AMV BBDO. For a period of time, all the work was sketches and storyboards on Post-its. I still remember one storyboard. The first frame showed the hood of a car. The second showed the car shaking a bit. And then it showed the whole car. And a line explained the shaking: "Introducing a bigger Volvo wagon for the family. It's time to make some babies." It gets the idea across without a high degree of finish. As my previous boss said, "If it's a good TV idea, you can sell it over the phone."

What about writing?

When they launched the BMW V6 engine, which was very powerful in those days, they used a line from a US president: "Speak softly and carry a big stick." It's a good line because it conveys that the engine is quiet but powerful. And there are a lot of expressions. If you can notice expressions and how people really talk and make use of that, it can be so powerful.

So headlines can be enough?

I think you need some [body] copy. I think long copy is getting more and more difficult. If something doesn't grab you and hit you over the head, you won't read on. I admire people like Neil French, David Abbott, and all those famous writers. The way they write is so punchy. And the rhythm is so motivating for you to read on. And, if you notice, they disrupt all the rules of grammar and conventional wisdom. And it's so engaging. But I must admit, in the Chinese copywriting arena we're lacking writing like this. And maybe it's a handicap of the language. Because the way we speak and write are slightly different. In Cantonese there will be a lot of expressions that are so colloquial. But when you put them in writing it is not as free and flexible.

Are print ads still important to you, or are you looking for more holistic, fully integrated ideas?

Personally, I like print ads. Because it's a creation that you can call your own. You can art-direct it. You can play with the type. You can write your copy. When you do TV, it involves a lot more people. Directors, film art directors, set designers, music composers, and a lot more people. You are trying to negotiate and compromise between all these people, and on top of that you still have the client. So print is more personal to me. And TV, digital, events, and everything else is a lot about collaboration.

But nowadays, the way I look at it, nothing is not digital and social anymore. Because if you do even a print ad and it's really good, people will share it. Whether you like it or not. Things can get famous overnight. The Evian Roller Babies had millions of hits in less than 24 hours.

What do you think of showing work that is not advertising?

When I was teaching, we had a program where students would work on real briefs. And we were working for the Hong Kong Airport Authority, trying to promote Terminal 2. And we had students from interior design, product design—not just ad students. So our solution was not what the brief was asking for. It was an installation and event. It was a giant chess board with airplanes in different colors. Like a playground. The whole thing was so unexpected that they decided to build it.

At Ogilvy, where I was trained, they had a saying which came from David Ogilvy himself: "When you hire people, hire people from other trades." The reason why he said that was that these people may see life differently. I think it's true. I feel that new ideas are when two old ideas meet for the first time. So if people come from other backgrounds, why not? I don't expect people I hired to contribute to the agency for the first year or 18 months. Because you have to invest a lot of time to train them. But this doesn't happen much anymore. Someone is hired and is put to work on a computer doing Photoshop or layouts or retouching, and after a year or two they become very good at that but they may not become a good communicator. Maybe what the industry is lacking now is investing in talent. And I don't believe the schools can do that. What you learn in school will be obsolete the day you walk out of school. Things are moving so fast.

"WHAT YOU LEARN IN SCHOOL WILL BE OBSOLETE THE DAY YOU WALK OUT OF SCHOOL."

One thing is to find programs where you work on real projects or ask tutors who are in the industry for real briefs. I don't know why, but when clients deal with agencies they are devils, but when they work with students they are angels. One example: Coca-Cola had a youth marketing project and they were so receptive to crazy ideas from students. Like letting teens create their own holiday and sponsoring it. Or making a vending machine that's like a piano, and when you buy something you can download music and that becomes a musical coupon to buy music from the web. There were a lot of crazy ideas, and they [Coca-Cola] were so receptive to students' fresh, unpolluted perspective. And even ideas that were fresh and unexpected and even dangerous.

Do you have any other advice?

Skills and craft and what you learn is not as important as a positive attitude. That is rare and hard to find. Sometimes if you ask someone why they joined the industry they cannot tell you. So I look for the right attitude first. Skills can be learned. BI

To see CC Tang's work, please visit http://breaking.in

DAVID CARTER
CHIEF CREATIVE OFFICER
CAMPBELL MITHUN
MINNEAPOLIS

What do you look for in a student book? And what impresses you?

Well, the first thing, regardless of if it's an art director or writer, is great ideas—pretty much that's it. Then, if it's a writer or an art director, it's "Is the writing good" or, "Is the design good or art direction good?" I mean, pretty simple…

If the ideas are good enough, could someone even get away with sketches? Does that depend on if they're the writer or art director?

I think that, in this day and age, people will expect you to have [finished ads]. If you're an art director, people will certainly want to see computer skills. Not like you have to be an expert in Photoshop, but you should know how to do that stuff. So if you don't have that in your book, it's probably more of a long shot. Unless the ideas are so great that somebody's willing to bring you in anyway. But I think it's important to show a level of craft, either with writing or art directing.

And on the writing side, is it important to have a long copy campaign or…

I don't know if I would say a long copy campaign, but even if there are a few lines in an ad, they should be well thought out and crafted just like the design should be. And certainly, if you're a writer, longer copy wouldn't be a bad thing if the idea is still good.

What do you think about putting things in a book that aren't ads at all?

I wouldn't necessarily look at that as part of the book. It might tell me, "Oh, they have other interests; they're not just an ad person." I think it would just flesh the person out more than anything. I wouldn't look at it as part of the book. It's like, "Okay, that's a great painting but have you solved any strategic problems?"

So maybe just for personality or flavor but you wouldn't really be evaluating the ideas on those things?

Yeah, I think it would just be a nice addition to get a sense for what kind of a person he or she is—the kind who wants to divulge their journal writings!

Do you have any other advice that you'd give to someone who is just starting out?

Putting a book together is a lot different today. I don't think people actually have physical books anymore, really. They just do everything online. I would say that fewer "great ideas" is better than more "okay ideas." I would try to solve some tough strategic problems. I think anybody can do a good ad for highlighter pens, or Wite-out, or stuff like that. I think it's more important if you can work on harder things. Unless it's just such a great idea no matter who it's for.

This is just my personal taste but I gravitate toward simpler [ideas]—the simpler the better—and more so in print than anything else. If it's a really "designy" thing, I don't have time for it, and I think most consumers don't have a lot of time for that anymore, so I think the ideas have to be more simple and clear. What else? It certainly seems like, in this day and age, having interactive ideas is very important too.

Do you have any thoughts on presenting those?

If you don't actually know how to build a site and it is just purely a spec thing, just comp a couple of the pages so you get what the idea is. As long as it is communicated clearly, I think [that's okay].

"...START WITH WHAT THE BIG IDEA IS AND THEN MOVE INTO DETAILS."

It seems like a lot of people are trying to do 360 campaigns that have tons of different elements. Do you have any thoughts on how to present those or what's important with those kinds of things?

Well, we struggle with that here on a daily basis—trying to present those kinds of ideas to clients—because they're really hard to present unless you have a really good client who can see the bigness of the idea and say, "Oh yeah! Okay, I get it." Because we've presented a lot of those kinds of things to clients and half an hour later you're still talking because there are so many different elements. So I guess I would say, start with what the big idea is and then move into details. I think, certainly here and at other agencies and maybe even in student books now, I think you fall into the trap of trying to come up with every single little thing that the idea could translate into. I don't think you necessarily need to do that as long as you have maybe three or four things where the idea is really clear and uses each medium to communicate that in the best way possible. So again, I think streamlining and keeping it simple is important so that, when somebody is clicking through the pages, they go, "Oh, yeah great TV spot," "Oh, yeah great web film," "Oh, yeah great event," or whatever it happens to be. Just so it's clear—that you can see the idea.

When people come to see you in person, do they have a physical book, or at that point have you already seen their website?

I think by that time you've seen it and you're just kind of talking to them. It's nice not to have to carry a big portfolio around.

Okay. Anything else?

Headhunters help. I don't know, the books that I've seen lately are—even in the past year—they're just too complex. I just clicked to it, and I didn't want to even look at it. Simplify, simplify, simplify! What is the idea? Communicate the idea as clearly, simply, and quickly as possible. And pare it down. I mean, if you had nine awesome, awesome things, there's no need for more. BI

To see David Carter's work, please visit http://breaking.in

NICOLAS ROOPE FOUNDER & ECD POKE LONDON

What form does a portfolio take for students and juniors who want to work here, usually?

They send a website. Because we're a digital agency I won't consider anything that's not. If they don't have a website then they're just not hired. It's as simple as that.Part of the process upon which we appoint people is: First, the portfolio comes in. It hits whoever at the studio it comes into. They have a quick skim of the site. If it's good, then they'll forward it to other people, and then, ultimately, we'll set up a meeting. So it's very difficult to get in without any folio. There has to be some kind of evidence of talent from a design or creative point of view. The same is true for writers, programmers, technicians, engineers. All of the evidence of their abilities should be available to see online, otherwise, again, they just aren't hired.

So what impresses you in a student portfolio website? What do you look for?

Originality and raw ideas, and some ability to form them into something usable. Communication is really a mix of all kinds of things. It is a mix of some kind of idea or concept and then that is channeled in a way to deliver a message or persuade somebody to do something. So really the evidence of both those things is important, i.e., the ability to have ideas that feel fresh and interesting, and appropriate, relevant, and resonant. And then the ability to use those ideas as a kind of vehicle to deliver a message. It's very, very simple.

A fluency with digital is also very important. Thinking digitally requires system thinking, which is never really there with traditional ad creatives. We don't just put pictures and copy lines together, we're designing complex applications to bring our ideas to life. If a creative can't think that way then it's a big limit on the scope of their thinking.

Do you have writers and art directors or designers? What are the different creative roles you have here?

We don't have creative teams as such, we have a number of floating creatives who plug into different people for different types of briefs, a kind of "hot teaming"—like "hot desking." It works like this because both problems and the solutions we have at our disposal are so broad that a single team would never be able to cover the necessary ground to think through every instance. One day they might sit with a strategist, the next a coder, the next an art director.

Poke does have art directors but not in the ad team sense. They're attached to the design department, although, as I said, they get put into the conceptual, creative work too when it's appropriate. We have a writing team too that works both on concept development and on the delivery side of things, so again, quite a different setup.

So for what roles do you hire?

Well, we hire conceptual creatives, writers. We hire strategists, information architects, user-experience people, designers, art directors, project managers, and engineers.

Designers who can code?

Yes, sometimes. But the "coding" thing is less important than the conceptual grasp of what they're

designing for, from an engineering perspective. It's more important that a designer has a really good feel for how things are going to fit together and work when the system gets "switched on."

It's like the architect-engineer relationship. It works better if the architect has sympathy for the engineering realities of what they're trying to create. What might be a great idea in theory is not necessarily one in practice and that's not a mistake you can afford to make too many times.

For a writer, I assume you want to see evidence of writing?

Absolutely.

In a digital format? Or just anything?

Not necessarily. There are lots of different demands on writers here, because we cover a lot of ground. From advertising communication through to editorial and publishing. And obviously, the demands on a writer are very different between those worlds. So it really depends.

And for designers? Or art directors?

I think that, in that area, it's much, much more important to have hands-on experience. It's so much more than just making compelling imagery. You have to have your head in it from a designer's point of view to really make compelling communications. And the constraints of all the various formats and just the way that users behave. And all the engineering possibilities…without having a firm grasp of all that stuff, you just can't be effective. It's critical to have good grounding in the mediums that we're working in.

How do you show off your technical ability? Is it just by doing something that's interesting or technically difficult? Or do you just want to see people say, "I know how to write HTML, I know CSS, I know whatever"?

No, no. If people are applying, we go on what they said about themselves but only up to a point. Then we'll actually send them challenges and ask them to write some specific, or to tackle, specific problems and then just look at the way they've handled it, ask them to take us through their thought processes to see their approach, and then make a judgment on that.

But as with everyone at Poke, the engineers wear two hats; in their case, their coding-craft hat and then their creative, problem-solving hat. The ones they need to put on when we're brainstorming the possible ways to attack an idea from a technical point of view. So we're also looking for signs of lateral thought and a passion for problem solving.

And are most of your designers also coders? Or is it separate roles and a designer hands something off to a front-end developer?

Yeah, it's quite separate. Only because people tend to be one or the other. We've got a few "hybrid" people around who do both. And they're great. They tend to get different types of work, though. Sometimes, on the smaller projects, they can literally just sit down and build out the whole thing. And then the bigger projects will get more dedicated disciplines. Just because of the way that, obviously, it makes it easier to work. If you've got 10 people, you don't need individuals to cover lots of ground. You can pass it around between people. So we don't really have a rule about that stuff. But certainly somebody who has both abilities is great. It's not just about what they can do, it's also how they think. A designer with a strong engineering bent can think through problems much more. It's not more creative, but there's more scope for their ideas to play out in other ways because, obviously, delivering an idea doesn't necessarily require a design as such. It can happen in a whole bunch of ways. So that's the real quality about ideas that come from more hybrid people.

Mixing it all up is the best thing you could aim for. Not trying to make a rule about, "They have to be this or have to be that," then you end up with a good mix of people who see things from different points of view. And then, providing you can always allow the good stuff to float to the top, then you're always going to get quality.

Do you like to see online books that include things that aren't necessarily websites, or even digital things? Or artwork, or products? Or just anything that just shows ideas?

Yeah, definitely. I'm very drawn toward people who can't not be creative. It's not just a career for them; it's something that's sort of built into their bones. And so I think people like that just can't not look at everything in their world and try to transform it in some way, or do something to it. I'm very reassured when I see that in a portfolio. In fact, I've hired a few people because of the stuff at the back of the book for that very reason.

We hired this junior designer a few years ago who didn't actually have that much experience. He had just graduated. He was building interactive sculptures and really interesting installation pieces in his own time and out of the college context. And one of the things that he built was a radio piano. So every key that you pressed on the keyboard, it just played a different radio that was tuned into a different station. It was just conceptually a really nice idea. Not particularly amazing, technically. But as an idea, it was great. He was just compelled to do it and he followed it through because he was interested in it. It was a demonstration of his open-mindedness, core creativity, and driving passion. And sure enough, a few years later, he's not just a really strong designer but someone who really shines.

> *"I'M VERY DRAWN TOWARD PEOPLE WHO CAN'T NOT BE CREATIVE. IT'S NOT JUST A CAREER FOR THEM; IT'S SOMETHING THAT'S SORT OF BUILT INTO THEIR BONES."*

And what do you think is a good way to improve?

I think from our point of view, the most important thing of all probably is a complete immersion in the digital world. Obviously talent is an important part as well. But I think immersion is critical. You forget, because we all live in the same world, that when a designer puts something together and sticks it on a poster, we're all drawing on the same references. We all have this consensus. And so you can be very sophisticated in your language in the way that you build these communications. In digital, not everybody is conversant because we don't all share the same histories as users; we've adopted at various stages and we've consumed very different experiences. But I think what's absolutely true is that, just like our physical world is a culture, the online world is a different kind of culture. And it has its own set of rules and reference points. And not just in terms of conceptual reference points, but reference points in the way that things work, the way that different systems make you feel. So if people, designers or writers, or whoever you're working with, aren't immersed in that world, then they miss all that. And then the communications will simply be less effective.

When you see something that's brilliant, it's about condensing something down to something very sharp, and very focused, and single-minded. But what allows it to be so sharp is the way that it's using those reference points to tell its story, if you like. So, in the absence of that, it's not as strong. I think when you see a lot of stuff coming out of agencies that I don't respect so much, a lot of it just feels crude. They feel very accomplished from a craft point of view but they feel crude in what they're saying, and how they're making it, and how they're building the communication. The point is simply that really understanding the culture and being ingrained in it just makes the work much better. BI

To see Nicolas Roope's work, please visit http://breaking.in

CRAIG DAVIS
FOUNDER
BRANDKARMA
SYDNEY

Interviewed at Publicis Mojo, Sydney.

What do you look for in a student or junior portfolio? And what impresses you?

I look for surprises. I look for the unexpected. I look for things I haven't seen before. And I try to look behind the work as well and see what's informed it. Because while the book is really, really important, I'd never hire someone on the strength of a book alone. I'm really interested in the person. I'm interested in why they're doing what they're doing. What drives them and what informs their work.

Is that something that you find comes through in the work?

Yes. It has to come through in the work. Advertising is a form of creative expression that's created by someone, and there's a signature to that which is individual. Or it should be. It's fed by their curiosity.

When I say I'd never hire anyone solely on the strength of a book, the quality that I look for in the person behind the book is curiosity. The extent to which they are an adventurer or an explorer or a magpie, and they pick things up. They're hungry to learn about stuff. Because in absence of that you're just doing tricks and you haven't got the raw material to work with. It's really important that you have lots of stuff to play with in your own brain and assemble in ways that only you can do. That's what makes a creative person and one different from the next.

How important is finish? Could sketches be enough?

I think sketches are enough to demonstrate an ability to think conceptually. For a long time that was enough, but I think the world has changed and there's now an expectation that people who can think can also do. Technology has democratized that in a big way. So it would kind of be weird if someone could only think but couldn't operate a Mac. Or couldn't create a film. It doesn't have to be high end. But those tools are available to everybody. Everybody is using them whether or not they are near a creative industry.

So, I'm interested first in how people think. That's the most important thing. But I am also interested in their ability to deliver their thinking in ways that are surprising. And that applies to writers as much as art directors. I don't think it's enough that people can just think conceptually and deliver that through a few words or a rough drawing. I think they have to be able to think through it executionally up to a point. And, of course, they have a lot to learn and that's why they're trying to get their first job in the industry, but those things are tightly aligned now.

Do you think writers need a long-copy campaign or some demonstration of writing?

Yes. I don't think you can say you're a writer if you can't put a few hundred words together. I think it's really important. And if you can't, it speaks to your level of passion and commitment to your craft. I think the whole thing about people not reading anymore is rubbish. I think people read a lot. They might read on different devices, but they still read. So the ability to write and engage and inform and entertain is still relevant. Maybe you're writing a script, so it's not going to be read, it's going to be performed and received by an audience live or via film, but the ability to write is still important for a copywriter. It's fundamental.

What do you think about including things other than advertising in a portfolio?

I think that's important. You can't just be a creative person in the confines of the advertising industry, no matter how broadly you define advertising. If you're a creative person, that's not a nine-to-five job or an eight-to-six job—it's a way of life. And I would think that really creative people want to find lots of ways to express their creativity and exercise those muscles. So things that they do that are noncommercial are completely legitimate. I like to see people who are passionate and driven and have enough in their system to get out that it manifests itself in other ways. So people are in bands. People have got art projects. People who illustrate or play with type or make films in their own time—I think that's all relevant. And there was once a time when people would leave advertising to pursue something else. "I'm going to leave my job so I can write a screenplay" or "I'm going to leave my job so I can record an album or write a book," and now I think your chances of making music or film or publishing are probably better inside the industry than out. In other words, all those forms of expression and kinds of content are high value inside the business now, so you don't have to leave to do that. You can do it on the inside.

Do you think print ads still matter as a demonstration of thinking and craft, or is print a dying medium and it's not necessary to show any print ads?

I think it's a great way to demonstrate the ability to think creatively. I think it's still a completely legitimate form of creative expression. In most

markets, it's a form that's falling out of favor quite rapidly. But it's a great shorthand demonstration of thinking ability, so I think it's still very relevant. But if that's all there is in someone's book then that's a problem. The ability to demonstrate creative thinking in other ways is really essential because people need to be capable of thinking in a cross-platform or trans-media way. It's essential.

"I LOOK FOR CONNECTIONS, EXPRESSIONS, IDEAS I HAVEN'T SEEN BEFORE. AND WHEN YOU'VE BEEN AROUND AS LONG AS I HAVE, YOU'VE SEEN A LOT OF THINGS."

Can you think of any common mistakes that students make?

A lot of student books are superficial in their thinking. And that's what I mean about looking for surprises. I look for connections, expressions, ideas I haven't seen before. And when you've been around as long as I have, you've seen a lot of things. So I suppose I'm a bit harder to surprise. But most of the work you see is predictable rather than surprising. Sometimes it's familiar or it's just skimming across the surface. It's not locked into anything that feels like it's culturally significant or insightful from a human point of view or got any emotional grunt—it's a quick gag that doesn't leave you changed. And, to your question about art, I think the rules that apply to art apply to advertising, which is they have to leave you changed. They have to leave you affected. They have to create a legacy of some kind. So, to that extent, they are very similar. So that's a common shortcoming.

Much better to have fewer, stronger pieces than to have more work but some of it is filler. Stuff that you're not proud of, don't put in your book.

Do you have any advice on how students should look for a job or get in touch with people like you?

I think they should be every bit as passionate, determined, and creative about how they go about it as they are about the work itself. It's hard. And it's not that anyone is playing hard to get, it's just that they're really busy. Being passionate and creative is really, really important. Determination and persistence really do count. And when you're a student and you send something out, you're kind of waiting there with yourbreath held for an answer, and when you don't get one it feels like you've been slighted, but the reality is that it could easily have just been missed or people are just too busy and, though they meant to, they never got back to you. You have to campaign yourself. And by that I don't mean you need three ads, you need to stay on the mission, without it getting annoying, which is why creativity is important. Be particular with who you want to talk to and then be persistent in the way you pursue them.

Being hungry is really important. The people who interest me the most are the people who are insatiably curious. I think it's hard to be a creative person without that. I think it makes you more interesting and gives you more to draw on. I think it's where creative energy comes from. So constantly find ways to feed that, and while you're trying to get an opportunity within an agency you need to draw on all the sources of stimulation and inspiration and perspective that you can. And never stop doing that because the second you stop doing that, you're toast. BI

To see Craig Davis's work, please visit http://breaking.in

MICHAEL RUSSOFF SONGWRITER & FREELANCE CREATIVE DIRECTOR LONDON

At the time of the interview, Michael Russoff was Creative Director at Wieden+Kennedy, London

What do you look for in a student book? And what impresses you?

It's not so much what's in the book as the person you're seeing in front of it. I always talk to the person for 10 or 15 minutes before I even open the book. Actually, usually after I've talked to them for 15 minutes, I can pretty much tell you what is going to be in the book. In a funny way, I can tell how they might think about something from talking to them. So I don't look at the book and then look at the person, I do it the other way around because the person is going to be who you employ; you don't employ a book. And the book is only what's happened in the last little bit.

So do you look for evidence of their personality?

Yes, and their heart. I want to be able to feel a person through a book. Like humanity. That's the main thing I look for in a book is humanity, because I think if you've got that, and if that comes through for different brands in your work, then you're going to touch people in some way. And then it's interesting. Then you'll connect with people. I'm not interested in arrogance or bravado. Or cleverness, even. I'd much rather see someone with a big heart in their book than a big brain. I think that means a lot more in a book.

What do you think of sketches or scamps versus finished work for books?

I actually prefer scamps. Somehow, if it's very finished you're sort of saying, "It's finished" as a student. It's like a full stop when you finish something really well. You're kind of saying, "Here it is, judge me, it's not changing." Whereas if you have a scrap of paper, there's more emotion, there's more fluidity. It's like, "This is just a stage. This is just a process. I know it's not about this. This is just to show you." It says more about the person—the attitude of the person doing it.

For writers, do you think that you need some copy in your book to show that you can write? Or for art directors, do you need to show any evidence that you can design?

I guess so. Do people still see themselves as writers or art directors? I guess that would be my question. Are you coming as a creative, or are you coming as a writer or as an art director? I'm kind of not so interested in whether you can draw, or whether you can write words. I'm more interested in an idea, or an interesting thought process, or an interesting way of looking at the world. If you can make me think differently about a product or about a category, then I'd much rather you did that than if you put three words together in a clever way.

What do you think about putting things in a book that aren't ads at all? Just journal writing, or art, or things that show something about you?

Yeah, I'd be happy if your whole book is that, actually. I wouldn't mind. I've seen books like that. They're very interesting. And I've seen people who have a book of advertising ideas and then a book of other stuff. And it's usually the book of other stuff that tells you more about that person or their creativity. So definitely, yeah. If you're a creative person you'll be creative in lots of different ways.

And so you're looking for personality, and a different way of thinking, and a unique mind?

Yeah. Someone who not only looks at things differently, but who can make other people look at things differently—because otherwise you're on your own and you're just an oddball. You might as well be sitting on a park bench with all your bags. You've got to be able to take people with you. To be able to make them see things differently as well. Then it's powerful. Then it's interesting.

"YOU'VE GOT TO FIND THE WORK YOU LIKE TO DO, AND THEN YOU'VE GOT TO FIND SOMEONE WHO APPRECIATES THAT."

If you had to give a piece of advice to someone who's just starting out, or just putting their book together, or trying to improve, what would it be?

I think, remembering when I was taking a book around—I think it was a pretty crap book as well—it was such a roller coaster because you would go and see someone, and someone would like one campaign

and they wouldn't like another. And then you'd go and see someone else the same afternoon and they'd like exactly the campaign that the other person didn't like. And they didn't like the campaign that the other person did like. And I think finding a way of explaining that, or learning from it, is the most difficult part of the process of putting a book together and trying to get a job through a book. I think the thing it should teach you is to value your own judgment. That's what it really is saying to you. It's saying that all advertising is subjective. It's got nothing to do with whether it's good or bad because, at the end of the day, you're going to show it to people, people out there are going to see it. They're going to like it or not like it. That's your book, really. So I think to be able to agree with some people and disagree with other people, and find your own balance within those two poles [is important]. You have to learn to make up your own mind about what good work is.

So it's developing a point of view on advertising, or on anything, that's yours. Is that correct?

Or just to know what work you want to do. What work you like. You might go to an agency and they like your work. I mean, that's the best thing: is to be able to go somewhere that appreciates what you like. There's no point in creating a book that doesn't feel like it's you, but you're doing it because this is a great job, or you really like this creative director, or you like the office view, or whatever. You've got to find the work you like to do, and then you've got to find someone who appreciates that. And then I think there'll be a flow between you and your first job. Because I think your first job is the most important. To get the right people around at the very beginning is the most important thing. And it's worth waiting, I think, for that moment where you feel it's really right. That's such a cute dog coming down the street.

Is there anything else you wanted to say or add?

Just put a cute dog in your work. ⊞

To see Michael Russoff's work, please visit http://breaking.in

KARA TAYLOR
MANAGING DIRECTOR, USA
FBI RECRUITMENT
BOULDER

At the time of the interview, Kara Taylor was Director of Creative Recruitment at Crispin Porter + Bogusky, Boulder.

What do you look for in a student book? And what impresses you?

Strategic solutions for difficult marketing problems that aren't compromised creatively.

How important is finish? If ideas are the most important thing, can sketches be enough? Do you look at physical books anymore, or is it all websites?

Finish is very important. Sketches are fine for one or two campaigns, but there should also be enough finished work in the book to gauge one's attention to detail, artistic vision, and overall love for the craft. We look at both physical books and websites.

How important is writing? Do you need to see long copy?

Very important. If a writer can't write, he or she shouldn't be a writer. Long copy, in some version, is great, but it's not the only way to judge someone's writing skills. Awesome headlines and TV or radio scripts can also clue us in on how well someone can actually write.

What do you think of showing work that is not advertising?

I've always believed that "artistic hobbies" should influence and be incorporated into the advertising solutions versus being showcased in the book as something completely separate. Isn't the ability to utilize one's inherent creativity a big reason why people get into this business in the first place?

Do you have any other advice for a student or junior trying to getinto the business?

Be just as passionate and strategic about your job search as you are about your work. Don't wait for the phone to ring. Get out there and pound the pavement. Be nice to everyone, and don't turn your nose up at any job. As long as there is one person in the building who you can learn something from, the job is worth taking. BI

DAMIAN ROYCE
CREATIVE DIRECTOR
WHYBIN\TBWA GROUP
MELBOURNE

What do you look for in a student portfolio? And what impresses you?

The number one thing is being able to identify solutions for brands. When a brand comes to an agency they are looking for solutions to their problems. So the first thing I ask when I'm looking at a folio is, "Are these ideas solving problems?" And, of course, "Are they doing that in a clever and original way?"

When you're looking at a portfolio, are you looking for big ideas that are blown out into every medium? Or are you looking for smart ideas and you're not concerned whether they are digital or traditional, or span different types of media?

Definitely the latter. Because the solution to a brand's problem doesn't always need to be driven into multiple channels. It could be a simple thing in one area. It comes down to seeing the thinking and the process that someone has gone through to come to an idea.

Do you think print ads are important?
Yes. It's still quite an important medium because people are still using that medium. And an idea for a brand can be summed up quite well in a print ad.

What if someone brought you a book of only print?

I would ask them why they chose to do that. In this day and age, where ideasare found in so many different areas, I would think it was quite strange that they didn't think outside of the print medium.

What format do portfolios take? What do you see and what do you prefer?

I mostly look at books online. It's quite rare for someone to bring in a printed book these days. I think the online medium is a more convenient way to look at a book.

When you meet with someone do they bring in a laptop or...

Over the past couple of years, I've just looked at the books online to immerse myself in their work and then, in the interview, I ask them some questions and it gives them a chance to explain the ideas in a bit more detail. The other side of the interview for me is to just have a good conversation and establish what sort of personality they have and what their views are about creativity and the industry in general—not just getting a picture of them through their work. I think it's actually a really good thing to be able to review a portfolio online before the interview because you can see the work and then get a sense for what makes them tick in the actual interview.

On that point, what do you think about showing other creative work that is not advertising?

I think it's a great idea. It shows that they are curious, creative people in general. And it shows how they tick. You see great ads every now and then, but it's often the things that aren't necessarily ads that really stand out and show a real insight into how a creative ticks. I've seen cool product ideas, stories, songwriting, and other creative projects outside of advertising. It's often these things that expose a person's true value or show an "X factor."

"HIGHLIGHTING THE PROBLEM, INSIGHT, AND SOLUTION IS A GREAT WAY OF SETTING UP WORK, WHETHER IT'S ONLINE OR IN A PRINTED FORM."

It's quite common now to see app ideas, which is great because aside from a differentway of looking at ideas for brands, it shows an entrepreneurial spirit and in some cases a really good business solution.

Is finish important, or could sketches be enough?

I think sketches could be enough. As long as the idea is clear. That said, I wouldn't present everything in a book as just sketches—you need to show evidence of being able to craft and bring an idea to life.

For writers, is showing evidence of writing important?

Number one is the idea. But the craft of writing is certainly important for people who want to be copywriters.

Do you have any other advice on how to build a better portfolio?

I think one thing is to be clear about what your idea is and what it's trying to achieve. That could be pointing out the problem it is trying to solve, the insight, the solution, and how that solution works. Highlighting the problem, insight, and solution is a great way of setting up work, whether it's online or in a printed form. It's something that I teach the creatives that I work with. In order to sell your work to a client, and that goes the same for a student selling work to a creative director, you take them through that logical process of how you came to an idea and why that idea is right.

Is that usually just a sentence in a book, or more?

There's no rule of how long it should be, but certainly keep it short or to the point.

Anything else?

Don't get caught up in the execution of ideas and trends. Your thinking needs to stay true to the problem of a particular brand and finding those great ideas that can solve that problem. And also don't focus on any one medium. An idea can come from anywhere, and it can be executed anywhere in order to capture an audience. BI

To see Damian Royce's work, please visit http://breaking.in

What do you look for in a student book? And what impresses you?

It's going to sound pat, but "good ideas." Stuff that you haven't seen before or thought of. Or if they have a new idea within something old. Just something that you're like, "Oh shit, that's great." I don't need the next greatest web thing or whatever...It's more about thinking than anything.

Do you think the level of finish is important? Or can someone get away with sketches?

I think nowadays everything is so finished that you almost have to have a finished piece because it gets distracting if it's not. You really want it all to be about the idea, and so, if someone has a sketch, it shouldn't affect it. And if it's really a good idea I guess it wouldn't affect it, but I just think that so many people have such put-together work now, you wouldn't really be doing yourself any favors if you don't get somebody to help you out with it. As a writer, I wouldn't know the first thing to do about Photoshopping, but I would probably find a friend who could help me out to put together some ideas.

"I THINK NOWADAYS EVERYTHING IS SO FINISHED THAT YOU ALMOST HAVE TO HAVE A FINISHED PIECE BECAUSE IT GETS DISTRACTING IF IT'S NOT."

What about copy? How important is it to show that you can write? What is the best way to show writing abilities?

I guess there's two different ways you can do it. I think you should definitely know how to write a headline. It's important to be able to get across a good, funny, intelligent idea fairly quickly. It's kind of what we do. And then you should also know how to write [longer copy]. So I guess you can show that through copy in a long-copy ad or other writing samples. Because I think it's almost like a lost art nowadays. A lot of people just do visual ads, which is fine. But I think if you're called upon to actually write something, you should know how to do that. So, in getting a job, you're going to have to show somebody that you can do that. Hopefully.

Do you think it's good to show things that aren't ads in your book?

As long as it has something to do with thinking. Let's say you shot a movie—that has something to do with advertising. It shows that you can put a story together and do that kind of thing. Say you wrote a book—that seems to me to have a very close relationship with advertising. And it's still pretty cool if you're an inventor and you made this new thing. It shows that you have some ability to think of new ideas. And some problem-solving skills and stuff like that—that's cool. So I think it should be somewhat focused on the job at hand...

As long as it's about ideas and thinking?

I think so. Just as long as it's relatable or it connects to what we do. I wouldn't tell anybody not to put something that they're proud of in their book. But I would say make sure that it's something that somebody could see and say, "All right, that's cool, and I can see how that can relate here."

And do you have any other advice for someone who's just starting out, either in terms of putting together a book or looking for a job?

I think a lot of people always want to go to the great agencies to start off. And I think it's good and it's bad. It's great to go to the good agencies because you get the recognition and you know you're working with the best people and all that, and that is awesome. But then if you go to a place that's too big or it's got too many great people, as a junior you're really not going to get a lot of the best assignments—you're probably going to get a lot of shit work. You're going to be doing that—which is fine, because you need to learn how to do that stuff as well. But if you go to a smaller place, I think you might have more opportunity to do more things. So I'm not saying go one way or the other, just don't be upset if you get one thing that you weren't looking for. And I think any job out there is still a job, and you'll learn how to do it. So if you're trying to go to a Goodby, or a Wieden, or a Crispin, and you don't get a job there for whatever reason, it's okay. You'll still be able to get there somewhere down the line, and you might even be better off for it because you'll maybe have a chance somewhere else that you wouldn't have had there. I always liken Goodby to the New York Yankees. They always had so many great people there that they weren't going to give them the shitty little retail ads. So juniors always had to do it there, which is fine. It's just that you may get a different opportunity somewhere else. But you also get to learn from those great people, so they're both good. [BI]

To see Mike Sweeney's work, please visit http://breaking.in

OLIVER VOSS
PRESIDENT
MIAMI AD SCHOOL EUROPE
HAMBURG

What do you look for in a student book? And what impresses you?

I think I'm old school. I like to receive books that I can either really flip through or look at them on a computer in a way that I see one page after the other—really structured, in a dramatic order. What I don't like is a website where you have to search your way through…from this project, and then you go back and forth. I really want the book to be well structured and, yeah, give me 10 minutes of entertainment. What I learned in one of the first agencies that I worked in was: start with the best and end with the second-best thing that you have.

And I think that's still true. And then in between, I'm looking for campaigns that work with clients that are not too easy to serve. So if I see a book that only has Tabasco and those kinds of products—condoms, or something like that—then it doesn't impress me as much as if somebody has a car in it or a washing detergent or something like that.

Do you want to see a book that's completely comped up? Or are scribbles okay? Or sketches?

Yeah. I think it's the idea that counts. It sounds a little bit like a lame cliché, but it is like that. But then, on the other hand, I think I am like everybody else. If something works immediately without me translating it from scribble thinking, "Ah it could look nice, so and so," then it probably hits me better. So the typical London approach where you only have scribbles in your book is not so much what I like and what we also do here at ad school [where] we really try to comp up this stuff in a slick way.

Okay. What do you think about copy? Is it important for writers to show that they can write?

I think it is important. But if I'm honest, I'm hardly ever reading long copy. I'd like to see it in a book, and I might read the first few sentences, but my day is just scheduled so tight that it's hard for me to concentrate on really long copy within all those busy meetings where looking at the book is one of those. And therefore I really like to see that somebody takes the task on and tries to write a long copy [ad], but I hope that others take more time and really read it all the way through. I am more up for shorter copy, something that hits you right away. And, of course, nothing beats a great headline.

What do you think about putting things in a book that aren't ads at all?

For me, that's fantastic when I see something like that in a book because that's the way I like to work myself. I'm not only focusing on advertising. I write for magazines and newspapers sometimes, or do my own little films for my own website that do not have so much to do with ads. And I think that is something that makes people interesting: when they do not only have this one-degree angle and only advertising fits in, but when they look at the world

360 degrees at what else is possible and what are other forms where creativity expresses itself. And I learn so much from those other disciplines; if it's music, or architecture, or feature films, or anything—I really love seeing that in books.

"I REALLY WANT THE BOOK TO BE WELL STRUCTURED AND, YEAH, GIVE ME 10 MINUTES OF ENTERTAINMENT."

What do you think of people who are still putting together books that are only print ads? Is print still a good way to demonstrate creativity in advertising, or is it a dying medium that you don't care about seeing?

Yeah, I still like print ads just as a challenge for creativity, where you just look at a page, and the page is always there, and it's always the same, and you have the same instruments to work on it. And that doesn't change and therefore you are always on the same level with everybody else. When photography became popular in art, then the paintings were not valued so high. But now it changes again that people like to paint, and like to look at paintings also. And I think it's something that will not vanish. And therefore I think if it's print, or outdoor, this kind of medium, they will always be there. And I like it because you can show your creativity…it shows the creativity of the person who gives me the book quite quickly. With Internet ideas, a lot of the times it takes a long time to explain them: what, and then this happened, and then that happened. So it comes back to the tight schedule that you have when you're a creative director. And print is a very good tool for that.

And about the book, and it applies to having a presentation with a client: if you have a campaign, you should show your campaign but you should show another, second campaign that advertises, or that sells, your advertising campaign. So in a way, you should put on a show. It doesn't have to be loud and it doesn't have to be aggressive or something, but it should be clever and interesting: the campaign that sells your book. So for example, one day I had a car parked next to my spot where I park my car in the morning and it had a message written on it for me or for the creatives here in the company with an email address. And I immediately sent an email to him, to the person who did it, and asked for his or her book. So I think some kind of teaser that's really made up for the person you want to work with is good. And I'm sure a young person has certain idols. So they might have one, two, or three people who they really want to work for. And I think it's good to not only send the book, like you send your book to everybody else, but to think of something that targets only this person who you want to work for—your dream creative. I would do that. But then the book has to be good. If you have a shitty book with a second campaign, then it's a disappointment.

Is there anything else that you want to mention?

I think that it's important to keep learning and to still always be in the position of the student. For me, at least, that's the way I work: for every problem that I'm facing and that I want to solve, solve it as I did when I was starting in the business, at 19 years old, when I had no clue and I just tried to make my way through and to get to the point. And I think to stay humble and to not think too highly of yourself, and that you will solve every problem, helps you. I still have a lot of panic when I receive a brief. Because I start to panic in order to get a solution. And I'm never sure if I will get one. Sometimes I don't. And to have that feeling of being naïve, and still being at the point when you start something and you don't know [the answer], that's very important for everybody and for students as well. BI

To see Oliver Voss's work, please visit http://breaking.in

What do you look for in a student portfolio? And what impresses you?

I think what impresses me more than anything else is just a point of view. It's interesting, a lot of young people come here who have been filtered through older people. So they come in and take me through work and I say, "Do you love this? Because I don't actually love this." And as soon as I push them in it they say, "No, I hate this, but I was told it would be really good." Or, "I was told you'd like it." And I get it because I remember being young and also being told to listen to everyone. But what you're really looking for is someone who can filter the information around them, even at a young age. So they can say, "Everyone told me this and everyone gave me this advice but ultimately I'm presenting you something having filtered it through my brain that I'm proud of." And I very rarely see that.

"YOU HAVE HALF AN HOUR TO SHOW THAT YOU HAVE INSTINCT, CONFIDENCE, THE ABILITY TO SEE A STORY, AND THE SKILLS TO TELL THE STORY IN TERMS OF CRAFT."

With students and even juniors, it's very seldom that you see someone passionately defend their work. I've been in the business for 25 years, and I remember, during one of my first forays into London when I was a student, I had to present to Tim Delaney, who was a fierce and massively respected creative director—one of the top creative directors in the world at that time. And I remember him just chewing up my book. And,

as the saying goes, he played the ball, not the man. So he wasn't hacking into me, but he was hacking into the work. And he asked me to defend it and there was so much I couldn't defend. And he said, "Come back when you have something from your heart that you can talk about." And if you're young I don't expect you to be articulate and I don't expect some technical defense. But I do expect a passion and belief.

One of the things I think is a huge mistake is juniors bring in too much work. And it goes back to what I was saying: they can't defend it. And, invariably, there is one piece they can defend and they love. And I've always said, "Bring that one piece." If you're lucky, there's three of them. But if there's only one, bring that one piece. And the worst that can happen is I walk out of the room saying, "I want to see more." And that's a great place to be. But if you're bringing 5 or 6 or 10—for some reason there's a strange idea in colleges that you have to have 10 campaigns with three ads in each, which is ridiculous—and 7 are shit, 2 are average, and 1 is great, it throws me. Because I think, "Is that one great because you're potentially great? Or because you fell on it."

I had an agency in Melbourne in the '90s, and I was desperately looking for a great art director. And I went through so many people. And none of them were that great. I was getting exhausted and I called up this headhunter who said, "I have one person who's really good but slightly insane." And he came in with a portfolio and was quite shy. In those days portfolios were fucking huge—as big as this table. And this guy had been in the business for 20 years, and at some really good places. And I opened his book and there was a beautiful photograph. And he didn't offer any explanation. And I said, "What's this?" And he said, "It's just beautiful." And I said, "Yeah, but is it a direct mail piece or part of a campaign?" And he said, "No, it's a photographer I've always wanted to work with." And then there was a piece of this silk gauze all folded up. And, same thing. I said, "What's this?" and he said, "Hold it up to the light; I just think it's beautiful and would really like to do something with it." And it went on. There was a bit of leather and torn-out bits of books and illustrations. And I started to get it. I said, "Have you got anything you made?" And he said, "I've been in the business for 20 years, and I haven't done anything I think is worthy." He actually had roughs at the bottom. So he had a kind of student book after 20 years. And he was a genius. As you can appreciate, he was a slightly strange character, but he was such a purist. He was saying, "You want me to be head of art and filter what is beautiful and not beautiful. And this book gives you an idea of my taste." He didn't say that, I had to work it out. And what was not in the book said a lot more than what was in. I hired him, and he went on to be an absolute legend.

You mentioned schools want you to have 10 campaigns of three ads. Do you feel that a book needs to have print ads at all?

The industry has changed. The cliché used to be three print ads with a logo at the bottom and a ridiculously simple proposition. Now it's the "something" project. The reason why those projects do well, whether it be the Tap Project or something else, is that the core idea is really strong and then it's just expressed across lots of different places. But a lot of kids get so excited about spreading stuff around in a lot of different places that they don't spend enough time on the idea. And sometimes there is both: a blindingly simple proposition that you'll never see once you get in the business— indestructible socks or edible pants—done in an overly simple way. And you get someone trying to be untraditional but, actually, they've missed the point and they're just spreading shit wide.

At the end of the day, I look for instinct. Even at an early age, you need to have an instinct. And it might not be perfectly attuned, but it needs to be there. And the other thing is craft. For those of us who've been in the business longer than 20 years, we miss craft. Once you've worked out the story, it still needs to be told beautifully.

Do you think someone could come in with a book of sketches?

I don't have any format in mind. When someone walks into my office, I don't have a contract that says, "You need to have three interactive campaigns, two outdoor campaigns, and one ambient." I don't give a shit about that. The contract is, "You have half an hour to make an impact." You have half an hour to show that you have instinct, confidence, the ability to see a story, and the skills to tell the story in terms of craft. And also people talk about engagement all the time. It's the same in an interview. If you can start a conversation and find some common ground and then say, "I wish it were thicker, but this is what I've done that I'm really proud of," I'm engaged. I'm not going to give you a job after half an hour. But when you walk out the door, I'll think, "That guy is interesting." We're in a creative business, so I don't care how you do it, but if you can't land all those things—storytelling, engagement, craft—in half an hour, then you're not going to be of much use.

Do you have any other examples of remarkable books that you've seen?

When I think of great interviews, often it's not the book, it's the person. There have been examples at Droga5 where the person's résumé has been outstanding and their work has been outstanding but, after meeting with them, we've walked away because we didn't think the person was outstanding. And conversely, I'm proud of the fact that there are people who've gone on to achieve their potential, but when I hired them it wasn't in the book.

At the end of the day, part of the value of a good creative director is that you can hire below the market. If I decide I want to spend 200 grand on every junior, it's not going to be a difficult job. But if I want the best juniors and the best middleweights and I don't want to pay through the nose, it's about growing them. It's about getting them just before they break. Just before they do the Grand Prix campaign.

So the book is like table stakes. If the book is shit, the conversation is over. If the book has got some real potential and the person fills in some of the missing gaps, we've got a conversation. If the book is amazing but the person is a nightmare, that's often difficult. And these days, work is more complicated than it was. We've had campaigns with 12 names on it genuinely. So it's harder than ever to navigate the work, so it puts more emphasis on the person.

What are the personal qualities you look for?

In this business, the line between success and failure is so thin. The line between conceit and arrogance and swagger is so thin. I actually think that you need to have a healthy amount of arrogance to be in this business. And I don't mean going around and being arrogant, but there's an arrogance to presume that when you look at this piece of white paper, you'll see something different from the millions of other people who have looked at that paper with the same brief. If you were full of humility, you'd just collapse on the ground and cry. Because you'd think, "Oh great, it's another four-wheel drive." There's an arrogance you need to dig in somewhere and go, "I reckon I can take this somewhere no one else has been."

What we sell as a company for a long time is vapor. For a long time before you see the gorilla playing the drums, it's vapor. Once you see the gorilla playing the drums and once it's gone viral and once everyone is jumping up and down, a lot of people will tell you how they always knew it was a great idea. But the reality is someone managed to tell that tale while it was vapor. And that takes confidence. That takes swagger. It's hard because what I look for is difficult to define. I don't want megalomaniacal monsters. At the same time, I don't want shrinking violets. I'm looking for people who find their own voice and find their own confidence and they manage to push things out in a positive way. It's hard to prescribe. But you can recognize it when you see it.

There's that old saying: make as many mistakes as you can, but only make them once. And I think that's really true of great creative people. I worked with some great creative people when I came through, and I hated being wrong in front of them. And I made sure I wasn't. And I know the best people I have are like that. If they bring me something and it's wrong and I point it out, there's a part of them that says, "Thanks, I've learned something" and a part of them that says, "Fuck, I don't want to do that again." And they don't do it again. The great ones grow. You don't see the greatness at first. You see the beginnings of it and it grows.

Anything else?

Sponges are overrated. If a guy came in here and gave the impression he knows everything, you wouldn't touch him because he doesn't know everything. But if a guy came in and said, "I don't know anything; I'm here to learn," then I don't want him either.

If people only take one thing from this interview it should be: If you got one great idea, bring it. If you got 10 great ideas, fantastic. But if you got one great idea and three that you're not sure about and two that you don't care about, just bring the one idea. Wear the pain of only having one idea. Because at the end of the day, we're not buying the book, we're buying your ability to see right and wrong. ⊞

To see David Nobay's work, please visit http://breaking.in

PAUL BELFORD
OWNER &
EXECUTIVE CREATIVE DIRECTOR
PAUL BELFORD LTD.
LONDON

Interviewed at This Is Real Art, London.

What do you look for in a student book? And what impresses you?

I don't know how much you know about "This is Real Art." We're not just an ad agency or a graphic design company or a digital company. We're all of those things. So that gives us particular problems in terms of recruiting creative people. Because you can never find someone who's great at all of those things. You can certainly find people who are great at ideas and strategies, but we have particular problems in finding individuals who have the capability to work across all the different areas that we do. Because we do everything. Digital work, websites, interactive in-store stuff, exhibitions, corporate identity, graphic design, magazine design, book design, film titles, a lot of moving-image work, cinema ads, films for the Internet, TV ads, TV idents, press ads, posters, etc. And students coming out of college are just not up to it. They generally can't come in and be immediately useful in terms of handling even a small project.

Where they can be immediately useful is being able to have lots of good ideas that can work across many different media. What we find at the moment is that we get people who've either been at advertising college or people who've done graphic design degrees, and there's really...they're entirely different kinds of beasts. So who are you aiming at? People graduating from advertising courses who want to get jobs in ad agencies?

Primarily. But I'm interested in your perspective on what you're looking for.

Well my perspective is they often have some quite good conceptual thinking in their books. Advertising students are just bad at execution. And I wouldn't expect them to be good because they haven't had much experience in doing it. Especially art directors. And I don't hold that against them. I mean, I'm happy to see a portfolio full of just scribbles as long as they're good ideas. The most important thing is good ideas. And then you take a gamble when you hire someone, whether they're going to become good at execution over a number of years or not. Some people will just have it and some people don't. I think you've just got to have the desire to want to improve how your ideas are executed. And some people honestly really don't care. They're happy that they've done a great idea and someone else can just kind of plonk it on the page and run it. I think that's a terrible shame.

So personally, I want people who have great strategies and ideas, and then also have the desire to execute those strategies and ideas to a higher level. So that's what I look for from advertising graduates. But I don't necessarily expect to see it in the portfolio. I just want to see scribbles and ideas. And ideas for anything actually, I really don't care. Just someone who can have ideas—interesting ideas.

So when you're looking at design skills, how do you want to see that, if not in the book?

I don't think you can judge it. I don't think you judge it in a young kid. They can certainly talk about it. I'd interview someone; when I was looking at their work, we'd talk about what kind of work they like, if they'd seen exhibitions, what kind of designers they'd like, if

they had any favorite designers, things like that. And someone who can articulate a point of view about design is certainly more interesting than someone who just kind of shrugs and says, "Oh, I don't know."

Right. It's interesting because in the US, no one really takes around sketches anymore. Everything is completely comped up.

I know and they all look like shit. I was in [New York] judging the One Show this year, and I did some portfolio reviews as part of that week. And I couldn't believe all these...I mean you're getting it more and more here. But I would say, "What's the point?" These people who spent hours on the Mac doing these kind of dreadful layouts with horrible stock shots and terrible type. And it just kind of puts me off. It's a good idea in there somewhere but it's got this veneer of awfulness over it. So I'm a kind of lone voice in that. I know that's the way the business has gone. American agencies would probably be horrified if someone turned up with some scribbles. So there's no easy solution to that.

But your point of view is the ideas come first?

Absolutely.

And sketches are fine for that. And then once they're in the business, they can start with creating things on a computer?

Yeah. And it takes years for an art director to become a good art director, I think. Years and years. So I don't expect it. I don't even look for it, to be honest. I just want to look for the desire to improve execution. Ideas certainly come way, way higher up the scale than the ability to know what buttons to press on the computer.

Okay. And about writing and demonstrating the ability to write...do you hire writers here?

I'm currently looking to hire a writer. We have interns who have been on advertising courses. But one thing that really frustrates me when I'm looking at student books is the lack of copywriting ability. You often see entire books, even without any attempt at headlines. And I don't think every campaign should be constructed that way, but I think it's a really important skill to have. It's a useful string to your bow if you have that ability, just to write a decent headline. I think it's a fashion thing, it goes in cycles, and everyone does really simple, visual ideas where the only words usually are an end line explaining the strategy and then a logo. And that's the kind of way most student campaigns are constructed these days. And it's fine, but it's just one way of doing it. It's good to demonstrate a breadth of skills in terms of how you execute campaigns.

"I WANT PEOPLE WHO HAVE GREAT STRATEGIES AND IDEAS, AND THEN ALSO HAVE THE DESIRE TO EXECUTE THOSE STRATEGIES AND IDEAS TO A HIGHER LEVEL."

So, for a place like this, what kind of work do you want to see in a book? Ideally, all the kinds of things that you'd actually do here?

If I were hiring a student team who'd been on an advertising course, I obviously wouldn't expect them to have magazine design. People who've been on graphic design courses need to be able to demonstrate design skills more than people who've been on advertising courses. If ad students do turn up with great design in their book then that's a bonus. That's great. But I'm pretty sure it would never happen because people who've been on advertising courses have been thinking about strategies and ideas more than how they're executed. But I would expect them to have some great strategies for real products, executed in different media. By executed, I don't mean finished up. I just mean ideas for their execution. So little four-frame storyboards for moving-image work that could be a TV ad, it could be an Internet film, it could be a moving poster screen where there's no sound but little simple, clever storyboards on good strategies and ideas. I would expect press ad scamps—just scribbles for press ads and posters. And then it

would be great to see specific ways in which that strategy and idea can be taken digitally. Applications that do clever, useful stuff related to that strategy. And it's not just using it like another screen. It's using that specific medium in a clever way. So if they can demonstrate that, then that's a major, major bonus. And there isn't enough of that that I see at the moment. Ways in which ideas can be dramatized across different media.

And what do you think about things in a book that don't have anything to do with advertising, or even design? More like just thoughts, or journals, or scraps…?

Yeah. A clever idea for products that no one's thought of yet. Wonderful. Yeah. Really impressive. I like all that.

What about just kind of doodles and kind of journal thoughts? And things that are less structured but maybe show some thinking?

Provided it's clever; it's got to be clever. And entertaining. If I'm engaged by it, then that's a major, major bonus, isn't it? That's the whole point of showing me something. You're turning a page; you're showing me something clever. Because we do so many things. One of the things we do is we go to a client and suggest stuff that they haven't asked us for. So it's really good to see, in student books, just ideas. To show that they're kind of sparking and can generate a lot of stuff.

And then one last thing, do you have any advice or thoughts for someone who wants to get into the business?

Have a point of view about what you like. Obviously, look at communications in the wider media, in popular culture. Think about it. What do you like? What don't you like? I dislike 99 percent of it, for example (and, if anyone cares to listen, I can talk at length about why I hate it). Absorb the wider culture. You succeed in stuff that you're interested in. If you're not really interested in the latest movie, or art exhibitions, or you have a favorite author and their latest book. If you're not interested in that stuff, then you're probably not right to do this job. You have to be totally interested in popular culture, I think, to work in communications. So ask yourself if you're really interested in this stuff. I mean, I keep stuff—I have shelf-fulls of scrapbooks that I've photocopied from books or ripped out of magazines, gigabytes of stuff on a hard drive. You should be intuitively doing that anyway. And then I think you're right for the job, and you should be interested in ideas and have lots of ideas. If you look at an ad and think, "That's crap," and immediately think about ways that it could be better, then you're probably right for the job. ⊞

To see Paul Belford's work, please visit http://breaking.in

MONICA TAYLOR
FREELANCE CREATIVE DIRECTOR
PORTLAND

Interviewed at Wieden+Kennedy, Portland.

What do you look for in a student book? And what impresses you?

First and foremost, great thinking. Intelligence, craft, and a certain level of joy or passion evident in the work. So many books are the same. Are there any surprises?

Ad schools' books can have a formula to them. After you see a bunch, you are keen to see someone with a flash of originality—some kind of spark, something you haven't seen before, a new angle on an idea. That includes thinking in many different mediums. Digital and social ideas are very necessary to have right now. Show ideas beyond print and TV. Too many books are still just print and TV.

With an art director right out of school, I also look for a love of typography or design, or just some kind of flair that makes it stand out from the others. With a copywriter's book I like to see words. Enough headlines and body copy to see whether or

not they can actually write. You wouldn't want to see a copywriter's book full of visual solutions only, with no copy. Don't laugh, I've seen it.

"AD SCHOOLS' BOOKS CAN HAVE A FORMULA TO THEM. AFTER YOU SEE A BUNCH, YOU ARE KEEN TO SEE SOMEONE WITH A FLASH OF ORIGINALITY— SOME KIND OF SPARK, SOMETHING YOU HAVEN'T SEEN BEFORE, A NEW ANGLE ON AN IDEA."

It's almost a double standard. In an art director's book, you want the concepts to be great, which usually translates to the writing as well as how the book looks. So I'd have to say there's an onus on the art directors a little bit to have a more complete package. I've heard people say about copy books, "Ah well the layouts look like crap, but he's just a copywriter." But I don't hear the same prejudice working in favor of the art directors. If you see a book that's not full of great concepts but the art direction's great, you tend to think of them as a designer. This, in the current ad world, tends to translate as "not conceptual," with my deepest apologies to my truly conceptual designer friends. I think that tends to happen. But then again, I'm an art director, so I am certainly prejudiced.

You mentioned for art directors that the finish is important. Do you think a stack of sketches can work for a writer?

You know, it's just one of those things. If the writing is absolutely brilliant, people will forgive anything. We all hear stories of this great guy that was discovered by writing concepts on a napkin, and I think that's awesome. I actually know that great guy. But that's probably in keeping with the rest of his or her personality, naturally. It can happen, but if you're one of those people you probably already know it, and you're not reading this. Most of us aren't that brilliant, and it ends up looking like you're trying to be cool. You'd dress up nicely if you were going for a job interview in a traditional office. So why don't you make your book look nice to show that you really want the job? It would be "hipster-PC" for me to say, "Yeah, your book can look like anything, just express yourself!" But I don't think that would service most students who are really looking for jobs at most places.

Do you think there are common mistakes or traps that a lot of students fall into when they're putting their book together?

It's not about completely tailoring yourself to what you think a particular agency is looking for. It's more like dating. Be yourself—in the form of your book—and find a place to work that appreciates what you have to offer and is attracted to your work. And vice-versa. I think creatives are pretty good at saying to themselves: "I like this agency, and I want to work there. And I think their work and mine are a really good fit." Keep that in mind when you go to meet the person from that agency, rather than thinking, "What are they looking for? How can I twist myself to be that? How can I change?" Take their notes, sure. They know what they are looking for, and can help you. But don't lose yourself. You'll be happier in the long run.

The power of editing is really important too. Sometimes what you leave out of your book can be just as important as what you put in. I hear creative managers, when they review books, going through the pages, "Nice ad, nice ad, nice ad, nice ad. Horrible ad in every way, horrible ad in every way, and then an okay ad." It makes them doubt the creative's judgment. Can the creative tell the difference between good and bad? And usually when you ask a student about an obvious weak link in their book, a student will say that some teacher told them they should include an ad that really got produced, or an assignment that was for a particular category that is supposedly good to have, like cars or financial services, or, if they are looking at Wieden, Nike. Not a good idea. It's not about the category, it's about showcasing your abilities and potential.

Do you think it's important to have long copy in a book for a writer?

I think it's great to see long copy. You just get to show off more of your chops. Especially if that's what you love doing—if that's what you do. It's a talent most CDs miss having onboard. Although there aren't a lot of long-copy print ads being produced now, there is a lot of writing needed—brand manifestos, digital content pieces, stuff like that. Same skill.

Do you think it's good to put things in a book that aren't ads? Like other art, or other writing?

Sometimes. I'm trying to think of when it's really helped. It's really helped when I've seen junior books from people who don't work at very creative shops. People who need to show a little bit more of who they are because it's not in the work they've been allowed to work on. And sometimes it helps me decipher their aesthetic. But too much of it, and I'm thinking, "Just work on your ads. Just make the ads better." And I also personally expect that stuff to be very good because there are no constraints. There's no client. It's art. And that can be tough, because then you're dealing with my subjective taste in art, or photography, or whatever. I like knowing what photographers you really admire, or designers, or what books you're reading, or something else that draws a portrait for me about your general creativity and taste. With certain people the creativity just spills out of them and they can't contain it in their ads. And they want to do this, and they want to do that. That's always great. It inspires me. And when it's genuine and authentic in a book, you can totally feel it, and you want to see more and more and more.

Do you have any tips for someone who's trying to get into the business?

I would say this business is a lot about persistence. And people love improvement as much as they love someone who's great from the start, because it just shows you could grow to be fabulous. So, if you don't succeed the first time, just keep working on your book, and come back, and come back, and come back. With new stuff.

What was it like when you were just starting out?

I graduated into a huge recession, a lot like it is today. It was extremely tough to get a job in advertising.

I was living in Boston after graduation, taking my book around, and I remember the Boston Globe ran an article then, about the collapse of the advertising industry. They had a quote saying it was "easier to get a job in Boston as an actor than it was to get a job in advertising." And you know how many acting jobs there are in Boston? Not many. I'd tell you more, but it was just too depressing. It was a Grapes of Wrath start in advertising. I finally got a job more than a year later, at a very small retail agency. I did coupon ads and circular covers, and I was grateful. And I'm not kidding, everyone wanted my job.

People I came up with through the business, we've spent a lot of time drinking and grousing about "how tough we had it" and, "kids these days have it easy." Sometimes we whittled while we complained. Typical old-person stuff. While business was booming, the career paths of graduates were fast and high. We were just jealous. Jobs were much more plentiful. Now again, it's tough out there.

I want to tell students: We all lived through it and had careers, and you will too. You can't control what economy you graduate into. You just have to be more competitive.

The upside is I do think the talent that gets the jobs in this economy will have a huge advantage over people who started a few years ago when things were flush. When the money gets tight, agencies only keep their best people, and hire the best people. There aren't a lot of people coasting through anymore. That's a good thing. Five years from now, you could be sitting at your desk at some great shop, looking to your left and right at your peers, and be part of a deep team of amazing talent. And I hope to be sitting anywhere near you. Whittling.

A story: When I got a job here [Wieden+Kennedy], I had a little portfolio epiphany. It was the morning of interviewing here. I was nervous. I was taking a last look at my book before leaving, and I remember there were about four or five elegant print ads that I thought my book needed to make it really full and nice. They were good ads, but there were a few other comps that I had in my back pocket. They were spec ads for Converse. My creative director didn't like them, no one ever thought they were any good, but I just

loved them. And it was getting late, and I had to leave for the interview. I ripped out the elegant stuff and I put in these Converse things, because I thought to myself, "If I'm going to go down, I'm going to go down with the stuff that's closest to my heart." And it was a wonderful moment because Dan Wieden looked at my book, and he got to these things that no one ever loved but me. And he said, "Wow!" He loved them. They made an impact on him, these spec pieces. And I don't think the others would have. And it made me think, "This place is different than all the other places I've ever been to. I really want to work here. I can do more of that stuff here. The stuff I always wanted to do." It had a huge effect on me.

So it is like dating. Be yourself.

Yeah, but sometimes people don't know who they are. So that's not as easy as it seems. And it doesn't mean, "Just relax." It means, figure out who you are and put it in the book. It's a creative person's life story. I'm still working on it. ⊞

To see Monica Taylor's work, please visit http://breaking.in

PETER GATLEY
CREATIVE DIRECTOR
GREY
LONDON

Interviewed at Fallon, London.

What do you look for in a student book? And what impresses you?

Stating the obvious, your book needs to stand out and be remembered. This is, after all, what our clients want us to do for them. When I look at a book, I'm open to being surprised. And I'm hoping to see that you're smart. This is your chance to show me. What impresses me most is a book that shouts, "I'm smart" and belongs to someone who has enough humility to not be too sure.

Are sketches okay if the ideas are good enough?

Anything is okay if it fits a brief of being able to surprise me and convince me you're smart. Don't spoil good ideas by producing them badly. The smart thing to do is show a good idea some respect. Sketches are fine as long as the sketches couldn't be done much better.

In terms of writing, do you think it's important for a writer to show that they can write, either with a long-copy ad or some other piece of long writing?

Play to your strengths. If writing long copy is your thing, do that. As long as I'm left feeling you're smart, it doesn't matter. It could be that someone called me on the same day and asked me if I've come across anyone who can write good long copy for a project or position. Who knows? Be the best you can be and see what happens. If writing long copy isn't you, don't do it. Write some short copy that makes me smile. Or show me you're smart in another way—your way.

If a writer came in with no real copy, do you think that would be a problem?

It's not a big problem for me. However, I might be left thinking all the bases haven't been covered. The next guy might have a similar good or brilliant book and some really nice copy. They're going to look smarter.

What do you think about putting things into a book that aren't ads at all?

All the better. Perhaps you've made an absolutely charming two-minute film—you might look more well rounded and perhaps more in touch with humanity than someone with a book that simply has one ad after another. I would rather look at a book full of good ideas than a book full of ads. How can variety be a bad thing?

So you said you want to see that they're smart. Do you also want to see their personality come through?

Enthusiasm is infectious. That would be good. And humility more often than not belongs to people who always want to learn and do better.

And do you have any advice for someone who's just starting to put together a book?

You might only get one shot at a person, or a place. Don't cut corners. Don't write ads until you have a really good strategy. And then write dozens of ads. Try and get to a place where being totally obsessive about your book feels healthy and not weird. Don't make a film until you've worked out all the details first, so it's a perfect film. Your book has to be the best it can be, so keep going until it is. BI

To see Peter Gatley's work, please visit http://breaking.in

DYLAN HARRISON FILM DIRECTOR FILMGRAPHICS ENTERTAINMENT SYDNEY

At the time of the interview, Dylan Harrison was Executive Creative Director at DDB, Sydney.

What form does a portfolio take usually? And what do you prefer?

The work comes in largely through links online, and I think that's absolute table stakes. You absolutely need to have a presence online. If you're fortunate enough to get in front of the ECD, the first assumption is that he's incredibly time poor. Links are great because they can look at it on their own time or when they're traveling or on downtime. Even the way that work is arranged on a link is very important. You don't need to be overly creative; think about priority of information. So, snapshots of information, big visuals, easy navigation. Make it easy to get through the work.

I did over a decade in London when I started out and it was all about reverence for the craft. How valuable your work is is how valuable you tell someone it is. And part of that, when I started out, was putting your book in a very impressive, leather-bound portfolio case. As big as you can. And I remember how proud I was when I spent my rent money for the month on a large, leather-bound A0 folio with my name embossed on the front. And it's kind of like a dare. It's a challenge, and you think, "Now I have to actually write ads good enough to put in there." And the point I'm making is I think you need to have the online portfolio but, increasingly, something tangible that students can bring to an interview is really important. And if you're going to do something physical then there needs to be a sort of reverence to it. How you present the work to me is telling me how valuable you think the ideas are within those pages.

And do you prefer a physical book, rather than someone bringing in a laptop and showing work that way when you're meeting with someone?

It depends on the nature of the work. Print and outdoor lend themselves well to a physical book. It's rarely done these days, but it's very impressive when it is.

When people are starting out they don't have any kind of production experience, so it's usually scamps and visualizations of ideas. It's good to get access to it online for speed and efficiency. But what's the most reverential way to present that work when you're up against books with finished, produced work? So, if all your work is scamps, it's important to present them in the best possible way.

It's also important in that initial meeting for an ECD or creative director to be able to turn the page every two or three seconds. You feel it when you go through hundreds and hundreds of books and then you come across one where you can turn the page every two or three seconds. You know you're dealing with someone who gets it. Whereas if you have to stop for a few minutes and ask, "What's going on here?" and "Who's the client?" then you know they are a long way from being ready to work in an agency. Because they aren't producing work that works.

If students can go out and shoot content and finish up work, then that's going to be more engaging than just scamps. And it's all these things that you need to be doing.

There's also something you can do with a book that you can't do online. It's the rule of tens. People say you need to have 10 campaigns of three to five ads. And in order to come up with 10 good campaigns you need to write 100. And in order to have three to five good ads within a campaign, you need to write 30 to 50 executions. So, once you start doing the math, you're talking about writing thousands and thousands

of ads in order to get to this document, which is a summary of your best thinking to date.

"YOU FEEL IT WHEN YOU GO THROUGH HUNDREDS AND HUNDREDS OF BOOKS AND THEN YOU COME ACROSS ONE WHERE YOU CAN TURN THE PAGE EVERY TWO OR THREE SECONDS. YOU KNOW YOU'RE DEALING WITH SOMEONE WHO GETS IT."

Now, the sleight of hand is that you go and see an ECD or a creative team—and it's often better to go see a senior creative team before you see the ECD because you can get initial buy-in from them, you can make the work better, and what you're doing is you're actually collaborating with that senior team and bringing them onto your side so they become advocates for you. And when you see the ECD, you're not going in cold, you're being brought to the ECD by that team. When you're working with them, you take in your book, and often the first question they'll want to know is, "How long did it take you to generate this book?" And, if they took a portfolio course or ad school, it might be 6, 12, 18 months to two years writing all the ads in there. And the reality is you want someone who can come in, take a desk in the hallway and churn out that many ads in a month. In two weeks. So a really good trick for students is to not just have one book. But have two books, three books, four books. That's what I did when I was starting out. Walter Campbell, a CD at AMV at the time, who wrote the Guinness "Surfer" ad amongst others, and was at the absolute top of his game, told me to write four or five books. Because then you can go to a creative team for feedback, and at the end you can say, "Fantastic, I'm going to take all of that onboard and can I come and see you in two weeks with some new work?" And they'll say, "No, come back in six weeks when you've had a chance to do some real work."

And you say, "Split the difference, how about four weeks?" And you still try to go back in two weeks. And you just send another book. And then in another two weeks do it again. And they'll think you've just written it and you're incredibly prolific. And after four or five rounds of this, if they haven't decided "This person is incredible," then it's time to try a different agency. But it's an easy trick to do, and you can't do it online.

What is the primary trait you are looking for in a book?

What I'm looking for above all is an understanding of and curiosity around what makes people tick. Just what motivates people. The trap when students start out is they start to write ads or emulate great ads. Creative execution is much easier than creative strategy. Creative strategy—being about to write a good endline, which is a campaign thought—requires an understanding of what motivates people.

As they begin to execute that, I need to see the beginnings of craft. There are many different tools within the creative arsenal, and I want to see them starting to use all of them. As traditional as it sounds, I love seeing a really strong headline campaign, because if you can write strong headlines, there's a good chance you can turn your hand to any platform. Engaging in reductive thinking and achieving simplicity is hugely important, and that can be applied to any medium. I love to see a simple image narrative with just an endline. I like seeing ads with an interplay between the visual and the headline and they work together as one idea. I like seeing a variety of tones: really funny, really irreverent, something serious handled tastefully and tactfully, work that elicits an emotional response. And, if you can get just four or five different tones in a book, then you're doing really well.

And do you like to see a variety in media as well, or is print enough?

I think a mix is really important. Students and juniors absolutely need to demonstrate that they can author a really interesting, irresistible idea that is media agnostic and translate it across different media and show me how those channels are interlinked. But, funny enough, in this day and age, that's more prevalent and now turning up in all the right channels is table stakes and everyone can do it. What's more important is, "Are you being interesting when you're there?" The reason I still like to see strong poster, print, or outdoor campaigns balanced by broader social thinking in a book, is that it shows me that you can be interesting in three seconds. And there is an appreciation for the craft of writing.

To evaluate ideas I have five criteria which have a descending order of importance. I ask, "Is it simple, is it relevant, and is it original?" And most people fall over on the simple hurdle. The nice thing about print and outdoor is you can quickly demonstrate simplicity in your thought. That two-to-three-seconds rule I was talking about earlier. The next thing I look for is relevance. You can show me an image of a guy standing on his head, but unless you're advertising trousers with special pockets so your change doesn't fall out, it's probably not relevant. It's a wasted opportunity. It needs to be relevant to the persuasive argument you're making. The third is, "Does it feel original and fresh, or does it feel clichéd and familiar?" And students often immediately want to do stuff that looks like award-winning work. So they choose clients like Nike, VW, Coca-Cola, and immediately those ads compare unfavorably to the real work. So I tell students to take those clients out and do ads for your local bakery or baked beans or a local pound or a business innovation idea. The types of clients you don't usually see in award books.

Those first three really determine if you've got an idea. And the next two determine if you've got a really good idea. I ask, "Is it surprising?" and "Is it engaging?" For the first one, is it stopping me and making me think? Is it pulling a pin on a grenade and launching it into my brain so it will be something I'm thinking about for the rest of the day? Does it surprise me in a satisfying way? And "engaging" is where we start to talk about the use of emotion but also the capacity for participation in the idea. Is it a big, deep, long idea that can start to author a conversation rather than something that is transactional or a two-second kind of engagement and, after I turn the page, I've forgotten about it.

What do you think about putting personal work that isn't advertising into a book?

I think it's important to put that work in, but it's a question of balance and it also depends on how impressive those outside projects are. If there is great thinking involved, or great craft skills, or you're demonstrating that you understand people and what makes them tick, and how to be really interesting, then, by all means, put them in. But don't exclusively do that because I also need for a student to demonstrate to me that they know what life in an agency is like and what the day-to-day business is like. And so I need to see that they can write a great headline, write a great TVC, have a great social idea, they can elevate something from the everyday into a more interesting conversation about people's lives. Funnily enough, having the discipline of having a brief to respond to actually makes for better work for a lot of students rather than just operating in a vacuum with no brief at all.

Do you have any advice on job hunting?

I can tell you the wrong way to do it: stunts. There's stories of people sending a fossilized foot and saying, "I'd like to get a foot in your door" and other bad puns. I was sent a brick recently with the message, "I'd like to build the agency with you" or something like that. I'm kind of disappointed they didn't go further and throw it through a window if they really wanted to create impact. And my favorite was someone sent a fish, saying, "I want to get a place" in your creative department, the pun being around "plaice." Unfortunately, the ECD had gone away for a fortnight and the mail was sitting in his office for two weeks and he came back to a rotten, decomposing fish.

What is important is to use the networks available. Recruiters are really important. Often there are industry bodies set up to support students. D&AD does an excellent student program in London. I did their student workshop twice and learned a hell of a lot and it led to a placement at DDB London and then they hired us. In Australia they have what's called AWARD School and it's an important process for students to go through. Basically, if you're not good enough to get into AWARD School yet, you're not good enough to get into an agency. Even then, a lot of the people who go to AWARD School are not ready for an agency—they need to put in more work—but it's a first port of call.

It's important that students are ready to take advantage of the opportunity to work in an agency when they get a placement. They're going to learn a hell of a lot, yes, but they are going to be judged from day one. So you want to be in a position to turn up and basically operate like any other junior team on the floor. In fact, you want the other junior teams to feel you nipping at their ankles because you're cracking briefs and getting work made. That's the fastest way to get a job. So before you get a placement, you need to be used to getting your work critiqued by CDs, taking on that feedback, and improving your work.

Something I didn't go into before on "traps that students fall into" is writing the same ad three times. It's really important to demonstrate that you can write a great creative strategy but also execute it in ways that are original each time. The other is that students write ads but they don't show it to anyone. If your mother, girlfriend, boyfriend cannot look at an ad and tell you what's going on without you helping them, it's not ready yet. Once you can write ads that are clear, then you can go to AWARD School, then you can start contacting agencies and recruiters and start down the path of getting a placement.

Anything else?

The industry is moving to where creatives have to wear a lot of different hats. So show me that you can do the grunt stuff: you can takes briefs for boring products or clients and say something interesting about them and churn out some well-crafted ads around that in different media—print, digital, TVC, promo, activation, etc. Also show me some thinking outside the box—personal projects. And if you can do that and then attach a client, then it becomes much more powerful.

Also, is there one thing that you want me to remember? Is there one thing that is going to be your calling card? Make sure you have one thing in your book that is potentially wrong but stands out from what everyone else is doing. You're being judged against hundreds of other hungry students who are trying to get in the door.

Do you think that's an ad campaign?

That would be wonderful. Because then it's close to the reality of what we do. But it could be anything. It could be the way you bring that book to life. It could be an idea or initiative in it. It could be a song you wrote. It could be a range of action figures you've designed. I don't know! But what is the stand-out thing that no one else is going to come through the door with, even if that's just a calling card to get you in to have a conversation about the other work. In the next decade, you need to show that you can do a lot of things, that you're driven by a creative urgency, you have a restlessness about you, that you're prolific with ideas, and that you understand what makes people tick. BI

To see Dylan Harrison's work, please visit http://breaking.in

RAJ KAMBLE
FOUNDER &
CHIEF CREATIVE OFFICER
FAMOUS INNOVATIONS
MUMBAI

What do you look for in a student book. And what impresses you?

The first thing I look at in a student's book is the ideas. It's somebody who can convey the idea very well. Who understands the problem and creates a solution properly. I look for something that has never happened before. A completely new strategy, a completely different way of looking at it. That's what I look for in a student's portfolio.

If the idea is the most important thing, does the level of finish matter or can someone come in with sketches?

See, I don't mind if somebody has nice sketches as long as you can understand the idea. But if you're an art director then I expect some level of finish because your job is to explain the idea. You're like a director of the movie. You have to know how to get the picture from a website, and how to put a headline on it—basic things. I'm not saying you have to do the most

amazing Photoshop, but as long as you can put it together well and convey the idea.

And for writers, do you need to see copy? Do you want to see evidence that they can write?

Yeah. I think people are writing less and less. And I think it's sad because copy is important. But I don't believe in long copy or short copy. I believe in the idea. If the idea requires writing short copy, write short copy. If the idea requires writing long copy, write long copy. So it depends on the idea. If a young guy comes and shows me he can write amazing copy and that product requires copy, I'd be really happy because that shows he can do an amazing job in the future. And, with a guy who can write long copy, there's a very good chance that he can write short copy too. So if someone has a long-copy ad in his portfolio, I will read that copy to judge him. It is very tough to judge a writer based on one or two lines. So, if you're a writer and you have long copy, I think it's a great idea. But again, don't write long copy for the sake of writing long copy. Write it if your idea requires long copy.

And then what do you think of putting things that aren't ads in a portfolio?

I think it's interesting because those one or two pieces show who you are and what your interests are. So I think it's not a bad idea. But I would put it at the end of the book—one or two pieces. Not more than 10 percent or 15 percent of your book. Show what you're interested in…maybe you shot a movie or you wrote a movie. I don't mind if you write a small synopsis or if you show one or two pictures or illustrations, if you do illustration. So I think it's a good idea to have something extra, showing that you can go beyond advertising. I respect that.

And do you have any other advice for someone just starting out in the industry?

The most important thing in this business is you have to be nice. Doesn't matter how good you are. You can improve. Many times people improve and they're getting better and better, but you have to be nice to other people. If you get a chance to talk to somebody, or show your book to somebody, respect that person. I would definitely recommend that you go online and find out about that person you're meeting. So you know who he is, what he did, all the information, so maybe you can impress him. "You know, I saw your campaign…," and he thinks, "This guy really knows who I am and he wants to work for me."

Number two is don't do campaigns for a product that does not exist. But don't do a big campaign. Don't do a campaign for Nike again because it's very tough to beat what they have. So choose a small brand that never made it big-time, and find a unique selling point they have, and create a personality for the brand. Choose a second-tier brand and make them a first-tier brand.

Number three: I think this is the best time in your life to find the right partner—a copy partner or art partner. So if you're a copywriter, keep your eyes open when you're looking for a job to find the right art director, because when you find the right partner, that's half the battle. That's very, very, very important. And always choose a partner who is better than you. And that's it. That's the secret of this business. [BI]

To see Raj Kamble's work, please visit http://breaking.in

COLIN BYRNE
CREATIVE DIRECTOR
VCCP LONDON &
KEVIN RUSSELL
CONCEPT DEVELOPER
DIGITASLBI
LONDON

Interviewed at AKQA, London.

What do you look for in a student portfolio? And what impresses you? And is it always a website for you?

CB: In terms of ideas, an appetite to explore channels other than print and TV. In communication terms, make sure it's easy to get to. A recipient wants to get to the work as quickly as possible, so make sure that the work is not buried as a link, within a CV, that's password protected, and doesn't work in Internet Explorer…Make it easy. Create a PDF of your work and make sure the PDF is given as much love as the rest of your work.

KR: Yeah. And for me, it's the formulaic, "Here's the three print posters with picture, headline, logo, or strapline, logo." Very conventional. But one of the problems we're working with the D&AD [Design & Art Direction, a British educational organization] to try and rectify is the fact that things have moved along over the last, 10, 15 years in advertising. It's not just about filling boxes. It's not just about communicating to consumers. It's about engaging them, and getting a two-way dialogue. And keep that going for three months with a limited budget, and get them involved in something. And some of the tutors don't have an idea of how that works. Some have come from 1970s advertising school. What we like, and what I like to see, is a bit more of a fresh perspective on integrated stuff. The students should be the next generation of creators, and for them to come in with something that looks like [something that's been done in the past is not good]. In terms of agencies, look at Goodby and Crispin Porter. You've got these fully integrated ideas, and it doesn't necessarily have to be, "Here's your TV ad, and here's your this and that." It's like the "fast" for the [Volkswagen] Golf. It's an actual toy that [Crispin Porter + Bogusky] built to create desirability. So fresh ideas that totally buck the trend and just go against the grain. That's what I look for. And it's not just about websites. Definitely not. It's just ideas.

Do people bring in sketches of print ads? Or do they bring in things that are comped up on a computer?

CB: Both.

Or websites? What do you prefer to see?

KR: As long as the ideas shine through, we're really not pushed. A little bit of effort does go a long way. But a very badly drawn scamp makes it look like they couldn't be bothered, or they've just knocked it out that morning. And sometimes they have.

CB: If they have just a really beautifully polished piece of design, that has its merits too. To survive in this industry you have to be versatile. Being a creative thinker, capable of originating ideas and then bringing them to life beautifully, makes you more employable. The same applies to being able to write and bring the idea to life through language. Don't think that agencies are merely looking for creatives who can originate ideas—they want people who have a point of view on how the finished product should look and behave, also.

"DON'T THINK THAT AGENCIES ARE MERELY LOOKING FOR CREATIVES WHO CAN ORIGINATE IDEAS—THEY WANT PEOPLE WHO HAVE A POINT OF VIEW ON HOW THE FINISHED PRODUCT SHOULD LOOK AND BEHAVE, ALSO."

KR: It really goes a long way as well, to show that they've got Photoshop skills; they've got a passion for design and layout. If you can clearly see, "Right. That person's going to go in an art direction." Because the creative teams these days are all saying, "Oh, well we do a bit of both" [art direction and copywriting]. Sometimes it gets to that point where it's like, "Well, we need to hand it off to someone." And they've only done, maybe, 40 percent of the job.

For copy, do you need to see evidence that someone can write copy?

KR: Yes. Someone who's got a good handle of the written language, and someone who's got a good handle of design and a passion for design. Because the ideas are very important but I think there's been a lot of focus—too much focus—on just pure ideas and not enough on art direction and design, basically. And they've been treated as completely different principles but…

CB: "Get a trade, Son," my dad always said. Writing is my trade, and if all hell breaks loose and

this industry goes belly up, I hope I'd be able to turn my hand to churning out brochure copy, pamphlets, parish newsletters—anything to put food on the table. If you can write or design, you'll never go hungry.

What do you think of things that aren't ads and don't have anything to do with ads?

CB: It's great to see if someone has other skills that could be put to use and nurtured within the agency. Some agencies look at non-advertising skills and interests over and above industry experience. It's a creative business so showing some individuality is key, right? I like to see what people are interested in—that they have a geeky side or a techy side. That stuff can be nurtured and put to use; it's a bonus. If they keep falcons, or got a bronze medal at the Lithuanian Ball Dancing World Cup in 1996, I struggle to see why that makes them more employable.

KR: It's about commercial gain, isn't it? We've got a hell of a lot of talented people here. When you keep finding very talented people, they tend to be talented in more than one field. We've got a lot of good illustrators, really talented photographers, animators, musicians here—published people, people who spend half their time traveling around doing that sort of thing.

Do you have any advice for someone who wants to get into, or is interested in, a digital agency, but they're coming from a traditional portfolio school?

KR: Definitely. Do veer away from, and spend two projects at least trying to veer away from, the "three-print, one 30-second script" execution of a campaign. Because I think traditional agencies, even now, are starting to think, "Well, we need to start getting like Crispin," and becoming a bit more integrated and a bit more off the wall with our thinking in terms of format.

So, do attempt digital. You want to display your thinking through digital in some way. It still could be a scamp and stuff—you don't need to work up a website—and do some coding, or anything like that. They hire the experts to do that for you. It's just about this engagement. It's a very simple principle. And the very simple difference between the two is one is push messaging—TV, cinema, press—where you have a captive audience and you're pushing it out, not expecting any response. You can't measure it. With digital, you are expecting a response. You're expecting them to come further into your website. Go 'round, watch this film, send it on to a friend, do that. Enter your email address. And it's very much an active relationship. And you're asking a hell of a lot of the person. So that's the thing we need to see. Can your thinking engage someone to that level where they spend seven minutes with this brand, and leave their email address, etc., etc.? So there's a lot more to ask. And it's very trackable.

CB: Explore new places your ideas can go. You don't need to have an expansive knowledge of emerging technologies and all the latest trends, just an awareness of the tools available to you and a desire to test your ideas in such places to see if they can work harder, sing louder, or simply become even better than they were. Show that you think outside of the TV/print box and you'll get noticed. BI

To see the work of Colin Byrne & Kevin Russell, please visit http://breaking.in

CROCKETT JEFFERS
CREATIVE DIRECTOR
BBDO
SAN FRANCISCO

Do you think books have changed recently?

From when I put my book together, and I finished at the Ad Center [now VCU Brandcenter] in 1999, it's changed so much that I feel like I kind of got in when it was still relatively easy to get a job in advertising. Because it was just print ads, and you could do spreads and maybe you might have an outdoor idea like a bus shelter, or a billboard, or something like that. But this was before people started putting guerrilla ideas in their book or anything interactive. It seems like that came not too long after, but now you have to. I think you have to show so much more of who you are and show that

you're an interesting person and can think beyond just the page. Like a print ad, I think now, is pretty boring to a lot of people; but at the same time we still do a lot of print and you still have to know how to write a headline. And so I think there's probably some sort of balance or a sweet spot in there where you can show that you do a headline, and a great headline, and then you also can do a website and write in the interactive space.

How do you think you should show your personality in a book? Through ads, or through other things than ads?

Well, both. I think that if you're a funny person, you should have work in there that shows that. And that makes it seem like you would be a good person to have around. You understand what's funny. Because it is a fun industry. And people like to have fun people around, which is a sort of silly statement, but it's true. But beyond the ads, I love seeing when people have little things that they've invented, or designed, or published. Like poetry or something—it just makes you seem more interesting and makes it seem like, as a writer, you have an appreciation for more than just the language of advertising. I think it's really cool and it's almost a lost art nowadays. So, anything that shows that you're, and I hate to use this word because it is so overused, but that shows that you're a "creative person." I think that is really interesting and you kind of have to have it now. It's hard to get hired on just a traditional book of advertising. At least if you want to work at a great place. I mean, especially like Wieden, they like to hire interesting people. And I know that—I'm speaking as someone who has never worked there, who's gotten my book sent back several times, but I feel like a place like that intentionally looks for people who are artists and creative people, more than just good at advertising. But you tell me, I mean, you worked there.

Well, I want to know what you think, though.

All right.

What impresses you in a student book other than having personality come through? What do you look for?

I like to see people who try to have something difficult in their book. I've seen so many books from ad schools where it's just these really great, simple, a lot of times visual solutions to products that really aren't that hard. And it's just like in the real world, you're not going to work on, you're not going to have clients like that, 95 percent of the time. So I think it's nice when someone's got a bank, or a utility, or something like that and you can tell that they really made the most of a difficult assignment. Because it shows that they're ready to step in and tackle the business problem and that's really what it's all about. You don't start working at an agency and it's Mad magazine, you know? People are looking to you to solve their business problems, and if you don't know how to do that for a real-life client, then you're not really adding much. So I like to see students that really have some smart solutions for hard products.

Do you think it's possible to get a job with a bunch of sketches? Or do you think a book needs to be laid out nicely on a computer?

It depends what you're trying to do. If you're trying to be an art director, I don't think you can because so much of it is you have to be able to, on the first day, sit down, and they give you a computer, and you need to be able to lay something out. I think a writer can. And I think that…everybody always says the idea is king. And that's still so true. So, if they're great ideas, probably so. But I like writers who are good designers too. And I like art directors who can write. And so it's hard to show that you can really play on both sides of that if you're handing in sketches. Great ideas are awesome but you've kind of got to show that you can just step in and do it. Because you're not going to give the client a marker comp, you know?

Do you think long-copy ads are important?

No, I don't. That's one thing that has definitely changed since I came out of school. I had some long copy in my book—nobody read it. I think one person read them. And I just felt bad for them, just sitting there, out of courtesy, reading all of this copy that probably wasn't even that good and they just did it to be nice, I think. It was like an excruciating 10 minutes that they spent on these three ads. And then, in the almost 10 years

that I've been in this industry, I've never once written a long-copy ad, or I've only been around a couple at the agencies where I was working. It's kind of a thing of the past. As a requirement for a student book, I'd much rather see work in different media. Like, "Where's your outdoor campaign" and, "Where's your interactive?"

And do you have any tips for someone who's just starting out?

Well, then I guess I have two answers. One, for the person who's just putting their book together: It's just so important to put yourself in your book because it's your only chance that you have of showing this agency that you want to work for, probably more than anything in the world at that point in your life, who you are and that you're an interesting person. Make them want to read more and more. And then it just comes with time, and re-crafting, and making it just as smart and fun, and engaging as you can make it. And you have to be hard on yourself because there are so many people out there who want the same job and who are going to those lengths. And it depends where you want to work. If you want to work at a really great place, I think that's kind of the price of entry. There are probably plenty of places to go where you don't need to go to such lengths.

"IT'S NICE WHEN SOMEONE'S GOT A BANK, OR A UTILITY, OR SOMETHING LIKE THAT AND YOU CAN TELL THAT THEY REALLY MADE THE MOST OF A DIFFICULT ASSIGNMENT."

And then for the person who does have their book together, and it's exactly how they want it, and they've just really put all they can into their book, I would say timing is just such a funny part of the business. You have to get a little bit lucky that they're looking for somebody at your level. And you have to stay strong and keep knocking on doors because it can be so deflating and just so hard on somebody when they're not getting anywhere with showing their book around. That said, if you keep getting feedback on your book, and it's consistent, that this isn't working or that isn't, you have to be open to changing it because it's just…maybe you didn't think about something a certain way when you were putting it together. And even though you thought it was perfect, maybe it wasn't. And you have to be okay with going back and totally redoing something, or dropping something that you just thought was great, if your feedback is consistent. And it's hard, because also, to a certain extent, you have to believe in what you've done, and that it is cool, and that there is a place that is going to think it's cool too, and maybe that's the place for you. But again, if the feedback is coming back consistently that this or that's not working, you might want to…

Don't get too attached to the way it is now?

Yeah. And it's hard, because if your art director goes in one direction, and they got a job, and they're working, and you're like, "Gosh! I don't have those files" or, "I don't know how to fix that" or, "that means a new illustration." It's hard. It's a pain in the ass, but it's worth it.

I think it's good to look at other books when you're first starting out. I guess, especially, it's good to know what a bunch of student books look like. It gives you a sense of where "the bar" is. Especially look at books of people who got hired. If you have the chance to go to sit with someone at an agency, and they still have junior books. Or even books from some of their mid-level and senior people, if they still happen to have those lying around. That's really a great way to understand where the bar is for that agency, or at that level of agency, I think. I remember when we were interns at Wieden one summer, and it was the first year they were doing interns. I looked at these books and then Jeff Kling's book, which was that famous sketchbook of funny lines and stuff. And that was really helpful to know what you needed to do if you wanted to be serious about getting a job. That was very cool.

I guess if you're starting out, the award annuals are still a good place to start just because you start to understand the language—the way that ad language works. And the flow of a headline,

and why something's good. I used to sit down and look at an award book, and look at an ad and say, "What is it about this that I like and why did it work so well?" So I think that's a good thing to do: to understand why you like something, and why other people liked it. And then I think you start to put some of those techniques into your own work. And I think another hard thing is keeping your book going once you get a job. So I'll look at my print now, and it feels terrible, you know? And I think you've got to keep trying to add to it. Even though it's not all that old, it just starts to kind of sit there.

Just always be working on it and updating it?

Yeah, because everybody else is. Everybody who wants to work at the places you want to work is bringing in better and better stuff. It seems like you've got to just keep building it. It's hard. You feel like you get to one level and you feel like you're good there, and then you want to go up but you have to have the work to show that, and it keeps going and going, and that kind of never stops. You're always rebuilding. 〔BI〕

To see Crockett Jeffers's work, please visit http://breaking.in

**GREG FARLEY
CREATIVE DIRECTOR
Y&R
NEW YORK**

**What do you look for in a student book?
And what impresses you?**

Talent in the basics. Show me a writer that can write or an art director with a unique visual point of view and I'll gladly work with you. I'd rather see a perfect print ad than a poorly written or designed social media idea. Being good at your specialty doesn't make you a dinosaur.

How important is finish? If ideas are the most important thing, can sketches be enough? Do you look at physical books anymore or is it all websites?

Finish is a fact of life. These days there are stacks of near-professionally crafted books lining the offices of every recruiter. Take the time to make your book sing, but do it online. No one should be killing forests for advertising anymore.

How important is writing? Do you need to see long copy?

This is very important: If you choose to be a writer just because you don't want to be an art director, then pick another career. Embrace writing. Whether you write long copy or headlines, you will stand out if you're good.

What do you think of showing work that is not advertising? Things like art, journal writing, photography, hobbies, etc.

Yes, do that. Make sure it has its own section in your book and only include your best. If it doesn't look as polished as the rest of your book, leave it out.

Do you have any other advice for a student or junior trying to get into the business, either in putting together a book or how to actually start looking for jobs?

Design and build your own site. Don't just plop things into a pre-installed web template. Your site should be a book piece in and of itself. BI

To see Greg Farley's work, please visit http://breaking.in

EUGENE CHEONG
REGIONAL CREATIVE DIRECTOR
OGILVY & MATHER
ASIA PACIFIC
SINGAPORE

What do you look for in a student portfolio? And what impresses you?

I want to see five great things. Too often students try to bulk up their books, which only shows a lack of judgment and good taste. Ideally, I'd like to see a couple of posters. They are the ultimate test. Any fool can blow up an idea, but it takes a great deal of skill to boil a thought down to a few words and a single picture.

I was going to ask you if you thought print was still important...

I now read mostly on-screens. Print has to evolve into a digital interactive form. A few apps have shown what's possible. The industry, as usual, is stuck with printing-press print, which looks godawful on the iPad. The day will come when it becomes mandatory for print to come with motion, music, effects, animation, and interaction with fingers.

How important is finish? Could sketches be enough?

Creative directors have [an] incredibly short attention span. Present your ideas in the most efficient manner and forget about all the craftybits. As long as the idea comes across crystal clearly, roughs are fine. Of course, platform ideas need to be explained. The best way to do that is with a concept board, which, funnily enough, is not too dissimilar to a good old-fashioned press ad.

You're known for long copy. Do you think it's necessary to have that in a book?

I don't think I necessarily want to read long copy during an interview, but evidence that a person is comfortable with words is important. Writing is refined thinking. A writer is generally more adept at constructing an argument, laying out a story, and, consequently, changing a mind.

So, good writing is evidence of good thinking, which is always useful.

Good writing is a learned skill. If you want to write well, you must do two things above all: read a lot and write a lot. You can only learn to write by imitation and practice. Unfortunately, copywriters only spend about 10 percent of their day writing. Meetings, conference calls, and talking in general tend to take up the rest of their time. As a result, the quality of writing in the business is dismal.

Are there common mistakes that juniors make?

The biggest mistake young people make is underestimating how brutal the world is out there. A semi-glamorous business like advertising attracts wannabes like flies to a rotting corpse. They buzz into the business in one dark endless swarm, but after 20 years or so, only a handful survives. It's a super competitive business. In Brazil, if you don't make creative director by 35, you leave the industry to do something else. I think laying pipe or digging trenches is easier than writing ads. When you first start out, there is no life, apart from work. You have to be able to take rejection without taking offense. If you don't love it, you won't stick around for very long.

"I WANT TO SEE FIVE GREAT THINGS. TOO OFTEN STUDENTS TRY TO BULK UP THEIR BOOKS, WHICH ONLY SHOWS A LACK OF JUDGMENT AND GOOD TASTE."

What do you think of showing work that isn't advertising?

I've been in the business for 30 years, and in all that time I've only seen one beginner with a decent book. That's not surprising, I suppose. After all, you only learn to do ads once you are in the business. I'm always fascinated by the obsessions of young people. Adrian Chan showed me his amazingly intricate drawings. Claire Chen her cross-stitching collages. And Ashidiq his drum and bass mixes. If they can focus their energy like a laser into doing great art, they can, most likely, refocus their mental power into doing great advertising.

Do you have any advice on job hunting or getting in touch with the right people?

Whatever you do, don't write an email to a creative director. Not only does the guy have a short attention span, he's as busy as a one-legged man in an ass-kicking contest. I usually get other people to "shortlist" books for me. That way, I don't waste my time on the mediocre majority. There are no shortcuts: the only way through the door of an agency is with a good book. Even if a creative director doesn't have a space for you, he'd recommend you to his CD pals.

You talked about editing before. Do you have any advice on how to decide which campaigns should go in when you don't really know yourself?

Show your book to a bunch of people you trust. If they even hint that a piece of work is crap, bin it and start again. Young people need to learn to disassociate themselves from their work and not take criticism personally. If the work is merely okay all the justification in the world won't make it great. Crush it up and start again. To achieve quality, there's just no substitute for quantity. On an average day, I can come up with about five decent ideas. In two weeks, I'd have 50 ideas. I pin all 50 of them up on a wall and I get a few good guys to help me pick the best ones. We usually end up with about 10. My ratio is roughly one to five. When you're starting out your ratio is closer to 1 to 50. But take heart; your ratio will improve with time. ⬛BI

To see Eugene Cheong's work, please visit http://breaking.in

**DAVID DROGA
FOUNDER &
CREATIVE CHAIRMAN
DROGA5
NEW YORK**

What do you look for in a student book? And what impresses you?

It depends on what needs we have. For me, the most important thing is—and there's a couple of high-level generic things—but I'll drill down. Obviously, there's no question it comes down to their thinking, and the diversity of their thinking, and the originality. I think a lot of students spend their time trying to emulate what's been done before, and to be on a level that's in sync with the certain agencies that they're going into, or stuff that's won awards in years gone by. And for me, it's not about that. For me, it's about the broadness of their thinking and really just seeing how they tackle something in a lateral way.

Obviously, being a student is a fantastic thing because you can cherry-pick any brand and work on anything, right? The canvas is huge and completely open-ended. And I think I like to see the degree of difficulty that they put in their book as well. I said the broadness of their thinking, and how they've brought it alive in more than just a couple of mediums. For me I'm not seduced by the finish of the work. If I'm looking for someone as a designer then I want to see aesthetic sensibilities and all that sort of stuff. But if I'm looking for someone purely on a conceptual level, I really don't care how it's mocked up. It's more just to see the diversity and the degree of difficulty. Because, as I said, I'm a classical advertising guy. I was sort of brought up in, and built my career on, TV and print. But now, particularly with what we're trying to do now, while we still do that and I still believe in that strongly, there's so much more out there than that. So I want to see the different canvases that people play on. That's what I look at. And the thinking within those.

You mentioned the finish of the work. What about just sketches? Can that be enough these days?

It can be enough. There are some books that I've seen where the finish is so extraordinary. They've put so much effort into how they've mocked something up and brought it to life. But the idea—the foundation of the idea—is so rubbish. So I feel bad for them that they've wasted so much time. Again, if it's someone who's going to have a heavy art-directional role or a design role, then I want to see their eye. No question. But if it's a conceptual thing, I don't care if it's on a…I mean, in London I've hired people who literally did have scraps of paper. Maybe that was a statement [from] them, but it was original. It was what was on those scraps of paper.

What about copy for writers? Do you want to see the evidence that they can write?

Definitely. I think copy is one of those things that goes in and out of favor all the time. But as someone who started as a copywriter, I see myself as a writer. I like to know that they understand the craft of writing. And I want to see their personality. How they write. Because whether it's long, long copy, or it's punchy, I still want to see that they understand the best way to convey something in their words. So, definitely. I want creatives to have a skill set. I don't want everyone to be so neutral that they're all vanilla.

We don't have departments as such. It's pretty integrated here. And people have certain skill sets. So the digital designer sits next to the old-school designer, or whatever you want to call them. But I like to know that people do have skill sets so they can mix it up a bit. I think just having a floor, just of concepters, sounds really exciting for the first phase, but when it's got to go live, you drop the ball if the nuance parts aren't crafted. So it depends who you're looking for. But, first and foremost, it's the thinking. And then I think it's a shame that the craft of advertising has disappeared. Because all the best stuff you admire, whichever, wherever it is, there's still a great craft to it. That's a shame because a Mac can't craft something for you. It can make things easier for you, but it doesn't craft them for you, it doesn't write them for you. So definitely, I like the old-school values with new-school outlook.

And what do you think about putting things in a book that aren't ads at all? Just personal work, or art, or journal writing…

I think if it adds dimension to who they are. If it's just trying to paint them as a wacky, interesting person, maybe. I look around my office and I've decorated it with some real Chinese contemporary art. It's a bit of who I am. If it adds some texture to who they are and tells more of a story so I can understand a little bit more about how they think, definitely. But if it's just things they like and they borrow from, if it doesn't manifest itself in their work and their thinking, then it's a distraction.

I mean their work that they've created.

Oh, absolutely. Our website is quite simple, but as much as we celebrate our work, we celebrate our people. There is a whole section which is what people do outside of work. And I don't judge what they do, but I love to know that people in our office are not just one-dimensional advertising people. Some of them have a passion for photography, and art, and movies, whatever. I just like people to be well rounded. So, if it adds that dimension, definitely. I think there's no downside to that.

Some people become such disciples of advertising. And they think if they can quote every ad that was ever made, and who wrote it, and who art-directed it, that makes them more interesting. Well no, that really just makes you a library of information. It doesn't actually make you forward looking. I like people who have reference, but I'd rather take one who has more dimension than just advertising because that's what we're in. We're in the business of communicating, and understanding emotions and people and trends, and all that sort of stuff. And you can't actually, really, sincerely get involved in it unless you have empathy with it, and an understanding of it. So I think that helps.

Do you have any other advice for someone who's putting a book together or just trying to get into the industry?

My thing is I'm not a big fan of people who do weird and wacky things to try and get in. Do you know what I mean?

Like stunts?

I always appreciate the effort. But I've often found, with the majority of people who do that kind of thing, their books are never as good, or as original, or as funny, as the stunts are. So I often get disappointed. And sometimes it crosses the line where it's almost like stalking and all that sort of stuff. I absolutely admire persistence. I think it's fantastic. I think really understanding who you're sending your book to and what they're about in the agency and all that is fantastic. So it's not just a mass mailing. But crossing the line where it's stalking doesn't really work with me. I'm sure to some people it makes them stand out. But only do it as long as your book is even better. I always find it more disappointing when someone does something funny and I get to meet them and their book is just boring and mainstream and all that. I think, "Wow, it's a shame you didn't put more effort into your book."

I remember way back when I was in Australia and London there were a couple people who were relentless, persistent, showed work ethic, showed understanding, showed learning, all that sort of stuff. And they just bombarded us with new thinking for…it's almost like they redid their book every week and sent it over. And, in the beginning, I didn't even like the stuff, but after a while the ideas got better and better. And I just thought, "This person is unbelievably persistent." And they did it for something like three months. So they're prolific. They're prolific and the work got better, and I just thought, "That's someone who's seriously keen." Realize it's not an easy thing—just hoping that lightning strikes straight away. And I hired them. I was like, "This is the type of work ethic and person that I like." Obviously, as I said, I liked their thinking because it's not about just creating a sweatshop. But I think being tactical and smart about how you get in, as opposed to just, "I'll just send my book out."

And also sometimes students think you have to target just the creative director. Obviously the person at the top does make the final decision usually but sometimes it's smart to work your way up through the agency. If you befriend someone in the agency who can give you some advice [that can work]. So, you navigate your way through the agency to get your book in there. I think definitely, obviously, in the new world, most stuff is done with links, which is always a good way. Because it lets people navigate through in their own time.

Do you prefer a website to a physical book?

I think a lot of the time I do. Just because I think you can actually show more and it can be done on my own time, without the awkward silence of looking at someone's book while they're sort of sitting there being nervous. And if I like what's on the website, then I'll see them in person.

"I THINK THE ONES WHO ARE MORE FAITHFUL TO WHO THEY ARE AND THEIR OWN TONE OF VOICE DO BETTER. THE ONES WHO ARE A LITTLE BIT BRAVER AND BOLDER ABOUT WHAT THEY DO."

But that's not saying the website has to be done with Flash and [be] over the top. To the principle we're talking about, about scraps of paper, I don't mind if it's pretty rough around the edges, as long as it works. Again, if the thinking is great, that's the thing. I think a lot of people are so desperate to be of the standard of advertising, that it makes them mass market. And almost mediocre and the same, do you know what I mean?

Because they're trying to fit into whatever?

Well, they're looking at the industry thinking, "Well this is what's acceptable." And everyone's looking at the same barometer of benchmarks. They all aspire to the same thing. They all end up being the same. And I think the ones who are more faithful to who they are and their own tone of voice do better. The ones who are a little bit braver and bolder about what they do. But I understand it's not just about who writes the funnier stuff and who writes the more shocking stuff. Everything has to be grounded in great insights and creativity. That's what I look for.

I've always known, for the last 15 years, when I see a book, I think, "God! That's really interesting. "And you just know straight away if it's someone you want to talk to and meet. I think restraint is a really interesting thing as well. There's not a lot of restraint in portfolios. I'd rather see a book with five great thoughts and nothing else than 25 average thoughts. Because the first question I always ask when I see anyone's book is, "Do you like your book?" Because that tells me a lot. If a student says that, "I absolutely love it," and I look at it, and I think, "Oh, that's rubbish" then I'm thinking, "Well maybe we've got different sensibilities." If they say, "Well, you know, not bad, but I think I could do better." Or they know what they like, and they know their weaknesses, then it's sort of more an open and honest conversation. Anyway, I'm a rambler, so…

No, that's great; that's what I want.

What else?

Well, I'm out of questions but as long as you want to ramble…

It's an interesting time. I'll just ramble on some more… The industry has changed so much, but clearly, the principles in the industry are still very much the same. You know, connections, and selling, and all that sort of stuff. But there are so many different influences now. We can influence so many different industries and collaborate with more industries. I think it makes it more exciting. And I think you're getting a lot of interesting people wanting to come [into advertising] you know? A lot of the young people in the last decade sort of weren't interested in advertising. They drifted off to these other, seemingly more glamorous industries. And I think advertising is getting more relevant again. And I think a lot of the sparky young people want to get back into it. Just from the diversity of people that I've been talking to. But we need students. I'm a by-product of an advertising school in Australia. And it's the backbone because they're the only thing that keeps us all along on this ride. BI

To see David Droga's work, please visit http://breaking.in

MATT ORSER
ASSOCIATE CREATIVE DIRECTOR
CRISPIN PORTER + BOGUSKY
MIAMI

What do you look for in a student book? And what impresses you?

I want to be jealous. If I see something that makes me think, "Wow, I wish I did that." That's it. That's all I look for. Because if I was inspired enough by one thing that I saw, that would make it memorable and make it good. It seems like it's easy but it's not. It's really hard to do.

Do you think a student book needs to be finished, or could it just be sketches?

I think student books definitely should be as finished as possible. And I think that everything in the book should be very easy to understand. I feel like I see a lot of stuff nowadays where we're doing a lot more integrated types of campaigns, especially within our books. And it is a trick sometimes to show it in the proper way, and if it is at all confusing, it just loses all of its importance. And that's why it always has to be really finished, and tight, and solid because I need to be able to just flip through it. No one's going to spend that much time. I think a book needs to be polished because then you just understand it quicker. That's it.

Do you think long copy is important?

I've always heard from everyone that writers should have long copy in their book and I think that that's true. I think they should have an element of some copy, and it seems like that should be a requirement. But that's the same way that art directors should have great, well-designed layouts. That's the craft of art directors and copy is the craft of writers.

I don't know if art directors need to have long copy in their book. It would be nice to see how certain art directors treat long copy because I think it's one of the harder things to approach when you're an art director. To do something new with it is really cool to see for an art director. I would be impressed by that as much as

I'd be impressed by a nifty visual solution. But both in the same book is really strong to me. You can't just do what you think you're good at 100 times in a row. You should have serious diversity in your book.

What do you think about things in your book that aren't ads?

I think stuff that isn't advertising in your book is really good to have. Actually, I would prefer that more people did it, but whatever it is, it's got to be interesting. It can't be trivial. I think it's especially about, "Does this person do other forms of art? And what do they do? Do they make films? Do they illustrate?" But that's cool to see because it just says a lot about who they are as a creative person.

> *"IF YOU'RE GOING TO GET INTO THIS INDUSTRY, YOU HAVE TO JUST COMMIT. IT'S NOT AN INDUSTRY THAT YOU CAN JUST TRY FOR FUN."*

And for me the people who have a life outside their job, creatively, are the people who I think just bring more to the table. And I think it's also just cool to see because it's inspiring what people do.

Do you have any tips on how to get into the industry?

There's the obvious, "Yeah, you have to go to ad school," which is what a lot of people say. At least get around someone who can help you make a book. All you've got to do is make a book. That's what you do to get into the industry. But the book has got to be good. But, above everything else, if you're going to get into this industry, you have to just commit. It's not an industry that you can just try for fun. If you want to be good at advertising, you have to commit right then, and move into your career with that full intention to be good. 🄱🄸

To see Matt Orser's work, please visit http://breaking.in

JAMES MOK
EXECUTIVE CREATIVE DIRECTOR
ASIA PACIFIC
FCB INTERNATIONAL
AUCKLAND

What do you look for in a student portfolio? And what impresses you?

I certainly like individual flair. I've always thought that the best creativity comes out of a person's ability to express themselves as an individual. I think it's really hard when you're young and you haven't spent a lot of time in advertising. You're still figuring out things, and you invariably copy a lot. You're mimicking techniques you're drawn to, so naturally your work is incredibly derivative, which is unfortunate because everyone is looking for something original.

"I LOOK FOR SOMEONE WHO CAN TAKE A BRAND'S POINT OF VIEW AND OVERLAY THEIR OWN PERSONAL POINT OF VIEW ABOUT THE WORLD, ABOUT SOCIETY, ABOUT PEOPLE."

I look for someone who can take a brand's point of view and overlay their own personal point of view about the world, about society, about people. Human insights, I guess. Then work has a bit more meaning. When ads are just a superficial gag or just a play on words, it doesn't really get through on an emotional level.

Can you think of an example that you've seen?

I saw a book with an idea promoting the impending arrival of a new elephant at the Auckland Zoo. Their insight was the elephant already at the zoo had

become socially awkward because it had been alone, so we needed to help it by making sure the public visited it before and after the new elephant arrived. I thought that was interesting—to empathize with the current elephant was a lovely take on the new elephant coming to the zoo.

Are there any common mistakes that you see in student portfolios?

The shit-piss-fart jokes, I guess. I just find shock gags and puerile humor tiresome. It says to me that the person lacks a maturity about how to sell a product. This type of work pulls the rest of the portfolio down. People's books are often judged by their worst work, rather than their best work. I'm looking for consistency. If I see one good idea in a book of 10 pieces, it feels like luck. Whereas if half the ideas are good, there is something going on.

Something that has been Mac-ed up, but is weak, is unfortunate. They have to show that they've worked out what a good idea is pretty quickly. I remember when I was starting out I don't think I had a clue, so I'm grateful I started in easier times. But there are more people trying to get in now, so the consistency says a lot. Either cut the crap ideas and have a smaller book, or make them better. Never assume that your book is your final book. It's a constantly evolving thing. Change something every week.

I wanted to ask you about the level of finish you're looking for. Can sketches be enough?

Absolutely. Sketches are fine if the creative can posterize their idea. The first thing you're looking for is good ideas and I know that craft will improve over time. But you have to be passionate about it and that has to come through in your book. I want to know that they are as into their craft as they are into their idea. Because a great idea poorly crafted is a tragedy.

What do you think about personal projects, art, journal writing, and other things that aren't advertising?

I like to see it because you get a more rounded view of the individual. I like to understand the person's point of view on life. I like to see the stuff that they do personally and their interests. It doesn't have to be visual arts or popular culture, they could like karate—I don't really care. A person with a lot of life experiences is probably going to be better at empathizing and expressing themselves in interesting ways.

Do you think copywriters need to show the ability to write at length?

For sure. I like to see that the person's taken a bit of pride to show that they can write and that there is some delight in writing. I'm an art director, and I think I can write. But when I see writers write, I know I'm shit. In a team, I want to know that one is going to be the writer. A lot of them say, "We do a bit of both." Does that mean you're both as passionate about the same thing? Or that you're both ambivalent about making the writing and the art direction amazing. I just think it's important, if you've chosen to do something, do it incredibly well. And be enthusiastic and passionate about it. Even if the creative director doesn't like every piece in your book, at least show you're passionate about it. That passion will take you so much further.

Do you have any other advice for students or juniors?

Here in New Zealand, I'm aware that we're a long way away from the rest of the world. Apart from the truth that our work should talk to the great human truths, I'm looking for a New Zealand flavor. I'm looking for people who understand our culture and have an instinctive understanding of what makes our culture tick. And if we're constantly looking at overseas technique, trends, and language, I think the danger is that we forget what makes our people and our society tick. What they respond to, what they love and laugh at, in the pursuit of some sort of global language. I think that's a shame. Homogenizing advertising ideas is the worst thing you can do. Anyone who gets that—not in a jingoistic, clichéd way—but in a really fresh way, is great. And if anyone wants to come down to New Zealand from overseas with their book, I just want them to take the time to think about what makes us a little bit different.

How else can people improve their book?

Be careful about how many pieces you put in. Probably no more than 10 pieces. It also surprises me how little

digital work is in people's books. This is our future! And we're talking about kids who are digital natives, and yet so little of their work demonstrates a good understanding of digital ideas, which is a shame.

My sense is that ad schools teach traditional media ideas first because you get to learn how an idea can be expressed in three seconds—that's a good thing. But it would be good to show how you can express yourself digitally. Show how smart you are at "getting it." People coming into advertising don't have a choice now because everything will be digital in the future.

It's also good to see a bit of a creative rationale for the work. No more than one or two sentences to frame it. It shows how you get strategic thinking. It shows you're starting to get it. You're basing your creative thinking off the objective of the brief as opposed to creativity that exists in a vacuum.

This is a generalization, but I think creatives are not that into business. It's just the way we think. So you throw a bunch of 18- and 19-year-olds into ad school and the challenge is they might be channeling a lot of creative energy, but they're not channeling it with a purpose. When students can apply their creative thinking to a problem—how to frame a product, or persuade a person to think a certain way, or do a certain thing—it's a good thing. BI

To see James Mok's work, please visit http://breaking.in

**TY MONTAGUE
CEO
CO: COLLECTIVE
NEW YORK**

What do you look for in a student book? And what impresses you?

I always look for two things: Work that makes me uncomfortable and work that falls outside the bounds of what most folks would consider to be advertising.

What I tell juniors is that, for the rest of their career, they will have someone telling them why a certain idea is too weird or crazy to show to a client. This is their time to show what they really believe is great. I hired a guy once because he had invented a line of products that were designed to raise money for the democratic party…peanut butter, jelly, stuff like that. I thought it was a genius way to raise money and, at the same time, raise awareness for the cause while people are walking down the aisle at Walmart or Piggly Wiggly. It's not a crazy or extreme idea, just a really smart way for the party to communicate in a new way with people, and to raise money.

I also consciously look for people who have creative passions outside of advertising: photography or painting or poetry or music or whatever. I think that the more advertising draws from and stays close to the fine arts the better off we will be as an industry.

The third thing I look for these days is an appreciation for the possibilities of technology. I just read that the History Channel is using Foursquare to promote a show about the history of America by enabling little pop-ups that tell you about the history of the location where you are checking in. Genius. Very much advertising, but advertising that is completely contextual and hyper-local. A book with ideas like that in it goes a long way with me.

How important is finish? If ideas are the most important thing, can sketches be enough? Do you look at actual books anymore, or is it all websites?

I'll look at anything. If the person is applying as a designer or an IA or creative technologist, then some work in that specific area is important. If they are applying as an idea person full stop, then that's what I look for. Are the ideas good? I don't care so much whether they are really slickly executed. And really slick execution minus great ideas is even worse. Having said that, the tools for making stuff have never been more available. I was at a friend's house the other day—this guy is a well known and very successful commercial director—and he was making a short film in his living room using a digital still camera. At this guy's level he could have chosen whatever tool he wanted to make his film, and he chose a tool

that is available to pretty much anyone. My advice to students today is: make stuff. Make a lot of stuff. And keep making that stuff better. Your "book"—or your body of work—is never finished. If you're talented, you should plan on spending the next 20 years making and remaking that body of work. Hopefully for a significant fraction of that time someone will be paying you to do it. But do it because you love it and do it because you're never satisfied with anything you do.

How important is copy? Do you need to see long-copy ads?

If I'm hiring someone to be a writer then, yes, copy is important. The idea swirling around lately that words are dead is, I think, pretty silly. What do you spend most of your time on the Internet doing? Reading. Texts, emails, blogs, whatever. I predict that that behavior will continue, so the ability to string together a coherent argument using words will get you a very long way.

"IT'S A RACE. AND IF YOU WANT TO WIN IT, YOU NEED TO WORK HARDER THAN ANYONE ELSE."

I think of good copy as salesmanship in text. The questions I ask myself are: Can this person put together a persuasive argument to get me to lay down money on this product? Do they make me want it? Do I get to the end feeling entertained? Informed? Wanting more? Those are the hallmarks of great copywriting. Still relevant and valid today, I believe.

Do you have any other advice for a student or junior trying to get into the business, either in putting together a book or how to actually start looking for jobs?

Get work. I mean anywhere. Don't be too picky too early. My first creative job in the business was at Grey. I figured I'd be better off working on my book on somebody else's dime than wandering around in the street waiting for Jeff Goodby to call me. The key to getting better at anything is practice. Use the early time in your career to figure out who you admire, and work your way steadily toward them. But don't turn down a paying gig because you feel like you're above it. That's a good way to starve. It is also a good way to get run over from behind by people who are spending their days inside an actual agency somewhere getting practical experience.

Once you have a job, remember that that's not the end, that's just the beginning. It's a race. And if you want to win it, you need to work harder than anyone else. Get in early and leave late. Volunteer for the tough assignments. Avoid gossip and politics. Show up and be helpful. Eat your vegetables and call your mom every once in a while. She worries about you. BI

To see Ty Montague's work, please visit http://breaking.in

STEVE YEE
GROUP CREATIVE DIRECTOR
DAVID&GOLIATH
LOS ANGELES

Interviewed at TBWA/Chiat/Day, Los Angeles.

What do you look for in a student book? And what impresses you?

The thing that impresses me is strong thinking. It's the answer any creative director will say. I see lots of books that show off how funny or how clever a creative can be, which is good. But the thing that I also look for is maturity. Show me you can think beyond a funny headline and attach it to a bigger thought that makes me think the product is cool.

Can someone get a job with a book of sketches these days, or does it need to be finished work?

A good idea is a good idea, so, yeah, I think a person can, but that idea better be amazing. With everything going multimedia however, a sketch may not be enough, particularly for art directors. I have to see your ability to design to properly measure you.

Do you think long copy is important to have?

I think so. Every writer needs to be able to write copy and every art director needs to know how to typeset long copy. Too many times have I seen creative directors compensate for writers who aren't able to craft copy. Or craft type for art directors who don't understand kerning. It can be frustrating.

What do you think about putting things in a book that aren't ads?

I think it's great. I actually prefer that stuff. I heard of one guy who got hired, I think at Wieden, who worked for a skate shop and all he did was make really dumb, funny videos of skaters. That conveyed so much more about the guy than a traditional portfolio. I don't see this often enough.

Do you have any tips on how to get into the industry?

Go live an amazing life. Fill your head with amazing experiences and meet lots of people. Understand culture from every walk of life and appreciate it. You only have unique thoughts if you have unique experiences. If you're a boring person, you have a boring portfolio. So I'd encourage anyone to…as much time as you spend thinking about ads, spend more time trying to fill your brain with things to put into those ads. And you'll always have something that's fresh. BI

To see Steve Yee's work, please visit http://breaking.in

**GREG BELL
DIRECTOR
BACKYARD PRODUCTIONS &
FOUNDER
VENABLES BELL & PARTNERS
SAN FRANCISCO**

Interviewed at Venables Bell & Partners.

What do you look for in a student book? And what impresses you?

Here's the truth: the vast majority of student books suck, so students are already going in with a strike against them. Usually, you're opening it thinking, "Oh God, here we go—a bunch of stuff that will almost certainly be hard to understand, almost there, and rough around the edges." So usually, your expectations are pretty low. You just see so many books as a creative director. It's mind-numbing, really. I'm looking for something that wakes me up. Something surprising. Something that screams at me to pay attention. Even just one ad.

Are there any traps that you feel a lot of students fall into? Or what would you not look for in a student book?

Yeah, being crass for the sake of being crass. Thinking that if you put the word "ass" in your headline the ad is automatically edgy and cool. You can tell when somebody is trying too hard, and it's frightening.

It certainly doesn't mean that I'm looking for conservative stuff. It's just that there are people who have good instincts about what other people find funny and interesting and cool and then there are people who don't. Those who try and fall on their faces. If you can't do it well, don't do it at all.

Do you think that just a book of sketches can be enough these days, or do you think books need to be finished?

It's such a cliché for a creative director to say, "It can be on a napkin if it's a great idea!" Yeah, maybe when you've already got a job! In the world of today's portfolios, you're competing with so many people—the drudgery of looking through all the books that are out there…your chances are not improved if you're peddling sheets of notebook paper. It's just human nature. When you're on the cereal aisle, the generic boxes don't get your attention, do they?

"YOU JUST SEE SO MANY BOOKS AS A CREATIVE DIRECTOR. IT'S MIND-NUMBING, REALLY. I'M LOOKING FOR SOMETHING THAT WAKES ME UP."

So it's sad but it's true, the schools that emphasize polish really do have an advantage. The great ideas that also have polish make a CD think, "Ah! I could hire this guy today and put him to work on real-live ads tomorrow." The guy with the homemade-looking book, you don't have that same confidence.

What do you think about long copy? Is that important to have in a book, either in ad form or in some other sort of writing?

It's a double-edged sword. As a creative director, you get a little nervous when there's not any in a copywriter's book. Writers' books that are all visual solutions or tricky one-liners make you sort of wonder if they can truly write. A little bit of well-crafted body copy can really give somebody an edge.

On the other hand, I've seen writers' books where they just cram the book with a lot of long copy, and it makes you think, "Wow! Those guys are missing job one: jumping off the page and getting people's interest." It can backfire if it seems like you rely on longer formats to do anything decent. My rule would be: put together a kick-ass book and then throw in a couple of long-copy pieces to seal the deal.

What do you think about putting things in a book that are not ads at all? Things like artwork or other writing or other projects?

It depends. Sometimes it works like a charm. Sometimes it gives somebody a personality and you just love them for it. Other times, it indicates a deficiency. If you have somebody that bills themselves as an art director yet they also include a separate design portfolio, you think, "You know what? They are really a designer. They're putting that in because they know they're not that good as an art director." It's the same with illustration, which I personally hate seeing in art director portfolios. I haven't felt the same way with photography. With photography I think, "Oh Cool! Maybe I'll be able to shoot some stuff in the agency!"

Don't try to hedge your bets in your book. If you put design work in there, you're going to be considered a designer. If you want to be an art director, be an art director.

Do you have any other tips for someone who wants to get into the business who's just starting out?

Spread like a virus. What was the classic old '70s shampoo commercial where, "They told two friends and they told two friends" and so on and so on and so on? It really works in terms of doing your job-search blitz. You need it to be a quick blitz when you're out there because you get put on a time clock the moment you get a job offer. "Oh shit, Grey is offering me a real, living, breathing job in advertising and they want an answer, but I haven't even had my interview over at Goodby!" I always tell students: Put your list together, aim for the best places first, your B-tier places second, C third. Say, "I just want an informational interview" and, "I'm trying to break into this business. I'm not asking for a job, I just want some information." Then make sure that, for each person you see, you get two or three names out of them. Then, from each of those people, get more names. If you're not an asshole or a complete hack, they're going to feel for you and cough up some names. It works every time because it's not cold calling. If a friend calls a friend, you get your meeting. Definitely use all your school alumni contacts, friends-of-the-family contacts, anybody who will get you in front of people you couldn't get in front of yourself. BI

To see Greg Bell's work, please visit http://breaking.in

**JOEL CHU
FOUNDER &
CREATIVE DIRECTOR
COMMUNION W
HONG KONG**

What do you look for in a student book? And what impresses you?

Students in Hong Kong are trained in illustration, design, and executional things. Not in conceptual thinking or advertising strategy. And when I meet students it is disappointing. They have beautiful layouts but when I ask a question about the idea or strategy, they aren't concerned about it so much. Their world is limited and they don't even have a little knowledge about marketing. This is a common problem here.

So you're looking for strategic thinking?

To be honest, I'm looking for attitude. I can't say I know someone completely after meeting them, but I will try to meet with them for one or two hours and I will sense something about their character. The portfolio can demonstrate skills, but it's hard to get a sense for their attitude from it.

In the past five years I have had bad experiences with young people who don't feel a sense of responsibility to the job or to themselves. They don't take it seriously. I try to make them afraid: "Why would you want to join this field? If you have a girlfriend or boyfriend you will break up soon because you won't have time to see them." Some people will say, "I don't mind," but others will say, "I have to stay past 8:00? I think I can't work here!" Because they are treating it like a job, not a career.

I don't want regrets. Some people just want it to be done. But I want it to be as good as it can be. And I want to find other people with the same thinking. Sometimes I try to push them. But I really want people who will take action by themselves. When you love the job you don't think it's a job, it's more like a hobby; and hard work isn't a hardship—you enjoy it. I want people who love the job.

Do people bring you work that isn't advertising? Like personal projects?

I like it. But advertising must have an objective. I want to see a balance. I want to see someone's artistic passion and personal point of view, but it must be applied to your job. And you must be concerned about society and what happens in the world, not just yourself and your own interests. I want people who are open minded. Advertising has a responsibility to educate society. It presents options to people. I used to see ads and think, "This is beautiful and different from my life. Maybe I should improve my life like this." I don't mean to say that advertising is so important. But advertising can be more than just getting people to spend money. It can have a good message.

I like creativity. I don't try to define what is advertising and what is design and what is book design. But advertising trains you to have balanced thinking. It must be logic and emotion combined. That is necessary to convey a clear message. It is good training for anything.

So it's the attitude and the thinking that are important, because they will come through in your work. These are real things from your heart that will be reflected in your writing, painting, and even in advertising.

"YOU WILL KNOW WHEN IT IS NOT GOOD ENOUGH. AND IF YOU LIE TO YOURSELF, YOU CAN'T IMPROVE."

Is there anything else you want to say to students or juniors?

Read more books. Read more newspapers. Be more concerned about the world. You will become better not just at advertising, but you will become a better person.

You can tell lies to other people, but you can't tell lies to yourself. Even if people tell you something you did is good, it might not be. You will know in your heart whether it is good. You will know when it is not good enough. And if you lie to yourself, you can't improve.

When you work you have to apply your whole self. When some people work their thinking is far away. When I am making things I am very focused. Not just for advertising. For everything. And that is the kind of person I am looking for. 🔳

To see Joel Chu's work, please visit http://breaking.in

BEN WALKER & MATT GOODEN EXEC CREATIVE DIRECTORS CRISPIN PORTER + BOGUSKY LONDON

Interviewed at Wieden+Kennedy London.

What do you look for in a student book? And what impresses you?

BW: I definitely look for something that's different. That's the first thing. It's amazing how much is very much the same. And what impresses me most is a wide range. Like someone who shows that they've got a real voracious appetite for everything to do with communication. Not just banging out a few ads, I think.

MG: Yeah, the thing I look for is a big idea that can travel across everything. And maybe…a bit of insight and understanding of what a brand is or could be. We do these brand books here. I usually end up taking them through those and trying to make them understand and delve into a brand and understand it. Before you start doing communication.

BW: Tone of voice is definitely something I look for. That they've got a good grasp of tone of voice so that they can apply that to different brands. That's quite rare, actually. But most of all I look for someone who's just a bit enthusiastic and comes in and is listening. Half of the time I prefer seeing books that aren't very good, but the people are taking it all in and come back a month later with new stuff. I like people who smile and are enthusiastic.

And then with books, do you like to see ads that are finished? Or are sketches okay?

MG: Sketches are fine.

BW: Sketches are fine.

MG: And ideas. I want to see ideas. I don't really care if they're finished.

BW: Although I have to admit, when people do finish stuff to an amazing creative standard it makes me feel much more comfortable about their work. I still think, "Wow!"

MG: I think it just makes me feel insecure about my own abilities as a designer. Some fucking kids are brilliant, aren't they? These kids are so good.

BW: If it's done creatively, you just think, "Wow, these people"; it's like this "voracious appetite" thing. You just know that they care. So although I'm quite happy to see absolute scamps and the worst thing is people that knock up ads as if they've run...I don't see a point to that. But people that do an amazing lot of design work to show their new idea, I like that because it shows that they're enthusiastic. But it's not necessary.

MG: I prefer to see time spent on thinking rather than execution. And I think that's rarer as well. I don't know if teams feel that they need to finish stuff up. I remember what happened with us at college. We had to finish stuff up for the fucking course, really. And it was done more for the tutors who tick their boxes and pass the course rather than [for us]. We probably wasted a lot of time in reality. Because the ideas could have maybe done with some more time thinking about them.

With copy, do you feel like you want to see a long-copy ad? Or a campaign in there to show that writers can write?

BW: No. I think hardly ever, I have to admit. Hardly ever necessary.

MG: I think it's quite rare to find writers. But I don't care if they...even if they wrote a bloody song or something. [Something] that just shows their writing skills rather than copy. If they wanted to show that they care about writing and they're into that craft, then that would be great. And I think it's quite rare as well to find those people. It's bloody difficult finding good writers.

BW: It's not often you see good writing in a book. It might be best expressed by, say, "I wrote this screenplay" or, "I wrote this introduction" or, "I wrote this piece in a journal." I much prefer to see that than some bogus long-copy ad where they go, "Oh, I'd better show my copywriting skills."

And how do you feel about things in a book that aren't ads at all?

BW: Yeah, I do like it.

MG: Yeah.

BW: I think that it's starting to go full circle now where people have caught onto the idea that certain people want to see other stuff. And they're just banging in stuff for absolutely no reason. And that's a bit stupid. So you do get those people now that go, "Oh, fuck it. I'll bang in, a..." God, I don't even know what. I can't remember. But like if someone's got a serious interest in photography or they have made some sort of textile things, and something is really creative, I think it's great to look at it in a book. And it breaks it up as well.

"I ALWAYS END UP SAYING, "WHAT'S THE PROBLEM?" AND IF THEY HAVEN'T IDENTIFIED THAT, THAT'S WHAT'S GONE WRONG."

MG: You sort of just want to see a creative person, don't you? But then also how they apply that communication as well.

BW: It would help. That's what I was saying about that "knocking things up" thing. I think if they prove that they're artistic people that's always a good thing, isn't it?

But you want to get a sense of who the person is and then just their ability to communicate?

MG: Yeah.

BW: Yeah, definitely.

MG: Big ideas.

BW: For me, if they're enthusiastic people with an appetite for creating and communicating then I think you're halfway there. Even if the book's awful, I almost guarantee that they could do a good job after a while. But if they've got a good book, full of nice ads, but they're not very communicative or artistic then I could almost guarantee that they won't be much use to a place. Well, not a place like this, anyway.

Do you have any advice on how people can either get better or get a job?

MG: Some of the books I've seen recently have been very traditional…like advertising, print ads, and a TV ad. And when I started to talk about brand and blah, blah, blah, and how to delve into it and stuff, I started suggesting that they should start with a website idea. And I wonder if that is quite a good way to think now because it broadens your thinking. And, I don't know, that was my tip to them.

BW: Yeah, I think that's good. My tip would be, have very big thoughts. Don't come in with campaigns for little, tiny things. I'd much prefer to see someone's take on what Virgin Airlines could do to revamp their business if it needs revamping. So think big. Always.

MG: And always work out what the problem is with a brand. If there's no fucking problem then you can't advertise.

BW: That's my one piece of advice that I always give to people when they haven't got a good campaign or what I think is a good campaign. I always end up saying, "What's the problem?" And if they haven't identified that, that's what's gone wrong.

MG: A writer here has been suggesting that we get a hold of AC/DC, because they're going to release a new album, probably do a tour, and he's saying we should do the advertising for that. And I thought,

"Yeah, that sounds great." But the fact is, if they announce a tour date, they're going to sell out. So you ain't got a job to do.

Is there anything else you want to say?

BW: Problem solving, I think. A lot of people don't realize that they're problem solvers. That's the main thing. And most people that I see with their book—we'll see three books a week. And over a year that's 200 books almost. So just try and make it different in every way you can. Layout, format, and what's on the front…I saw a good book the other day with an antelope's fucking things coming out the front, and it looked great. I remembered it. It sounds really stupid but it's true. Do something different! [BI]

To see work by Ben Walker & Matt Gooden, please visit http://breaking.in

**JUSTIN DRAPE
CHIEF CREATIVE OFFICER
& CO-FOUNDER
THE MONKEYS
SYDNEY**

The first thing I want to ask you about is what form portfolios take, how people get in touch with you, and what you prefer.

I hear from headhunters quite frequently, and a lot of creatives also make direct contact via LinkedIn, email, and occasionally mobile. It often depends on where they're coming from and whether or not they know somebody who already works at The Monkeys. Most people send through a link to their website. And, as long as it's easy to navigate and it showcases the work, that's a good starting point. If I can see there is unique thinking there, we'll do a follow-up phone call or interview and take the conversation further. If somebody is genuinely talented, I don't mind how they contact me, I'm usually just glad that they have made the effort to do so.

When you bring someone in, do they bring a laptop or a paper book?

A laptop or iPad is easier, considering a lot of work is sold in the form of AV case studies these days. If I'm looking at the work with the people who created it I like to hear about their process, what their involvement was, what they're happy about with a particular piece, and what they may have done differently. A link to the work is easiest because I keep a talent file. If somebody sends me their work, and I like their thinking, I'll include it in the file. It may not be right for that moment in time, but I can always go back to it later. Circumstances change all the time in our industry, and when new creative opportunities arise I can make contact and see if somebody is interested in making a move. Especially for international talent because we get a lot of interest from people overseas, and it's a big decision to move out to Australia so you want to make sure everybody is certain there is good chemistry, a similar ideology towards the work, what they want out of working at The Monkeys and what we'd like from them.

What do you look for in a student or junior portfolio? And what impresses you?

Unique thinking and a willingness to learn. I don't think you can teach either of these things, so it's really important. I've met some juniors who are interesting thinkers but they have attitude problems and/or a sense of entitlement that will not sit well within our company culture.

Also, in regards to their unique thinking, it doesn't necessarily have to be advertising work. If somebody has a unique take on the world, you can see that through a piece of writing, a new business idea, or a personal art project. If they are showing initiative and a willingness to experiment, then that's the type of person we want in the agency. Some of their work might not be perfect, but if they're trying new ways of doing things, that's important to us. It's okay if you try and fail, but it's never okay if you fail to try.

Do you think it's good to put that stuff in with your ads or keep it separate in another section?

At the moment it feels like everything in the industry is converging, so I'm always interested in seeing creative thinking beyond advertising. At The Monkeys we've created quite a few projects without brands. We've created TV shows, a couple of art installations, books, etc., and they don't have brands attached to them. We have people that have come onboard from various backgrounds. One of our art directors, for example, was a designer at Mambo and helped set up Deus [Deus Ex Machina] which is a unique brand, and when he came to see us he actually had his sculptures on exhibit downstairs in a well-known gallery. He brought in some examples of his sculptures and we were really impressed by that. He hadn't worked in advertising before but, after joining just on three years ago, he's now won awards from all of the major shows around the world. He's just focused his innate energy and talent on advertising projects.

How important are polish and finish? Could sketches be enough? Or do you need to see design skills?

It's interesting to see where people will take the work in execution. But, ultimately, you're going to focus on the thinking and the idea, because you can teach people how to craft various communications. There's potential for people to grow there so it's not the be-all and end-all. Although it can be impressive, and a pleasant surprise, if somebody conveys an idea beautifully with their execution. I love it when somebody shows me a unique way to bring their idea to life.

What about copy?

Truly talented copywriters are hard to find, so I get pretty excited when somebody who has a fresh voice is interested in joining us. Lately a lot of copywriters have been submitting pieces that they've written for blogs, magazines, and newspaper publications, and I find that a helpful and interesting way to see how they can flex their skills, because a lot of people claim to be writers but, when it comes to writing more than a headline, they're not very talented. Some "writers" submit work with an introduction page full of typos, and it's like: "C'mon! At least use your spell check."

If you see a book with no copy in it, or very little copy, is that a red flag?

If the book belongs to a copywriter, yeah. Otherwise it depends on the role we're looking to fill.

Can you think of any examples of portfolios that have stood out?

Sure. The best portfolios stand out because of the thinking inside, but occasionally they stand out for other reasons. I received a personalized app last week. The team went to a lot of effort to bring it to life, so it was interesting and showed good initiative. We didn't end up hiring them though.

"IF YOU CAN OBSERVE, LEARN, AND ABSORB EVERYTHING FROM SOMEBODY WHO CREATES GREAT WORK, IT SETS UP THE FOUNDATIONS FOR THE WAY THAT YOU WILL APPROACH YOUR WORK IN THE FUTURE, AND OSMOSIS IS A POWERFUL THING."

A while ago a young creative from South America sent me [a package] containing a Photoshopped picture of me standing between two transvestites, a pair of silk boxer shorts with my name embroidered on them, and a letter attached claiming that he [the sender] was my love child. It was funny albeit slightly disturbing. The letter explained how his mother is a professional samba dancer who came to Sydney for a show about The Carnival of Brazil. Apparently after the show she met me and we spent the night together. According to his claim, "The next morning she had to catch an early flight back to Brazil and wasn't able to say goodbye. Nine months later I was born in São Paulo." Not sure how my wife would feel about that one.

And what do you think about this type of approach? And stunts in general?

I think some of them are funny but not necessarily in a positive way. You can't blame someone for trying to stand out, but I do think the smartest, and most effective, way to get noticed is by just showcasing clever creative thinking. I'd prefer the effort be focused on examples of creative work, and hopefully that will say enough about you.

Do you have any other tips for someone about getting in touch with Creative Directors?

Use all of the contacts and resources that you have, and if you don't have any then find out who some of the most influential and trusted headhunters are and show them your work so they can make contact for you. And only try to get in touch with a CD whose work you respect. You'll hear a lot of advice when you're starting out and not all of it is good. If you can observe, learn, and absorb everything from somebody who creates great work it sets up the foundations for the way that you will approach your work in the future, and osmosis is a powerful thing. ▣

To see Justin Drape's work, please visit http://breaking.in

CRYSTAL SACCA
FREELANCE CREATIVE
SAN FRANCISCO

What do you look for in a student book? And what impresses you?

Unexpected ways of solving an expected brief.

How important is finish? If ideas are the most important thing, can sketches be enough? Do you look at physical books anymore, or is it all websites?

Anyone can have a good idea, but not everyone can follow through on execution to make it great. Craft is important. Especially for art directors, but almost as important for writers too. Writers should have well-executed, finished campaigns in their book to demonstrate their level of taste and how they can collaborate with art directors. That being said, it doesn't hurt to have a few cocktail napkins.

How important is writing? Do you need to see long copy?

We're in the business of communication, so writing is über-important, even for art directors. Long copy never hurt and is a fun design challenge for an art director. Although, as an art director, I probably won't read your long copy to the end.

What do you think of showing work that is not advertising? Things like art, journal writing, photography, hobbies, etc.

It can show depth. And personality. Since student books all start to look the same, it's kind of nice to see someone's talents beyond making ads. But only if it's good.

Do you have any other advice for a student or junior trying to get into the business, either in putting together a book or how to actually start looking for jobs?

Don't forget to go surfing. BI

To see Crystal Sacca's work, please visit http://breaking.in

BOB GREENBERG
FOUNDER, CHAIRMAN & CEO
R/GA
NEW YORK

So, first of all, a very basic question: what are the different roles at a digital agency for creatives?

The different creative roles are separated into three categories at R/GA: visual design, interaction design, and copywriting. Visual designers represent the largest design group here that I'm aware of—about 110 people—so it's quite large. They come out of Pratt, Parsons, Portfolio Center, or Savannah College of Art and Design—those types of programs—and are looking at the ways design integrates with various digital scenarios and is split

between marketing and platform (which could be either a campaign or a more systematic program). Generally visual designers go to digital agencies, branding agencies, branding companies, or traditional design shops.

Our second category consists of interaction designers, sometimes called information architects or ID experts. These people might have found their way into an IDEO, a Microsoft, a Google, or whatever, or to a digital agency like ours. We have a fairly sizable group here too—more than 85—and these people design the user or customer experience. At R/GA they also play a more strategic role and tie into our whole planning process, but that's a separate discussion.

The final creative competency is copywriting, with another large group of close to 70 writers. They typically would have gone into magazines or newspapers, and some could have wound up writing copy for a traditional advertising agency—but they've come here, and they're writing across multiple platforms, a different skill set. I set up special training opportunities internally, since universities do not train one to work across multiple screens, multiple devices, or multiple platforms.

And what constitutes a portfolio for each of those roles? What do people show you?

In the past, visual designers coming out of school had fairly traditional portfolios, but that's changed now and they show us a mixture of things: websites, applications, a unique, visually designed RSS feed, and so on. We're looking for conceptual thinkers with portfolios that reflect the work of problem solvers—whether they're in information design, visual design, or copy. We've become used to seeing different things— and occasionally somebody who's really great. Universities now train students to do a much better job, so portfolios are being upgraded as a result. But we have a recruiting group, with tools and expertise that give them a unique ability to judge portfolios, and they're better than I am at telling you what we're looking for.

That group then gets tied into an allocations team that knows what we need for our client. And it's different for SC Johnson than it is for L'Oréal, not the same for Chanel as it is for Nike. We have an 80/20 kind of thing that's a little different from Google. We want people to work 80 percent on one client but perhaps 20 percent on another. That requires a pretty sophisticated system for which we offer what we call R/GA University training to teach the basics, among other things. A lot of people come from the outside to talk about all kinds of things. For example, the layout group from The New York Times—about 200 people—spoke this past week about the interesting things they're doing.

"PEOPLE WHO COME OUT OF UNIVERSITY NOW AND GO DOWN THE PATH OF A TRADITIONAL AGENCY ARE, TO ME, MAKING A HUGE MISTAKE."

We recently added planning to our coursework, brought in MOTH, a sort of viral writing group, and did something with mobile analytics…so it's always something. When people come here, they can get trained in things their university didn't necessarily do a good job at. They can get more training in areas of interest, and then we give them not just one client to work with but a range of clients bringing a range of challenges.

So if someone comes out of an ad school who's an art director or a writer, and they have a traditional book, is that something you want to see? Are the art directors roughly similar to visual designers and the writers to your writers?

Our business is no longer about a copywriter and an art director who go off to figure things out, come back with a TV spot and a print ad, and believe they're doing what the client or consumer needs. People who come out of university now and go down the path of a traditional agency are, to me, making a huge mistake. Titles are not important, and their books are perhaps

not exactly what we need, but if they're good, then it would take between six months and a year to train them before they come up to speed.

At the end of the day, it's not really about what we need; it's what the consumer wants. So, I think the problem with some agencies is that they're looking at managing the client and not really looking at what the consumer wants. Our approach is different: we look at what the consumer wants and then we get measurable results back to the client. We have some clients that are 90 percent marketing based and 10 percent digital platform, and certain clients who are just the opposite: 10 percent marketing and 90 percent systematic applications and platforms. It shifts. We're probably almost a flip of Crispin Porter + Bogusky, where that agency might be, on one account, 30 percent platform and 70 percent marketing.

What do you mean by "platform"?

Platform would be like a Nike+, Nokia viNe, HP.com, or something like that. It's systematic, digital applications for websites, digital marketing, and advertising, or it could be an application that ties into community—that kind of thing. On the other side of that, it may be very campaign led and marketing focused. We don't advertise it, but we're taking a lot of the budget from the traditional agencies. I was asked recently to judge television commercials for an organization, and I said I didn't think I should be the person to do that because I don't really believe in them. But we have done 4,000 commercials here, so it's not like we or I don't understand them. I'm very much for storytelling, which we do a lot of, and we have many people from traditional agencies— probably 100—who could be an agency on their own. I get very passionate about what we should be developing in terms of university curriculum so that graduates can actually get a job, not just at an agency like R/GA but at a company or traditional agency that has to make the transition. I don't see the business being the same a few years from now.

We still partner art directors and writers here; on the marketing side, we think this structure works very well. But these people are one part of a team (visual designer, writer, and art director) that also includes an information architect, a media connections planner, a technologist, and a planner. So the team is a very comprehensive group.

It's a much bigger team.

It's a much bigger team, yeah, and the ideas often come from technology. As an example, the person who runs our Nike business, which is about 164 people, comes out of technology. We work across marketing, e-commerce, retail…

So let me ask you this. What do you look for in a student's portfolio who's just starting out, and what impresses you?

Well again it goes back to looking for conceptual thinking and problem solving. We pay attention to work—even if it's not exactly like what we're doing—that indicates the students have talent that would fit in here and be appropriate to a particular client, so if we're looking to fill a position, perhaps we can tap that candidate. But I recall that even in the earliest days—when R/GA was doing basic motion and graphics, before there was the name "motion graphics"—I could look at a static print portfolio and know whether there was implied motion in the work candidates were doing, even when they'd never done any actual motion work. One acquires a certain amount of skill that, as I mentioned, goes across allocations of people. Recruiters, department heads—they can spot talent, even when specific experience is not reflected in a portfolio.

And that's my next question, about the finish of work. Is it okay if there's potential there, or there's a big idea there, for work to be less finished? Could it even be sketches on a piece of paper? Or does it need to be a nicely produced website?

We'd be more interested in their ideas because, obviously, if students came here, we wouldn't have a problem supporting them in whatever they needed. But they should have some examples of their design skills, visual interests, and relationships with color. I think that it's probably both: they need to have some finished work to show what they're capable of, from a craft perspective, and they need to have something that shows how they think. For example, a really good idea that comes out of a loose storyboard would be better than a well-executed storyboard without a good idea.

And for writers, I think you mentioned, it's a little different skill set that you're looking for in writers here. How would a writer best show you what they've got?

We're going to look at their writing. And if they do venture out to write things for, let's say, a mobile application or a mobile format like a wireless website, or even if they write something for a magazine, I know that we're really good at judging whether they'd be capable of doing the kind of writing we need, which is really not just one thing but writing in multiple platforms across multiple devices. We can't train people to write or put words together, but we can tell if they're good writers and capable of learning what our clients require.

Headlines are still important, so we like to see headlines. Or if they venture out to do a commercial, that would be a good thing to see. We're not against commercials, by the way. It's just that most of today's commercials are about metaphor, and we're more about moving into a combination of metaphor and demonstration. For example, if you think about the Apple iPhone television spots, they're demos. But if you think about the Apple "Mac Guy versus PC Guy," that's a metaphorical description of a product and service. And they're both great…the best of what our business offers. We have so many different social platforms we're connected to, which we develop for just about everybody, that it would be helpful if they had some experience there. I'm sure they use Twitter. We don't read their personal stuff but we would look at what they do there or on a blog. What we're trying to do is mirror what's happening with people and thus our consumers.

And what do you think about putting things that aren't ads in a book? More like what people are interested in, or their hobbies? Maybe it's journal writing, or maybe it's art that they do on the side, or photography?

I think it would be great. In a meeting I had recently with our head of HR, he told me that a colleague in his department is a kung fu expert, and I wouldn't have known that. I think martial arts connected to HR is probably a good thing—not the protective aspects but more the theory behind it. So I believe if students and candidates can present in an innovative, interesting way whatever they're interested in, that would be a plus. It doesn't matter what it is. Critical skills are involved in creating interesting, appealing portfolios and résumés, so we would be looking at both closely.

So are you looking for a design sense there, or are you looking for innovation in terms of how it's all put together?

Well, you would know from your experience working at agencies how important it is for somebody to be able to present well. The way they present what they do and the passion that comes through—they're both important. The portfolio itself says an awful lot about the people we see.

Do you have any advice for someone who's just coming out of ad school?

Well, I always read a thank-you card…especially one that's handwritten. I think that means something—at least to me! It doesn't matter what your handwriting's like. A handwritten note impresses me a lot these days. ⊞

To see Bob Greenberg's work, please visit http://breaking.in

ASTRID BOESZE
FOUNDER
REGARDING RESOURCES
AMSTERDAM

Interviewed at 180 Amsterdam.

What do you look for in a student book? And what impresses you?

What I look for is originality of ideas—big ideas. And then what impresses me is the personal piece. That's a big thing we look for. Not just making spec work and what the young creatives think the recruiter or the agency wants to see, but showing a piece of themselves. So whether it's photography, or personal projects, or things like that. That's big for us [at 180].

Are sketches enough, or do you want to see finished work?

Nowadays, more finished work. Sketches are now almost old school for us. And we really look for craft as well. So, in terms of art direction, there needs to be some design influence and hands-on capability and for copywriters as well, no longer just little script ideas, they've got to be able to put the whole thing together.

So for art directors, you want to see designed pieces?

Yes.

And with writers, do you want to see copy? Do you want to see long copy or other evidence that they can write?

Yes, that's key. Actually, come to think of it, we're always on the lookout for copywriters. There seems to be a shortage of copywriters coming out of the schools nowadays. Everybody says they do everything. No longer is somebody just an art director or just a copywriter. They're sort of both. Or they work together as a team and they both do both. That's happening more and more. But, from the copywriter point of view, yes, we like to see writing samples in the book, actually. And long copy.

So what do you think about people who say, "I'm both," or teams that say, "We're both art directors" or whatever? Is that cool with you?

It's definitely cool with us. I think it's just trying to pinpoint, though, what exactly they're doing. I have no problem that both create. I just need to get a sense of what they can do. For example, one of them is writing, maybe in another example, one is more concepting and the other is more executional…sometimes it gets a bit vague. And when I feel like I can't see through it, it's a bit of a turnoff, actually.

You mentioned personal pieces in a book. A lot of students hear that and think, "Oh, what does that mean? It could be anything…" and get stressed out. So could you just talk about what people have done or what could work for that?

Sure. Somebody did a travel journal. And there was writing in it, and he interned at different places along the way, and made a book about that. Published a book, actually. I thought that was really original. Some people have dance, or art, or sculpting, or something like that, which is fine. It's not making something up; it's just showing another piece of who they are. Some people love movies. They might just have a list of movies they like. It doesn't have to… it's not meant to create more work, it's just meant to give a little bit of a glimpse into the person, because I think coming out of the schools now, they're trying so hard to make spec ads. And you're seeing these spec ads done in 360 or done [in] integrated [campaigns]. They're trying really hard. So then it's nice to see the other piece—who they are. And sometimes that actually helps balance them trying so hard.

If you were to give a piece of advice to students just starting out—either on putting a book together or getting a job—what would that be?

Well, from my perspective, purely from a recruiting point of view, the best advice I could give is stay in touch via email. Phone calling gets a bit difficult sometimes, because we have so many people that call in and it's just hard to keep in touch with people that way. I think emailing is a better and more effective way. Also, the biggest piece of advice is to put your book online. And send a link and make sure it works.

It's just faster and easier than physical books?

Yeah, and it's so much easier to share with CDs or with other creatives who you want feedback from. Leaving physical books for people to review is just not happening.

Oh, and the other piece of advice is: be a team. I think sometimes hiring an individual is difficult, especially at a junior level. They get plopped into the creative department and they can get lost really quickly. So either present as a team, or make sure that you get hooked up with somebody in an agency and don't be left to float around.

One other thing: make sure your work isn't too "ad-y." I think nowadays more than ever, the work can be cool ideas. They still have to be big ideas. So sometimes the one-off execution on something,

while it's really interesting, is hard to translate into a bigger idea. So, big ideas but less ad-y. And persistence. Because timing is so important with this whole thing. And also networking. That's a big one because so much of what's happening in the industry is word of mouth.

So just try to meet as many people as you can, and get in front of as many creative directors…?

Yes. And if you're using a recruiter, make sure you inform the recruiters of who you're working with because sometimes what happens is people double-send and then it gets messy and it can become a "hands-off" [situation] because it's just too messy. So just be careful with that. I would say pick one or two recruiters.

So, there is one thing I have done if the agency I'm interested in is in another city. I felt like if I made a trip there, then people are more likely to see me and see my work because I'm showing up and I'm going to be there "from this date to this date," so it sort of forces them into action.

Very good point, actually.

Does that work?

Yes. It would. Yeah, that's a really good point. It also helps because sometimes, when you send a blind email and the work is interesting, you might lose being top of mind [if there is no urgency]. But absolutely, that is a really good way to get in front of people. Set some dates and just say you're in town. And probably, I would say nine times out of 10, it's going to work. If the work is halfway decent.

Any other tricks?

Keep the tone casual. And just know that it's not personal. Sometimes people feel very offended [if they don't get a response] but you don't realize that there are so many emails coming in. Sometimes they even get stuck in the spam filter. They don't all make it through. So, if you keep emailing, just keep the tone neutral, friendly.

Friendly and casual.

Yeah. And what you said...making a trip, if you can. That, and networking.

Is there anything else you want to say?

No, just remember the personal piece. I think that's huge for us. Show who you are. 🄱🄸

BRIAN FRASER
GLOBAL CCO & CHAIRMAN
LAND ROVER
Y&R
LONDON

Interviewed at McCann London.

What do you look for in a student book? And what impresses you?

Freshness. But that's a bit broad, isn't it? I think the most difficult thing about putting a book together is to put a book together that looks and feels and sounds different from other books. And that in itself is really hard. Because I think part of the problem is you've got—as it is now—you've got an advertising course. What tends to happen, particularly in this country, whether it be Watford or Hounslow or whatever, a lot of the students come out looking and feeling the same. So that's kind of a downside to that course, I guess.

But it's a point of view of freshness—a way of thinking about solving a problem in a lateral way, really, because that's what we do. I mean, we get paid for solving problems as creatively as we possibly can. Ability to think across media platforms is a given, I guess, and it's obvious. Even though, surprisingly, you still don't see a huge amount of that in student books.

For me, I have a bugbear about a lot of student books. I just did a D&AD [Design & Art Direction, a

British educational organization] workshop, which I haven't done for about 10 years, but I thought it'd be interesting to see. Simon and I did one and about 26, 30 of them turned up—a great bunch of kids, very bright. Fantastic ideas. But I said, "Who's the art director? Who's a copywriter?" No one put their hands up. They did both roles. So I think if you want to make a difference putting a book together, to have some sort of cross skills is a huge advantage. Particularly some sort of art direction skills because what I see a lot of is the inability to be able to put things together. Having great ideas isn't enough. If you can't convert them, then they're not great ideas, they're bad ideas. So that's worth thinking about when you put a book together.

> *"HAVING GREAT IDEAS ISN'T ENOUGH. IF YOU CAN'T CONVERT THEM, THEN THEY'RE NOT GREAT IDEAS, THEY'RE BAD IDEAS."*

I'm always going on to people in my department because they don't get to the cinema enough. Don't go to galleries enough. Don't read enough. It's all that sort of shit, you know, that you retain—those images, that information, those stories in your head. And it's that ability to put them down on a piece of paper as opposed to just putting an idea down on a piece of paper. Really push it further. So I think a book with good ideas, and well executed, will show the ability that you're thinking about how you could execute them. Or give you a good head start for what I'm seeing around.

You may have just answered this, but what do you think about scamps or sketches versus finished work?

I'm not saying you have to slave over [layouts] though I did, actually, and that's just because of the way I used to be. But that's not required. It's the ability to have a point of view about how the idea is expressed. I don't mind if you can draw that loosely, but it's how things are put down on a piece of paper. It's the order of communication. Where am I supposed to look first? Where am I supposed to read first? What am I supposed to think, what am I left thinking? That's what art direction and communication's about. It's about order as much as anything else, isn't it?

And then on the writing side of it, what do you think? Do you think writers need to have copy so that you can see if they can write?

No. I don't really care. I mean, to be honest, you want a point of difference. Someone coming with a book, all of long copy, I guess that's a point of difference. Whether it's good or not [is unclear]. It's certainly good if it's well written, you know what I mean? I don't look for the ability to write long copy [print ads]. But frankly, if you're going to write a script or a three-minute film or five-minute film you've got to be able to write.

So I think you need to demonstrate the fact that you can write. And if you're going to put a book together, six campaigns, six products, or whatever, one campaign can have dialogue, and another campaign, for example, just be more about direction. I think it's just showing you have the ability to write like that in different styles.

What do you think about putting things in a book that aren't ads?

Fine. I'm totally all for that. I mean, design a bridge, I don't care. Also I've got a thing about advertising courses at the moment. Because I didn't do advertising, I just did fine art and some arts. When I joined, the business attracted more eclectic people and I think we're not so good at that now. Creative departments should be creative departments. They should be full of different people. It should be a catholic department with different tastes, and abilities, and styles because that's what makes it interesting. So I don't really think it matters, really, where people come from. As long as they want to do it, I think.

It's just on the visual side, I think some sort of ability to understand filmmaking or how to put a picture together, or a layout together, is required. But I don't think there's any point in coming into this business unless you're going to love it. I love the challenge of a new brief. I love putting a film together no matter whether it's going to go on content on a site, or whether it's going to be pumped out on TV. It's the same challenge, really. I think you've got to love the craft of it. Love doing it. That's almost more important than anything else. Because if you don't love it, it's harder to deal with the rejection because, let's face it, most of the time, most of the work gets rejected.

So the first thing you said was about making your book stand out. How do you do that?

It doesn't have to be ads. Advertising doesn't have to live on a press ad or TV commercial. It equally doesn't have to live online, either. It can live in lots of places. So demonstrate that. For example, you see a lot of books with really great one-off ideas. But the really difficult thing about what we do is to come up with big ideas. Big campaign thoughts that drill down into lots of different areas. That's the real challenge. And if you can demonstrate you can do that, then you're going to stand out. BI

To see Brian Fraser's work, please visit http://breaking.in

KC TSANG
ASSISTANT PROFESSOR
THE HONG KONG POLYTECHNIC
UNIVERSITY
HONG KONG

What do you look for in a student portfolio? And what impresses you?

I would look for something special. Gwen Yip sent me not a portfolio but a booklet full of comics and some writing. It was different. Not normal. Not just something that was done as a school assignment. The other thing I would look for is insights in the work.

Is that quality something that could come through in advertising, or are you looking for work that isn't advertising at all?

Not even advertising at all. It's better not to be advertising.

Why?

If you want a job at an advertising agency and you don't send me advertising, that is special, and different from all the other candidates. It shows bravery and an attitude that is unique, and if the content of the work is good then this candidate is in good shape.

Are you looking for craft skills or writing?

When I first started interviewing people I would just look for good ideas. But then later I decided that the idea is important but it is not the only thing; craftsmanship is important. And later on I decided that craftsmanship was even more important because if you don't know about advertising and what a concept is, I can teach you. It's easy. You can pick it up in one or two years' time. But I can't teach you craft. That is something inborn. You have to spend 10 or 20 years to learn it. So when I saw a candidate I would ask myself: Are they special? Do they have craft skills? Do they have good taste? Do they have an attitude? And the last thing is concept or ideas.

Do you have examples of special portfolios that you can think of?

One of the internship students sent me her real ID card. You are supposed to carry your ID card every day in Hong Kong. The police will stop you...

So, just the fact that she sent you that meant that she didn't have it and...

I had to ask her to come in so that I could give her back her ID card. When I saw this I felt so stunned. Like I discovered a dead body. Because an ID card means a person.

So you thought that was a clever way to make sure you would meet with her?

Yes.

Do you remember any advertising work that was especially good?

I don't remember any ads; I just remember the people. I remember the personality. There is a guy named Lo Fai. He was very precise. Very targeted. He showed me a portfolio of only five print ads. But they were stunning ads. But I didn't hire him because of the work. I hired him because of his attitude and his way of doing things. You can never hire someone based on a portfolio because they are so young. It's all about their personality as reflected by their portfolio.

Is writing important for writers?

If I'm hiring a writer, I'm looking for writing and I really want to read longer pieces. But I'm usually disappointed. Most of those who are good at writing do something else. Actually I hired two from this school. But they are art students—not writers. But I still hired them because they showed me a lot of essays. They wrote them by themselves even though they were never asked to. They had a passion for writing, and they were interested in writing.

> *"IF YOU WANT A JOB AT AN ADVERTISING AGENCY AND YOU DON'T SEND ME ADVERTISING, THAT IS SPECIAL, AND DIFFERENT FROM ALL THE OTHER CANDIDATES."*

Are there common mistakes that students make?

Just putting together campaigns of print ads from school assignments. It's just their homework. And they will include the brief and don't bother to explain the strategy. And they will show the thinking process—the mind-mapping. I'm not interested in seeing the process; I just want to see the result.

Do you have any other tips for someone just starting out?

I think you have to be precise about who you are, what your personality is, and what your strengths are. So you choose some work that can reflect your personality. The work can never be good in the eyes of a creative director, so you shouldn't worry about making it perfect. But it should be unique and reflect who you are.

Gwen Yip, who I mentioned before, made a travelogue to show her way of looking at the world. It was illustrated with writing, and it had emotional expression. You could see the personality there. [BI]

To see KC Tsang's work, please visit http://breaking.in

LESLIE ALI
FREELANCE WRITER, DIRECTOR
& CREATIVE DIRECTOR
NEW YORK

What do you look for in a student book? And what impresses you?

I look at what their interests are outside of advertising. I think it informs you more than the actual work itself, because students don't yet have a body of work that defines them. And the briefs that come out of most ad schools are similar. So it is quite nice to see what they do and what their true passions and interests are outside of advertising.

How would someone show you that?

I'm seeing more and more of it. Maybe people just know that that's my thing. But the books I'm seeing generally have a space for work and a space for play. You can usually find something that runs through both, and you get a sense of the person, their tonality, their sense of humor—something that allows you to believe that this person could be a great lateral thinker.

And do you also want to see a variety of styles and tones?

I need to see that the person can apply themselves to any brief. I have more faith in a young creative that can bring something special

to a brand and give me a lateral solution to any problem; it's about knowing that they have the capacity to think in many ways. It's interesting that you find writers especially who get stuck in a certain tone of voice. Which is fine for a bit. Especially if they're a genius at that. But they will be asked to explore other sides of themselves, and I just think it's a good thing to do this early on rather than after 20 years in the business.

"I NEED TO SEE THAT THE PERSON CAN APPLY THEMSELVES TO ANY BRIEF."

Can you think of any examples of portfolios that have done this successfully?

Lately I've seen a lot of people who are doing different things in the world to express themselves and make some sort of statement. A lot of people are working on their own business initiatives, or raising money for causes they believe in, or creating products that they really like. I think that is where advertising is going anyway: coming up with solutions to clients' problems by creating interesting products and tools for their brands. I hired a team who had a project for the BBC they were pitching that was trying to create bridges between the classes in the UK. They were trying to pair up street rappers, or poets actually, with politicians. A way to let the politicians express what they thought was important in a different voice. It was just great.

What do you think about craft and polish? Are you looking for design skills, or could sketches be enough?

I'm old fashioned that way. I don't really care. I just want the idea to be great. This applies to art directors and writers. I think you'll learn your craft as you go. I think you can just tell when someone is a conceptual thinker, and that to me is more important than craft. I think you'll learn to improve your art direction or writing if you have a better grasp on concept first.

Are there any common mistakes that students or juniors make?

I think they often try to show you that they can create across any channel. Any medium. Just give me your favorite stuff. The stuff that makes you happy. The stuff you're passionate about. It gives me a clearer idea of who you are. Less is more, really.

What's the best way to get in touch with creative directors?

Having an online portfolio is an absolute must. If you send an email to the creative director (or the person who's helping the creative director get through their day), I think you'll stand a better chance if your portfolio is one click away. I'd also be really careful about how you construct your portfolio so it doesn't take a lot of time to get to the best bits.

Make it simple and fast.

Simple, fast, and succinct. If you have a lot of setup, preamble, and description to your ideas, I won't believe that you have enough faith in your ideas. So, less description and just show me the work. I also think it's valuable to have a strong sense of yourself and what you want to do, because ultimately you're going to have more success in an agency culture that suits you. There's no point in going to an agency—no matter how fabulous or how great a name it has—if the culture doesn't work to your strengths. So be discerning and select places where you're excited to be part of the culture as opposed to just thinking, "They do good ads" or "They have won so many awards." It doesn't really work that way. You'll find your right match.

I don't have any more questions. Is there anything else you want to say?

Getting into advertising is tougher now. Just be really clear about why you want to get in. Because it's a rough ride, and you'll have amazing, incredible highs, but equally you'll have some really challenging lows. You really have to be in it for the ride and love it all. BI

To see Leslie Ali's work, please visit http://breaking.in

**JAMIE BARRETT
CREATIVE DIRECTOR
BARRETTSF
SAN FRANCISCO**

What do you look for in a student book? And what impresses you?

I look for at least one piece of work that is undeniably great. I think a lot of students make the mistake of putting together a solid, smart, A-minus book but don't have the one thing that separates them from the pack. Whoever I hire, I want to feel they have potential to do something genius, not just the potential to do good, smart work. Life is short, and it doesn't reward singles hitters.

How important is finish? If ideas are the most important thing, can sketches be enough? Do you look at actual books anymore, or is it all websites?

Sketches are enough, generally. If it's a predominantly visual idea, then obviously, it'd be nice to see it more fully realized. But it's not critical. On a day-to-day basis, creatives don't come in with "finished" ideas. So creative directors are more than used to evaluating work that is "unfinished." We often use reference, though, and that could be a good thing for students to consider…including visual references for some of their concepts. But generally, I'd much rather hire a diamond in the rough than a polished turd.

As for paper books, I rarely look at them these days. It's predominantly websites now.

How important is copy? Do you need to see long-copy ads?

I don't need to, no. But if you're a writer, show me you can actually string words together. You can prove that in any number of ways, not just in the form of long copy. I'd say more than half the copywriters employed today are not true "writers." If a student can show they are masters of the actual craft of writing, that's a real differentiator.

What do you think of showing work that is not advertising? Things like art, journal writing, photography, hobbies, etc.

I'd say go for it. But just make sure your non-ad work isn't a chore to go through. As you put your book together, picture the creative director, who will look at it as someone who doesn't really want to. More often than not, going through portfolios is time consuming and dull. So you're going to want to entertain that unmotivated CD. You're going to want to make him or her feel like it's worth spending more than 90 seconds with your book. Your "journal writing" may be brilliant, for example, but it better be brilliant in the first three sentences, or you're going to lose the ADD crowd, which is 90 percent of us.

Do you have any other advice?

It's not new advice, but it holds up: Don't do the advertising book you think will impress someone else. Do the advertising book that impresses you. Your take on the world. Your take on a car. Your take on maxi pads. In short, your take—your voice. I want to hire an original. Show me you are exactly that. ⊞

To see Jamie Barrett's work, please visit http://breaking.in

LUKE SULLIVAN
CHAIR OF ADVERTISING
SAVANNAH COLLEGE OF ART &
DESIGN & AUTHOR
HEY WHIPPLE, SQUEEZE THIS: A
GUIDE TO CREATING GREAT ADS

Interviewed at GSD&M Austin.

What do you look for in a student portfolio? And what impresses you?

Okay, so I was just interviewing a kid for his first job, right? Kid had just gotten out of a very good ad school. As we clicked through his book he said,

"I'm sorry there's not much advertising in here, but..." I interrupted him and said, "Dude, you had me at 'sorry.'" No, there wasn't a lot of advertising in there. But his book was filled with fascinating things, interesting content, and yes, pretty much everything except what I might call traditional advertising. And I loved it. What a book needs isn't cool advertising. Just cool creative stuff. Yes, ultimately the work needs to have some sort of a commercial aspect to it, it has to report to some sort of purpose, some strategy...but show me something cool, something interesting, that's what I need to see.

How important is finish? Can sketches be enough?

The short answer is, if your ideas are incendiary —I mean if they are hair-curlingly great—yes, you probably can get away with a less-than-finished look. But when you have a less-than-polished book, well, you have human nature working against you. It may not seem fair, but the better-looking books have an advantage. It has ever been thus. Remember the handsome stupid guys in high school? Dumb as a bag of scissors, and they still attracted all the great girls? Get over it. Anyway, I don't care how you do it, but find a way to make your great ideas look like great ideas. I'm not talking about kick-ass finished art, but if you can go a level or two beyond stick figures, go for it.

Do you look at actual paper books anymore, or is it all websites?

I was once a fan of paper books. But I'm old school and I fondly remember turning the pages to see beautifully rendered print, outdoor, etc., one page after another. But I realize now it's time to get over it. Today, I agree you need only a link to your portfolio and that's pretty much it. Yes, a leave-behind can't hurt once you land an interview, but if you can't afford to print it beautifully, don't do it.

How important is copy? Do you need to see long-copy ads?

No, I do not need to see long copy, as long as the rest of your work convinces me that you can write. I am seeing many books from copywriters where the concept is visually driven. Cool. I like writers who can think visually. But the thing is I need writers who can write, and not just create cool concepts. When you first start as a young writer in this business, it's likely you will take on tons of jobs where there is no photography budget. And what artwork or visuals you do get to work with are usually stock shots of, say, the latest handset from Verizon or a three-quarters shot of a car. In which case, you cannot solve the problem visually. You will need to do something cool with words. I'll put it this way. All books need to be conceptually great; that's a given. But when I look at art directors' books, I look for people who demonstrate the craft of art direction—of type, design, and the ability to make any page or screen look great. And when I look at writers' books, I also look for craft there. Meaning, I want writers who can write.

What do you think of showing work that is not advertising?

Showing work that is not advertising, or business related? It all depends. If you have something that is mind-roastingly cool, by all means, show it.

Do you have any other advice for a student or junior trying to get into the business?

I put most of my advice in Hey Whipple [Hey Whipple, Squeeze This: A Guide to Creating Great Advertising]. But I would advise kids these days to look at what other students are posting online. Many of the ad schools have their graduates' student books online. Look at what your competition is doing. Know what you are facing and then deliver a product that is as good as or better than the other guy's. BI

To see Luke Sullivan's work, please visit http://breaking.in

**SAM GLATZER
CREATIVE RECRUITER
SAM & LORI
NEW YORK**

What do you look for in a student book? What impresses you, and what do you think impresses creative directors?

When I look at a book—and I think that it's the same for creative directors—I look or original thinking. And I think people tend to evaluate a book more critically if they see recognizable brands. So when I look through a book and I see a Nike ad, or a Coke ad, unless it's so beyond brilliant, you tend to think that people are relying on the existing brand for their ad rather than coming up with something clever.

I think it also depends on a copywriter's versus an art director's book. I think that people are pretty critical about art direction looking like it could've been produced. But I think for the most part, my sense is that people are looking for original ideas and original thinking. Even if it's not executed really beautifully, I think that people react to, "Oh wow, why didn't I think of that?" or, "That was really clever." And I think people react positively to campaign-able ideas, as opposed to one-offs.

And what do you think about the level of finish?

I think it depends on the creative director. Now, everybody needs a website. But I think people, especially juniors, should still show up for an interview with a paper portfolio because I think relying on the Internet to showcase your work can backfire. Because the Internet can go down and then you have nothing to show.

I think things have to be finished. I don't think that people need to spend $10,000 on a beautiful portfolio. But your portfolio is your calling card. And it shows that you care. And it shows that you took the time, and if it doesn't reflect that then I think people react to that. Having said that, there are creative directors who say, "If it's on a napkin and it's the most brilliant idea, I don't care." So it's probably case by case, but I would say more often than not, you're competing with people who have the best books with really great ideas, and they are put together well. And I don't know if you were going to ask this, but I'm going to say it anyway: I think one of the things that's really important with the junior portfolios is that they represent something outside of just who they are as it relates to advertising. So when people put together their books, if they are a screenwriter, or if they are an artist, or if they have a T-shirt company, or if they walk dogs on the side—whatever makes someone memorable—I think when that's included somehow in their portfolio, it gives whoever is interviewing them something to relate to other than an ad and it gives them a talking point. So if you have something that's interesting—that you grew up on a horse farm or whatever it is—then people are like, "Oh yeah. I remember that person's portfolio, isn't that the guy who grew up on the horse farm?"

That was one of my questions; you answered it.

Oh, there you go.

What do you think about long copy? Is that important these days?

I think so, especially with the web. I think portfolios need to play to somebody's strengths. I'm a firm believer that it's not the library of everything you've ever done; it's your ad for people to hire you. So I think you want to give examples of things that are beyond one word so that people can see that you can actually write, if you're a writer. But at the same time, if that's not somebody's strength, they shouldn't put it in. I think this happens even with junior portfolios, that people will ask for more. If they see something in it that they see potential in, or they see some good ideas, they might come back and say, "Do you have any long body copy?" Or radio or whatever it might be. And then that person has an opportunity to show more than what they have put into their portfolio.

Do you have any other advice or any tips for someone who's just starting out or looking for their first job?

Put together a portfolio that's easy to navigate, if it's online, which I think most people have to do now. I think people get encumbered by wanting to put together fancy, beautiful websites with interesting navigation. And when people get lost, or they're waiting for things to download, they lose their patience.

"...I THINK THAT BEING ORGANIZED IN THE JOB SEARCH IS HALF THE BATTLE..."

But I think that being organized in the job search is half the battle, to be honest. I think that you have to know where you sent your portfolio. You have to know when you sent them your portfolio. You have to know how to oh-so-gently, casually follow up on whether or not they looked. You have to be scrupulous about note taking so that they know you're not…there's a fine line between stalking and oh-so-gently reminding somebody that you exist, and following up.

Also, make sure you have no typos in your book. And networking: In the end it's about relationships, and people like to help people who they know. And alumni connections can be really helpful for people. But because of websites, you can send stuff so frequently. And I think creative managers and creative directors get inundated. So it's very hard to figure out: how do you make yourself stand out? And it's a really tough… anything clever can help. I mean there was a junior team last year that they did some crazy video that they were sending around with their portfolio. And they got a job. But they did something really clever, and really smart. And it was more than the "Hi, I need help, looking for my first job," which I have 100 of in my inbox right now. BI

What do you look for in a student portfolio? And what impresses you?

For a student portfolio I'm not overly fussed about the craft side of things. I'm more interested in whether there are interesting ideas that are coming through. Actually, what's more important for me is what the person is like. I get a much better sense when I meet someone whether it's someone I would want to work with. And what I look for is feisty, interesting characters. Not people who are submissive or too amenable—you want creatives who have their own mind. Not someone who is going to sit in the corner and do what they're told. I want people who can think on their feet and show initiative.

In terms of the book, as long as I can see they have the capacity to think of ideas and translate that into an ad of some kind, that's the most important thing. If someone shows a few neat ideas and interesting insights, then I'll say, "Let's get them in and have a chat." And then I find the meeting more important. I'd rather get someone in and work with them to help them grow and become a creative.

You mentioned craft isn't so important to you. Could sketches be enough?

It's very important to me now, but when I was starting out, my book was hand-drawn. I'm an art director who came from a typography/design background. What I wanted people to hire me for was my ideas. I really wanted to separate the fact that I could art-direct and do typography—because I had a whole book of that stuff—from my ideas and insights. So for me, sketches are fine when you're starting out.

If someone does choose to craft things up, and it is really beautiful, then that's cool, as long as they've got great ideas. If their thinking isn't great, then it makes it a lot harder to hire them. If we had a great copywriter who was a great conceptual thinker I might try them together. But, the first thing I would want to see is still ideas. Because we've got people here who can do that [design], and I love that stuff so I can help people grow that side of themselves.

How does a book end up in front of you?

It's a whole mixture of different ways. Recruiters will send stuff. People will email me directly. It's tricky in this business because we're so busy. It's a bit like ads: you have to really stand out and make yourself different from all the others. Anything you can say in your first blurb that makes people say, "I wonder what this person is going to be like?" will help. If someone does the stock standard, "I'm looking for a job; here's my portfolio," it will depend on my mood and how busy I am. But I think you've got to do a little bit of work to get CDs to look at you. And that's the whole thing about advertising: doing something that makes you more appealing.

Do you get many stunts?

I've had some. You hear about those stunts where the CD says, "That is brilliant; bring that guy in—I want to hire him now." I've never seen a stunt that made me feel that way. Someone sent a box of oranges once and there was nothing clever about it. It was just a box of oranges. That was a missed opportunity. I've had people leave ransom notes that were silly and didn't help at all. I'm waiting for one that's really bloody good so I can say, "Get them in here right now!"

For writers, do you want to see long copy or evidence of writing ability?

Copy is a bit different; we can cover for an art director, we've got designers and typographers, but a copywriter needs to be able to show a gift for writing. So, when a writer comes through I'll spend a bit more time reading the copy because that's a skill that is very hard to cover for.

There aren't very many really good copywriters. I don't think it's something that, at a junior level, we really cultivate. So it's almost something that happens by accident. I don't think we do a good job teaching that, as an industry.

What do you think about showing personal work that is not advertising?

Personally I love seeing other creative things. And that applies to anyone I work with. When a photographer comes in I love seeing their personal work—what they do without a client sitting over the top of them. I love seeing what creatives do on the side too. It might be a kid's book or a website; it shows a highly motivated creative person who can't stop creating. Naturally good creatives will just do everything: Write poetry, make things, do comedy, and have a heap of different outlets. It's more interesting to me than someone who's just in advertising and it's all they want to do.

Do you think that should be separate from your ad work or all together?

I quite like it all together because it surprises you. If you know you're going to be looking through a whole bunch of ads and they are throwing in these other things, it makes for more entertaining reading.

Can you remember any examples?

On a team's website they had a collection of their work but when you moused over it, it changed to all different kinds of pork and sausages and cuts of meat. It was just silly and funny, and I liked that they brought a sense of humor to their book.

Another guy had taken a year off to paint, and in his paintings he had very interesting concepts. His book was really good but his personal work excited me a lot more, and the fact that he'd taken a year off to do it made me think he wasn't just a run-of-the-mill working person.

Are there any common mistakes that students make?

From the moment a candidate walks in the door, you're assessing them as someone you would work with and put in the department. So it's the clothes and the hair and the way they mount their book. And you're asking yourself, "Are they taking themselves seriously? Do they really want to do this? Are they putting in the effort?" I've had kids come in with a shopping bag and scraps of paper, and, if the ideas had been brilliant I would have forgiven the presentation and just thought they were a mad bastard. But they were the same sorts of ideas as everyone else, and he didn't have anything interesting to say about his work. So put a bit of effort into making yourself look good and presenting your work. If you're showing to an art director, don't have double spaces in your copy—art directors will just think, "All these little mistakes make me think you don't care about your work." You can really undo yourself in an interview, and you just want to show that you're smart and creative, that you have a few things going on in your life, that you can talk about all the pieces in your book...you should never have that dead silence in an interview. You should have something worked out to say for every piece in your book.

"YOU'VE REALLY GOT TO DECIDE IF IT IS WHAT YOU WANT TO DO EARLY ON AND THEN PUT 100 PERCENT EFFORT BEHIND IT."

I don't have any more questions. Is there anything else you want to say?

We need great creative people in this industry, and it's very, very hard to break in. You've really got to decide if it is what you want to do early on and then put 100 percent effort behind it. If it doesn't feel like it's your thing, don't push it, just get out. We need really committed people. I think a lot of people stay in the industry too long and they get jaded and cynical; it's clear they aren't enjoying it anymore. Advertising can be an amazing job, but some people choose to get bogged down by all the knock-backs. It is a fact in this industry that you are constantly being knocked back; you have to learn to get on with it, bounce back, and have fun. 🄱🄸

To see Mark Harricks's work, please visit http://breaking.in

ALVARO SOTOMAYOR
CREATIVE DIRECTOR
WIEDEN+KENNEDY
AMSTERDAM

What do you look for in a student book? And what impresses you?

What I really look for is personality. How you make an idea yours. Not just how you do an ad, but how do you make it an individual thought—that's what I look for.

Do you like to see finished work that's been laid out on a computer or are sketches okay for you?

I like to really look for personal stuff—personal diaries, drawings, or photography—it just shows more character. You need to remember that the basis on which you are going to get hired is 50 percent skills and 50 percent how you fit with the culture of the company.

Is it different for writers and art directors? For art directors, do you want to see some design ability on a computer?

I look for bravery overall in ideas as well as in design. But for art directors, I look closer for a sense in space, color, and type. Photography is so overused that I really react to other expressive crafts like illustration.

Do you think it's important to have long copy in a student book?

Long copy is great. I think it also shows depth in the thinking, which is very important. Communication at the moment is more about conversation in various points, so flexibility in tone and having a personal tone is a must.

Do you think it's also important for art directors to show that they can lay out long copy?

The question makes it sound like long copy is evil… at this time, in the age of the iPad, I think knowing where to place relevant information is a must.

You've sort of already answered this, but do you like to see things that aren't ads?

Yeah, definitely. For most of the people I hire, I do it because of their ideas outside of advertising.

What kinds of things?

Some people have an innate passion for ideas, ideas that want to change the world. A one-shot camera, a water barrel that helps cool itself, iPhone apps, miniseries, book ideas, funny ideas, quirky ideas all have a greater chance of landing you a job than any print ad you might have done.

Do you have any tips for someone who is just starting out?

Really follow your gut. Really try. It's all about intuition, so just really follow that independence that you carry with you and use it to make work that, for an audience, is worth their while. Companies are desperate for ideas like that. [BI]

To see Alvaro Sotomayor's work, please visit http://breaking.in

DAVID COVELL
CREATIVE DIRECTOR
JDK DESIGN
NEW YORK

What do you look for in a portfolio coming from a student or someone who hasn't worked in the industry before?

For students, I look at fundamentals. And I find that it's really hard to find students now who [have that]. I don't know what it is—whether it's the university courses that are being taught now or what—but it seems like those fundamentals are going by the wayside in lieu of what I see as "style," especially illustration style. There is this weird thing happening now in design, where the designer has become the artist. Where selling your wares, as, say, a T-shirt designer, has become the thing…the utmost in the young students' minds. It's too bad because I find that a lot of the fundamentals like grids and typography, and even mark-making, has really gone by the wayside. Just simple, formal training, like how to create tension in the composition—you don't really find that as much anymore. So that's what I look for: typography, the ability to make a clean, beautifully drawn mark that also has good content in it as well. Not just for style's sake, but just a very good story within the mark itself.

So if someone came here with a book that was not done on a computer but was just sketches, and the ideas were good enough, would you consider hiring them? Or do you really need to see layouts?

If the ideas are strong, they speak for themselves. But it would be fantastic to see the thinking behind a project, and I would probably like to see both sketches and finished work. We're a design firm, so process is important. But we are also about communications, marketing, and advertising. So I do appreciate really good storytelling within a book itself as well. And if someone brought both sketches and finished work, that would be a powerful thing.

What do you think about seeing things that aren't design in a book? Like photography, or writing, or other things?

I think designing and writing sort of go hand in hand a bit. And it is important for a designer to be able to direct a photographer, so I guess, if you already have a photographic eye, then yeah, that would be great to see. I find less inspiring people's personal artistic endeavors. Paintings and things like that usually are not so great and often distract from the design part of it. You can sort of see books where the designer wishes he or she were the artist. And to me there's a real distinction.

Do you have any tips for someone who's just starting out on how to improve or how to get into the industry?

Edit. Be really ruthless on what you put in your book, I think. Because I find a lot of books that go on and on with weaker projects. It is better if you only show me three great projects as opposed to six where three of them are just mediocre— that always distracts me a little bit. And, just in the book, think about being as professional and clean as possible. I would take a cue from a photographer's book, actually. I respond more to books where you just show me the work in a really clean, pristine way. I think the work should speak for itself and not necessarily have overly done packaging behind it. I think a lot of students get wrapped up in that kind of thing. BI

To see David Covell's work, please visit http://breaking.in

NICK WORTHINGTON
EXECUTIVE CREATIVE DIRECTOR
COLENSO BBDO
AUCKLAND

What do you look for in a student or junior portfolio? And what impresses you?

The first thing I do is I look through it really fast and I don't talk to the student. And I get an impression about how clear their thinking is, how original the thinking is, and a good overview of their thinking. Then I'll go back and go through each campaign and talk about the strengths and weaknesses and maybe offer some advice.

What I'm really looking for in a book is original thinking. And I'm looking for people who could potentially come into the department and not replicate what everyone is doing. The most disappointing books are the ones where you know every idea in there could have been done by anyone in your creative department. So really they are bringing nothing new. If you're just coming into the industry, you should be full of ideas, opinions, and points of view, which might not be practical. They might be completely outlandish, but they should communicate something fast, have a clear point of view, and do so in a way that is surprising.

The other thing is I want a depth of thinking. I'd say 90 percent of the books I look at have one really great thought. And then they have nine other campaigns which are kind of fine. And the books that really stand out are the ones with 10 really great thoughts. It's really hard to do, but it is the thing that students wanting to get hired—not just wanting an internship—have to do. If they can do one great idea, they can do two, they can do three, they can do four; they just haven't done them yet. I think a lot of students accept ordinary very quickly in the work that they show.

"WHAT I'M REALLY LOOKING FOR IN A BOOK IS ORIGINAL THINKING. AND I'M LOOKING FOR PEOPLE WHO COULD POTENTIALLY COME INTO THE DEPARTMENT AND NOT REPLICATE WHAT EVERYONE IS DOING."

Then, to a lesser degree, I'm looking for glimmers of hope in writing or crafting art direction or finding interesting ways of presenting those ideas. But, to be honest, in a conversation you can find out about their background, what they're interested in, their references, and you can get a real sense of what they might bring to that work if they were able to execute it with an agency helping them and the best photographers, the best illustrators, etc. The craft side of things is something that is very secondary at that stage.

One of the most beautiful books I saw was from two girls who had been to art college, then gone off and had babies, and in their mid-30s they said, "We're going to do what we always wanted to do." They got back together and created a portfolio at home, and they had been making stuff with their kids so it was all sticky-backed plastic and stuff snipped out of magazines and hand-drawn stuff with crayons. And the design was so original. I had never seen a portfolio

like that. We didn't hire them in the end, but it was incredible to see somebody who wasn't going through the AWARD School machine and pumping out stuff that looks the same as everybody else.

I know we're looking at the ideas, but one of the first things you need to learn in this industry is, "Don't do what everybody else is doing." Try not to work on the same briefs that everyone else is working on. So often the same briefs are given out and all the students in all the colleges are working on the same briefs. Do them for sure, to get your grades, but work on some other stuff. Because we do get bored.

It sounded like you were talking about people bringing a physical portfolio to you and you looking at it with them in the room. Is that how it usually happens?

Ultimately the process would end with me meeting with the person and looking at a physical book or looking at it on a computer. Quite often it's on a computer.

Do you have a preference between those two?

No, I don't really. But people do send me emails and ask me to check out their work, and I'll look at it really fast, but they aren't there and there's no opportunity to have a dialogue. If I'm interested, the next thing would be to ask them to set up a time to have a chat, and that's where all my judgment will happen. It's difficult for international people but the best way is, if they are coming to New Zealand, come see us then. For more senior people, they have some work under their belt and it's easier to evaluate their abilities and also we can offer them a proper job. If an intern is in Australia or Asia and they really want to work in New Zealand, then they're going to get on a plane and come around and see all the CDs.

The resources and commitment from some students I've seen lately is phenomenal. We had one team who came out of college in the UK and they got in touch with a bunch of agencies around the world and said, "We're going around the world for a year doing internships, and we think your agency is amazing so we'd love for your agency to be one of the ones we visit and we're also visiting these others and we've already been to these." Just the scale of ambition from them made them irresistible. They ended up being fantastic and went on to Wieden, Droga 5, here, and ended up getting job offers from pretty much all of them.

So don't play by the rules. Just work out what you want to do and how you might get there. Students always come and see us when the college course finishes, and they all show us their books at exactly the same time. If you're smart, you'd forge those relationships while college is going on, and some students do that and they end up being the ones who get on fastest. But they don't wait for the world to line itself up for them—they go out and organize it for themselves.

This is a wonderful business for young people to be in because it's such a meritocracy. There really are no rules about how fast you can go. If you are bright and continually surprise people with great thinking, your trajectory through the business is going to be meteoric.

Do you have any other advice?

I had a friend in college and every time we went out he'd end up with a girl at the end of the night. And it happened again and again and again. And one time in a pub I asked him, "What's your secret?" And he said, "Your problem is you ask out one girl a year...I ask 10 girls a night and 1 of them will say yes. Sometimes it's the first and sometimes it's the tenth. It would take you 10 years to be as successful as I am in one night." And I didn't apply that to the pursuit of women, but I applied it to my advertising portfolio. He was a 90 percent failure, but I assumed he was 100 percent brilliant. So if I have a book with 1 brilliant campaign in 10, people think I'm 10 percent brilliant. But if I want people to think I'm 100 percent brilliant, I just need to do 100 campaigns. And I can fail 90 percent of the time, but the creative director doesn't need to know that. And that liberated me to not worry about failing. I stopped worrying about cracking every problem, and I just kept moving forward fast doing ads for anything I could find. And I went to see a couple of teams in London and they helped whittle it down to 30 and then 10 pieces eventually. And we put that book into the agency we really,

really wanted to work in and we got a job. And it completely and utterly changed my career and my life. And I wasn't any different. I was the same 90 percent failure. I just approached things differently.

Then, when you get a job and you have to solve problems, do 10 and then go see your creative director. And there will probably be one brilliant one in there. A lot of people stop and go, "Here's an idea...that's the one I thought of." Another thing: When we were trying to get our book together, we'd spend a day and go into the city to a massive department store like Selfridges on Oxford Street. And we'd go there with a notepad and look like very strange people. Security would come talk to us after we'd been there for two hours. We'd walk down the aisles and go, "Whoa, look at this product; wouldn't it be awesome to do a campaign..." Because you go into the pet department and there are all these really fantastic products that have a great reason to be and no one has ever advertised them before.

So you go through the whole department store reading the labels and the backs of the products, and you make a list. And you each find 100 things in a day that we could potentially advertise and write down a little tiny bit about the product. And then get together later and swap those lists. And then you sit down independently and work on each one of those things. You write down as many ideas as you can, and when you run out of ideas, before you get to the despondent stage, you cross that thing out with a marker so that you can't read through it. Because it's human nature to want to go back and try to solve things that we couldn't solve. "Maybe I can think of something now!" Forget it. Dump out all the thoughts you can in half an hour and move on. And work your way through that list over the course of a few days, and when you get to the end you've got hundreds of ideas sketched out. And we would swap piles, sit together, and go through each other's piles, and mark anything that's great with a marker. And we might end up with 15 things that we thought were hot. Then we'd ask ourselves, "Can we build a campaign around this?" and some of them develop into really good thoughts, and some would wither and die. And we'd take the 10 or 12 campaigns that came out of it and go show them to a team that we respected. And then we'd do it again. But you need to balance the crazy stuff with some solid stuff.

Solid stuff meaning more boring clients like a bank or a utility?

Yes. Be careful with things like extra big bubble gum or hair dye or grass that grows slower. It's good to think of stuff for a bank or just something that no one's thought of doing. But, really, creative directors just want to see ideas that they wouldn't have thought of themselves. And starting with a problem they've never had to solve before is a good place to start.

As far as media goes, do you want to see "360 ideas" blown out? And do you need print?

It's very easy to see the potential of an idea across media channels, so really I'm looking for the idea. Press ads and billboards are still completely legitimate. And particularly billboards are very reductive—you have to really boil the thought down to its most basic form so it will communicate fast. And that helps get the idea really quickly. I don't want a preamble. I don't want a long explanation of the problem. I don't want to dig and dig and dig. I want them to recognize what the idea is and get it up front.

If you're working with technology and you've got a great idea for an app or something that changes people's relationship to the brand in some way, show it in that format. I don't need to see the same idea blown out across lots of different media. That's something that could come up in conversation if I met with that person. If it were all print, that would seem limited. So a variety of media is important, I suppose.

Do you need to see long copy or evidence of writing?

One of my favorite pieces of work before I got into the industry was "lip-smacking thirst-quenching ace-tasting motivating cool-running..." whatever it was, for Pepsi. And that was a billboard that wasn't English and wasn't writing and was a complete corruption of language to create a message. And I was trying to do English at school, and it was "rules, rules, rules." And there's someone communicating an emotion and a feeling, and it was beautifully liberating.

So it depends on what you want to communicate. Sometimes there's a role for long copy. It's fantastic to see great writing. But you can see great writing clearly in a four-word headline or an introduction to an idea. If someone writes a long-copy campaign just to prove that they can write long copy, I'm not interested in that. Brilliant long copy is rare, but it's delightful when you get it. We've got a young team here with some long copy work that is fantastic, and it will remain in their book for years and years and years. If it's great, put it in. You've got to be able to master the tools of our trade, which are basically words and visuals and using them across different media.

What do you think about including personal work that isn't advertising at all?

It goes back to what I was saying before: you don't want a templated book. You want them to have a personality or point of view on the world. If somebody has made a bunch of films, that's fascinating. If someone is an amazing illustrator/typographer and has great skills there, it is fantastic to see.

Do you have any other advice?

There's a really interesting thing that happens with the brain: when you're working on a particular problem and you're stuck, you're unlikely to solve that problem, but you'd probably solve a completely different problem. So if you're trying to think of something for apples, you're bound to think of something for bananas. And so you can forget apples, because no one needs to know that you didn't solve that brief, and if you've got an amazing thought for bananas, do it for bananas.

You can change the client as a student.

As many times as you want. So work fast, and don't worry about those gnarly problems that you didn't manage to solve. Keep moving until you get thoughts that really excite you. We don't need to know how many times you fail.

And the last thing I'd say is don't give up. Because it is tough. And it's easy to get despondent, and it's the determined people who ultimately end up learning how to do it and get the furthest. ⊞

To see Nick Worthington's work, please visit http://breaking.in

What do you look for in a student book? And what impresses you?

I definitely look for clever. I want to be surprised and entertained when I look at your book. First, I want to know that you know how to engage an audience. After that, I want to see that you have a good understanding of the people you are trying to reach. If the book has both of those things, then yeah, I'm impressed. You've managed to get my attention, and at the same time, demonstrate just how insightful you can be. You'll probably be getting a phone call. But then, if your clever, insightful book is also a well-crafted one, you'll have this creative director at your doorstep on his knees, begging you to come work with him.

How important is finish? If ideas are the most important thing, can sketches be enough? Do you look at actual books anymore, or is it all websites?

Back in the day, I remember spending hundreds of dollars on thick laminations and felt backings, so as not to scratch the laminations, for each one of the ads in my book. Today, such an expense is highly unadvisable, given the opportunities you have to present yourself digitally. Online portfolios and PDFs are faster, more efficient, and cheaper to produce and send. Your student work won't stay in your book forever, so don't bother with the fancy portfolio case. There's no need to spend all that money on packaging. Spend it on important things like food, rent, and finding out Gerry Graf's home address.

As for your ideas, well, that's another story. The care and thoughtfulness you put into executing your work matters. Every ad is an opportunity to show your love for your craft. And no, it doesn't mean I won't take your book seriously if it's made out of cocktail napkins. I'll probably look at that one too. But it does help to know you take your work seriously. Well-crafted writing and art direction say a ton about your talent

and work ethic. And to be honest, nobody has ever sent me a book made from napkins.

How important is copy? Do you need to see long-copy ads?

The question is, "Would the audience you're trying to reach appreciate or require long copy to get the message of your campaign?" If the answer is yes, then I might need to see long-copy ads. Otherwise, shorter copy, headlines, and samples of your writing will most likely be enough to let me know you've got the goods. Besides, I'm far more interested in a writer's ability to create a seamless marriage of words and images. My first creative director, the late ad legend Diane Rothschild, once created an ad for the Range Rover that showed the vehicle driving speedily through a shallow pond. The headline read, "We brake for fish." Always remember the first rule of copywriting: less is more.

What do you think of showing work that is not advertising?

Personally, I love it when candidates have blogs. The ideas and thoughts you share about yourself can often tell me more about the way you think than any ad in your book. On the flip side, blogs have turned me off from certain candidates even though their work was stellar. Everything you show is a window into your personality. In that way, yes, photography, art, and writing can give you a great edge on the competition. Or not.

Do you have any other advice for a student or junior trying to get into the business, either in putting together a book or how to actually start looking for jobs?

These are strange days for our business. Massive shifts are taking place and nobody is entirely sure what the agency of the future will look like. I imagine there's a ton of pressure on students to demonstrate their ability to keep up with everything new. But proceed with caution here. Sometimes, the best idea isn't about new media, it's simply a new idea. There's no substitute for a smart human insight. So rather than treating your book like an emerging-media check box, think about your audience and what place your client's brand has in their lives. Think about ways for brands to add real value to real people.

"SOMETIMES, THE BEST IDEA ISN'T ABOUT NEW MEDIA, IT'S SIMPLY A NEW IDEA. THERE'S NO SUBSTITUTE FOR A SMART HUMAN INSIGHT."

Also, consider the fact that you'll be competing with hundreds of portfolio school students who have presumably given a great deal of thought to self-promotion. So don't be afraid to be yourself. We go into this business because we think differently than other people. Have faith that your difference will be appreciated, welcomed, and, ultimately, celebrated.

Lastly, I would also suggest you find the right crowd to work with. This business is full of passionate, wonderful, talented people. Find them. Surround yourself with them. Learn from them and remember to return the favor someday.

Best of luck to you. BI

To see Ari Merkin's work, please visit http://breaking.in

**FREDRIK CARLSTRÖM
FOUNDER
C&CO
NEW YORK**

What do you look for in a student book and what impresses you?

Original thought. Which, I'm aware, is not a very original answer. But I look for a presence of thought and I'm surprised that there are not more people

who will just come with a sketchbook and show lots of ideas. I know most people do carry a notebook, whether they're art directors or copywriters.

That was actually my next question: Do you think work needs to be finished on a computer? Or do you think a collection of sketches is enough?

I think what I am about to say is true whether you're a student or a seasoned professional who is about to go into a meeting: it has to be either-or. Either it is absolutely perfect, or it has to be rough sketches. If it's in the middle, it doesn't work. People don't get, "It will look like this, but nicer." They see an ugly ad.

Do you think a student book needs to have long copy?

I don't think it really "needs" to have anything but I understand why the question is there. It's like you're going to a party—if you don't know the social codes you're not going to be social and relaxed. It's the same going to a job interview and students often ask these types of questions.

The very unsatisfactory answer I always give is that I don't think there are any rules about anything other than the rules that apply to everything in life. Show up on time, don't look homeless, be prepared, know who you're seeing, know what the agency is doing, reference back to something they've done, don't steal stuff from the conference room. If you go to an agency that's famous for its long copy, maybe you show something you've done with long copy. But then again, some ideas require copy, some don't, and I think it all comes down to how you thought about it. And how you solved the problem. At the end of the day, you have to walk in with your ideas and think that they are good, and if you don't get hired it's because the person who met with you didn't. So what? You will find someone who does like your ideas and that's where you want to work.

What do you think about seeing books with things that aren't ads in them? Other writing, or journal entries, or photography, or art projects?

Good and bad. If you are looking for work in advertising, show that you know how to do advertising. If you can explain why your diary or poetry is relevant to me and why I should hire you based off them, kudos to you. But sometimes you see a book with lousy work, but great photography, or great something else, and you can't help but think, "Maybe you should do this instead because you're obviously better at it and you like it more." Again, show anything that shows that—and how—you're thinking and that you can speak about intelligently.

"EITHER IT IS ABSOLUTELY PERFECT, OR IT HAS TO BE ROUGH SKETCHES. IF IT'S IN THE MIDDLE, IT DOESN'T WORK."

And do you have any tips for someone who's just starting out and trying to get into advertising?

Don't. "Getting into advertising" is too broad. I think you need to identify what it is about advertising that is interesting to you and try to go into that. Because advertising has changed so much. I don't know what they teach you in school now, because half the agencies don't even know what is going on right now. I just came from a meeting today where very senior people didn't know anything about very fundamental things—the Internet, digital, media, programming, how people communicate. I think you should think about why you'd want to go into advertising because it's not the way it used to be. It really isn't. It's changed a lot and it's about to change even more.

Why did you go into advertising?

I think most people—maybe not anymore, but then, anyway—didn't know there was such a thing as advertising agencies. People thought that companies did their own advertising. And I remember seeing this ad for a Swedish airline. You know how airports have these three-letter codes, like "LAX" and "JFK"? They had written this ad; it was a very simple ad. The message was something basic, not very interesting copy or anything, but it was written in a

way that divided up the copy into these three-letter words. And I was a kid, but I recognized that form. I recognized the three-letter words. And I just thought it was really clever and I wondered, "Who does that? That's interesting. That seems like a fun job to me to think stuff like that up."

Ultimately, I think any creative person, a film director, or a designer, or a fashion person, or whatever… anyone who is good at communicating with people are similar. They go to a bar, and they go, "I wonder why he ordered that drink that way?" Or, "How does this door handle feel in my hand?" Or, "Why do I come off as arrogant when I am feeling insecure?" And all those small insights about yourself and other people is the basis for stories, films, design, ads. I've worked with some really fantastic people in my life. The good ones are all curious and have some self-awareness.

Advertising people get a lot of flak. And a lot of them should. But some of the best people I've met in my life are people in advertising. Because they're well rounded, articulate, and really funny. They know that what they're doing is not that important. It's not like they are saving the world. But they try to find the best in the product and bring out the best in a business. I remember working for an optician's chain in Sweden. And our strategy was to break them out from all these other kind of lousy opticians. And the concept was "A Real Optician." We created this guarantee that, if your glasses broke, you could bring them back and get new ones—no questions asked. Perhaps that's not groundbreaking. It wasn't going to cure a disease. But for people who had glasses that broke, it made their life a little bit better. [BI]

To see Fredrik Carlström's work, please visit http://breaking.in

PAUL CATMUR
PARTNER & CREATIVE DIRECTOR
BARNES, CATMUR & FRIENDS
AUCKLAND

What do you look for in a student or junior portfolio? And what impresses you?

I look for work I wish I had done. I look for work that shows a creative maturity. It's not just copying the latest scamps from Cannes. It's work that's actually designed to look at problems in a different way and probably sell a product or to change people—whatever the brief calls for.

Can you think of any portfolios that have done those things?

I did see a portfolio a couple years ago that stood out from all the others and that I thought was exceptional. But, in talking to the team, I didn't think that they were exceptional. I thought that they had the wrong attitude. I would rather have people with the right attitude who aren't brilliant than brilliant people with the wrong attitude. It's not just about the book; it's about the people.

Once I hired a design student who had a portfolio that I thought was exceptional. He came here, worked as a designer, and is now doing very well as an art director. But I don't think my portfolio, that I did with my art director, was exceptional. It probably had a degree of maturity that student books often don't have. But our attitude underneath it was very good.

Do you recommend that students write their own briefs and make their own strategies or can they find briefs?

I think that creative teams these days need to be generous. The best and smartest teams will write the strategy on their own. To me a lot of planners would be creatives if they had whatever difference it is— maybe it comes down to hard work sometimes. You need to be really smart to be a planner, but you have to work really hard to be a creative—probably harder than planners. I'll get in trouble for that.

Are there common mistakes that students make?

Some agencies like to see scamps. They like to see ambient rubbish that is designed to appeal to the 10 members of an award jury and not to change the thoughts of members of the public. But it depends which agency you go to. If you come here, personally, I'm not interested in them—I think they're a waste of time.

When I was growing up in London, you had to tailor your book depending on which agency you were going to see, and I think that probably holds true today.

Do you think that's a good idea?

I think it probably is a good idea. And there are some people who will say, "I only want to work at such-and-such agency," and maybe there are people brilliant enough to pick and choose which agency they want to work for but I haven't found that very often. Generally I find you need to get into the industry and do some work and then take a long-term view if there is a particular agency where you want to work. It's a lot easier to move around from inside the industry than outside it, I think.

Is the level of finish important? Can sketches be enough?

They can. You can see the idea in a sketch. But we're a small agency and currently we have two creative teams. Both of the art directors are very good with a Mac, and that saves a hell of a lot of time and messing around. It's a complete waste of time to have an art director sitting over a designer or Mac operator telling them what to do. So I think the ability to produce reasonably polished work is very good. There are an awful lot of ideas littering the award books around the world that are purely based on being well-put-together rather than great ideas. So for an art director or team to be able to put things together well is not going to do them any harm and is very beneficial.

And what about writing? Do you need to see long copy?

Writing is writing. I think if you can write interestingly in any form—be it a film script, be it articles, be it a diary, be it a letter complaining about something—if you can write well you can write well. It's a very tricky one because that can, to a certain extent, be taught. I didn't start in advertising until I was 30, and I had forgotten to write properly between leaving school and going to advertising college in London. I had to learn it again. Inspired writing comes, to a certain extent, from inside, but not every piece of communication needs inspired writing because inspired thinking can make up for that.

"THE BEST AND SMARTEST TEAMS WILL WRITE THE STRATEGY ON THEIR OWN."

Most long-copy ads in student books are incredibly dull. Copywriting doesn't mean you can write a lot of words. Sometimes it means you can write three words but they're very, very good.

What do you think about putting personal work in a portfolio?

I like people who have done interesting things before [advertising]. I find that much more exciting than someone at 16 who decides to do advertising because you get to go to parties, wear whatever you want to work, and turn up late; so it's cool to do and so they've gone to advertising college. I prefer a richness of experience. And evidence of writing or illustration or other work can show that. And I don't mean someone who says they like books and going to the cinema and eating Italian food.

Do you have any tips on how students and juniors can get in touch with you?

New Zealand is a small country, and, while we're a small agency, there is a relatively small number of students here. So I try to support them and support the agency by seeing as many as I can. Because you never know when you might need someone. So I do keep a not-particularly-well-kept collection of URLs and CVs on the computer.

Do you have any other tips on building a great portfolio?

Say you're in a college and everyone is working on the same brief. Then you have a show and all the ECDs come and see all the same campaigns—it just gets very dull. You don't want to do another Super Glue [ad].

Which brings me to my next point: when I started, all the students used to do the world's strongest glue or the world's fastest running shoe or the world's longest-lasting battery. Stop it. You don't get those briefs. The Asian award shows are full of that kind of thing, but it won't get you a job at any decent agency. It might, but it shouldn't.

Be yourself and be nice. It was a tenet of Bill Bernbach that everyone who worked at DDB had to be nice and talented. To that I would add "hardworking." Get those three and you'll do well. And make yourself indispensable. If you get a placement at an agency, just do everything.

I think your book has to show evidence of everything. The days when you could have a collection of campaigns of three print ads with the odd TV or possibly radio are over. It doesn't cut it anymore. We name beers. We design beers. We think up the whole concept. Big campaigns. And integrated mini-campaigns seem to be the thing now. The "matching luggage" of campaigns has dropped off, and now it's about one simple, single idea—almost tactical—that takes place over a few months and then you move on from—

[Phone rings. Paul takes the call.]

...There you go. That was a creative team who will start Monday. Daniel, my business partner, saw their work at a show and they emailed it to him, he sent it to me, and I thought it was the best work I'd seen at that show. So I got them to come in. One of them had a big beard which I thought was a good sign. They're from the bottom of the south island in New Zealand, which means they probably aren't too flashy and are down-to-earth guys. So they'll be here Monday.

Fantastic. Before you were talking about integrated campaigns.

We had a junior team here who were brilliant in coming up with ideas, but couldn't actually do ads. And they were probably more useful. When we needed an ad for "$50 off a flight to Fiji," they would struggle. But when it came to doing an all-encompassing campaign for garnering industry support for the advertising standards authority via Web, digital, and DM [direct mail], they were brilliant. So when the "$50 off flights" briefs came I would do them. If there's one thing an old advertising creative can do, it's average work very quickly. Which somebody needs to do. It's an important part of the agency. If you can do the simple ones simply and easily, it creates time to do the hard ones better. ⊞

To see Paul Catmur's work, please visit http://breaking.in

JOSÉ MOLLÁ FOUNDER & ECD LA COMUNIDAD MIAMI

What do you look for in a student book? And what impresses you?

First of all, students have to keep in mind that the main thing creative directors don't have is time. To me a book should show where your standard and criteria is. I don't care about quantity that much. I'd rather see seven or eight ads that are really good than 20 that are okay, because with your portfolio you are saying, "Okay, this is what I think is really good." Of course it's great if you have 20 great ads but I think it's also good to leave someone wanting to see more.

The first page of the book makes a big statement, and it can change the way you see the rest of the book so it should be really strong. The end is also important because it will drive the desire to want to know more about you and your work. So, choose your best ads for the beginning and the end, but make sure what's in between doesn't kill the thrill.

It's also important to try and show good ideas on different platforms. Something that worked for me when I was starting out was to describe TV ideas, for example, with just brief paragraphs, telling the core of the story, using as few words as possible. Keep your audience in mind—you are talking to people who are accustomed to imagining things, that's what they do for a living. Never ever have long scripts; believe me, nobody will ever read them. Make sure you have a healthy mix of print, out of home, TV, interactive, some guerrilla, even some radio is nice, only if it's good, though. But don't overdo it. Less is more.

Do you think it's important to have TV in a student book?

I think it's key to show you can think in TV and interactive terms. Here's another good tip when it comes to TV: don't try to shoot stuff. There's a reason why directors and production houses are so expensive. Good TV is very hard to produce. The democratization of technology is not helping students. Knowing where you place a camera or how to shoot a spot is not what will open doors for you as a creative. Coming up with great ideas will, and that's what will give you the chance to work with the best directors and editors who you will eventually learn from after many years.

Just write, in five lines, what the idea is and end with the concept and VO. The idea will always look better in the creative director's mind, especially if you are talking to the right creative director. And if you are not, then you don't want to work for him or her anyway.

Do you think just sketches can be enough? Or do you think ads need to be produced and comped up?

Please don't be pretentious when it comes to the actual book. When I see really fancy, expensive books, immediately I think, "Wow, the content better be good." So it can actually backfire because it sets expectations high even before looking at the work. And, if the content is not good then it makes it even worse. On the other hand, when I see a book that is "normal" and I open it to find some great ideas, the surprise is very pleasant. Students get too obsessed about their books and they redo the same ad 35 times and they spend lots of money they may not have. Personally, I think sketches are okay. Again, the imagination of a creative director can be a powerful ally.

"...DON'T TRY TO SHOOT STUFF. THERE'S A REASON WHY DIRECTORS AND PRODUCTION HOUSES ARE SO EXPENSIVE. GOOD TV IS VERY HARD TO PRODUCE."

Another piece of advice is to be careful when deciding what products to put in your book. This is basic. A good ad for laundry detergent is ten times stronger than a good ad for condoms and it looks more professional.. Stay away from funky products and brands and choose more "serious" advertisers. Also, stay away from iconic brands. Every time you see ads in student books for Nike, Apple, MTV, etc., it's impossible not to compare it with all the great work that has been done for those brands before. So all that great work will go against you. Having good ads featuring serious brands adds more to the equation. You should make us think, "Wow, if he or she can do a good ad for a product like this, imagine what they could do in other categories." It should create the feeling, again, of wanting to see more.

When I taught, I would give my students an assignment and tell them, "Okay, you have to develop a campaign for a shampoo with only one condition: you cannot show hair." And the stuff I would get was actually much cooler despite them being shocked in the beginning. They would come in with the perception that it's much harder to do a good shampoo commercial than a good condom commercial. But in reality, both are equally hard.

So for art directors do you think sketches are okay as well? Or just writers?

Well, sketches are good for communicating an idea. Having said that, I'm always looking for crafting,

something harder to find in this digital era. As an art director, even if you don't have great ideas yet, nice art direction can open doors for you. It's the same with writers. When a writer knows how to write, even if the ideas are not great but the copy is really good, he can get a job. But try to show some range so that everything doesn't look the same. Choose a few executions to prove that the crafting is there, and sketches to communicate other ideas. Of course it helps when you see a very nice idea that is finished properly, but a lot of people spend months working on one ad and they forget that the idea is just okay. And it doesn't matter how many times they try to change the art direction, it's still going to be just an okay idea. So I would spend that month coming up with five good ideas that maybe you see in a sketch form.

Again, if you have five great ideas well produced—awesome. But don't waste your time, the better a bad idea looks, the worse it is, because it means you really, really believed in that bad idea.

Do you think long copy is important to have in a book?

Yes, I love when I see writers that can actually write and it's one of the boxes I always try to check. Make sure to have at least one campaign with great copy.

What do you think about things in a book that aren't ads at all?

It's very important, especially in today's world. Advertising can be claustrophobic and is always late on trends. People who have their minds open to other forms of creative expression are always the most likely to bring fresh perspectives to the table. But you have to make sure it makes sense in your book. One time there was a guy who heard that we liked stuff not related to advertising. He had an interview with my brother in Buenos Aires and he created a puppet that was basically his penis with some eyes and a mouth painted on it, telling different stories to the camera. After a few minutes, my brother Joaquin finally spoke and said, "Can I ask you something? Why the hell is it that I have to be sitting here staring at your dick? Is this supposed to be funny?" The guy was shocked because his whole presentation was based on this supposedly artistic thing. For the record, we ended up hiring the guy under the promise that he won't let his penis do the talking ever again. The moral of the story is that whatever you show as extra work has to somehow be related to our industry, even if it is indirectly. I think it's great to finish a book with, "Hey, I write poetry, here are a few examples. I do photography or I paint, here are more examples." But avoid getting into, "I like hiking." Who cares?

And then do you have any tips on how to get into the industry?

Getting your first job can be tough. I was lucky because it wasn't too hard for me but, generally speaking, you need a lot of perseverance. I've seen a lot of gimmicks sent by creatives and we get some at the agency every now and then. Most of them are just that, gimmicks, and the ideas behind them are not very good. So, again, you see all this effort spent on a bad idea and that only makes it worse.

One of the best cases that I've seen was at Wieden. Someone sent a well-written letter to all of the partners saying something like this: "Hi, I'm handsome. Very, very handsome. Yes, I know I'm not supposed to say it but I'm incredibly good looking! So much so that girls love me. Not just random girls, I mean every girl in this world loves me. So here's what could happen. You stay late at the agency working on whatever project and I go to your house and knock at the door. Your wife opens the door and, as soon as she sees me…well, you can imagine what could happen…So here's my proposal: You hire me. I stay working late instead of you, so you can go home early and enjoy your lovely wife. Deal?" He was hired the next day. And it was only a letter: a piece of paper, an envelope, and some copy.

Another piece of advice is not to go to every place out there. Where you work first is the place where you will learn a lot and that is crucial. Decide which are the three or four great shops you really want to work at and keep trying. You may hit a wall many times before you find the door. But if you want it badly enough, it will happen. BI

To see José Mollá's work, please visit http://breaking.in

ALI ALVAREZ
CREATIVE PARTNER
THE BROOKLYN BROTHERS
LONDON

Interviewed at Fallon, London.

What do you look for in a student book? And what impresses you?

Originality of ideas and something that shows who they are as people. For some reason, students are all being given the same briefs and so you see the same kinds of products—and work—in their books. So I think they should try to find the products that just don't feel "studenty," something they're interested in, and focus on great ideas, really. Although it's nice to see things executed well, it comes down to ideas. Good Photoshop skills don't count.

Do you think it's important for things to be finished? And specifically for art directors?

I guess for art directors, it's more important. But I don't know. I'm driven by ideas here. At Fallon it would definitely be more about the idea. And many places have got a really strong design department, so I definitely think I'd rather see strong thinking and help develop the execution.

Do you think it's important to have long copy in a book?

Depends what you consider long copy. A very traditional ad with lots of words—no. The campaign Fallon did for Tate Britain that won the Grand Prix at Cannes was a long-copy poster, but was surprising because of who it was for. I want to see that people can write; there are lots of ways of showing that.

What do you think of putting stuff in your book that is not advertising?

I love it. Yeah, I really want to see it. In fact, if you didn't have that in your book I'd be worried, "Is ads all you do?" I was just going to say too, about the long-copy thing, that doesn't need to be an ad. It could be a short story. Or it could be a film that you've written and shot. I think these might be more well received if it were that kind of stuff than [advertising] because that doesn't seem like as much of a chore to read. But I definitely, definitely want to see stuff that's not advertising.

Did you put stuff in your student book that was not advertising?

I had two pieces. This fine-art piece and a really stupid little homemade movie that I had done, that a teacher told me to put in there and I was horrified about sharing it with any big creative directors. But everyone loved it and it made them laugh. So, my teacher was right. Thanks Craig.

Do you have any tips or advice on how to get better, or how to get into the industry?

I think the best advice I could give is that you really have to edit the work. It's much better to have four to five brilliant ideas than eight mediocre ones, or three that drag the rest down. And the only way you can edit it is by showing it to people. I made a list. Make the B list and A list and show it to everyone on the B list, be ruthless about the crits, and get it down to your best work. Show it again, be ruthless, and then start showing it to the A list. And keep editing through your whole career. BI

To see Ali Alvarez's work, please visit http://breaking.in

POLLY CHU
CHIEF CREATIVE OFFICER
JWT
BEIJING

What do you look for in a student or junior portfolio? And what impresses you?

When I look at a portfolio, be it a young guy or a very experienced guy, actually I'm not looking at

something that he already did. Because sometimes it is meaningless. People always want to do something great. But they have some restrictions because of the environment or the agency where they are working does not have the right account for them, or the kid at the university doesn't know how to express himself. If I just look at the portfolio and judge this guy based on what he's done, it's not fair.

I will talk to him and ask him questions based on the portfolio. "What is the idea behind this? Why are you doing that? Tell me a story about the work you did." Something like that. I'm trying to find out about his thinking—the logical part and the nonlogical part—which is actually what I'm searching for: the creative part.

The person who is very creative should have some potential that I can see in the thinking behind his ideas. There may be a lot of things he wants to achieve, but maybe he doesn't have the technique or maybe he isn't allowed to do that work because his boss doesn't like it or the client doesn't like it or whatever. So, from his story I know "This guy has a lot of thinking" or "This guy has a lot of passion" or "This guy has a very strategic mind." Then I can see if that is the person I need.

Do you think print ads are a good way to demonstrate thinking? Or do you like to see integrated campaigns?

Let's put it this way: if it is a simple project, print ads are a very easy way to judge his craft. However, for more interesting, out-of-the-box thinking, a fully integrated campaign will better demonstrate your creativity.

No matter how breakthrough a print ad is, it is just about the headline, art direction, and strategy. But with an integrated campaign, there are so many more things that you can play around with. So, if you like music, you can inject that. You can bring more interesting thoughts and more of your personality into it. And if a guy is mature enough to control all these elements—events, PR, Internet games, whatever—then he really has potential. Of course this is very difficult. It is something that requires a lot of knowledge. But this is now the trend, and when we get in touch with university students, they are very into this type of multimedia communication. And some are very good. When we have workshops with university students, they can both lay down the strategy and also the creative, and also they have very good presentation skills.

Are there common mistakes that students make in portfolios?

I remember seeing some young guys and they didn't edit their portfolio. They put in everything they had ever done. That's the first thing.

The second thing is a totally unorganized portfolio. I interviewed a guy showing me work on a computer. And there was no PDF or PowerPoint with his work in it. Everything was on the desktop and he had to find the file and click to see the video but he had the wrong file. So the interview just gave me the impression that this guy is totally unorganized.

On that topic, do you like people presenting work to you on a computer or a physical book? And how much do you look at someone's website vs. their printed book?

This is a good question because in China they don't have a printed portfolio anymore. Most of the time they show me work on their laptop. Sometimes they don't even get out their computer. They just give me a USB drive. Some of them have websites. The site should not be very big. The work should not be long. If you give me a 10-minute video, I don't think I can get through it. It has to be very fast and organized. Or give me a short version so that I can understand them in a short amount of time. They need to organize the website in a way that is very easy for us to see their work in the way they want to present it. The navigation should be very easy.

Okay. Sorry, I sidetracked you from the question about mistakes.

The third mistake is they will present the most finished work. No matter how finished it is, you are not a professional. When we look at a student portfolio, we are not looking for professional technique. So they have a misperception about that. We're not looking for someone to do beautiful Photoshop work. We're looking for someone with

the potential to be a very good creative thinker.

> ## "IF SOMEONE IS NOT CREATIVE, IT DOESN'T MATTER HOW MANY YEARS YOU TRAIN HIM, HE CANNOT GET THOSE ABILITIES."

So how can we see if a person has potential? It means looking at sketches or thumbnails. It means looking at some interesting video or a nonadvertising piece. If they have something very interesting, they should not be shy about showing it. Even if it is very naive and nonprofessional, they should not hide it. Just show it to us. Or if they have an interesting hobby they can put it in their portfolio.

Technique can be learned in training. Within six months or a year, a guy can start from zero and become a very professional computer operator. However, if someone is not creative, it doesn't matter how many years you train him, he cannot get those abilities. So we're looking for someone who is very curious about everything. He is very interesting, is interested in many things, and has a lot of lovely ideas. Show us.

Do you have any examples of the kinds of nonadvertising work that people have shown to you?

There was a guy who liked to travel. So he wrote his own travel book—a travel journal—about his experiences. And he wrote it in a very naive way. The writing was lovely, and it was 100 percent better than the copy he was writing in the advertising. Another was a girl who showed me some embroidery. That was also impressive because the person who can do embroidery like that must be very patient. Sometimes this can impress us. It's doesn't have to be all ads and storyboards. And if the person has the right character, this is really treasured.

Do you have any other advice?

I'll tell you a story. When I was in Shanghai, one day a young guy knocked on the door. He was a media person, but he wanted to be a creative. So I said, "How can you prove to me that you have the ability to be a creative?" Because he didn't even have a portfolio at all. But then he showed me a notebook in which he translated all the ads from Archive magazine from English to Chinese. At that time there was no Chinese Archive. And then, he rewrote every ad, using the same visual, with his own thinking. And he told me why he thought his ideas were better. These were just thumbnails. But he was so passionate about advertising and he was trying to write in his own way.

This really impressed me. And then he said, "Since I don't have a portfolio, what if I work here for free—you don't need to pay me." So I let him come in. And he would come in every day and write the leaflets, which everyone hates to do. And every day I could see that the work was improving. Every day. He wrote every sentence with passion. And after a few months, I thought, "I can't let him go." Even though his technique is not very mature, I thought, "I have to find a way to let him stay." So he did, and three years later he became one of the most famous creative directors. In just three years' time ! The story behind this is that it is not the portfolio that really matters. It is the attitude that really matters. And when we look at a portfolio, it's not about the content, it's about the character behind it.

And the last thing is to know who you are talking to. A lot of students don't, and that is a disaster. Know something about the person you are talking to. Sometimes people email and I agree to meet them. And then I find out in person that they know nothing about the agency, and they know nothing about what they want. At least go on the Internet and learn about what they are doing and why you want to come.

When a student makes a portfolio they need to get prepared. They need to think about what parts of their life they want to expose to the interviewer. It should be the most interesting parts. The most creative parts. The most organized parts. The most passionate parts. It's those parts they need to expose to their future agency. ⊞

To see Polly Chu's work, please visit http://breaking.in

HAL CURTIS
CREATIVE DIRECTOR
WIEDEN+KENNEDY
PORTLAND

What do you look for in a student book? And what impresses you?

The first thing you always look for are good ideas. Good thinking. I'm an art director so I'm probably more severe in my criticism if I'm looking at an art director's work. I'm harder to please. But it's always about the idea. You look for craftsmanship and alongside craftsmanship you look for passion. I want to see a unique voice. Someone who's an individual. The best advertising talks to you like a person—not a company. So good writers, they have a unique voice. A distinct voice. And you can see that in a book. In a good art director's book you see a unique style. They just have a certain something that makes them stand out and makes them interesting. Good books can be very traditional, or they can be very unusual, or they can be very organic. You can see, when you look at a book, someone who's really excited about the craft. You can also see when someone doesn't really know what they want to do yet. But, to sum it up: You look for strong ideas, good craftsmanship, passion, individual voice, and style.

So, do you think it's really important to have finished work? Or do you think sketches are okay?

I've seen it happen both ways. I think, for an art director, you need to show somebody who's going to give you a job that you have an understanding of the fundamentals of art direction. That you understand composition. That you understand typography. That you know how to lay out a page. That you know how to compose a television frame. That you have an understanding of those things. So many art directors don't. Particularly ones who've gone to just ad schools and haven't studied art. The fundamentals. They don't have a passion for or knowledge of typography. They don't know how to draw. They don't understand color, or chroma, or value, and the basic tools of art direction you use every day. And if you don't understand them, you're at a real disadvantage. So I think for art directors, you should go to art school. You should either have an undergraduate fine-art degree or at least have attended art school and studied before you go to an ad school and put together a portfolio. Draw, paint, make a film, take some pictures, learn the art part. Then put together a book. So for art directors, you must demonstrate craftsmanship.

For writers, I don't think showing finished work is as important. I do think you can get a job with just tremendous headlines scribbled on napkins. Or a journal of just thoughts and scripts. You know, Jeff Kling got a job here as a writer with just a sketchbook. It had style and a unique voice. It was full of drawings. But it was mostly just writing. And it was this really intriguing book of ideas. There wasn't an ad in it.

That was actually another question I was going to ask. So what do you think about "non-ads"?

Well, it depends on where you want to work and what kind of writer or art director you want to be. If you're an insane person, like Jeff Kling, and you want to work at a place like Wieden+Kennedy, it's a good thing. If you are a more traditional type of writer or art director and you want to get a job at a more traditional type of agency, it's probably not a good thing. But you know what? If you're good, you can have both. I've seen both. I've seen books that come in and they had 10 really great ideas, but they had this really interesting sketchbook of just fucked-up thinking.

Okay. And long copy: do you think it's important for writers to show that they can write?

I do.

And do you think it's important for art directors to show that they can lay out copy?

I do. Now, some people will tell you it's probably not as important as it used to be because we don't do that kind of advertising as often anymore. But I think, as you get online and art directors become more, and more, and more a part of what's created in the digital space, it will become important again. But yeah, I think that when you're trying to get a job it's like going through the NFL combine. They put them through every skill test imaginable. Speed,

strength, skill, you name it. They want to see how they do in each of these different areas. Same with a book, the more talent you can demonstrate, the better. The more areas of craftsmanship and execution you can show that you're fluent in, the better. So if, as an art director I come in with long copy that shows I can handle typography, and I can show you, through another campaign, that I can do traditional work, but over here I show you that I can be organic, and handmade, and cool, and appeal to a different target, and over here I understand the digital space. The more skills you can demonstrate in your portfolio, the better.

"THE BEST ADVERTISING TALKS TO YOU LIKE A PERSON—NOT A COMPANY."

Tracy Wong, a wonderful art director, went to Art Center where I went. And he was at Goodby in the early days when they were doing so much really tremendous print work. Now has his own agency in Seattle. He used to say that when he was putting his book together, he wanted it to be like, for each ad or each campaign, a different art director had done each piece. He wanted to be so versatile that his style was to not have a style. That he was so skilled he could execute any style. And he was certainly that kind of art director—is that kind of art director.

Do you have any tips on how to improve or how to get into the industry?

Well, I think it's really important to have someone who cares about you—someone who is in the business already—to be a mentor to you. So you can attach yourself to that person and learn and have someone to walk alongside you as you develop a book. For me it was Mark Fenske. Seek out a person like that and establish a relationship with them. It's, I think, a really terrific way, while you're in school, to make your book better and learn. But also once you get out, have somebody who will take an interest in…making a phone call. This is a relationship business, and that's really important. And most creatives like talking about the craft. And I had people who did what I'm doing with you, and what you're doing for other people, do it for me. And I'm happy to. I mentor kids from the University of Oregon, and we have interns here every year. And Kevin Proudfoot, who's ECD of our New York office, was an intern of mine. And so, if you seek out a person whose work you respect and just send them work, they'll—more often than not—engage with you. So that would be my best advice. Find someone early on, and ask them to look at your work and tell you what they think, and kind of help you put your book together. Find someone whose work you respect. Then work hard. ⬚BI⬚

To see Hal Curtis's work, please visit http://breaking.in

YANN JONES
WRITER/DIRECTOR
TH2NG
& ASSOCIATE LECTURER
CENTRAL ST. MARTINS
COLLEGE OF ART
LONDON

Interviewed at WCRS London.

What do you look for in a student book? And what impresses you?

Well, that's a very difficult question to answer in a short sentence.

It can be multiple sentences.

Okay, multiple sentences it is. I think books come in different leagues. I'm not sure where this analogy is going—I'm just thinking off the top of my head. Books from advertising colleges used to consist of seven or eight campaigns with four ads in each campaign. Each ad had a different headline and a consistent thought in a strap line at the bottom. This is now a very old convention of a campaign, you won't get into a decent agency with a portfolio full of these. Some students make the mistake of thinking that advertising is a comedy sketch or a

gag with a logo at the end. If you're going to do your job well, you'll have to go some way beyond this. For me this is a "division three" portfolio. I'm talking first, second, and third division, not the new "Premier League," "The Championship League," then "First Division" as we now have in football. That's very confusing so you can delete that bit. I don't even like football that much.

Yes. And Americans will be very confused.

The better students move past this convention up to the second division. They understand the fundamental structure of advertising: proposition, substantiation, audience, things like that. They've put their own personal perspective on advertising and dug deeper into strategy. They've explored less conventional media: digital, ambient, social, or even better, they've taken a more holistic approach to communication strategy. So these are the second-division books—these can be very good books. You could get a junior position or placement very happily with one of these portfolios. But to get into the first-division category, it takes something a little bit indefinable—a characteristic specific to the team. These are the one-in-a-hundred books; and I probably see 100 portfolios a year.

But remember, your book is only half the equation if you're trying to get your first job. A book gets you through the front door, for a placement or a trial. Then it's how you get on in the agency, how you perform on projects, and how you interact with other people. Agencies like to live with you and see how you operate. That's the other half of the equation. Curiously, good portfolios don't automatically deliver good agency teams. Some very creative people are simply not suited to an agency environment.

So, in terms of scamps or sketches versus finished work, what are your thoughts on that?

Twenty years ago, it would nearly always have been a scamp-based portfolio. The old adage goes that "If you have got a great idea, you could scribble it at the back of a cigarette packet and you should be able to sell it." Hmm, cigarette packets, that's how old that adage is. Of course the reality is different: agencies look for a more multifaceted skill set. Most students are digital natives, technically proficient. It's good to see scamps and some hands-on technical ability, fifty-fifty. I would caveat that by saying polished art direction and a knowledge of web-building software is not a substitute for good thinking. An agency has resources to support presentation, but it can't do your thinking for you.

"...IT TAKES SOMETHING A LITTLE BIT INDEFINABLE—A CHARACTERISTIC TO THE SPECIFIC TEAM. THESE ARE THE ONE-IN-A-HUNDRED BOOKS; AND I PROBABLY SEE 100 PORTFOLIOS A YEAR."

For writers, do you want to see much writing in a book or are you more just concerned with ideas?

It's not high on the list of priorities. You get a sense of someone's writing in their concepts, their thinking, and their headlines. I don't need to read a slab of body copy.

What do you think about putting things in a book that are not ads? Things that give a glimpse into what that person's identity is? Do you find that in the "division one" books you're talking about? Or are these things maybe just irrelevant? What are your thoughts?

I think that the identity of any team or creative should come through in their work. I don't look for specific pieces of work that say, "This is who I am" and, "This is what I am about."

Well, it could be that, or it could be just some ideas that they have, or journal writings they did, or photographs they took.

I think that could be a part of a good portfolio. But it comes down to the specific content.

Well, if that content were good, is that something you'd want to see?

Yes.

And so what sets a first-division portfolio apart? What differentiates the one-in-a-hundred books?

As we've said, a student who has proven that they understand the basics and then moved beyond them, developed their own personality and original thinking. Smart branding is overlooked by many students—and agencies. Understanding different tones of voice. And creatives that appreciate that the portfolio itself is also a piece communication.

I remember one student built a complete 3-D model village to represent her portfolio; she created a journey through the village with each location delivering a different campaign. An advertising version of Michael Bentine's Potty Time. It was hilarious.

If you could give one piece of advice to someone who's just starting out, trying to get into the business, or putting a book together, what would it be?

There's nothing worse than wading through a portfolio of semi-realized, confusing ideas. No matter how complex, original, or sophisticated your thinking is, the book itself needs immediacy and simplicity. ⊡

To see Yann Jones's work, please visit http://breaking.in

JEFF KLING
CHIEF CREATIVE OFFICER
FALLON
MINNEAPOLIS

What do you look for in a student book? And what impresses you?

Well, in a student book, I look for a point of view. And I like to see an individual's voice emerge. Separate from that of every single one of his cookie-cutter ad school peers. Because anybody can parrot, of course, all the ads that appear in all the annuals. And everybody can write in that One-Show-Penciled voice. But I like to know who I'm hiring. I like to see some evidence that, if push came to shove, and we had a big important pitch, somebody could write an ad-like object in the accepted understanding of what an ad is. But well beyond that, I want to know what specifically this person brings to the table over that person. That's it.

I like to laugh, too. I don't mean to say that laughter is the only emotion that I want access to from advertising or from communications. But I've got to respond in some way emotionally. I want a book to make me laugh or to amaze me or to make me drop my bacon sandwich. I don't want a book merely to provoke cold verbals like, "That's funny. That's clever. That's interesting." When I feel something, I know it. And like it.

So the next question that I ask most people is, do you think the work has to be finished? Or do you think sketches are okay? But now I'm remembering that your student book was just sketches, right?

Yeah.

Not even ads.

I guess mine was sort of a unique case because it just really took the piss. So I did fake ads, ads that I quote, "Thought would be great" unquote. Or, "This is the best ad I can possibly do for this, that, or the other thing." And they were just super naïve. I really want to know what kind of answers you've been getting back because I think people pay huge lip service to "the sketched-out idea." And it's "all about the idea." But if you show 100 percent of creative directors in advertising the sketched-out idea on a fucking napkin they won't even fucking look at it. They won't do it. And they'll probably either lie and say it's all about the idea, or they'll say, "Well there's no reason why somebody nowadays shouldn't have access to slick production and desktop publishing, etc., etc." That's definitely true for art directors and designers. But a writer?

I mean, come on. Words can appear a lot of ways. So that's what I'm interested in. That's not to say a book should only be that, but I don't mind that. I don't mind that at all.

> *"I NEVER, EVER WANT TO HIRE AN AD WRITER, EVER. SO, I DON'T NECESSARILY WANT TO SEE A LONG-COPY AD BECAUSE, IN A STUDENT BOOK ESPECIALLY, THEY SUFFER—THEY FALL INTO THAT "AD-Y" RHYTHM."*

Do you think you need long copy in the book?

I don't know. I don't think it matters. I mean, there's only copy that's too long, you know? And I like to see that somebody really can write. I like to hire writers. And people who are writers first…and then, because they're a writer, they can handle the subset called "ads." I never, ever want to hire an ad writer, ever. So, I don't necessarily want to see a long-copy ad because, in a student book especially, they suffer— they fall into that "ad-y" rhythm. But, if you want to put in a play you wrote, or a thing you got published in McSweeney's online, or whatever. Something like that in there? Yeah, I really want to see that stuff.

That was my next question. Do you think things that aren't ads are good? And I think you're going to say yes. So then my follow-up is: Do you need ads at all? What should be the balance between ads and other work?

I guess it depends on what you're going for. It's a question of intent. Part of being a copywriter or art director is having the gall to say that that's what you are. "I do this." So you're saying, "I am capable of accepting money from you in exchange for this skill set." So you're declaring that that's what you are. So show it. You don't absolutely need ads. I could discover a filmmaker or artist as a creative director and say, "I want that guy on my project." But that's very different from that guy saying that what he is is a copywriter or art director. So technically, no. Ads aren't needed but if you want to say that that's what you are, and that's what you're capable of doing, then the burden of proof is on you to show that, yes, that's what you can do. So I do need to see that. But I don't need to see that over and over and over in three-ad "campaign" bursts. Show me that you can do that a little bit. And then anything else. I just want to know what your voice is as a writer. That's it.

Do you have any tips, either on getting in the industry, or how to improve as a writer and art director?

Good God! I mean, anybody trying to get into advertising nowadays has my profound sympathy. I guess my biggest piece of advice would simply be to make your own luck. You've got to get into the conversation. I'll give you an example. When I got a job at Wieden in Portland, I would get calls from people in a past life saying, "Hey, I got this great idea for a Nike ad." And you quickly learn that from the legal standpoint you're not even allowed to hear that idea because if some version of it comes out, even by accident, in any form, you're suddenly subject to a lawsuit. So you hang up the phone. But one of my old bosses who fancied himself a bit of an athlete called and he had a couple ideas. And, the thing about advertising is, as lame as it is, and it is extremely lame, not just anyone is allowed to do it. That's kind of a cool thing about the system. You have to be serious enough about doing it—even if ultimately all you ever do is really shitty crap—you have to be serious enough about it that you're going to align your whole life, or your professional life, so that you're in a position even to do ads. And I think that's good. It's kind of a very natural winnowing process. And so I think it's important that you go through some kind of process to align yourself to be able to do ads. And I think the best way to do that is simply to introduce yourself to people who can help you get into that position. I mean, you introduced yourself, right? I mean, I didn't know who the fuck you were. I got to know that you existed because you let me know that you existed. All a book is,

is a request for a conversation. I mean, if I look at a book, then I kind of go, "Okay I'll talk to this guy." That's all it is. That's all it has to do is be something that gives enough evidence that I should talk to this person—I should get to know this person a little better. So that's all that has to do is just open the door. And then you walk in and extend your hand. 🄱🄸

To see Jeff Kling's work, please visit http://breaking.in

SCOTT NOWELL CO-FOUNDER & EXECUTIVE CREATIVE DIRECTOR THE MONKEYS SYDNEY

How do portfolios come to you? Do people email you links? Is there a recruiter who brings them to you? Is it all online, or do you see physical books anymore?

The answer to that is yes. You get all of that. We try to get people to send a PDF or a link, and that way you can narrow it down easily because we get so many. Otherwise you'd interview people all week and never do anything else.

And in an interview do people bring in laptops?

Laptops, tablets, paper, leather...as long as it's a coherent presentation of their work it doesn't matter what it's on. You'd be surprised how many people will come in with something like a paper portfolio and then they'll have a couple MPEGs on their computer, but they can't find the ad they want to play you or suddenly they can't play it and they're sweating and you're sitting there thinking, "Geez, you could have played this better."

Do people email you directly?

Yes, all the time. It's fine. Every day we get someone saying, "I'd love to come and see you" or "I love what you're doing; is there a chance of me coming from Brazil and getting a job in your agency." We're getting people from Brazil and Peru and all these strange places...not to say those two countries are strange. But it's amazing the amount of direct emails you get.

So once you're looking at the work, what impresses you?

For a junior book you just want to see some interesting and fresh thought. I think a lot of students' books have what that person thinks you need to see. But really you want to see what kind of thinker they are. We hire people who have hardly any ads in their book but they've done an amazing blog and we know they can write, or they've got a clever business idea or solution. You just want to see a fresh take on the world, whether that's in advertising or in another pursuit that could be applicable to what we do here.

It's got to stop you. Like a consumer [seeing an ad]. If you can engage a jaded creative director then you're most of the way there.

You mentioned showing work that is not advertising. Do you think someone could show no advertising? Or a mix? And should it be separate from the advertising work?

My feeling is you put your best thinking together. If you've got ads in there that work, great. That's always a comfort to a company that does make a lot of ads. But advertising is branching out into other fields, so it's great to see people who can bring something else to the table. But some people talk about private stuff or they just talk about what they do and, if it's not very good or done to the level of your ads, then don't bother.

Can you think of any examples of when it's worked well?

One girl here came from AWARD School and had a lot of design work, having previously worked as a designer. And she had a few design and business projects that we just loved, and then she had her ad school stuff which demonstrated that she could think in that concise advertising way. But in combination it was a much stronger package than if it was just the ad work.

You just want to see a fresh take on the world. And that's what advertising is. You've got to have a fresh take on a car or chocolate milk. It's always good to see people who are obviously into what they are doing. We had another talented girl who came in with ads, but she also had a website where she was selling products, and some of those products had gone into the Museum of Modern Art. We were sold on that website.

"DON'T DO CREEPY THINGS. DON'T STALK [CREATIVE DIRECTORS]."

One of our other guys started here after working as a designer for a company called Mambo, which is an Australian surf label. He'd worked on ads for Mambo but never for an ad agency. We liked the way he thought and the design skills he brought and hired him.

It is a wide-open thing; you could do anything. But it makes a person more interesting. If someone comes in with a bunch of ads and says, "And here are some bike designs; I'm building a bike." If it's presented well, that's great. I don't know how I'm going to apply it now, but we might be able to apply that kind of thinking.

Should it reveal something about their personality?

Yeah, but it doesn't need to be a personal bio. If someone's written a short story and they want to be an advertising writer, it's really valuable for a creative director to read. So it doesn't have to be autobiographical, but if it's a valid form of creative thought then it's worth seeing.

What do you think about polish and finish? Can sketches be enough?

Yes. As a junior you can bring in sketches. As a more senior person you can't get away with it because you want to see produced work.

For a junior art director, is it also okay?

When you meet someone, all you're looking for are ideas and attitude. That's pretty much it at that level.

If they've got the right attitude they can learn the craft. If you've got good people in the company, then they can learn from them.

What about writing?

Advertising has been full of writers who don't know basic punctuation or grammar and it's incredibly annoying. If a writer brings in sketches of ideas that's fine, but if they've written a blog or an article for the local paper...it's good to see that stuff because you can see how they express themselves.

Do you have tips about getting in touch with creative directors?

Don't do creepy things. Don't stalk them. No Photoshopped pictures with the creative director's head on it. I just wouldn't do that sort of stuff; you'll be seen straightaway as a freak. Just do good ideas and be open to what people have to say about them. It can be confusing when you first start out because you'll go to one person and they'll say, "That's great; you'll get a job soon," and then you'll go to someone else and they'll say, "This is rubbish; you're nowhere."

The best thing to do is keep working. Get briefs and keep working on them. If you can go and meet a creative director and you seem to be getting on, just ask them for a brief. If it's alive or dead it doesn't matter. If you come back with work it shows a bit of initiative. Attitude is so much of it. If you've got people who are sitting there with decent ideas and you can tell they've got a bit of talent and they've really got drive and a good attitude, you know they'll make it. But if you have talented people and their attitude isn't good, they'll either have a reality check and do well, or they'll just fade away.

How do you deal with the problem you mentioned: some people love it, some people hate it. How do you decide which pieces to put in your portfolio?

Pick the people whose opinion you value most and go with their opinion. And your own. I think that's the only way you can do it.

I'm out of questions. Is there anything else you want to say?

Just on the attitude thing: we've met quite a few people who come in and say, "We've been at this place and it's terrible...they kill good ideas and we want to work somewhere cool like your place." The reality is it's hard everywhere. And you never want people who slag off where they have been. It is acknowledged that it's difficult to get work through at certain places, but there's no point in bad-mouthing anyone or anything. And it's always good to see people with a positive attitude, even if they're working at the worst place and they say, "We keep trying; it's pretty hard, but every day we try to come up with new things." So attitude is a major factor. Good ideas and attitude. And don't be afraid to put stuff in that you think is good that is not advertising at all. ⊞

To see Scott Nowell's work, please visit http://breaking.in

**KARA GOODRICH
SENIOR CREATIVE DIRECTOR
BBDO
NEW YORK**

When you see a student book, what do you look for and what impresses you?

Originality of ideas. Taking on some products or services that are a little deeper than the usual superficial stuff. It's also easier to do good work for something that has more substance or story to it. Also I look for range. If they're a writer or art director, do they have a schtick or can they really find the right voice and the right look for a brand?

What about things that aren't ads? Do you think it's important?

I personally do not want to see fiction writing or screenplays or art—that doesn't do anything for me. If it's advertising-related work, like guerrilla, alternative-type things that ultimately have a marketing purpose, yeah, but as far as your hobby, writing, painting, or poetry, no.

Do you have any tips for someone who's just getting into the business?

Well, I've always said, "Hold out for as long as you can for the best first job you can get." Which is sometimes easier for kids who either are from the city they are searching in and can live with their families still, or have enough money or whatever to hold out for awhile. Your first agency experience can really shape the direction of your career. But many entry-level people I meet are reaching the end of their financial rope and need a job, any job. I understand that, too.

So my secondary advice is: If you have to take a job and it's not "the" creative shop or you're worried that it's not the best shop, give it six months maximum. If you haven't gotten book-worthy stuff at six months, work that genuinely replaces your student work with better work, then you have to look for another job. Actually, that piece of advice was given to me originally by David [Lubars] when I was just starting. And it seems really simple, but it's true. The most productive years of your career go by too fast to waste [more than] six-month increments. The award shows…when you're doing something and you realize that you can't enter until the following year, that starts to press on you. You begin to feel that time ebb by, and you want to get your career moving a little faster than that. Try to hold out for the good first job.

How did you get into this business?

I went through a bunch of crappy agencies. I was one of those who couldn't wait for the best thing. I wasn't interested in New York because frankly, the best work was coming out of San Francisco, Minneapolis, and Portland. I muddled around for five years in at least four different agencies, but I forced a couple good things out of each place. Good enough to get me my "break" at a great shop.

When you started, did you do any classes or ad school?

I have a degree in advertising. I went to Syracuse. I'm not sure if Portfolio Center [an ad school] even existed then. But I did focus on advertising, so I had a portfolio coming out of school, which is important.

People try to put their portfolios together while they're working—it's hard. It's really hard. I feel for them. Especially to get that finished quality when you have no access to all the things you need to get your work looking finished and polished, much less build a website. I think the ad schools help. They direct your energies quickly, in a productive direction. ▣

To see Kara Goodrich's work, please visit http://breaking.in

STEVE ELRICK
FORMER EXECUTIVE CREATIVE DIRECTOR FOR ASIA
BBH
SINGAPORE

What do you look for in a junior portfolio? And what impresses you?

Originality. Freshness. Raw, bleeding talent. You do get to a stage where you see a lot of portfolios. A lot. So, similar to advertising in general, you're looking for something that really stands out and has impact. Add to that, when you see similar portfolios from ad schools: because they work on the same briefs, there's an even higher wear-out factor.

You become hungry for something that is really fresh and stands out. It's increasingly tough to do that. We've got the BBH tagline which is, "When the world zigs, zag." And we have a lot of respect for doing things differently and coming at things from a different angle. When I'm looking at books I'm looking for a really fresh, original take on stuff.

I don't look at portfolios as a record of what you have done. I look at them as an indication of what you could do. It should be a signpost to, "Ah—wow, that's the way that person thinks or approaches a problem." I want to think, "I never thought about it that way before."

There was recently a very junior team where I just met the writer first. And he came along with a school exercise book. And I said, "Is that your portfolio?" I knew they had gone to ad school so I was expecting to see finished work. And he said, "I do have some finished work in here," but he preferred to talk me through the ideas. It was scribbles and scamps. It showed the process and the progression of the thinking. Here was the brief. Here was our thought. And it would be sketched out in very basic terms, but because he was so confident and articulate in how he talked about the idea, at least I was able to understand the way he thought. And even if the idea wasn't necessarily that brilliant, I could see the "zag" to it. That's a really good, interesting starting point. And I thought it was a really good way to get across his personality and not just sit there with a portfolio of ads.

Is it a good idea to have a setup line to explain the thinking before a campaign?

It all depends. I think it used to be, "Don't explain anything, just show us the print ad or the poster and I'll make a judgment call of whether I think it's good or not." And you could flip through a book and subjectively make a quality call about how good it was. Nowadays a lot of the presentations are "Here is an integrated, 360 campaign we did for a restaurant." And, almost by definition, people have to describe the brief and describe how they approached it before one can see the project as a whole.

It's tougher now to make a quick judgment call about a book. But my guidance there would be to still sum up an integrated campaign idea quickly, and then go into the detail. One of the things I loathe is having to sit there as someone explains the campaign idea across multiple media only for us to realize it probably wasn't worth the effort. Quantity is no substitute for quality. It's great that you did a Twitter feed and interactive posters and teasers for the TV and a Tumblr page, but it's just not that good. So keep it simple and short with a description of the work that precedes everything. That's a skill that a lot of people should learn when they're presenting.

Do you think ideas need to be fully integrated like that, or could a great print campaign or a great website idea be enough?

I think nowadays if someone's got a portfolio of just print and TV, it's going to be severely limiting. But I don't think everything has to be 360. You can still shine brilliantly in distinct channels. That's often a problem we find with clients now. For every little project it's "Give me 360." Well, you can't afford to do it properly across 360 degrees; how about a brilliant 36 degrees?

As a whole, across a portfolio, people do need to show how they think across all different media. Gone are the days when someone can walk in with even a beautifully crafted print poster or TV portfolio and expect to get a job where the ideas have to live in totally different media 50 percent–80 percent of the time.

I still think you're able to tell from print, poster, or TV how good a writer is. Or how good an art director is. But I think you need to show that breadth of work that really uses the other media to full effect. There are now so many different things you can do with mobile/online/interactive mediums that it's a massive advantage if you can show you know how they work and how people use them.

I have a friend who is an engagement planner in New York and purely on the basis of his status updates on Facebook, I would give him a job as a writer. He's funny. He's witty. He's entertaining. He's "on brand." And he has a quality cutoff...he doesn't just post shit. He crafts everything.

We've got an old-school copywriter here who was almost dismissed. I don't mean fired, but dismissed as a person who could not write interesting digital content. But there was one campaign where he just blew everyone away. Not by doing anything particularly different but just by transposing the whole idea and the way he wrote around the idea in a different medium.

For people breaking in, if they're coming in as a writer, a blog can be great. I wouldn't go so far as to say, "Just show us your blog about what you did today." But show us writing that you're proud of that shows you can communicate. And if it is something other than advertising, great.

Over the years I've seen different people like journalists who want to break into advertising. And they can show me clippings of articles they wrote; and that's great if it's great in that medium. But you also need to show some willingness or passion or interest in doing it for advertising. I reckon I can write advertising but if I suddenly wanted to change tack and get into journalism I think I would know better than to just turn up with a book of ads.

One of my other questions was going to be about showing work other than advertising, but it sounds like you're saying it is useful but needs to be in addition to ads.

Yes, back to my initial thing about freshness and originality: if it's visual media and he shows he can paint or draw or do animation, filmmaking, graphics, type—anything above and beyond that shows he can communicate and express himself in an original, fresh way—that adds to the cachet of having that original thinker working in the agency. And applying that to agency life. It's sometimes a tricky one. If someone wants to take me through a book of amateur photography that's not that great, then it has a negative effect. But showing a breadth of talent in any way is a good thing. It's more appropriate now than it used to be just because the breadth of disciplines that you might be working in when you're in advertising has become so much more disparate.

I have a mate who was and is a good stand-up comedian and comedy writer. But he was an agency guy for a long time. He was a funny guy and that came out in his work. So if your advantage, for instance, is being funny and witty, then, of course, you should show 10 minutes of your stand-up routine or a funny article. Anything that shows how you can express yourself is always a good thing.

Are there any common mistakes that you see in student portfolios?

There's the classic one about picking easy, scamp propositions. The strongest glue ever invented. Extreme hyperbolic propositions like that. The torches that light up the moon. The batteries that never run down. It's propositions that you'll never get in the real world. The "edgy" condom ad. Controversial pro bono stuff. Also propositions that have been done 50 times by other brands. To me, these things are not worthwhile to show.

I quite like it when people choose the tough products: consumer goods, washing powder, or whatever. Stuff that you might actually be working on.

It's a double-edged sword, but I actually like the people who have the balls to come in and present ads for the brands you have in the agency. Quite a high-risk strategy! But, if people have done the research before they see you and tried to better some of the work that they see coming out of your agency—and of course it might be off brief—but I think it shows a nice chutzpah to come in and show five ads for Axe "That I think are good and are better than what you're making." It's got a nice ring of confidence and also shows that the person has thought about who they are presenting to.

"IF YOU BRING A REAL ENTHUSIASM, AS LONG AS IT'S MARRIED UP TO SOME TALENT, IT GOES A LONG WAY. PEOPLE WILL WANT TO WORK WITH YOU."

That would be another mistake: coming in and knowing fuck-all about the agency and who you're presenting to. Because to me it just says you don't really care about which agency you get a job in. You're just doing the rounds and not even doing five minutes of Google research into what kind of work the agency produces and the people who are there. Do your research. Know who you're talking to. Try to at least customize your pitch to them. That's just common sense and politeness.

I think being cynical is a cardinal sin. We've got enough cynical people in agencies as it is! The last thing we need is people coming in with that ironic, cynical attitude toward advertising. People who are "too cool for school" and say, "I'm really into these other things, but I probably need a job in advertising" versus "I really want to work in advertising and specifically at this agency." I personally find it a waste of my time if people come in and bitch about the business before they've even got into it. We've got a quote up somewhere: "Cynicism is the opposite of creativity." It's a tough business and you get beaten down, but unless you're willing to get back up again and approach things with a sense of freshness and positivity, take your cynicism elsewhere.

Just attitude. Because you're looking for fresh, enthusiastic people to come in and learn from. That's the other thing for me. You can almost have very junior books that are too considered and too crafted. And seem to fit within the trend lines very well. I prefer to have people with disparate, different thinking. We've got an intern team and their brief was, over 10 weeks, to do good famously. And the brief was to try to bring to the fore some of the issues with migrant workers in Singapore. So they came up with lots of ideas, but one of the guys said, "I think the best way we can get their issues out there is for me to go and live and work as a construction worker and sleep in a dorm which is a converted container." And he's done it. What a great way to show passion and originality and jumping into a project with both feet. I think it was brave of him, but it was also the attitude of "I'm going to go for it." I'm less judgmental about whatever content that they produce because of the attitude with which they've approached it. You can't be too enthusiastic when you want to get into the business. If you bring a real enthusiasm, as long as it's married up to some talent, it goes a long way. People will want to work with you. The beneficial effect on the department can almost outweigh the content they produce. It can really enliven the rest of the department.

Do you have any advice about getting in touch with creative directors?

I think links are a godsend in many ways because at least you're not walking in with a stack of laminates. The downside is if those links don't work well or it takes too long for a TV ad to load then you quickly lose interest.

One killer idea can be enough to make someone say, "I want to try that person out." Don't put everything in your portfolio just because you've done it. If you've got one campaign or three campaigns that are head and shoulders above the rest, use that as the way to get your foot in the door.

Sometimes I'll go through a book and I'm usually quite nice until someone says, "No, actually that's really good. I took this in to another creative director and it was his favorite campaign." And I'll say, "Go back to that person and get a job then." But I suppose it's galling to people when they get conflicting advice."

What's your advice on dealing with that?

It's mostly a subjective game. Even million-dollar ads that are made and pass through Wieden or BBH or whatever. You can see them on TV and think they're crap. And that's going to happen with your portfolio. I'd not take it personally.

But there's another example where I said to this guy, "I think you've got three great campaigns in here; kill the other six or seven." And he said, "But some people like this one." "But did they like it more than those three?" Because keeping average-y stuff in your book, all it does is pull down the rest of it and it starts to seed doubt in the CD's mind.

I often ask people before I tell them what I think, "Tell me why you think it's a great idea." And you'll often find people talk themselves out of the campaign they're presenting. You've gone through that process and you can hear it as you're saying it—you're not convinced. If you're not convinced of your own work, take it out. Don't expect people to see some hidden genius in your work that you're not quite sure about.

Only present the work that you passionately believe is great. You might get a lot of disagreement from a CD, but at least if you're showing commitment to the idea, then I think that says a lot. I would prefer that people argue back to me and try to convince me it's good than to say, "You're right; maybe it's not that good." Then why the fuck did you put it in there? So that self-belief, even up to the point of arrogance, is a good thing as long as you're taking on board other opinions. If you've seen six or seven creative directors and none of them have picked your campaigns as being good, there's a certain point you need to say, "This is impressing no one; time to take it out."

Tenaciousness is another thing that I find works well. Maybe it's ego, but when you're a CD and you vent your opinion on some work, you'd like to think that people are taking it on board. Whether they agree or disagree, at least they are open enough to hear your opinion. A couple of times people come back with some tweaks and say, "How about this?" Maybe you said one out of six was the stand-out ad and they come back with five other ads. I find that impressive. And it's a clever way of keeping in contact with CDs and engaging with them. I think maybe CDs are looking for a freshness and a passion that they might have had beaten out of them over the years. You want to get an energy from people that makes you think if you stick them in the creative department, not only will that amplify the energy in the other teams but also within yourself. ▢

To see Steve Elrick's work, please visit http://breaking.in

KASH SREE
FREELANCE CREATIVE DIRECTOR
NEW YORK

What do you look for in a student book? And what impresses you?

What impresses me? Clarity of thought. Freshness of thinking, too. And sometimes those two can fight each other. Just getting it. Stopping power. What's happening now is there's a lot of the "Crispin-ization" [Crispin Porter + Bogusky] of books as everyone goes 360, forgetting that what you need is an idea first of all that then spreads out. Not, "I've got all these bases covered." So I personally like to see a strong idea that's got some sort of legs, or can resonate. This is something that Crispin actually does, but students misinterpret and just scattergun weak ideas across different media.

I've got three rules that I like to apply when I'm looking at print ads, or any ads. And that's, one, does it stop me? Two, is it original? Because you don't want to be advertising someone else's product. And three, does it make me buy into the product? Now by that, I don't mean, you're not going to rush out and go and grab it off the shelves, like they did in the sixties. We were still getting out of the war and were just not used to

having stuff. But you're creating this relationship with the products. So if your ad makes people reconsider— it's like, "I wouldn't mind hanging out with that product." And when you need a product of that type, that one will be on your list. That's enough. That's what I want them to do. So that's my three rules.

"...CHANGING THE WHOLE BOOK MIGHT TAKE TWO MONTHS. WAITING FOR SOMEONE TO SAY IT'S PERFECT MIGHT TAKE FOUR YEARS. AND IT WOULDN'T BE A VERY GOOD PERSON THAT SAYS IT WAS PERFECT."

Other student-book things: don't create pollution. A lot of people want to do things like, "Oh, I'm going to do something in a lavatory. Or I'm going to do something just outside your front door." Unless it's really engaging, unless I really am interested in it and it enriches my life in some way, I'm going to be five times to 20 times more angry at you for encroaching on another piece of my life with a piece of bullshit fucking advertising. Make it something that enriches my life, not fucks it up a bit more.

Other things for students: be prepared to listen. A lot of students come and say, "Well, someone else liked this." I said, "Well, why didn't they give you a fucking job, then? They're being nice to you." It's way easier to go to a student and say, "Oh yeah, that's a really nice book. Yeah, keep trying. See ya!" And then not take your calls anymore. It's a lot harder to be a bastard and sort of say, "Okay, this is going to be confrontational. It's going to hurt. And it's going to hurt me saying it." Because you do get tensed up. But you say, "This sucks, because..." But you've got to say the "because." And, "This is how you can fix it. And this is good because..." But you've got to be ready to hear someone say, "I don't like this." And then do something about it. Even if it took you months to put together. Put another one together. It's slower to think, "My book is perfect."

I've seen guys do this—quite good guys—say, "My book is perfect," and wait for someone to say, "Your book is perfect." Rather than change the whole fucking book. Because...changing the whole book might take two months. Waiting for someone to say it's perfect might take four years. And it wouldn't be a very good person that says it was perfect.

Do you think it matters between just having sketches if the ideas are good and having finished work?

No. I prefer it if you could just show me some outlines, or some sketches, or marker things. Just so I can get the idea, great. I know now books have gotten a lot more polished. And they want to see them finished, and okay, some people do that. Personally, I say, with all that time that you're doing it up you could've come up with a better idea.

What about long copy? Do you think that's essential?

I think there's need for long copy. We have got a shortage of people that can write. And we're finding that industry-wide now. We can't find people who write. Because all the award shows just give awards to people with your logo on the bottom as the answer. That's great. But there's still a place for a reasoned argument. And for a fun reasoned argument at that. They're just not awarding it anymore so people aren't doing it. So I'd say yeah, definitely there's a place for it if it's compelling.

What do you think about putting things in your book that aren't ads?

I would say put that in a different section of your book. If your book is bad, and then I've seen that you've taken my time to show me your poetry, I would say, "So why don't you go and be a fucking poet then?" If your book is good and then you add more depth to you by saying, "And I'm writing a book. And here's a film I made. And here's my DJ-ing skills," I'd say, "Cool. Here's a cool person." But that's icing. First you need a cake. So I'd almost keep it in a separate book and say, "Here's my book, and here's my extracurricular activities." This is the sort of thing that, if everyone has similar books, you can use to help differentiate yourself.

And do you have any tips on how someone can improve as a writer or an art director?

Yeah. Do another book in a week. It stops you from being precious. It makes you work harder, you get faster. Once you've done that, do another book in a week. You build muscle. Don't be afraid to just work your ass off. Because you're building muscle now, and later on when you have to do it, it'll come much, much faster. It's painful and it seems futile to begin with. You get two, three hundred percent better. Do a book a week.

And any tips on getting into the industry?

Know who you're talking to. Whenever you ring someone up—or email someone. We've all got egos. Say, "I love this ad that you did." Or, "I like this ad, or, "I remember you from this." And it opens the door. I've had people sort of say, "Here's my work, tell me what you think of it." And I delete because I don't have the fucking time. You've got to sweeten me up a little bit. Tell me I'm good looking. "I could tell by email that you're a very handsome man!" That'll work. BI

To see Kash Sree's work, please visit http://breaking.in

TONY LIU
GREATER CHINA PARTNER
M&C SAATCHI AEIOU
SHANGHAI

What do you look for in a student portfolio and what impresses you?

If I look at a portfolio, I look at ideas first. I think most creative directors will. But if you then prove that you can execute it well using a computer, it's even better. It is important to make the creative director understand your way of thinking. And also to show your variety of thinking. You have to show that your thinking is very broad, not narrow.

Nowadays many people are into techniques. We can always hire people to do Photoshop or retouching and so forth. And that is important, but I'm looking for people with thinking. Everything doesn't have to be comped and finished, but if you have just a few at the end to show that you have those art-direction skills and to show you can use computers, it helps.

In the old days art directors could lay it out and give it to a visualizer so you had to imagine everything in that rough sketch. But now, with a computer, they can try this and try that. They don't think of the whole thing at once, they just try different things. It's good and bad. But in this business you really need to narrow down the idea first. Drawing with a pencil and gathering references forces you to think and to imagine. And that is the most important part of the process. Nowadays some people are thinking about the technique right from the start.

How do people get in touch with you? Do you look at mostly physical or online books?

I still think a portfolio is the most important thing. If your house caught on fire, that's the thing you grab. In the old days, we would mount our work and use a marker to black out the edge because it's white...these small things about how you present your work. Nowadays people come in with their computer. It's okay. But people don't do it right. People look in different folders and it's messy. That tells me they are not in love with their work. They don't know how to sell themselves. The presentation is also a very important part of this business. So I don't care if it is a paper book or online book or showing work from a computer as long as the presentation is good and they have shown attention to detail.

Advertising people want approval. You want people to love your work. If you are not treating your own work this way, you're not that in love. I don't think schools here teach people how to do it.

What do you think about showing work other than advertising?

I hired someone with no knowledge of advertising but she had a sketchbook, and I hired her as a copywriter. Later she became more interested in making beautiful visuals, so she turned into an art director. And now she is a very good creative director.

Sometimes students have doodles—a small drawing—and next to it a paragraph or small poem. And from that you know that they live. Advertising people need to live life. Without that, there is no way you can have inspiration. You don't have to always write advertising headlines. If a person loves life and wants to put it down on paper for themselves, that person has merit. As a Chinese creative director we are like a jade finder. There is no way I can know everything about you, but there is something in you that makes me think you have a chance to turn into jade. And I am responsible to help this person develop and turn into jade. And if I'm a student I want to find someone who will do that for me.

What characteristics do you look for that tell you someone might become jade?

People who are easily inspired by a lot of things. By life. Music, books, movies, hobbies, friends, everything. If you don't have that I don't think you stand a chance.

How do people show that?

That's why the interview is very important. You ask questions and see how they respond. "What's your hobby?" Maybe from that you will know if they are very narrow or very open to the world. Or maybe they get excited talking about music. Some advertising people may have technique, but without those ingredients, there's no chance. Even if I give you a formula, if you don't have a life, you don't have any ingredients to put into that formula. You look at Hollywood, they have formulas to get people to feel empathy. If you don't have that human insight, you've got nothing to become different.

Can you see that in people's advertising work as well?

In China, no. You can see their technique and their computer skills. Students in China have big problems because they don't know what's outside China. Maybe English is their hurdle. But they are a little shallow and not worldly, and it limits their imagination.

Creativity is all about mixing different things together. New combinations to make new things.

I always encourage people to read more because whatever you read will be a box. A movie you watch will be a box. An ad that you see and analyze how it works will be a box. A friend who shares his life story is a box. Once you have the technique, you need all those boxes to try different things. The more boxes you have, the better. In this business you try out 100 options in your head. That's how to do something good: try 99 options and see that one is better than those. If a guy comes in with just one idea, it is probably the same idea everyone else had.

"GOOD ADVERTISING PEOPLE LOVE LIFE. THEY LOVE TO TALK TO PEOPLE AND SEE THINGS. THEY GET EXCITED ABOUT EVERYTHING."

Good advertising people love life. They love to talk to people and see things. They get excited about everything. Creative people, not just advertising people, should be like that.

Can you see evidence of this in the work?

Yes. And I also want them to learn one thing: always analyze work and why it makes you feel good or why you like it. If you analyze the work you like, then you will understand where the idea comes from. Even look at Shakespeare. People still love to read it. Why is his work so likable? And you realize there is human insight in it. You have love, hate, jealousy. If you analyze it, you will see the components and understand why people love it. Hearing a joke and understanding why people laugh will help you tell a different joke with different components. And it is different in China and the West. And you start to understand the culture. The more you understand, the easier it is to do brilliant work.

Do you have any advice for Chinese students on getting into advertising?

I went to school in the States. One assignment was to draw 50 logos. Not for a company but for yourself. You were the client. And when we went to show them to the professor, without even looking at them he said to do 50 more by tomorrow. Sometimes he would take a lighter and burn your work and say it is rubbish. This hurt a lot of students' feelings. But this is the business. Each week we would see the sun come up doing homework. And it is the same thing working. You burn the midnight oil. A lot of students in China don't know about this. They don't know what this business requires. So when they graduate and see this, they don't want to do it, but it is already too late. In my school we started with 40-some people and only 8 graduated. And only 3 are still working in the business. The more toughness you encounter early on, the better you can cope with it once you get into the business. Maybe they can understand this a little bit when they read this.

In China, because of the way exams work with getting into universities, you get students who go into advertising to get into a particular school. They may not want to do advertising or know anything about it. In the States, people will have an understanding of the curriculum and do it because they want to.

You know if you are in love with it or not. Just like you know with a man or woman if you are in love or not. Don't ever cheat on yourself by pretending you like it. It will be very painful for you. How do you make sure you love it? Go read One Show, Communication Arts, D&AD, and if you get fascinated by what's in it and want to start making your own work like that, then you have a chance. If you love it, it doesn't mean you're going to be successful. But if you don't love it, then you stand zero chance. ⊞

To see Tony Liu's work, please visit http://breaking.in

TYLER MCKELLAR
FREELANCE COPYWRITER
DRIGGS
IDAHO

What do you look for in a student book? And what impresses you?

I look for someone who is clearly enjoying what they're doing—whether it's a serious ad or a funny ad or something in between. You can tell fairly quickly if someone is just cranking out an ad to please an ad school instructor or if they're giving their work the tender loving care that can only come from truly enjoying writing and designing.

How important is finish? If ideas are the most important thing, can sketches be enough?

I think it's critical that some ads be thoroughly finished—as a way of showing you've got the stamina to effectively see something through to the bitter end. But the reality is creatives are almost always showing ideas in very rough forms to their clients, so what would be so surprising about seeing that from students in their effort to break into the business? Great ideas will always win, whatever form they may currently be in.

How important is writing? Do you need to see long copy?

You hardly see long-copy print ads anymore, but the web has opened up even longer writing opportunities. Proof that you can keep 'em laughing or crying or thinking for a good 500 words or so will go a long way to proving you're not a fluke who's relying on a few snappy headlines.

What do you think of showing work that is not advertising? Things like art, journal writing, photography, hobbies, etc.

It couldn't hurt—as long as the hobby doesn't involve a mandolin. I can't stand those things.

Do you have any other advice for a student or junior trying to get into the business?

If you've got anything that's actually original, most people will hate it. But remember that you're not trying to get a job offer from everyone. Stick with what you like and someone—some*one*—will like what you do and give you a job. 🄱🄸

To see Tyler McKellar's work, please visit http://breaking.in

WARREN BROWN
EXECUTIVE CREATIVE DIRECTOR
BMF ADVERTISING
SYDNEY

What do you look for in a student portfolio? And what impresses you?

I look for clarity of thought. I like a combination of logic and madness. We work in an industry where we solve problems, and trying to define what is the problem that we're actually trying to solve is quite often the biggest challenge. So I like people to have a very analytical way of approaching a problem and figure out what is important and what isn't. If there's a logic to the construct of your argument or idea, then you need to deliver it with a sense of irreverence and madness. And not fall into the trap of delivering it in a dry fashion that won't catch anyone's attention or get them interested. It's a very "yin and yang" thing; if the fundamentals of the thinking are sound and given a "sticky wrapping," then they will engage people.

That's interesting that the problem is figuring out what the problem is. Is that something that you can see in the finished work? Or do you think it is helpful for students to write a sentence about the problem they are trying to solve? A setup line?

I think that's key to how powerful your idea will be. There are two important things you need to be successful. First, find something interesting to say. That's the basis of any great idea. And once you've identified that, it is important that you find an interesting way to say it. It's very hard to be original if you can't find something interesting to say initially, so I place a lot of emphasis on what that nugget is. I think most people, when they are given a brief, just rush headlong into trying to please the client without stepping back and saying, "What is the real issue here? What are we really trying to address?" The client will give you a set of challenges that they'd like to have met, but there might be an underlying thing that will wipe all those other concerns out and give you a much stronger steer on where you need to go to create a bigger impact or solve a problem that even the client hasn't quite identified yet.

What about finish? Can sketches be enough?

I think principally it's about ideas that fire the imagination. There's a great quote I heard years ago: "A child's mind is not a vessel to be filled but a fire to be kindled." And I look for people who fire my imagination with ideas. The more breadth and scope of the thinking and the greater the creative territory that they've discovered, the stronger the idea— that's what's inspiring. You can transport great ideas into any medium. Into any nook or cranny you like and they are unbelievably sticky. They stay with you. You can't shake them off. And that can be presented on a scrap of paper. I never get seduced by wonderful presentations that are highly finished and may have dressed up something that is essentially quite boring. I always look for "What is the key nugget? What is the leap they've made creatively? What is the fresh insight?"

For art directors, do you look for design skills at all?

I think you've got to be able to do everything these days, but if you had to put an emphasis on one thing I would make sure your ideas are sound, well thought out, and you articulate or present them in a way that gives the viewer an indication of how you see it developing creatively. And you can do that by getting reference material, if you can't create it yourself. There's enough information out there now on the Internet that you can pull stuff together to say, "Okay, this is the sort of territory I'm in, but it's not going to

be quite like that, it will be more like this." Because if you're truly original, what you're trying to present might not exist. So you've got to find a way to fill in the blanks for me with material that is relevant and will help illustrate the idea.

"JUST BECAUSE YOU'VE GOT A FEW TERRIBLE THINGS IN THERE… FAILURE ISN'T A BAD THING. AND IF YOU MAKE PEOPLE TERRIFIED OF FAILURE EARLY ON IN THEIR CAREER, THEY'LL NEVER BE ANY GOOD. PEOPLE NEED TO BE ADVENTUROUS."

If you're a good creative director, you have to have a pretty well-developed theater of the mind anyway. Good creative directors can usually spot something within an idea, and you might find that that should be the focus. Sometimes people come with a fully formed campaign and they believe they've done a wonderful job. And often a creative director will say, "You see this little bit over here? That's the great bit, and you've surrounded it with all this crap." So you need to be quite aware that editing is key to getting a great result. Because it's not what you put in, it's what you leave out that will make your idea stronger. And most people actually think that the more they put in, the more it will enhance their chances of impressing someone. But it doesn't work for me or for anyone I know. It's all a process of reduction and finding the essential bits that will empower an idea.

Do you need to see evidence of writing ability for copywriters?

I think what you need to see is people who can actually write down an idea that has a flow of logic so you can understand what they are trying to say. I usually get impressed by people who can write a sentence and string together an argument using just the English language even though very few people tend to rely on that these days. We live in a very visual world. I always believed that if you're a really good art director you should learn how to write, and if you're a good writer you should learn how to art-direct. Because you never know how the idea is going to be best expressed. We're in the business of communication, so it's really important that, if the only medium that you've got open to you is words and you want to express your idea, you want to be articulate enough to choose the right words that will empower your thinking. Rather than getting it lost in a spray of adjectives or what-have-you. Or if you're stuck in a visual space and you're a writer, you've got to be able to think visually to find what will work best in that discipline. But I think these days to succeed you have to be the fully rounded article.

Understand basic grammar and how sentences work, and then you don't always have to rely on it. Picasso was a classically trained artist and then basically threw it all away to explore a new visual language. And I think it's a lot easier to do that if you understand the fundamentals and what underpins everything, and there may be times when that knowledge is very important. It also helps in presentations; if you can write well you can usually speak well, and if you can articulate your point quickly and succinctly to clients it is very helpful.

What do you think of including personal work that isn't advertising in a portfolio?

I have this question I normally ask people in interviews who are trying to impress you with how professional and buttoned down they are: "What's the craziest, maddest thing you've ever done?" Because I think you need to know the personality of the person and also how far they are prepared to go to do something quite mad. If they've never done anything that is exciting or has gone against the accepted norms and conventions and busted out and done something wild, then I get a bit bored. So I like to think there is a strong personality there that is almost being wrestled into business. It's like having a wild horse, and you're sort of breaking it in to work in a more commercial sphere. I think great creative people are a little bit like that. They can be, not wild in their behavior, but really out there in their thinking, trying to

commercialize that creativity and make it relevant to brands' and clients' problems is a fun challenge to have as a creative director. So I'd rather guide or channel people into that space. Trying to make people who think they are creative more creative is difficult. If they're too buttoned down and wary of every client concern, then you'll have a pretty dull creative department. You want a bit of a wild ride with a department that can come up with unexpected, single-minded, and effective ideas.

Can you think of any examples of remarkable junior portfolios?

Not specific examples. But what I normally find is students will have a book of maybe 30 pieces of work—about 10 campaigns with examples of how the idea works across different mediums or platforms. Because you want to see that they aren't relying on just one good idea to get by. If they get knocked down, they need to show they're able to get back up. If an idea they think is the best they've ever had gets killed, they need to come back the next day with something even better. Good people can do that. Not-so-good people will get crushed. But it's important to have at the very least two or three things in the book that stand out.

John Hegarty explained [this] to me once when I was a junior in London showing him my book and he got to the end and he just smiled. And I thought, "This interview is going really well." And he said, "You know Warren, I think you can be brilliant or terrible, but right now I don't think you know the difference." I'd rather see a book that is a bit up and down because people are exploring and trying. Just because you've got a few terrible things in there... failure isn't a bad thing. And if you make people terrified of failure early on in their career, they'll never be any good. People need to be adventurous. Experience in the business will help them to know when they are being terrible or good. But you should never be frightened of failing. They need that unfettered gush of creativity. Don't rein it in or be too politically correct. But, on the other hand, don't go out there and do attention-seeking stuff just for the sake of it because that won't win any votes either.

Are there any common mistakes that students make?

The biggest mistake a lot of them make is to try and produce work that they think the other person will like rather than doing what they like. So they haven't been true to themselves. And it's much easier if you say, "This is me; this is the type of work I can produce; this is the type of work I like and admire." I think it's important to maintain a personal integrity and an honesty. And if the CD interviewing them doesn't like it, that's okay. What's accepted in our industry is pretty wide ranging, so there's nothing wrong with being quite individual. If you're good and talented, you will find a niche within this business that will accommodate you and allow your creativity to blossom.

Do you still like to see print ads these days?

Not necessarily. I quite like poster ideas because you're forced to reduce your thinking down to very few elements. So that's a good discipline to start with. And most great ideas you could write down in a sentence. A lot of great movies you could write the proposition in a sentence. Whether that turns into a print ad, poster, online film, content, whatever—it doesn't really bother me. But Idon't place a huge emphasis on print anymore. A complete print book would not get a job here.

Do you have advice on how to actually get in front of creative directors?

A lot of people send funny stuff in the mail. That normally ends up in the bin. A well-written email can sometimes work.

Pointing you to an online portfolio?

Sometimes. But it has to be really good. If they somehow coerce you into wasting your time, you get quite angry, and they've burnt their bridges before they've really had a chance. Referrals are really good. If a friend I trust says, "You really should look at this person," I undoubtedly will. When I was trying to get a job, I just hammered John Hegarty for several weeks—rang him up nearly every day. And came into the agency with a new campaign nearly every day. If you want to get into a particular company or work for a particular CD, persistence usually goes a long way. You can

wear them down and they'll give you a shot, and if you impress them enough in that one meeting, don't disappear for three months, come back the next week. And if they don't like your book, come back with a whole new book next week. People love that sort of persistence and energy and creative drive. Because if you're running an agency, you want people like that. It's like striking oil— people just gushing ideas. That's more impressive than a beautiful, finely honed book where the thought of changing anything in it puts the fear of God in them. If your book is preventing you from getting into the agency you want to get into, then chuck it out. Do another one. It's tough, but it shows that you're really keen and you're really sure about what you want. You're actively pursuing a position where you feel you belong.

Don't ever give up. Usually you'll get to a point where you think, "It's too tough; I tried everything and nothing seems to work and I'm destined for failure." That's the time when everyone gives up. And that's actually the time when you should keep going. You've just got to push through that barrier. The ones who keep going that little bit longer are the ones who succeed. No matter how tough you think it is, it's always going to get tougher, and trust me, once you do get a job it's way tougher still. You have to have the hide of a rhino. But if you can clearly identify the type of company you want to work in and the type of people you want to work with, it makes it a hell of a lot easier, and then it's just down to dogged persistence. And if you try hard enough, you should be successful. BI

To see Warren Brown's work, please visit http://breaking.in

AKASH DAS
EXECUTIVE CREATIVE DIRECTOR
LOWE LINTAS & PARTNERS
MUMBAI

What do you look for in a student book? And what impresses you?

Freshness. Freshness in terms of the projects they have done and also how they have compiled their book. I remember hiring two people onto my team…one just showed me some thought-through book covers and the other a scrapbook full of ideas. Newness in the idea is what I look for.

How important is finish? If ideas are the most important thing, can sketches be enough? Do you look at physical books anymore or is it all websites?

I believe skills can be learned over time, from your seniors and from people you admire in the business. As a newcomer, people should focus on ideas. And for the second part, I get to see both websites as well as physical books. But I feel a personal interaction is always better.

How important is writing? Do you need to see long copy?

A good long copy for writers seals it. I can only talk about the Indian agencies, but here it is difficult to find good writers. There are kids who can come up with good ideas but they lack that craft. A healthy mixture of copy and ideas is always better.

What do you think of showing work that is not advertising?

In the new age, communications is not bound to any particular medium. Things like photography, poetry, illustration, etc. give me a picture of how differently the person thinks. But be very selective with what you want to show.

Do you have any other advice for a student or junior trying to get into the business?

Only good work can take you places. [BI]

To see Akash Das's work, please visit http://breaking.in

ERIC SILVER
CHIEF CREATIVE OFFICER
SILVER + PARTNERS
NEW YORK

What do you look for in a student book? And what impresses you?

Something that displays a unique way of thinking. Creative directors at "creative agencies"—and there are not that many—see tons of books every day and, unfortunately, many of them start to look alike. Perhaps because ad schools are teaching with the same methodology or perhaps because ad annuals and award shows tend to all look similar. The truth is even just one brilliant campaign can lead to a hire.

Can a book of sketches be enough, or do ideas need to be comped up nicely?

I personally don't care if it's a writer. But if it's an art director, the ads need to be comped up nicely and have a great sense of design to them. This is imperative.

Is it important to have long copy in a book?

Long copy feels like more of an '80s trait. To be candid, I don't want to see any long-copy ads in a portfolio.

What do you think about including "non-ads" in a book?

Again, it's subjective. For me personally, "non ads" will go further than any advertising that's in a portfolio. Again, the job of the applicant is to set themselves apart from the competition by any means necessary.

When I was hired at Wieden in Portland, I had a decent book but Dan Wieden hired me based on a comic strip I worked on called "Smear."

How did you get into the business?

I went to one year of law school and then did a clerkship in Los Angeles. During that job I was reading a statute and just couldn't digest it. It dawned on me that I had zero aptitude or interest in my chosen profession. So I quit that day and started working on a portfolio. I always loved the idea of being able to create mini-movies. It's a career perfectly suited for my attention deficit.

I took my first advertising job at a day rate of $25 a day. It's very hard to get that first gig but, like any profession, it's on the job that you'll really learn the craft. So it's critical that you start out at a great agency with smart mentors who will steer you in the right direction. It's cliché, but don't worry about money when you first start out.

Do you have any tips for someone who wants to get into advertising?

I would study all of the advertising annuals you can get your hands on. You should at least be familiar with all the work that has been done previously. Once you've done that...then forget it all. Go about the business of charting brilliant new avenues. BI

To see Eric Silver's work, please visit http://breaking.in

TONY DAVIDSON
EXECUTIVE CREATIVE DIRECTOR
WIEDEN+KENNEDY
LONDON

What do you look for in a student book? And what impresses you?

It's different to when I was a student. Back then press, poster, and TV campaigns were all the rage. Today there are far more options, and I think it's important that a book shows that you are thinking of media-neutral ideas that solve clients' business problems. The technological revolution has led to everyone trying to jump on the latest technology. I think it's important to be relevant—not simply innovative. Finding the right voice or doing the right thing for the particular client you are working on is what defines a brand from any other. I try to judge the person as much as their portfolio. This is not an excuse for not doing as much work and working on your personality more, I'm just interested in the person and what makes them tick outside of this business. Am I rambling too much?

No, no...it's good.

As I said, a book used to have to show that you could do a television, press, poster, and radio campaign. There wasn't even much ambient back then, although one of my favorite bits of work from the '50s is when bread crumbs were laid out in a famous square, so that when people were taking photographs looking down at the square and they had their photographs printed and developed, it spelled the word "Kodak" with pigeons. Now that's a good idea. If I saw that in someone's book, I'd remember it and them. In the end, you're trying to get me to remember something about you from your work. And you remember good ideas like that.

It's easy to have one good idea but much harder to do campaigns. In the end, as you climb up in this business, you get rewarded for being able to develop and lead brands forward over a period of time. Like Bill Bernbach did back in the day with VW, or John Hegarty did with Levi's. There's a consistent tone or feeling around those brands. I think Wieden has achieved it with a number of brands, like Nike and Honda. It's not just one ad that happened. It was a whole tone of voice and point of view.

Many students don't interrogate the brand enough and just write ad jokes. I'm not interested in award-winning gags. I want to see people that get hold of the brand, understand it and what it stands for. A lot of work at the moment, when you look at Cannes and advertising festivals, feels to me like just jokes. And I don't necessarily think that they were really caring about the product, they were just writing a joke to get to the product. And also, we tend to hide stuff at the moment. I'm amazed that the amount of stuff

I watch which is 59 seconds of, "What's this? What's this?" and then, "Oh that's what it's for." It never used to be that. We used to be more honest about advertising.

Do you think craft is important these days?

Yes. And with people coming out of school I think maybe there's a lack of craft and a lack of core skills. I don't see as many great writers as I thought. I don't know how writing is being taught now, and maybe it's because advertising, the industry, isn't as exciting as it was, say 25 years ago, or as attractive to people.

"I'M NOT INTERESTED IN AWARD-WINNING GAGS. I WANT TO SEE PEOPLE THAT GET HOLD OF THE BRAND, UNDERSTAND IT AND WHAT IT STANDS FOR."

I think it is good to see writing because I want to see the person behind the work. I really want to feel it. In the end, you're supposed to express yourself in some way. You're digging into somebody else's brand and culture and you find out about it and make sure you understand that. But then, when you express it, a little bit of you comes into your work. Otherwise we would all be robots. So you're trying to feel that, "Oh this person's got something to say to me. I can feel it in the way they're trying to show me their writing or art direction."

And with art direction, I think it's tough now to come into this industry without some of those core skills. If you can't art-direct on a Mac and do layouts for all media, it's hard to be an art director. Originally, in advertising, there was this studio of designers, and they were classically trained in design. And then there were these writers, who were separate. And the writers used to write stuff and stick it under the door and the art directors and designers would design it up. And then someone had the idea of putting them together—so we'll make a creative team. And what happened is it all became about the idea. But maybe some of the design and the writing

skills have been watered down a bit, lost a bit.

So I think having these core skills, and having the ability to present your stuff digitally or having an idea about art direction and really surprising me with designs that are fresh but relevant and don't lose the message, will obviously benefit you over someone else. But in the end you have to find what your love is, what your passion is, because that's what will drive you. If your passion is writing, you should have a love for writing.

The difficult thing is you've often got to communicate yourself and your work without being in the room. And the thing that the CD would remember is probably a brilliant idea. Or brilliant copy. Or art direction. Or brilliant use of social media. But you have to give him something to remember you by and you have to do it pretty quickly.

So, with craft, that traditionally comes through in print ads, but now, as you said at the beginning, a lot of ideas are based around technology and there's really not a lot of craft there, until the thing actually gets built. In a book, it's a lot of explaining what the idea is. So how do you reconcile those two, and what's your advice? Do you still do print ads so that you can show off the craft or do you just come up with ideas and explain them in a book or do you do both?

I think it's a good discipline to learn both. Look at "The Tap Project" that Droga did. When you go to a restaurant in America, and you get a glass of water, normally you get it free but on the bill it says, "Do you mind paying a dollar? And the dollar goes to water in a country that doesn't have any." Well that's a good idea. But he also art-directed it beautifully. If you'd had that idea, at least attempt to show me what it would look like design-wise, as well as having the idea in front with a sentence to explain it. But if you could then further that with the art direction of it and then further it even more if it actually worked, that would be even better. Wieden always says, "It's not just what you say, it's how you say it." The way you present that idea is interesting as well. And that comes down to the art direction of your portfolio, be it physical or online.

What do you think about long copy in a book?

It's a little bit of conundrum that, because people don't

have time to read it. But if that's your problem, you're a writer and you're frustrated that nobody reads your work then, one, think about how you're art-directing your words. Maybe they could be laid out in a way that is more engaging. The other thing is, if I were doing it, I would probably write something on the first page. Try to find an interesting way of making the point that you're a writer. But if every single ad is a long-copy ad, you'd kill the CD because he doesn't have time.

But it's a shame because I do think the power of the word is underestimated and undervalued at the moment. You've got J. K. Rowling—she's written these books and every kid's reading them. If you think about the labels on Innocent Drinks; Dan Germain is the writer of all that stuff. And that writing sort of holds the values of the brand. The Old Spice YouTube video response campaign is a great example of what great writing can do for a brand, not to mention its use of social media.

But if you're a writer, you shouldn't just be able to write copy. You should be able to write dialogue. You should be able to write for a bit of film. Like the YouTube video that they did for Sheffield United when they got relegated in the premiership and they took the film Downfall and rewrote the subtitles so it was all about football teams. This thing is very, very funny and that's writing. That's the stuff where everybody's going, "Whoa! Have you seen this on YouTube?" So, in your book, you should have some stuff that is competing with that stuff and better than that stuff. I just think you have to break out of the formulaic thing that we got used to. Again, it doesn't discount you doing three beautiful press layouts for a wonderful company.

And with press ads, you said before that you like to see—especially for art directors—design skills and the fact that they can use a Mac and all that. But in London, a lot of people have sketches and some creative directors think that if you have finished layouts it's kind of like saying, "I don't have any more room to improve. This is perfect." What do you think about sketches versus finished work?

It kind of comes back to that whole argument about what's the most important thing and the answer is the idea. I sort of sit somewhere in the middle because I think, obviously, if I see a great

idea, that's number one. But sometimes a great idea can be caused by the art direction. And if you work with brands like Nike you understand that texture is important and I think it's something you should be taught.

I think one of the problems is that a lot of the ideas that get highly finished aren't that good and that's the problem. And maybe what you should do is concentrate on ideas and be very honest with your portfolio. And if I were doing it now I might go see a really good art director. I would go see someone who's in a digital company. So you can take in a book of just ideas, because you are not going to creative directors. And when you know you've got the idea that everybody is going, "Oh that's a good idea, that one's really good," then maybe you should start thinking about doing it up. But there's nothing more frustrating than seeing a really shit idea that has been highly worked up.

Also, I'm not even sure that the future is a writer and an art director [team]. I get a sense that the kids coming through want to do a lot more. They want to be an animator, they want to be a director, they want to be a writer. I love the idea of a hybrid-ideas person who can move between disciplines, is independent, and when you put them with someone else on the project that's right, it works. So I wouldn't want to stop anybody from doing just a scribble.

When you and Kim were starting out, how did you do it?

When Kim and I first started, we had amazing talent all around us: John Webster, Frank Budgen, Bill Gallagher, John Pallant, Peter Gatley, these were all multi-award-winning clever, smart people. And we used to run in with our ideas to them and be very open. It was like, "Oh, what do you think about this work?" And they would cross out 95 percent out of what we'd written and go, "There, that's your idea isn't it?" And then we'd run back and work some more. So share your ideas with people around you—friends you trust and respect—and then go and see the sort of teams who are doing good work at the moment. They're not creative directors but they're doing good work. Get their opinions and keep going to see them.

What do you think about putting things in a book that aren't ads?

There's a guy here called Michael Russoff who went to the Portland office with Chris Green. And they came back with this film about all the chairs of the Portland office. It was just them sitting on all the chairs and it was called 110 Chairs of Portland. And it just made me smile and feel something about those people who had bothered to do something outside their day jobs. But you will find different agencies looking for different things. Some good agencies are looking for the more traditional ad campaigns.

I'm much more interested in what makes someone interesting and drives them, than what awards they've won. It always amazes me when I see the CV and it's all awards. I think the most interesting people are people who have got something to say. And they're creative and they're trying to find an outlet to say something. And what you've got to teach them is strategy and the discipline of making it relevant for that brand. But beyond that, if they haven't got anything to say about themselves and they're just regurgitating old advertising, I think that's all they're going to do once they get in.

It seems like a lot of students are really nervous about putting lots of non-ads in their portfolio.

Well maybe do two books then. There was an art director named Joseph who came in to see us and he had a scrapbook that was separate from his ad book. He was an art director and some of the layouts were really interesting. You could see the way his mind worked with layouts and feelings and a lot of them had ideas in it. We took him on a placement just on the strength of that scrapbook.

Another team we took on that went on to Mother was Tom and John. They came in and had a reel of these mad films. One of the films…I can remember it now, you see? It was about how Tom and John solve problems, and they just filmed a car park with a very, very low rail around it. And they just filmed themselves getting over the rail in different ways. And it was like, "Normal people do it this way but we do it this way." They were very funny. They were doing silly lifts of each other over it. And it was just

done with music and editing and it was really funny. And you came away from it going, "These guys get comedy timing, they get humor," and then, when you meet them, you feel their personality. They presented something in a completely different way to every other team that was coming in. It didn't feel like "a classic advertising book."

When Dan Wieden asked us what we were doing when we first met him, Kim and I were leaving to set up a website because we were interested in the web. And we had this idea about wobbling jellies all around the world and playing them online. And I think Dan probably thought we were mad, but at least we were trying to play in a new medium that we were intrigued by.

"THERE SHOULD BE SOME REALLY MULTITALENTED PEOPLE COMING OUT BECAUSE EVERYBODY NOW HAS THE CHANCE TO BE A CREATIVE."

There should be some really multitalented people coming out because everybody now has the chance to be a creative. That's basically what the Internet has done. That's why 99.9 percent of the stuff on YouTube is absolutely shit. But the 0.1 percent is really good. A lot of it is being done by people in their bedrooms. And I'm interested in some of those people, and you're competing with some of those people to get noticed. I don't know how hard is it to go shoot the "OK Go" video ["Here It Goes Again", with the treadmills]. It's not massively hard. There's nothing stopping you now to present a pop promo idea within your portfolio. I think people are looking for ideas, and ideas are everywhere.

The other thing that is quite impressive is when those ideas have actually come to fruition and they've actually been made or happened. We hired some product designers here recently and they're very good at making stuff happen. Because if you're a product designer, you have got to go and find out about it and execute it and make it happen. Then, when you give them problems that are not products, they work out how they're going to make it happen. And that's quite an interesting thing, which you don't often see in an advertising-student portfolio. But I don't think you should be frightened of showing a bit of yourself and what you want to do. I would think if you are creative, you would have something beyond just an advertising portfolio. I'm interested in the other things that drive you creatively—that make you who you are. And sometimes you can utilize that to your own benefit.

What do you think is a good way for people to improve? How would you suggest that people get better?

The way you learn is by being surrounded by interesting things and better people. Go to venues, go to galleries, be inspired, surround yourself. Just be curious about stuff and soak up other creative influences around you. It's part of your day job when you actually get one: to get inspired. And it's not about copying. It's about being influenced. Andy Warhol was influenced by [advertising]…the artists are influenced by us, we're influenced by them, and we're both influenced by culture.

Second, and most importantly: See people that are better than you. Get surrounded by people who are better than you. You have amazing access in this industry, I think, to good creative people who have come through the same process. So go and see them. If you like them when you go and see them, keep coming back and seeing them without annoying them too much. Kim and I, in all honesty, managed to get somewhere only because we've been surrounded throughout our careers by good people. We went to Leagas Delaney and saw Tim Delaney. He's a fantastic writer. He forced us to write a lot more. We had Dave Dye, Paul Belford—they challenged our art direction. And then we went to BBH where we had John Hegarty for the first year before he went off to America. And he was incredibly helpful on Levi's.

I would also encourage you not to only see people in advertising agencies. It is important that you have aspirations, I think, beyond that. You might know an architect who is really interesting. You might do some ideas with him or products or whatever it is. The great thing is now the solution doesn't have to be a press ad or a radio commercial. I think you can open your mind up and go, "Here is the business problem," because that's what a client really brings in or should do. And you can solve it in any way. So if you got 5,000 cars sitting in a field, the answer doesn't have to be, "Oh, stick a press ad in local press saying we've got 5,000 cars." You might think of an event. You might think of something, some really clever, smart way that is relevant to that brand tonally, to clear that field. And that's where I get excited. When I see people who are actually taking business problems and thinking about clever ways of solving them.

If you were just starting out now, what advice would you give yourself?

If I were starting out, I'd be experimenting loads. I'd have my own website and be making my own things. Daniel Eatock, who did the Big Brother logo, is just constantly loading [his site] up with things that he's doing. Just random things, like car alarm dancing. He just stands in front of car alarms when they're going off and it's hilarious. He takes photographs of trees that are at angles but he straightens all the photographs so the tree strands straight. He's not trying to solve an advertising problem, he's just putting stuff out there that interests him and he's got that side to him. He's a lovely, lovely guy. He's got something to say and I hope one day we can utilize him to do a project with this stuff. But he's found the thing that he likes doing and he's doing it. In the end that's what we all have to do as creative people. If you want to get into advertising, then you have to find out what level of advertising you want to get into. Because some people are quite happy sitting in a big agency churning out stuff. Other people want to be in a high-end creative place pulling their hair out. I don't know how much you want it and how much you don't. People have to find where their creative outlet is and how they're going to utilize it.

Any other tips or advice?

Every student sends links to their site but, a lot of times, they fail to edit and presume that creative directors have time to check all their work. Editing is an important part of being a creative. It's good if the subject matter and brands vary. Show that you can do more than one tone of voice. And it's probably wise not to attempt to do work on brands that have already got brilliant advertising, as your ideas will immediately be compared to that work. And that's part of the trick is to find that tonality and then deliver whatever it is that you're doing so that it feels like it's coming from the brand.

Here's another thing you can do: When you get a portfolio of ideas you think is good, throw that portfolio away and start again and do another portfolio. And then throw that one away and do another portfolio. And then go back and pull all the good ideas together from all the portfolios. And you might have a really great portfolio.

I think, as a creative, you have to be really, really prepared to constantly come up with new ideas and new thinking and not get too stuck on one thing. People tend to tweak things only a little, when actually there's a better idea out there. So you have to be not too precious with your ideas. And be careful about doing up the first idea that you've had. But I think when it comes to seeing a creative director, hopefully you will have been guided by the people you've seen before. I'm always wanting to be surprised. You know, it was what Bill Bernbach always said: "If you're not surprised or you're not being challenged, you'll never notice anything." In the end, I'm looking at a lot of these books and they all feel quite the same. Perhaps because a lot of people go through the same courses, get the same briefs, and then they continue with that product. So you're even competing against other students who've got the same products. I would pick stuff that no one else is doing because then at least you're not competing with them. BI

To see Tony Davidson's work, please visit http://breaking.in

What are the different creative positions here, and what form would a portfolio take for those positions?

You're starting in the most complicated place. Why it's complicated is the difference between the answer to that question 10 years ago and now is incredible. We've gone from a very simple media environment to a very complicated media environment. And because we map our talent against the different media opportunities out there, we have a matrix of talent that is mind-bogglingly diverse. When I started here in 2001, we had three creative departments: Copywriting, visual design, and interaction design. And just as on the traditional side of the house where they have copywriter and art director, what those three aptitudes did was pretty much the same no matter what client we engaged.

We did websites. There are templates in traditional media that people have been making for 50 years: 30-second TV spots, magazine print ads. And even though the templates we were working against were probably more complicated and variable, a website was a website. Back then, if we were hiring a visual designer, I would look at a portfolio, see how they designed a home page, how they designed a more editorial page, a more photographic page, see how clear their hierarchy was as far as interaction was concerned. But I could tell quickly if they could work here, and if they could, they could probably work on anything that came through. Same with interaction design: Look at a few wireframes, see how they think. Same with copywriting: Were they clear, descriptive, etc. And now, if I look at how we engage our clients, each one has a unique collection of diverse aptitudes working on their unique collection of business problems. Because now there has been a proliferation of contexts that people engage media with. In the old days, we did one thing with media. We consumed it. And advertising did one thing: it interrupted you while you consumed it. And now media is a membrane of everything that doesn't just send us entertainment and content. but it is applications and it enables us to make transactions; it gives us the ability to create our own content; and it's also deeply informational in a way that traditional advertising isn't. So we navigate through this media membrane in all these different contexts, and it's so complicated that our role as agencies is just as much about managing complexity as it is about telling a message. So when I'm looking at portfolios...it depends!

We still have those three disciplines: Visual design, copywriting, and interaction design, which is basically pictures, words, and designing pictures and words into experiences. But the difference now is I have visual designers who are more classic art directors that know how to be on a TV shoot and know how to craft a print ad. I have visual designers who know how to design interfaces on mobile devices. Visual designers who are very good at motion graphics. Visual designers who are more brand-identity designers. Visual designers who are very good at physical space and they might work for the retail group. Visual designers who are good at visualizing data. And the list goes on.

And copywriting is the same thing. And not only that, but you add interaction design and you also add technology, because a lot of the people who work in technology are fundamentally creative. The Zuckerbergs and Pages and Brins of this world are creative. So there are other creative cultures that are part of the agency world now that 10 years ago wouldn't have even been recognized as creative. So, why the answer to your question is complicated is that the process of working with clients is. We figure out what their problem is, we curate a team that is best suited to solve that problem, and then we choreograph that team and all the pieces around it. So, we could hire someone because they fit into an existing offering like a visual designer and they might do one thing really well or a few things really well. They might be really good at designing retail spaces. We have generalists and we have deep craft-driven positions.

But there are three things I look at no matter what discipline they come from: Great craft, great concepts, and the context of their work needs to make sense. That last thing is new because

in traditional advertising the context was fixed. The template was 30 seconds and it was always consumed in the same way—you interrupted someone. You never had to ask, "Why is someone watching this ad?" And now, because there is an interface in front of every piece of content, you have to ask the question first and foremost, "Why would anyone give a fuck about this?" If you can't answer that, then you haven't answered the context question. So the evaluation process is around those three things, but those three things manifest themselves in so many different ways.

Do you see students and juniors coming to you already specialized in a chosen field? In something as specific as, let's say, mobile copywriting?

It depends where they come from. If they come from a classic ad school, they come to us with the budding ability to come up with narrative concepts. Not systematic concepts because they haven't been exposed to enough software development. So they aren't balanced in that sense. They come with the belief that a lovely story will solve every business problem which just isn't true anymore. But we take in people who are good at that, pair them with people who have been trained in something else somewhere like Carnegie Mellon or ITP [at NYU] and are taught to be innovative in the medium itself. So, the classic team is copywriter and art director. Here it is a storyteller and a systematic designer. That's more of a whole creative brain than words and pictures. It's rare that we see work that is complete. We look for pieces and then bring them in and combine them in interesting ways.

Are there common mistakes that a lot of juniors make that are preventable?

If they come from advertising school, the biggest problem is that they write ads in the vernacular of advertising. All good advertising doesn't feel like advertising. Doesn't look like advertising. Doesn't taste like advertising. Competent, solid advertising can do that, but it tends not to be very effective. Apart from the fact that media has become so fragmented and it's more and more difficult to do classic interruptive advertising, there is this other thing happening in parallel which is a cultural disruption. As a result of the proliferation of brands and messages, people have become fatigued. People are generally pissed off and annoyed by advertising, and they find the vernacular of advertising so easy to decode. The rhythms and textures in the language and visuals make it look like advertising, so we switch off immediately. And the problem is that if you have gone to a school that lives in that vernacular, you can come out spewing out the same stuff. So you have to ask yourself, "Why would people care about this?" and it's not going to be just because it has a clever tagline. Or some lovely alliteration. You might feel clever for doing it, but it doesn't answer a human need.

"ALL GOOD ADVERTISING DOESN'T FEEL LIKE ADVERTISING."

When we get more digitally focused creatives, the most common problem is they don't signal the functionality well enough. When I see an interface, I should already understand, because of the way the interface is designed, what I'm going to get from it. Apple is a great example of a company that creates interfaces that you have a Pavlovian response to because you know what you're going to get. A lot of the younger designers want to be clever. They want to create interfaces with branded language instead of descriptive language. They get the hierarchy wrong. They fall into their own vernacular. There's a vernacular in website design which is: Logo top-left corner, global navigation along the top, feature space... and if I see another bloody design like that for a website I'm going to go fucking crazy because it doesn't respond to a need. Like the feature space that takes up half the page is dead—we don't use technology like that anymore. We'd rather have a grid of things we can interact with than one big, luscious photo.

Another is people include bad work. And the reason is usually, "I wanted to show you I could do brochures or websites or whatever." I would rather see two pieces of work that are well done than 50 things that are mediocre. Because when you're looking at a portfolio, you're always thinking that they'll do the worst thing in that portfolio for you. When people walk away from a portfolio they

usually remember one thing. So, after your best pieces, all the other stuff can only make you feel worse about them.

Do you like to see a big idea that is blown out into all different media, digital and traditional, or do you like to see ideas that just live digitally?

I don't distinguish ideas by traditional or digital because even traditional media is digital now. TVs are shipped now with applications installed in them. So it's an interactive medium that isn't any different than opening iTunes. And there are no print ads now without a URL or QR code. So print ads become doors into these deeper interactive worlds. So I won't judge it by whether it's digital or traditional; I'll judge it by whether it's a story or a system. A story is intended to make people feel something about a brand. Systems are intended to make people behave within a framework of a brand. So systems tend to live in digital mediums more because there is more interface there and more of an expectation that you interact with it.

So it depends what the problem is. If a client comes to us and says, "We already have a well-known brand—we want to shift perception of it," I would argue the best way to do that is to create a behavior and then create communication around that behavior. When we partnered with Nike and came up with this innovative behavior of Nike Plus, there was a real reason for runners to try the shoes again. And in the wake of Nike Plus, I think they went from second or third back up to number one, and no ad was going to do that.

So, there's always a play between the system and the story. It's just that the story doesn't come first. Sometimes it does. When Wieden worked on Old Spice their intention was to exhume this old brand and make people feel differently about it. They didn't want to create ongoing habitual behavior outside of the product. There was no service layer that they built. And they did it by telling great stories.

So I'm not saying that there aren't times when leading with the story is right, but more and more we're finding our clients are in commoditized spaces where messages aren't enough to get people to try their products, so we create a service layer and then communicate about the service layer. The advantage of that, as opposed to advertising campaigns where you get a spike of awareness whenever you're running the media, is that the spikes of awareness get converted into ongoing relationships. It's two sides of a coin, and, at the beginning of a project, I'm looking for both. I'm looking for a brand idea that can be expressed in a message and a service-layer behavior that could be social media or a content hub or an application that will change the brand. Then I'll go back to the storytellers and say, "Stop thinking about the brand message; think about how to message that platform."

In a student portfolio, are you looking for both those things?

I'm looking for the ability to tell a simple, coherent story and I don't expect this, but when they work here, they learn how to tell a story that leads to a behavior. It's not just clever and makes people laugh. There are times when a funny ad is completely appropriate, but if you're going to work at R/GA, you're going to work with people who are able to build robust, interesting software. So, figure out a way to talk about that. And drop the metaphors, because metaphors are not good for changing behavior, although they may be good for making people feel something. So we might need that, but you should learn to write a nice, clean demo too that describes what the software or the behavior we've created does.

From the other side, what people from more technical schools learn from more traditional advertising people is they've got to make their experiences simple and human. Because they tend to be additive thinkers, as opposed to narrative thinkers who are subtractive. They must learn to make software that their grandmother can use, not just software that a Google engineer can use.

Is the ideal way to demonstrate your skills to invent a system for the service layer, or for the behavior layer that is a good idea, and then tell a great story around it?

Yes, that's right. And normally you would work with people who have different strengths. Twenty years ago a copywriter and art director could conceive of and make anything that the agency made: TV, print, direct, radio. If you take all the work that we produced last year, there aren't one or two people who are capable of that. So it necessitates a collaboration, and the more nuanced way to look at it is choreographing. You need to know when to lead and when to have someone else come in and lead. It becomes a very different process. There isn't much of a process in the traditional model. The process is you and your writer or art director go off to Starbucks and come up with some ideas. And then you outsource the production and Smuggler looks after it and you get Fincher to direct and you eat craft services. But for us there is a lot of process because there are lots of decision trees. And things can unravel if you have the wrong person with the wrong piece. So you need to be sensitive to the range of aptitudes and how to connect them at the right times with the right things. As a creative leader here, you need to curate talent and have a vision that corrals that talent so it arrives at a singular, coherent point at the end. There isn't really a templated way to do anything here.

"NOW YOU CAN'T BE A WANKER BECAUSE YOU ALWAYS ARE NEEDING PEOPLE TO HELP YOU MAKE YOUR WORK BETTER."

Any other advice?

For your online portfolio, don't get creative with the actual container. Make the website as simple as possible. No fancy transitions or bloated Flash stuff. Make it a bloody slideshow as long as we can see the work. That's the most important thing.

Also, look at your work as a complete piece. So, even if you're an art director, don't have poorly written copy. I see this with designers all the time. They'll have interfaces where they've got either Greek or poorly considered navigational language. You should care about that stuff, even if it's not your core sensibility; get someone to help you and make it feel very complete and tight.

And don't be a wanker. There was a time, 10 or 20 years ago, when you could get away with being a dickhead, because as long as your copywriter got along with you, you didn't have to get along with the client services people or anyone else, as long as you were doing good work. Because everything was outsourced and the collaboration was just with your creative partner. Now you can't be a wanker because you always are needing people to help you make your work better. If you piss people off, they are not going to want to do that. BI

To see Nick Law's work, please visit http://breaking.in

DANY LENNON PRESIDENT THE CREATIVE REGISTER WESTPORT

What do you look for in a student book? And what impresses you?

First of all, I am a "website" person, not a "book" person. Some people are still romantic about books. I am not. I like a site because not only do "ideas" have to come across clearly, concisely, and profoundly to transmit through that medium—as it is less tactile and emotional—but it really does ultimately become extremely poignant and engaging if the ideas are strong and, of course, that is the most important thing. Some may argue that the tactility of a hard portfolio cannot be beaten, but the fact is, we must understand and accept that the digital page is the current focus and the future. The publishing world is equally substantiating that as they go full-speed online. It also gives those who do not have as much digital experience an opportunity to express themselves in this medium and to show their skills in creating a user-friendly experience as well as their creativity.

Beyond the ideas, it will be the formation and character of presentation. It's individuality, it's craft, it's fluidity, and it's simplicity. It has to blend both your vision of who you are, whether by means of its craft or by means of its aura and impression tonally, with the power of the work. But, at the end of the day, you need to make it easy work for the recipient. If it is hard work, you will be passed over.

And, last of all, no segregation. I look for the power of ideas in its ability to reign across all platforms without compartmentalizing them. It should be unified, natural, and simply an assumed part of the creative process of engagement.

Can a book of sketches be enough or do ideas need to be comped up nicely?

I personally have no interest in books as the initial form of entry in the application to a position within a company. Sadly, no one has the luxury of that kind of time, and most people are continually in transit. Taking that into consideration alone means that your portfolio must be transportable, hence the convenience of sites. Any time, any place. That is if you are seriously on the market and wish to gain the attention of the right people. Anyone that has time to sit down and look at books…well…I wonder where they should actually be at that time.

Regarding "finish": I think that finish is important simply from your own inner sense of completion and desire to finish your idea and present it in a manner that will demonstrate more abilities than the idea alone. To see an idea in the best manifestation possible, demonstrating your own wide-ranging skills to implement it, is of course a distinct advantage, I think. So yes, I look for that. Finish also represents parts of your personality such as detail, presentation, ambition, fulfillment, and more.

Is it important to have long copy in a book?

I don't use the word "copy" anymore. It is not in my dictionary. I prefer to use the word "write." Copy implies a particular stylistic connotation to the concept of writing that was specific to advertising. Today, in the multiplatform and less-restricted world of advertising, it is about writing and yes, the demonstration of all abilities and variations of writing skills is without doubt an advantage. I encourage exposing one's love of words and the creativity it yields when leaving the door wide, wide open to interpretation of the individual as they see fit. I welcome all examples of writing across multidimensional platforms.

What do you think about including "non-ads" in a book?

I encourage showing anything that demonstrates your passion for creativity. That is the absolute beauty of websites. It allows you to expand your breadth in a visual and captive context to expose the many platforms of your desires, interests, and personality.

Do you have any tips for someone who wants to get into advertising?

Yes. It's not all about ideas and sites alone. That is only 50 percent of it. The rest is about how interesting you are as a personality, character, human being. They will be judging you in terms of how you fit into their cultures. Make sure that you do enough research on all the companies you are interested in, and try to understand those cultures to see if and how you would fit in. It is equally about presentation of yourself. How you talk, what you say, how you sit, walk, move, and what you feel free enough to emote. You are a package. Not just a site or a book. Be open. Be you. And be involved!

And lastly: Make sure you know what is going on around you. Keep in touch with "the street" of advertising. Get a grip on the future and the direction it may or may not go in. Have an opinion, or at least work on one daily, in response to what you see, read, feel, and experience. Your voice does not need to be accurate. But there has to be a voice. ⊞

TIFFANY ROLFE
PARTNER &
CHIEF CONTENT OFFICER
CO: COLLECTIVE
NEW YORK

What do you look for in a student book? And what impresses you?

Originality and work that makes me wish I'd done it. Something totally unexpected.

How important is finish? Can sketches be enough? Do you look at actual hard-copy books anymore, or is it all websites?

Execution is part of the idea. Everything can be executed in a million different ways, so it's an important part of the idea. A sketch will never give you the same feeling as a finished piece. Even a sketch is a type of execution so it can affect meaning. I mostly look at websites, but I still enjoy a good paper book.

I think it's more than that though. It's crafting. And some websites can still feel like craft went into them. So how you put it together, whatever medium, is important.

How important is copy? Do you need to see long-copy ads?

I like seeing copy for sure. But it doesn't have to be an ad. It can be a story or a blog or a love note. Whatever shows you love to write.

What do you think of showing work that is not advertising?

Yes. As long as it's great and shows your creativity and passion.

Do you have any other advice for a student or junior trying to getinto the business?

Become a fan of good work early on. Understand it and why you love it. Find places that are doing that type of work. And then, when you are ready to find a job, you'll know the type of place you want to go. It will also help you understand the kind of work you want to be doing. Find inspiration in things outside of advertising so you can bring a fresh perspective to things. ⊞

To see Tiffany Rolfe's work, please visit http://breaking.in

What do you look for in a student book? And what impresses you?

I think probably the first thing is just smart ideas and I think something a little bit different. And usually that tends not to come from a lot of the ad school students because I think they get set into a program of…They all seem to have, in my opinion, a similar look and feel, everything like the type is very, very small and the logo. And there's very little copywriting today and that's what I miss. I mean, I want to see examples that someone can actually write. Not that every ad is a long-copy ad by any means, but you seldom see that in writing anymore. There's a clever headline and that's as far as the writing goes, and I like to see a lot more than that. I think it's more just showing off their creative thinking—anything that shows off their creative thinking, whether it's a story they've written or paintings that someone may have done or a cartoon that they've…whatever. I just want to see how they think and solve problems.

"I WANT TO SEE EXAMPLES THAT SOMEONE CAN ACTUALLY WRITE."

It's probably the thing that I look for the most and something a little different. I think one of the biggest negatives to me is if they spent more time on the look of their book and the case that it's in or whatever than the interior of the book—the contents—there's a problem and you see a lot of that too. Kids that think flash is going to…some flashy wood box is going to make all the difference in the world, and no, it's the contents that it still comes down to in the end. We have problems to solve for clients and who can do that? But I look for people outside the ad

school realm a lot because I think sometimes they bring just a wider perspective. But we have kids here—young people here—from ad schools and some of them I think are better than others—come better trained. Some come in as technicians and there are the most amazing things they can do with Photoshop or Flash or Illustrator or whatever. But they can't really…they're not real idea generators. And then others are just a wealth of ideas, and the rest of the stuff…you can always find people to make the thing look pretty. I think it's solving problems and doing it in a different, unique way is the hard part— the hard thing to find. So that's what I look for: just good thinkers, problem solvers.

You got into this already but I want to ask you about writing. And is it important for you to see long-copy ads or do you want to see any example of writing no matter what format it is?

Yeah it doesn't have to be examples of a long-copy ad. I think, unfortunately, you see less and less of that and there's a common perception with advertising—and it's a pretty broad statement—but anything you do is like, "Oh, people don't like to read." They read if it's interesting. Otherwise there wouldn't be books. There wouldn't be newspapers and magazines. People read if it's interesting and I think the problem is we got lazy and don't write compelling communications to consumers. Compelling stories for them to get involved in. So I look for any kind of writing. We have a writer here who wrote for The Onion at University of Wisconsin and that was most of his portfolio and he's turned out to be a very, very good writer in any medium and especially radio and mediums like that where his imagination is allowed to really go wild. But yeah, I want to see something and that doesn't have to be ads. Almost more importantly, I like to see something that isn't advertising. If they're writing their great novel, or screenplay, or poetry, or just anything—ramblings of whatever. Just see how they, again, how they think and construct things and tell stories. Because it's what we're in the business of—telling stories.

You mentioned a lot of people come in with very polished books but the content is not necessarily great but…

…Or it's very similar to everyone who graduated from that school that year, and worked on the same clients. A lot of these same ideas, and they have a similar look and feel to them. It's usually a strong Photoshopped visual with clever headline and very small logo in the corner and it's like…there's more to it than that. It's too simple.

Right. What do you think about the other extreme of just hand-drawn sketches? Do you think that that can be enough these days?

Yeah, we've hired people from that. I said things don't have to be really, really slick and finished. It's the attention to detail in solving the problem, and it's not always just a visual with the clever headline. Sometimes there's more that needs to be said or shown. Just to show that they've taken the time to really make sure that whatever they're trying to communicate comes through. So yeah, but I mean, I started my book with just drawings because there weren't computers back then. So, I thought that it was a big deal to use the Xerox machine. To photocopy something—that looked really professional. And so yeah, it's ideas. But now, I think with the online space playing such a huge role I don't think I would consider…it'd be tough for anyone to hire anyone who doesn't have an understanding—not a complete understanding—but isn't somehow involved in the online space or at least, is interested and wants to learn that medium. Again, that changes a little bit of how you view things because online is very…it's kind of hard to show online in a sketch form. But again, it's still ideas and I've seen stuff that's done that way.

So do you want to see online ideas in a book?

However they want to present them or even if it's just, "This is my idea" and if it was just written out in a paragraph or whatever it took to sell the idea, or "I had this idea for this" or whatever. Again…they don't have to be an expert in Flash necessarily. Although I think most art directors now coming out of schools, if they aren't or don't understand that medium, they're going to have a hard time in the next three or four years getting a job. But whatever explains the idea, that is the most important thing. Again, it gets back to: you want people to solve problems for clients. There's always going to be people who can execute this stuff—that are the Photoshop whizzes or that can

build the website. It's the thinking that goes into it and the "why" and the understanding of communicating with someone—that's really something that is hard to find. It can be taught, be learned through experience, but it's nice to have some basis coming in. Of how people view stuff that's given to them, or how you interact with people, and it's changed a lot. It used to be you just told people what they wanted and whatever we wanted them to hear, and now you're engaging them in a conversation. There are people that understand people. A lot of psychology majors and people like that do well in advertising. Sociology, cultural anthropologists, and people like that. That's what this business is growing from. So I think people who understand people—because we do live in an insulated world—and I'm not trying to get into advertising philosophy here, sorry if I'm digressing.

No, no that's fine.

I don't think there's a lot creative people who could tell you what a loaf of bread costs or a carton of milk. I mean we live in a pretty insulated world and we kind of force our thinking on to clients and consumers to a large degree. And the consumers, they've had enough, and now they want to engage. They'll tell you, they're deciding what brands are going to make and what they aren't. You have to learn to engage with people now and start a conversation, hold a conversation with people. So, yeah, you need to be a conversationalist too.

Are there common characteristics of great ideas, unique insights that you see in books other than that?

Sometimes there's a lot of the obvious or things that look like a slight variation on something that's been done before. It seems in books I see that there's a lot of print and they tend to take on a poster format. Maybe you occasionally see some radio from a writer, and maybe TV if there's a storyboard or something…and they'll have almost the obligatory, "Well, here's a couple online things and here's some out-of-home ideas, and some stunt or something," but it always seems like an afterthought. And, to me, that's where advertising is going—those kinds of things. Something that gets closer and closer to the consumer so that you're face-to-face with them, you're asking them, engaging them in a conversation almost. That's where advertising is going. And TV and that…well it will always have a role. It's playing a different role than it used to. I think those things are more important in a book. It's solving a problem and finding a new way to get in front of people. Because I'm not an 18-year-old kid by any means and the way you talk to an 18-year-old is different than it was in the past. So, it's just people that understand that. Or that talk to a 25- or 35-year-old, people who understand how to engage with them, where to engage with them. Because I think now where you deliver the message is almost as important as what the message is, and it makes a statement. Because when you look at stuff and the sites that you go to or wherever you frequent in your daily life, there are certain places you're going to run into advertising or communication with you—someone trying to start a dialogue with you. And it's more meaningful if it's somewhere where, "Wow they really recognize me and understand me because they're talking to me here."

You mentioned putting other things in the book besides ads; do you have any tips on how to do that?

I think it's almost like a scrapbook of the way you think or what you like—what you're interested in. To me—and again, I'm very different than I would I think, a creative director at Grey, or McCann Erickson might be or whatever, and I can blame that on years at Wieden+Kennedy, I guess—that the most interesting things are the unexpected. Like Jeff Kling, I mean, like hiring him, it was like you're hiring this performance artist rather than a writer and he turned out to be a great creative guy—really great mind. He thought really, really differently than most people, the kind of person that we needed at Wieden at that time. And I remember I hired a copywriter who had never worked in the business before. He had come out of the navy. This was in Australia. He came out of the navy and he had a book that he had done. What he had done was written letters, because he had a lot of time in the Australian submarine corps. I think maybe they had three subs. And he wrote letters to companies, to the Queen, to the President of the United States, everything. And he kept all the letters and he kept all the responses from them

and he made a book out of it. And he had photos—like he wrote to the Mars Company about how much he loved…he wrote such intriguing letters. They sent him cases of Mars candy bars, Milky Way, and all that kind of stuff. He got dog food. He didn't even have a dog but he got dog food, and all this stuff. It was just…I don't know. They were just really interesting letters, and back then it was just photocopies in a book, bound. But I remember when I interviewed him. He came in and the creative director at the agency at the time—it was Ogilvy and Mather—said, "This guy is weird. He scares me. You should go talk to him." So I talked to him and I said, "So where is your work?" And he said, "Oh, you probably know most of my work," and I said, "Oh really? So tell me about it." Then he said "'Stop.' That was one of mine. 'Do not enter.' I can't take full credit for that because the original guy who wrote that said, 'Turn around you're going the wrong way' and I just kind of tightened it up." And he was dead serious when he was delivering this and so I was starting to think that, "Oh my God! This guy is crazy," and he went on and sighting all these things and after a while I realized, at least I was hoping that it was a joke, and then I started laughing and he said, "No, no. Seriously, I've never worked in advertising but here's my book." And he showed me this thing and I was looking through it and it was just so interesting. And you knew a guy like that…and he literally came in and there was just something fresh. He had no preconceived notions of what advertising was. It was…to him, "I got some time and the medium to entertain people and hopefully in that entertaining I can tell them an entertaining story that they buy into," and he ended up doing really well. He ended up going to Thailand and running a big radio station and stuff. But as a writer. And that was his love—radio. But still, it's just interesting.

"LISTEN TO PEOPLE; DON'T LISTEN TO EVERYONE."

I think the other thing is just constantly keep updating your book. Find something fresh. Listen to people; don't listen to everyone. I got told that

I was never going to make it and that I should quit and not even try to get into advertising. Maybe the guy was right but I seem to have fooled enough people. But it's like that and listen to the people that make sense, but you got to be true to yourself and not make your book...if you start making your book to be what other people want...and that's part of the concern I have about a lot of ad-school students, is that they're trying to make books that look like the work that's being done in agencies. I want someone that thinks differently. I don't want another one of me. I don't want another one of what I've already got. I want someone different who's going to shake things up and come in with a totally different perspective on advertising or not even... Advertising has gotten to be such a weird term. Just someone who can talk to people... talk with people.

My last question was going to be: do you have any tips for someone who's just starting out? But I think you've just rattled off a few right there.

Yeah, I'd say just stay persistent and put whatever you think is a good reflection of you [in your book]. As I said, I've hired people with literally scrapbooks. Some of the people from Wieden+Kennedy 12 [ad school connected to the agency], I've talked to a couple of them and they had those little books. It was so interesting to look at. I felt like I got to know more about that person from their little writings and things they've collected, and stuff they've stuck in there, whether it's like parts of a menu, or whatever, photocopies of an email, or something. I felt like I really got to know the person and knew more about them and their thinking. And again, it depends on what kind of agency you want to go to. It's not for everyone. Some people want to see a very ordered ad, and want to see that you can actually do ads. And I want to see people who can think and solve problems and talk to people—engage them. If you're engaging as an individual, I think you stand a pretty good chance of [being able to make ads]...and if you're interesting and you're always exploring and passionate about what you do... then I think you can set the world of advertising on fire. I think it's showing passion somehow for what you do. And if you get rejected one time,

go back, you get rejected a hundred times, but if you're passionate enough, eventually it's going to pan out and you'll find the place that's right for you. I think advertising is kind of like the mafia. Once you're in, it's kind of hard to get out because I'm amazed at the talentless people, in my estimation, that work in this business, that always seem to find jobs. But as long as you just love what you do, and are always exploring new ways of trying something new, you'll do well. BI

To see Vince Engel's work, please visit http://breaking.in

LISA FEDYSZYN & JONATHAN MCMAHON CREATIVE DIRECTORS WHYBIN\TBWA NEW ZEALAND & HEAD OF AWARD SCHOOL NEW ZEALAND

What do you look for in a student book? And what impresses you?

JM: Good ideas. Big ideas. Original ideas.

LF: Ideas that let the student's personality and humor shine through. And that are mature enough to solve business problems but remain creative.

JM: And it's better if these ideas can live beyond a single execution.

LF: Having said that, who can resist a cheeky one-off?

How do students get in touch? In what format do you prefer to see a portfolio?

JM: We are happy to meet with any creatives if they have made the effort to contact us and ask to meet. That way we can talk to them, go through their book, and try to help out.

LF: We don't mind how it's presented. Some show us stuff on laptops; others show sketches. Just as long as the idea is the strongest thing on the page. If it's nicely presented, then that's a bonus.

JM: Yeah, if it's just a sketch, just make it a good sketch. Having a bit of care with your presentation always helps.

LF: Students and juniors should get in touch with CDs by calling them or by email. And if you still can't get a meeting, pass on a simple website with your work.

What are common mistakes that students make?

LF: A lot of students can have similar books. Try to get real briefs from an agency (or agencies) you admire and work on them. Not only will it give you a different book, but it also talks directly to that agency.

JM: Another problem is showing too much work. Don't feel you need to show everything you have ever done. If you have eight great pieces of work, only show them. Don't ever think it's quantity over quality.

How important is the level of finish? Could sketches be enough?

LF: Very. Even when sketched, it should be a sketch that best represents the idea.

JM: Sketches can definitely be enough, as long as the idea is strong and it's easy to understand.

Is writing important?

LF: Writing is always important. But it doesn't have to be a long-copy example. If the best idea is radio, show it in a radio script. It could be copy on the back of packaging or on a website or for a TV script. There are many ways to show off the quality of your writing skills, but they must be attached to a great idea. The media is not important.

JM: I don't mind if there isn't any long copy, but when there is copy, as in a tagline or something, just make sure it's a cracking line or sums it up nicely. Needless to say, no puns.

Do you like to see "non-ads," such as art, hobbies, personal work, etc.?

LF: I like to see the personality of the individuals in their work. But if they have "non-ads" that also show this and a great idea, then go for it.

Do you have any other advice?

JM: You'll get a lot of varied feedback on your book depending on whom you show. But you must back your own judgment and put in what you like, and what you think will land you a job.

LF: Don't be shy. Take as much advice as you can handle. Ask to work on briefs from the agencies you interview at. Your book is never finished! [BI]

To see work from Lisa Fedyszyn & Jonathan McMahon, please visit http://breaking.in

MIKE LEAR
SVP/CREATIVE DIRECTOR
THE MARTIN AGENCY
RICHMOND

What do you look for in a student book? And what impresses you?

Great, simple thinking. In many different forms of media. I still see a lot of books that consist of print campaigns blown out into other media. And that's not what I mean. That just tells me they don't get it yet. I want to see great ideas, that are totally media agnostic. Maybe it's an idea of how to use Twitter in a way I've never seen. Or...well, just lots of digital. I personally think all ideas should lead with digital, and there might be posters and traditional stuff that support it. But never the other way around. And students: Please, please, please stop trying to do TV. It's never good. Ever.

How important is finish? If ideas are the most important thing, can sketches be enough? Do you look at actual books anymore, or is it all websites?

We never look at actual books here anymore. PDFs are how it starts, or websites. I don't remember the last time I saw a physical book. And the finish question...yeah, that's an important one. Some people, and schools, think finish isn't as important anymore because the thinking and the ideas are what we are paid for. "We can find anyone to build it how we want it," they say. Not so fast...I think you have to have both. And what's wrong with that? But ideas are the most important thing. I would rather see a sketch of something killer over a gorgeous piece of dumb. But the idea of, "I'll figure out my craft later," no way. You would be dead here. We need people who can hit the ground running.

> *"I PERSONALLY THINK ALL IDEAS SHOULD LEAD WITH DIGITAL, AND THERE MIGHT BE POSTERS AND TRADITIONAL STUFF THAT SUPPORT IT. BUT NEVER THE OTHER WAY AROUND."*

How important is copy? Do you need to see long-copy ads?

All I want is some sense of voice from a writer. Maybe it's long copy, but maybe it's just a few lines on a website that are lovely. But in my opinion, gone are the days of the mandatory long-copy campaign. Prove to me you can write well. That's it.

What do you think of showing work that is not advertising? Things like art, journal writing, photography, hobbies, etc.

As long as they're ideas. Journal writing: I don't think so. Photography: eh, maybe. But I am going to hire you because I see thinking that I wish I did. That's it. That's my meter. When I see a campaign that makes something inside me just a little sick, a little green...that's what I want. Sometimes I see a campaign that I just go, "Ugh...dammit." And that's it. You have me. So, no, I don't care if they're ads. The ultimate example is Banksy. He's an artist, sure. But what makes him different is he is conceptual. His ideas are sickeningly great and tight.

Do you have any other advice for a student or junior trying to get into the business?

Man, I think it's getting harder. And not for the economy and all that crap. It's just that people have found out that what we do is so effing fun. I mean, I literally got paid today for looking at different takes of a guy on the toilet. That was my job today. "Eh, I don't know, does it look like he's constipated or something?...This needs to be funny, maybe this one where he's on the phone and being coy...Yeah, that might be funnier." And then the check shows up in my bank account. You see? That's just awesome. ▫

To see Mike Lear's work, please visit http://breaking.in

TODD RIDDLE
CREATIVE DIRECTOR
FALLON
MINNEAPOLIS

Interviewed at BBH New York.

What do you look for in a student book? And what impresses you?

Creatively speaking, whether it's writers, art directors, or digital, the main thing is breadth and depth. So I can tell pretty quickly if someone is really good at one thing, and usually you assume that, by the time the book gets to you, there's something in there that's pretty good. But what really impresses me is someone who has various tones of voice in the work that they have. In other words, they can do something serious, they can do something funny, they can handle something more mainstream or a really tough brand but in an interesting way, and also, say, something that's really smart. And to give an example: The Economist is a classic example of a really smart brand that's able to show off a creative person's ability to write or think in a really smart way.

Something like Axe, here at BBH: is funny, guy humor, I guess. The Volkswagen stuff, whether it's from Arnold or Crispin, is sort of more mainstream, and sits somewhere in between. So that's just an example of three different kinds of voices that I can pick up pretty quickly if they can do more than one.

So if someone comes in and does all bathroom, guy humor, and the whole book is like that, it is pretty evident. So I'm really impressed right away by breadth. Also, I would say a lot of writers really aren't very good. A lot of writers who call themselves writers aren't really good at the craft of writing. Which is kind of just the ability to write something really insightful or pick up on a truth in the world. Or maybe it's irony, or a funny point of view on comedy, etc. But you can tell someone who has a point of view in their writing versus just writing a bland headline or digital idea or whatever. So, in summary: breadth of what they do as far as tone, breadth of what they do as far as mediums, whether they do a billboard or a print ad, or something interesting in digital. All those things play a role.

And in terms of finish, how important is that? Could someone just bring you a book of sketches if the idea is good enough? And also, how often do you look at actual paper books now versus websites?

I only look at websites now. In fact that is all I get sent. The reason being that anybody that's in the business, or trying [to get] into the business now, should be able to pretty much build their own website, or at least have access to building their own website.

As far as level of completion goes, there certainly are a lot of books that are really slick. They look really finished but when you look through the veneer, there's not much there. So I would say having to look good, be clean, and be decent looking is a must-have for books and the reason is because it communicates a couple of things. Number one, that you take yourself seriously and

that you see yourself as a professional. And two, that you show off your other skills: that would be your ability to communicate using technology or even shepherding or working with people who can use Photoshop, Illustrator, whatever kind of design software you want to use. If you have none of it yourself, at least you can show them that you have the prowess to work with people to get it done. So all those skills, whether you can do it yourself or you have people who know how to do it, you have to walk that walk before you can get a job, in my opinion. A really great idea that's just sketched out is a thousand times better if it's executed by spending a few hours on making it look really, really great.

And you've touched on this before but for writers, how important is it to show that you can write, and how's the best way to demonstrate that?

I guess for a writer, I would be really impressed with a writer who came in with some really, really fundamentally smart print or outdoor billboard headlines, but also thinking really visually. So writing isn't just about writing words, it's about thinking very sharply about communicating an idea. And it's clearly by having command of the language, but it's also having a command of communication and visual communication as well.

What do you think about putting things in books besides ads?

I think what's great about technology now is you can build your own website. In the past, if you were an art director and you wanted to share your photography skills or the fact that you can sculpt or the fact that you're in a band or the fact that you are good at macramé, or whatever you do, it was hard to put that into your portfolio. Just because of the sheer volume of the book. It would be like, "Half of what this guy or this girl does is photography—why is she sending this to us— I guess she wants to be a photographer."

Whereas nowadays you can have your advertising portfolio on your website and you can also have a link to some photographs that you took. Or, if you traveled the world with a friend, and did some interesting things, and wrote a blog about it. You can link to that blog also. If you wrote songs or music you could have a link to that—like if you were actually on iTunes. So I think there is a way now to make it very, very appropriate. And also demonstrate your breadth without being annoying or without looking like you don't know where your passion is. I think it's totally appropriate now to say, "I want to be in advertising but I also have these other skills and other passions and this is going to let you know who I am. Besides just 'number 456' out of this advertising school." So it's a way to personalize who you are and also demonstrate other skills that, more and more, are becoming needed and appropriate, and also just converging with what we're doing in advertising.

Do you recommend separating the ads from the other things?

Yes. I've seen a lot of websites where they'll have their advertising stuff—maybe a TV idea, some print, and some website designs—and then it will say, "What I do for fun." For example, there will be a whole thing of photography they shot in India. Or a blog that they've been keeping. Or a link to some other website that they made. It helps people understand who they are.

Do you have any other advice for anyone who is just starting out in the business?

Yes, and this is the advice I give to everyone, which is really hard to follow. The key when you're starting out is to surround yourself with the best people possible, for as long as possible. I don't want to say it's easy, but it's easier to get any job than to get a job at a really great place.

In the beginning, it's not about the money, even though money is clearly important, which is why most people go to work. But, long term, your first five years in the business is just an investment. It's an investment about creating who you're going to be 10, 15, 20 years down the road. So, just like a child born into one family is going to be very different than a child born into another family, this is different because you actually get to choose the family that you get born into. Think about yourself being born into a creative family. You get to choose who that creative family is. And you're better off

waiting for the right family to adopt you than to just jump in with whoever will take you first.

"YOUR FIRST FIVE YEARS IN THE BUSINESS IS JUST AN INVESTMENT. IT'S AN INVESTMENT ABOUT CREATING WHO YOU'RE GOING TO BE 10, 15, 20 YEARS DOWN THE ROAD."

My first job—I was offered a couple of jobs in the industry making not-much money. But I took a job that actually paid nothing for the first nine months. I interned for free. And that was after a college education. Because the people I was working with were the best people I could find and be around at the time. And I ended up staying there for 12 years. So, that's a good example of just waiting, because, whether you want it to or not, it will define how you think, how you view yourself, how others view you, what you think you're capable of, all of your experiences, what you create, and what you will create in the rest of your career. It's the most critical part of your career. And even more critical than the college or education that you got. Because everyone will forget where you went to college after two or three years—whatever school you went to, nobody is going to care. No one's going to care about your GPA. No one's going to care whether you graduated or not. No one's going to care about anything. All they'll want to know is what have you done in the past two or three years. And if you've been surrounded by really great, smart, bright, creative people, and that's rubbed off on you, and you've become a bit of them, then that's all you'll have to have really, in the end. 🄱🄸

To see Todd Riddle's work, please visit http://breaking.in

DAVID LUBARS
CHAIRMAN & CCO
BBDO NORTH AMERICA
NEW YORK

What do you look for in a student book? And what impresses you?

I look to be jealous—I want to see stuff that I wish we were doing.

Can a book of sketches be enough, or do ideas need to be comped up nicely?

You need to show big ideas and how they can be delivered across several channels. The more finished, the better.

Is it important to have long copy in a book?

It's nice to have any copy, writing seems to be a lost art. But, no, you don't need long copy—the best ideas can be summed up in a text message.

What do you think about including "non-ads" in a book?

It's good to show a range, especially today where content can take on many forms, from art installations to TV shows to whatever.

Do you have any tips for someone who wants to get into the business?

You have to want to work long, hard hours, and you need to possess a healthy degree of paranoia. BI

To see David Lubars's work, please visit http://breaking.in

HEMANT ANANT JAIN
CREATIVE DIRECTOR
CHI & PARTNERS
NEW YORK

What do you look for in a student book? And what impresses you?

I think to say I look for fresh ideas would be a cliché. I look for will power, you know? It's just so many people…many students who come and say that well, we haven't had the opportunity to do this or, we haven't ever had any exposure to advertising or whatever. I don't really see the merit in that because if you were driven you would produce ideas no matter what. And they don't have to be ads but they need to be ideas, and they need to be executed. They need to be produced, "I've done this, I have done this, I've done that," you know? I don't want to listen to the odds you've faced, I want to see what you've done because that's how I pretty much started. Nobody was giving me an opportunity to work in an agency, and whenever you go to an agency they say, "So what have you done?" And it's ridiculous because until the time you're in an agency, you can't do ads.

"…IF YOU'RE TELLING ME THAT YOU HAVEN'T GOT THE OPPORTUNITY… SORRY, THERE'S SOMEBODY MORE DRIVEN THAN YOU BECAUSE TALENT IS ONE THING, DRIVE IS ANOTHER. A COMBINATION OF BOTH IS WHAT IS GOING TO MAKE YOU SUCCESSFUL."

But what happens to all those twenty years, twenty-five years, twenty-seven years that you spent before joining advertising? What have you got to show for that? Some three poems, four stories, that's never going to cut it because there are young students who are fifteen years old or seventeen years old or eighteen years old that make fabulous work and [are] producing ideas. Especially in these times where the opportunities and the exposure and the kind of outlets are far too many. You know, you could pretty much make a YouTube video. You don't have to have experience of being a traditional setup to produce that. You just need a fucking mobile phone camera for all you care, and you can do your film. And in these times, if you're telling me that you haven't got the opportunity…sorry, there's somebody more driven than you because talent is one thing, drive is another. A combination of both is what is going to make you successful.

What do you think about finished work versus sketches?

See ideas…they're two criteria on which to judge people. One is ideas. So obviously, sometimes, the ideas would be so fantastic that sketches…forget about sketches, you can just talk about your idea and you can be in. But on the other hand, if you have not only thought about those ideas, you've sketched them and you've taken time out to produce and you…see, the thing about producing ideas, it's execution skills. It's like your designing skills or your filmmaking skills or your editing skills or whatever which really make a difference. Because thinking of ideas is…anybody can think of ideas. But knowing what to do with those ideas is also very important because that's what it is all about. Somebody thinks of a film and he shoots his YouTube film and puts on the music, puts it on YouTube, you see the finished product, and you say, "Okay, this is what this guy wanted to do." So your vision is not only about the idea, your vision is until the very end. And that's important. So I like to see as much work put into the ideas as possible.

What do you think about putting long copy in a book?

I don't believe in that. I think, if you're a good writer… you've got to see the writing skills. I mean, writing skills are important but if you're a good writer you can show that skill in two lines. You don't have to write a fucking full page of copy to show how good you are. I mean the best copywriters, if you're talking traditionally, really craft that one line of body copy really well. I mean you can see old work and see the great writers and you'll see that even the three lines

of body copy make a lot of sense. And, you see, the thing is, it's not about writers doing long copy and art directors designing long copy. It's about what are you doing with the ideas, what is the idea? If an idea requires an explanation of more than a hundred words, then so be it. But it has to require that. And long copy and short copy and all of those things are just tools. I don't think they're necessary or they're not. I mean if you hadn't had a word of copy in your portfolio and yet you had these very interesting ideas and not the very scam-ish advertising, that will still make a lot of sense.

What do you think of putting things in books that aren't ads at all?

That's definitely a thumbs-up for me because ads are only .0001 percent of your creativity. And thankfully advertising has become like that now. People don't like ads. People don't believe ads. So how are you going to engage them by not doing ads? And that's why all these agencies start saying that, "We don't want to do ads" because they know that, as tools of engagement, they've become outdated. They want to do stuff which is engaging and which also builds the brand. I think in a book, if you could start seeing different kinds of ideas—somebody's blog or somebody's illustrations— you're already starting to see that, yes, this person can engage your interest in many other ways than traditional advertising. The traditional, "Okay, this is an ad, and here's a headline, here's the body copy, here's the product logo," you don't have the luxury of using those tools anymore very effectively, I'm afraid.

And do you have any advice on how to improve or how to put together a book or how to get a job?

If you're enthusiastic and energetic, then it will show in your work. Whatever you bring to the table should reflect your personality, your enthusiasm, and your willingness and your drive to do creative and interesting stuff. If you're just bringing 10 ads or 15 ads, they aren't going to make a hell of a lot of difference. Going back to what I said, the YouTube video—people do that without anything. But still they create these fantastic little things: one minute, two minutes, things in which the entire world watches and goes "Wow!" I think if you don't have that kind of stuff in your book then you'll find it tough. Not tough to find a job. You'll find it very tough to succeed in these fields because they are extremely competitive fields—especially advertising. Because it is a business. It is a service business, and you're providing a service so there are constraints. And those constraints are roadblocks. You've got to cross them, and you've got to fight against them, and still have a vision and still produce to be able to get decent stuff. BI

To see Hemant Anant Jain's work, please visit http://breaking.in

MIKE HUGHES
FORMER PRESIDENT &
CREATIVE DIRECTOR
THE MARTIN AGENCY
RICHMOND

Sadly, Mike Hughes passed away in 2013. Thank you, Mike, for being a great person and a great teacher to us all.

What do you look for in a student book? And what impresses you?

I look for humanity that goes beyond cleverness. Although I confess that cleverness is very important. I want to see signs that the student isn't just trying to impress his or her fellow students. I want to feel that the work is strategically smart—and not just attention getting. I want to see a careful, thoughtful presentation of the work. I'm really turned off by misspellings, poor grammar, etc.

How important is finish?

Less important for a writer, more important for an art director.

If ideas are the most important thing, can sketches be enough?

Yes.

Do you look at actual paper books anymore, or is it all websites?

Both.

How important is copy?

Being able to write clearly and well is an asset for anyone. For a writer—even in these minimal-copy times—it is essential.

Do you need to see long-copy ads?

I like to see something that shows at least basic writing skills and the ability to express thoughts clearly. That's true for writers, art directors, strategic thinkers, etc.

What do you think of showing work that is not advertising?

Be respectful of my time: I'm not going to spend a lot of time with your journal. But, yes, I like seeing things that reach beyond advertising.

Do you have any other advice for a student or junior trying to get into the business?

Be enthusiastic. Demonstrate a willingness to continue learning. Let me know it would be fun, interesting, and rewarding to work with you. BI

To see Mike Hughes's work, please visit http://breaking.in

IDA GRONBLOM &
FABIAN BERGLUND
CREATIVE DIRECTORS
ANOMALY
NEW YORK

Interviewed at Wieden+Kennedy, London.

What do you look for in a student book? And what impresses you?

IG: Creativity on all levels, in any media.

FB: First you look for something that is sort

of half-decent, because a lot of books are quite bad and you want to make sure you have at least some positive feedback. But then, if you find that there's good work in the portfolio, then you start to look for really interesting strategies and interesting solutions.

IG: I think how people solve problems—that's what I look for. The thinking behind it and how they come to a conclusion. Not just, "Oh, it's a clever visual" or it's "a stunning image and a brilliant copy line together." That's just too old school. I think what's interesting to see is how you get your head around the brand and their business problem.

FB: A lot of students have books full of ads with smart visuals or fun copy, but they haven't thought about why they made the ads. What's the problem they are trying to solve? And is an ad the best way to solve that problem? The issue with a lot of student books is that they've made a lot of ads without a brief—without a real problem to solve.

"THE ISSUE WITH A LOT OF STUDENT BOOKS IS THAT THEY'VE MADE A LOT OF ADS WITHOUT A BRIEF—WITHOUT A REAL PROBLEM TO SOLVE."

IG: A lot of students just go, "Okay, we're going to create a campaign for like…"

FB: American Express…

IG: Yeah, American Express, and they end up doing advertising for a credit card, not American Express. You could just swap the product, you know? It could be any card, really. That happens a lot. We tell them to do your research, try to figure out the tone of voice of the brand, what makes it different from other brands doing the same thing. Is there anything you can dig up from the brand's history? What do people associate with this brand? I think this is something that, as a student, you're not that used to doing because you are looking for quick fixes. You get an assignment and then it's more fun to hang out with your mates and then, all of a sudden, you need to deliver it tomorrow so you go with an idea without having analyzed it enough. But what you really need to do is to get under the skin of the brand. This is the main feedback we give to students about their books. And when some students already think this way, then it's like, "Wow! These guys are great!"

What do you think about sketches versus finished work?

IG: Well, if you're an art director, I think you have to do everything you can to illustrate what the finished product would look like. Doesn't have to be the final execution. Could be a sketch, but then you have a few mood images to show what look and feel you are after. So it's fine if you do your own sketches, but then you have to show somehow that you can think visually as well.

FB: I think it's whatever gets their idea across the best. A lot of the time a sketch is okay, but sometimes, if you don't do a bit of art direction, you're not going to get what the idea is. Art direction can be a big part of the idea.

IG: It could be everything.

FB: We also ask a lot of students to do more copywriting. Because I think a lot of them just want to do a clever ad, a quick visual, and then put three words in the corner. They think it's enough. I think if they actually sat down and tried to write a radio ad or a TV script, and not just do the key frames for it but try to write it down in words, they would actually learn a lot more and it would also help them to realize if the idea really works or not. So we encourage people to write a bit more because we hardly see any writing in books nowadays.

IG: It's funny sometimes, I don't know if this is a British thing, but you see student books where every campaign is based on comedy. Having fun is fine but not for every project because not every brand does humor well—sometimes it doesn't fit with the brand. It's horrible when you see a book that is just one pun after the other.

You started talking about this already, but how does a student show writing ability?

FB: I don't think you necessarily need lots of ads with long copy. You can still sense if a student can write, even if the writing isn't in the ad. They should analyze the brief, write a manifesto or a radio ad or a TV script before they start drawing up key frames. For an integrated or online campaign a good strategic write-up of the idea helps. You might only want to put the visuals in to illustrate your idea in the end, but it will make a difference if you've written it properly before you start making it.

Also, I agree with what Ida said before about a lot of students being so hungry to get a job and so hungry to finish their portfolio, but a lot of them aren't willing to work hard enough. I have to say this is odd. It's as if they think it's going to be easy as long as they just get a job. They don't realize that the moment you start working for an agency you actually have to do even more work. And to get your first campaign out, it's fucking hard. You won't just automatically get loads of amazing campaigns out just because you're in a good agency.

IG: It's funny because we see a lot of different teams twice or three times a week, and the ones that take your feedback and have the energy to actually go redo the campaign and come back with something better really impress us. Because that's, in reality, what we're doing here every day. We have our ideas rejected on a daily basis and you always have to pick yourself up. And there's always, always a better idea around the corner. I get amazed myself that you almost always manage to come up with something new. It's only happened to me a couple of times that I've actually given up on something. So staying positive helps when you have to redo stuff.

FB: I think that's a very common mistake when you're a student. You think that you have the best idea you could ever come up with for something.

IG: Just because you have the best idea in your class.

FB: And it's very hard to get over an idea you really like—to kill a darling. But if you write it down properly and you sketch it all out, then that can help you see if the idea really works or not and when you've taken the idea as far as you possibly can. You also sort of get it out of your system and it's easier to start all over again. People are lazy sometimes.

IG: We're really harsh aren't we?

Yes. But it's good. What do you think about putting things that aren't ads in the book?

IG: Good.

FB: Yeah, I think it's good, but it should be…

IG: It should be 20 percent of the book.

FB: Communication ideas and not just something silly to be different. Not something that's like, "Why?" The point of the book is to tell other people that you have ideas and that you get communication and problem solving. So aim for ideas that do that. A business idea or a design solution for something or whatever [is good] but it can't just be something mad, you know?

IG: Or tiny, small, ambient ideas that would never have an effect. They're fine if you've got the big campaign and they're sort of the icing on the top. But you have to remember that they're the fun bits you get to do locally somewhere, and if you are lucky they get picked up by the media, but that's never a sure thing. So you can't present them as, "This is the big thing, the only thing we're going to do for this brand."

FB: Yes, a lot of students want to do nontraditional advertising but they end up doing very traditional nontraditional advertising. They have a lot of ideas for outdoor, ambient stuff, but just because you don't pay for the ad space doesn't make it a good idea. Ambient work should be thought through strategically as well.

What about creative things in the book that aren't ads at all, more like artwork or journal writing…?

IG: Yeah, that's good. Special skills that really show who you are and your personality because that's how you're going to stand out and be remembered.

FB: If you're a good photographer, animator, or graphic designer, I think you should show that in your book as well. Same with writing, you can have things like that in the back of your book and say, "I've written a novel," if you have. You shouldn't be afraid to show that you have a special talent. I think it's a balance of things and some people get the balance a bit wrong. I think it's hard if you only have wacky ideas or things that aren't advertising. It's hard to take that person in on a placement or for a job because you don't know if they can deliver on the everyday work you need them to do as well. Even if you are looking for someone who has the potential to be great in a few years, you also need to know that they can write some radio ads, make some posters today, or tackle a smaller digital brief, and if you have no clue how to do advertising because you only have a book with mad ideas, it's going to be hard for you in the beginning.

Do you have any other advice on how to put a book together?

IG: Constant improvement, I think. As long as you're trying to get into advertising, as long as you're jumping from placement to placement, you just got to keep making your book better. There's no other way.

FB: Yeah, it is a lot of late nights…

IG: …I mean, that's what we still do. That's what you do when you have a job. You're constantly updating your portfolio with better work, at least you should aspire to.

FB: It's hard for people to manage their book once they get their first placement or job. It takes up all your time, and you don't really have any time left to update your book. When you have enough good ideas, I would spend some time on the finish of them. And that's back to the question of just pen sketches—it doesn't have to be finished all the time. But ideas need art direction and you can either lift or ruin an idea with design, typography, photography, etc.

IG: I get a bit scared when people come in showing a book with only pen sketches. Not showing any design sensibility or art direction, then I get a bit scared because that's not really the reality of advertising anymore—that you just sit with a pen and pad.

FB: Another piece of advice is to have your best work in the beginning of the book because the first impression is going to influence what people think of the book. Think about the order of things too, so there's a natural flow. Mix up big campaigns with smaller ones. You shouldn't have too many "slow" campaigns after each other. Give them breathing space with lighter ideas in between.

"ALWAYS AIM TO SEE MORE JUNIOR PEOPLE, THEN WORK YOUR WAY UP—MAKE THEM RECOMMEND YOU UP."

IG: I wouldn't advise people to drop off their book at agencies. I know a lot of people do that but I think, when you meet the person, that's when the book comes to life—when the people talk about the projects, present them. I don't think it's very good to leave your book unless you're amazing, and it will stun anyone. Sometimes students try to see the most senior people in the agency, like the executive creative director. I'm not sure that's always right because, first of all, they barely have time. Chances that you're going to see them are slim. And are they going to be impressed by you? No. They look at a lot of books, and they look at award-winning creatives' books all the time. They go to award shows to judge. It's been ages since they were in school. So they're just going to think you're shit. So always aim to see more junior people, then work your way up—make them recommend you up. I think you might just burn all your bridges if you go straight up to the top if you're fresh out of university.

FB: It's better that someone else in the agency sends your work to them and says, "This student is really good." Because, again, they're going to look at your book with that in mind—that their colleague who they respect thinks your work is really good.

IG: And then, you know, usually in every agency there are a couple of younger teams that look at all the student books and they can judge it the best really because they see all of them.

How do you find these junior or middleweight teams that you can show your work to? How do people find you?

FB: Don't be afraid of phoning people. Just call the agency reception and then you just ask, "Who can I talk to about coming in and showing my portfolio?" and then they will hopefully direct you the right way. You build up a list of creatives that work for different agencies and you can ask them if there's anyone they think you should see in another agency. People always want to help students along, even if you can't give them a placement where you work. So just try to build this network of people you've seen. And once they like what you've done, they talk to their friends…

IG: We've come across quite a few people from overseas who can't come in and show their book and they send PDFs or they have a website, which is fine. Some people just beg. But in this industry, begging is worth nothing because it's all about showing what you've done and who you are. So don't beg. Be proud. Do good work and the rest will follow.

FB: And do read up on the agency you're actually going to see. We made the mistake of writing the same email to two different agencies…

IG: But we forgot to swap the name of the agency. I can't remember which agency it was. But we wrote something like, "Hi! We really want to work at Fallon" and sent it to Saint Lukes or something. We got a reply saying, "Well, if you really want to work at Fallon, why don't you contact them?" We were so embarrassed.

FB: So that's a mistake you shouldn't make. And don't expect people to reply to your emails. When you work in an agency you get hundreds of emails per day. So the best thing is to send an email to introduce yourself and then call them the same day. Because then, when you phone up the agency, you can refer to your email that they have in their inbox, fresh the same day. And don't be afraid of calling over and over again either. Because it's not that people don't like you, that's not why they don't return your call. It's because they are incredibly busy and not always in the agency, and I think it's hard when you're a student because you might not understand that. Because you have all the time in the world so you don't understand why they don't get back to you the same day.

And what do you think about self-promotional pieces to get into an agency? Didn't you do that?

IG: Yeah we did one. It was related to a brief set by the agency we had earlier worked on, so it got the agency's attention and we got the chance to come in and show our book.

FB: I think when you do them, you have to be very careful and do it tastefully.

IG: We did two life-size posters of ourselves attached to the front windows of W+K with us pressing against the glass, with a note saying, "We're still trying to get in." It was a follow-up on a W+K placement scheme interview and assignment we had been invited to earlier. We didn't make it to the final four for the scheme —we were too experienced—so we put up those posters to show that we were still keen on getting in. And we quit our jobs at our current agency for a month's placement at Wieden's. After a month we got hired. It was quite a risk.

FB: It's sort of a fine line when you do a stunt. If it's really tacky and a bit scary or if it's just clever and nice. And it also depends on who you're doing it for—if they're going to appreciate it or not, you never really know. So you do take a risk when you do it. Luckily it paid off for us.

IG: To be honest, we just thought basically, "It's all or nothing." We were in London, it was either we get our foot in here or we go home. We don't have anything to lose. So we were just like, "Okay, let's do something," and Tony and Kim loved it.

FB: I think you should just do something you can stand for and be able to take the reaction. Think before you do it and what kind of criticism it could give you, and then evaluate the trade-off.

IG: There's been some weird ones, like someone sending in a horrible, gory painting and there was that guy who sat on a Verner Panton chair outside in the pouring rain for hours demanding a book crit.

FB: Someone sent in something that was some kind of statement on good communication and it was a picture of the Twin Towers with the airplane crashing into it. That sort of attention-seeking stuff is not going to get you anywhere.

Anything else you want to mention?

FB: One thing we always say about going around showing your book: You get a lot of feedback, a lot of thoughts from different people. Thoughts like we're giving now in this interview. But, at end of the day, it's all just personal opinions. You have to believe in what you think is best and evaluate the things in your book from your own point of view, based on what kind of advertising it is you want to be doing. You just get confused if you listen to other people too much and change your book after every book crit. Because if you do, yeah, you might get into a place because you changed your whole book to be the way they wanted it to be, but it won't be fun to work there because you might have just lost yourself to get there. It's better to take advice and critiques that make your work better without compromising on your own gut feeling.

IG: At the end of the day, it's all about identifying what you think is good advertising, staying true to that, and true to the time you live in. That's a skill you find in great creative directors. ⊞

To see work from Ida Gronblom & Fabian Berglund, please visit http://breaking.in

JEFF GOODBY CO-CHAIRMAN GOODBY, SILVERSTEIN & PARTNERS SAN FRANCISCO

What do you look for in a student book? And what impresses you?

I look for things that no one I know, even myself, would ever come up with. If your solution is something that your friends or family might come up with, throw it away.

How important is finish? If ideas are the most important thing, can sketches be enough? Do you look at physical books anymore, or is it all websites?

I look mostly at digital books these days, but that doesn't mean there wouldn't be a notable place for a portfolio put together with Skil Saw, Dremel tool, and black masking tape.

Finish isn't important to me because I can imagine what the thing might be like. But the majority of creative directors care about finish, I think. They see it as a demonstration of taste and hand skills.

How important is writing? Do you need to see long copy?

How important is writing? Really? It's the way we communicate and organize ideas. Even if you're writing with pictures, you're writing.

I like to see some long copy because I believe that people who can write longer-form stuff are better at writing short form too. They know what to take out.

What do you think of showing work that is not advertising?

I love it. Much better than showing that Bagel Bites retail thing that never quite got produced.

Do you have any other advice for a student or junior trying to get into the business?

Try to look at the world through the eyes of a busy creative director who doesn't really care who you are. As David Ogilvy said, "When selling fire extinguishers, open with fire." ⊞

To see Jeff Goodby's work, please visit http://breaking.in

JI LEE
COMMUNICATION DESIGNER
FACEBOOK
NEW YORK

Interviewed at Google Creative Lab.

What do you look for in a student book? And what impresses you?

I receive lots of emails with students' portfolios. From both students and recruiters. So, for me, the first thing I look at in a portfolio is how a student organizes his or her work. Good navigation and ease of use are very important. No matter how great their work is, if I am lost in their website, if I have to take a few extra seconds to find something, then the person already lost me. This is also an indication of how well the person knows how to communicate his or her message. So, if I'm lost in the navigation, that tells me this person doesn't know how to use the web to communicate his own message. Lots of people these days use Cargo or Index Exhibit and they work well.

"THE FIRST THING I LOOK AT IN A PORTFOLIO IS HOW A STUDENT ORGANIZES HIS OR HER WORK."

Can you explain "Cargo" and "Index Exhibit"?

They are portfolio website templates. They're probably the most widely used templates for designers and people in advertising. The great thing about them is

that people can customize the way they want their sites to look and they don't have to know PHP or coding. It's a really easy way of showing your work.

Okay.

And then, once I am navigating the website easily, obviously I'll be looking for the quality of the work. And the work has to be well presented. Is it well photographed? Is it well designed? Is it well written? Is it concise and does it communicate the idea quickly? So there are a few steps even before the work; packaging an idea is as important, if not even more important, than the idea itself.

And while I'm looking at the work, I'm looking for the kind of work that is non-formulaic. I see lots of students' portfolios that are formulaic. Many students, for instance, do environmental work, like doing things on the escalator or revolving doors or on the sidewalk and appropriating objects and transforming them into some kind of brand message, which I think is fun but that's what everybody does. So I think it's fine to have a few environmental installation pieces but if the book is filled with those things then it feels that the person is not really exploring something beyond.

Same thing with the print ad: some kind of an intriguing image in the center and then a tiny logo at the bottom-right. That's the formula that I've been seeing over and over again over the years. So I'm not really interested in those kinds of formulas, I'm interested in big thinking. I'm interested in "idea people" who are really thinking about media. So there's a problem and there's a solution. How do you spread that solution creatively throughout different media? Do you know how social networking works and how you create a gadget that lives in Facebook and how you would really spread that idea?

And what do you think about print ads? Is that still important because it's a way to judge someone that's very standard among different books, rather than if someone just comes in with all new media?

Well, I think what a lot of people are looking for these days is 360-degree thinking. So I'm looking for someone who is not bound by medium but bound by the idea, and media is there to support that idea. If print is what works for solving that particular problem, that is good. But if the person is doing print because that's just the way things are done, then I think the person is still in the old school of thinking. So maybe the solution for that particular product or brand is creating a chair or creating an in-flight magazine or creating an event in Times Square, and maybe the print ad is not appropriate for that particular product. So I don't think that print is an absolutely necessary thing to have in your book.

I think ten years ago, because media was limited, you did print, you did TV and radio and outdoor. But nowadays, it's really wide open. There's gadgets, there are social networking aspects, rich media ads, and there is print and there is outdoor. But I think when we're creating these messages, we're creating it mindful that a consumer will experience this in many different layers of their lives. So when they wake up, they may listen to the radio ad, and then on the way to work, they may receive a three-word message about this new particular initiative of a brand, and then when they go to work, they may turn on the computer and they may find a Facebook post from another friend, and so on and on. So you know, it's a wide range of sensorial and media blips that we get. And so the person would have to really think about the whole thing. And the more 360-degree thinking that's in the book, the better.

And how have you seen people present these things, either good or bad? Because when you do a 360-degree campaign, it can be so many different things that it can be overwhelming for someone to look through and get the idea.

True. Well, I think it has to be self-explanatory, with very little text, living in your website. So the person never needs to be sitting next to me saying, "This is how I did it." I think what lots of students end up doing is that they are so used to presenting the work to their teacher in college, they automatically assume that is the format. And that is not true. You know, most of the time you're just sending the link in and you have to let the viewer figure it out on their own in a really easy way. I teach at SVA [School of Visual Arts] and that's one thing that I stress the most. Obviously, the packaging and then how do you explain this idea visually so that it stands on its own? And if there is a

complex project, then I think I would first introduce the brand or the product, and then set up the problem or the challenge, and then the solution. So, in one or two slides, you learn about this product, you learn about the challenge, and maybe you have to write that in very small, short sentences, and then you learn about the solution. And then you go on: "In this solution, there is an outdoor element, there is a print element, there's a TV spot," and so on.

> ## "...A PERSONAL PROJECT THAT COMES FROM THEIR OWN VOICE AND THEIR OWN PASSION, IT'S ALWAYS UNIQUE AND IT'S ALWAYS INTERESTING."

You mentioned that the presentation is very important in terms of clarity and that it looks good. Is the craft also important? For an art director, do you want to see evidence of amazing design, and for writers, do you want to see copy?

Absolutely. And I think this idea of writer versus or director versus designer is becoming blurry and blurrier. So I expect any presentation to have all that stuff and still look beautiful. It doesn't matter if it comes from a copywriter or art director. If it comes from a copywriter who cannot design, then I think it's the copywriter's job to find the right designer or a partner to make that look beautiful. Because we end up doing lots of presentations internally and presentation is, again, as important as the work itself. So we're looking for someone who can generate ideas and also present that idea in a really beautiful, simple way. So presentation, design skills, all that stuff is really important.

What do you think about including stuff in a book that is not advertising? Things like personal projects and art or photography or journal writing or things like that?

I think for me, personally, it's a huge plus. My personal vision is that personal projects are extremely important both for personal growth and also end up helping you professionally. I've done lots of personal projects like "The Bubble Project" or "3D Alphabets" or the "World Trade Center Logo Preservation Project" or "Goollery"...these are personal projects. And because of those personal projects, I was able to find good jobs in good places. You know, it's not because of my ad/design portfolio. If I only did professional projects, I wouldn't be in such a place that I would like to work for. So I definitely look for personal projects and I encourage young designers and art directors and copywriters to include their personal projects. Because that's where the real personality comes out and the passion and quirkiness, and that's where you can really see what kind of interests this person has. I've seen so many books with Doritos ads or some bowling-alley ads or condom ads. Those could be fun but I think the level of interest is very low. But then, if you found a personal project that comes from their own voice and their own passion, it's always unique and it's always interesting.

Do you have any more advice for someone who is just starting out?

The other advice that I have is to make it as personal as possible. So you can enclose your photograph, or tell your stories about where you come from, or if you have a rich ethnic background or special interests or if you're a climber or you're a collector of something, that is a plus. All those little quirks make me feel connected to that person because I have learned a little more about them.

And being open so that you can share...maybe creating platforms, open projects where you invite other people to participate in making things. Those little details I think makes me get a sense that, "Okay, this person gets the web." And by making a lot of the contents creative commons. The fact that he put, "So and so, 2010 copyright," makes me realize the person is still thinking old media. But the person who puts "CC," creative commons, makes me think, "Okay, this person understands open source" and the power of spreading ideas and all that. So that may be a very small detail but those things matter.

And there are other small things: Coming up with the URL of your website. If you have a long, complicated name with lots of consonants, then I would encourage you to think about another name. Like, in my case, "jilee.com" was already taken and so I had to think about another name and I came up with "pleaseenjoy.com." So when I talk about "pleaseenjoy.com" in a cocktail party, people are probably more likely to remember that than Ji Lee. You're building your own brand, so I'd treat your website and your business card, the way you dress, the way you present yourself, everything as if you're building a brand in a professional context. Would you like to be known as John Doe or would you like to be known as a unique brand name? There's no good or bad, but it's something that you should be thinking about. 🄱🄸

To see Ji Lee's work, please visit http://breaking.in

TOBY TALBOT
CHIEF CREATIVE OFFICER
DDB
SYDNEY

Interviewed at RKCR Y&R London.

What form does a portfolio take? And what do you prefer?

I usually see links to sites, most of which are pretty basic: "Work," "About," "Awards," and "Hobbies" (always my favorite section; boy can you tell a lot about a person by their hobbies). I haven't seen an actual physical book in years, which is a shame in a way. Websites can be desperately same-y.

How do portfolios come to you?

I am very blessed to have a team, Andy and Nicola, who are passionate about helping young talent get into the industry. They are the first port of call. Honestly, if I responded to every single email I got about a job, I'd be an HR director, not a creative director. Since joining, I have set up a creative internship program called "The Farm." Nic and Andy draw up a shortlist of the best teams out there, and every three months we revolve our intake. Three new teams come in. Three teams leave. If a team can make themselves indispensable to the agency in that time, we keep them on. It's working so well that Y&R is thinking of rolling it out globally, which is great.

In a meeting do people show you work from laptop or paper book? And what do you prefer?

I usually see the work remotely, to be honest. I'm pretty time poor. It's actually quite nice to look at ideas without someone feeling the need to nervously apologize for them. If I like the book, I'll meet the team. Their personality—and by that I mean their sense of humor, alertness, and passion—counts just as much as their work. Especially for teams that we're considering for internships. They need to light up a room, not be a wallflower.

"IF A TEAM CAN MAKE THEMSELVES INDISPENSABLE TO THE AGENCY IN THAT TIME, WE KEEP THEM ON."

How should students and juniors get in touch?

Through the dedicated channel on our website. Most agencies have that now. I'm not big on being stalked. It's a fine line between a team demonstrating unbridled passion and being a massive pain in the ass.

What do you look for in a student book?

Consistency is really important to me. Start with your best ideas and maintain thatstandard. Easier said than done, I know. But too many times I see a great idea first up, then realize three campaigns on that that idea was either a fluke or someone else had it.

You want to see ideas that stay with you long after you see them. Usually because they're so stupidly simple and contain a powerful emotional truth that you think, "Wow, why hasn't someone else thought

of that before? More importantly, why haven't I thought of that before?" Jealousy is a wonderful motivator in our business.

I will also tell you what I don't look for. There's an awful lot of "cr-app" ideas out there. I went to the Cream show at Mother the other night. Lots of apps on lots of tablets. Barely any proper ideas among them. Nine times out of ten, they were just silly gimmicks. Apps can cost a shitload of money to develop. Clients need a good reason to invest in one, which is why they rarely do. These are the commercial realities that students need to understand. It's tiresome that they plainly don't. [BI]

To see Toby Talbot's work, please visit http://breaking.in

PAUL KAMZELAS
CREATIVE DIRECTOR
BBH
NEW YORK

What do you look for in a student or junior book?

Simple, fresh, insightful thinking. I like to see "pure" ideas, ones that don't rely on a specific medium or just come out of exploiting the latest bit of technology.

What are common mistakes that people make?

Don't try to be funny or wacky with your ideas if you're not. Present solutions that pour out of you naturally. It will help match you with the right place. And more importantly, your job will be easier and more fun.

How important is the level of finish?

It's not essential for your work to look like finished ads. Your energy should be focused on generating ideas, not on Photoshop. What I will say though is, as a creative, whether you are art or copy based, you should understand how an idea communicates best. Is it a big headline over a visual? Is it a predetermined sequence of visuals or copy? Is it a sound over a colored background? Whatever…show that you've thought about it even if it's through handwritten copy and stick figures. To be honest, you'll know you have a big idea if it can be described in a paragraph without visual comps and still be exciting.

Do you need to see long copy or evidence of writing?

Writing is important. I believe that even if you are art based you should be able to at least write a half-decent tagline. Don't cop out by saying, "Oh, I'm a visual guy." But to answer your question, I think after a decade or so of formulaic, visually led advertising with tiny logos, the copywriter is back. I don't think you need to demonstrate it through a traditional long-copy print ad, but you do need to show that you can set a tone, tell a story, or initiate a conversation for a brand.

Do you like to see "non-ads" such as art, hobbies, personal work, etc.?

I do, but I look for certain things in them. Besides a passion for creative expression, I look for evidence of life experience—an understanding of people and the world around them. I believe it makes for a more powerful and insightful creative. A little pet peeve of mine is when I'm presented with a blog that is purely a curation of stuff from around the Web. If you are going to present personal work, make it personal.

"PRESENT SOLUTIONS THAT POUR OUT OF YOU NATURALLY. IT WILL HELP MATCH YOU WITH THE RIGHT PLACE."

Other advice about portfolios or getting into advertising?

Find ways to prove you are dedicated, keen, and passionate, especially if you've made contact with an agency you really want to work for. If someone you respect critiques your work, get back to them showing that you've taken their comments on board and re-looked at your work.

Ask for a brief, even if it's not a real one, and fire back a bunch of solutions. A good friend of mine had a gimmick when he started. He'd hand over his portfolio, which was then literally a zip-up folder. They'd open it expecting to see his work, but all they found was a blank layout pad and a Sharpie. He'd then suggest that they give him a brief and an hour and he'd come back to them with some great solutions. Pretty ballsy, but he became the talk of ad town and ended up with a job very quickly. BI

To see Paul Kamzelas's work, please visit http://breaking.in

DYLAN LEE
SENIOR COPYWRITER
WIEDEN+KENNEDY
PORTLAND

What do you look for in a student book? And what impresses you?

I look for big ideas. I don't have to see digital. I don't have to see TV. I don't have to see alternative media. If someone has great ideas, I know he or she can think of something for whatever medium comes up. I also love to see a book where someone has multiple voices. Because sometimes funny works great. And sometimes it doesn't. I am also always impressed by truths; those ideas resonate with consumers and go beyond gimmicks, word plays, and jokes.

How important is finish? If ideas are the most important thing, can sketches be enough? Do you look at physical books anymore, or is it all websites?

I want to say that I'm not affected by pretty books and execution. But it is advertising, and presentation is important. However, a good creative mind should and will see a good idea on a piece of toilet paper. If you have a great idea but not the time to make it look shiny, present it. As for websites, I'm torn. They make portfolios quick to view, omnipresent, and of course, "Everybody's doing it!" But I fear they do a disservice to the work. TV spots, print ads, and out of home were not meant to be shrunken down and viewed on a tiny computer screen. For a copywriter, it's sad to have well-crafted copy scrolled through in a way you would never read a real ad. I'm sure I'll succumb, but I'll always have a life-sized, tangible, more impressive book to show. We should make our ideas look amazing, captivating, and larger than life. Isn't that what our jobs are?

How important is writing? Do you need to see long copy?

If you are a copywriter, you will write. I guarantee it. Sometimes short copy, sometimes long copy. TV scripts, radio, websites, Facebook ads. If you don't have writing in your book—and I mean longer than a sentence or two—then you will run into problems in your career. I see juniors being hired who can't form a sentence. Or write dialogue in scripts. Or write their way out of a cereal box. If you're a copywriter, it will help if you love words. And well-written long copy means you're in another class of writer.

"...WELL-WRITTEN LONG COPY MEANS YOU'RE IN ANOTHER CLASS OF WRITER."

What do you think of showing work that is not advertising? Things   like art, journal writing, photography, hobbies, etc.?

I like this. A lot. It shows you're not just about advertising—which will make you better at advertising. Advertising shouldn't be formulaic. It's great to see you can bring outside creativity into your work.

Do you have any other advice for a student or junior trying to get into the business?

Don't curse as much as Jim Riswold. [BI]

To see Dylan Lee's work, please visit http://breaking.in

KEVIN RODDY
CHAIRMAN & CCO
RINEY
SAN FRANCISCO

What do you look for in a student book? And what impresses you?

I might be different than some in that regard because I look, first and foremost, at the thinking behind any creative solution. Even more than the idea or execution itself, I look at how they are solving the problem...what's the thinking behind that. Because what I find is that there are a lot of people who approach a problem in a straightforward way and, I think, when you do that you're on quite a crowded highway. A different way at the problem leads more easily to a different idea. A unique idea. It must be relevant to the problem but it will stand out to me more when its approach isn't something I've seen before or easily expect.

Beyond that I look at what I imagine are the clichés of portfolio reviews: quality of the idea and execution of the idea. But more so today than ever before, I'm never more disappointed than when I see a book that's filled exclusively with print ads, television spots, and maybe the occasional microsite thrown in. You'd be surprised at how many of those I still come across. Again, I think more than anything, and this goes back to the first point, I look for big ideas—big ideas that can and are executed in a lot of different ways. I'm never interested in ideas that are executed in a limited fashion. I don't want to see the limits of an idea, I want to see how unlimited it can be. I want to see it live in more than a couple ads. I want to know that the person behind the book knows the value of a big idea to a brand.

For that reason, among others, I don't like to see one-off ads in a book. To me that says the person had an "ad," not an "idea." And as I've said, I'm less interested in ads than I am in ideas. Big ideas. Enduring and engaging ideas. And a portfolio is the place to prove to me that a person thinks that way.

If it's the big ideas that are paramount, does the execution matter? Could sketches be enough, or does the finish matter?

No. I know I said that I look at "the quality of the execution" before. But in that I don't mean its "finish." I mean that, for me, it's important that a book show me that the person understands how to execute an idea. How to think executionally. A great idea can fall apart at any stage of its development, so I want to know that everything matters.

That said, sketches don't necessarily show me a person's finishing ability—but that's okay—I don't judge a book that way. Unless it's something that's actually been produced, I won't judge the level of finish. Only the quality of thinking. I believe "finish" can be taught. But "thinking" is inherent. Someone has to have that or they won't get a job from me.

"I DON'T WANT TO SEE THE LIMITS OF AN IDEA, I WANT TO SEE HOW UNLIMITED IT CAN BE."

I just saw a book yesterday that wasn't at a good degree of finish but I also could tell pretty quickly that the ideas just weren't good enough. So any degree of finish wouldn't have made that good. On the other hand, great ideas will pop out. So all I require is a degree of finish that, one, expresses the idea so I can understand it, and, two, lets me understand that you understand the value of execution.

So, again, that doesn't mean that it has to be heavily finished, but it does mean I have to see what you want to do with it executionally, how you're going to bring it to life, and make it more interesting and engaging. We all know that any idea can be executed in any number of ways, so I want to see the way you do it.

Also, if I'm looking at a copywriter's book, I want to see good art direction, and vice-versa if it's an art director's book. If a writer doesn't care about the way an ad is art-directed, or an art director doesn't care how it is written, they aren't doing their job. Whether the lines between the two are blurring or not, it's a team and they better have a point of view. My art director always made my writing better, and I hope I always made my art director's art direction better. These aren't the days of "I'm going to slide the copy under the door and let somebody else do it." So if the art direction is bad, and you're the writer, you have to take responsibility for that.

That's a good segue to my next question, which is about copy. Do you think it's necessary to demonstrate that you can write?

Absolutely. I think we're losing the copywriter's craft.

Is it necessary to do in a longer form, or are just really good short headlines enough?

Interestingly, I saw a résumé recently where the person had a ton of long-form experience. Great experience from television, Conan O'Brien, Broadway theater, and publishing. Very impressive stuff. But when I met with this person and looked at their advertising work, it wasn't very good. So just because someone can write good long-form stuff doesn't necessarily mean they can write advertising. So I want to see advertising writing.

That said, however, I do love to look at long-form writing as well. It shows me that the person can write. And it also shows me that the person probably loves to write. And I find that important however you do it.

As for advertising writing, I like to see examples of headline writing. A well-crafted headline is a lost art. I love to see people who understand a great headline. I remember hearing stories of how Tom McElligott used to make writers rewrite a headline a hundred different ways, just for the discipline of headline writing. And to ensure that it was crafted in the best way possible. I love that story. I love that kind of discipline. It makes for stronger writers and better advertising. I'm a big believer in not thinking your first draft is your best draft. In not thinking that you can write perfectly, quickly. I love the discipline of writing and rewriting. Walking away and coming back. It's important.

Craft is about really, really hard work. It's about pushing yourself. It seems that the days of doing dozens of layouts to get to one, or writing dozens of versions to get one, are gone. I don't know whether it's the computer, laziness, or just a belief that, "I'm good. Therefore, I only have to do it once because that's going to be the best." Whatever it is, it's just wrong. Put in the work and you will be rewarded.

What do you think about putting things in a book that aren't ads at all?

Love it. Happy to look at it. It goes back to my first answer: "I want to know how your brain works, I want to know how you think, I want to know how you approach a problem or an opportunity." I just want to know that.

Not that long ago I hired a young guy out of school not only because I thought his ad work was quite good, but in large part it was his thinking and his design and the stuff he had done beyond advertising…and the way he had approached it. So yeah, I would encourage you to do all of the above. But definitely not in the absence of things closer to the advertising world.

Do you have any general advice for someone who is putting a book together or trying to get in the industry?

Yeah. My advice would be this: Never think your book is good enough. Ever. I don't care if you've gone to two years of school and paid a lot of money and you now have a book that you think is pretty good and it's time to shop it around. My point of view is, as soon as you leave school, either make the work in there better or do more of it. Always refresh your book. Always look to make it better.

"NEVER THINK YOUR BOOK IS GOOD ENOUGH. EVER."

I believe that if you get a great job and that job is allowing you to do fantastic work, then you're golden. Your book will improve via that. However, most first jobs won't allow that. So I say, work on your book at night. If the job isn't allowing you to do the work you think you are capable of, then do it on the side because I want to see what you're capable of, not necessarily what you're doing. If you allow the agency you work at to define your work, you could potentially be screwed.

When I got my first job, I knew I wouldn't ever be able to show what I was capable of doing. I was writing headlines for a Bed, Bath, & Beyond retail newspaper ads. The visual was dozens of tiny product pictures with prices. I told myself, "This isn't all I can do—if I don't show that I can do more than this, I'll never get out of here." So I kept working at night. And when some work I'd done got me my next job, it still wasn't going to be enough. So I kept working at night. I kept doing work on the side, selling it to clients and getting it in shows until, eventually, I got to a place where I actually was doing the kind of work I thought I was capable of doing.

But if you ever believe this business is easy, if you ever believe you're great, if you ever believe your book is good enough, you're dead—absolutely dead. There are too many people who are better than you. I don't care who you are, there is always somebody better. And so you can't stop. Never ever stop working on your book. Even when you get a job. Keep working on it. Keep making it better. 🄱🄸

To see Kevin Roddy's work, please visit http://breaking.in

MICHAEL SIMONS EXECUTIVE CREATIVE DIRECTOR WIEDEN+KENNEDY SHANGHAI

What do you look for in a student or junior book?

I think, primarily, I look for evidence of a lively mind. Is this somebody who is interested in the way communication works? Are they inquisitive and have a desire to solve problems in interesting ways? I look for a kind of uniqueness in how they see the world, how they use words, how they construct images, or how they use technology.

Are there common problems that you see?

I think an interesting issue you will face if you are a student or just starting out is the variety of opinions your book will elicit. Every one of the luminaries you expose your work to will have a different point of view about it. This can be confusing and disheartening. But the important thing is to stay true to your own unique view of the world. Obviously, you need to listen, take on board what you think is relevant, and reject what you think is not, but try and stay true to who you are. The messed-up way you see the world is what will eventually make someone think it might be a good idea to offer you a job.

"THE MESSED-UP WAY YOU SEE THE WORLD IS WHAT WILL EVENTUALLY MAKE SOMEONE THINK IT MIGHT BE A GOOD IDEA TO OFFER YOU A JOB."

How important is the level of finish?

Sometimes a lot, sometimes a little. If you are demonstrating your ability to think conceptually, it doesn't matter if you write your idea on the palm of your hand. If you are demonstrating your ability to create beautiful design, you probably want to finish your design to the highest standard possible.

Is writing important? Long copy?

Again, it depends. If I'm looking to hire someone who will work on an account that requires a lot of longer copy, then it's very important. If not, it's not.

Writing for film and writing for print and writing for digital are totally different tasks, and many people are only good at one. And I think that's perfectly okay. It's also okay to have a book with no long copy at all.

Obviously, being versatile is the ideal. But it's pretty damn rare. Also, keep in mind, there are many brilliant writers in the world who are not wordsmiths.

Do you like to see "non-ads," such as art, hobbies, personal work, etc.?

I'm kind of suspicious of people who don't have that stuff in their books. A book should be a demonstration of who you are. If your entire life revolves around advertising, you probably aren't a particularly interesting person. And your ads will probably reflect that.

One of the best junior books I ever saw was Joe Staples's book. He'd finished four years at St. Martin's, traveled around the US with his skateboard, and followed his girlfriend to Australia. He had no specific idea what he wanted to do, other than do something in design or art. I opened his book, and he said, "This is a typeface I made out of torn-up London Underground tickets." I turned the page, and he said, "This is a typeface I made out of bent paper clips." I turned the following page, and he said, "I took these photos underwater with a cardboard box with a hole in it." I turned the next page, and, referring to the blurry images I was looking at, he explained how he'd spent several months with a video camera attached to a motorcycle helmet whilst riding a skateboard trying to replicate the effect of looking out a train window because he thought it would animate images the same way film does. I didn't need to turn any more pages. I said, "You're hired."

What happened next was kind of interesting too. All his friends from St. Martin's were starting their own design companies and were working on amazing projects. Being a designer or art-based creative was important to him. So I made him a junior art director. After six months of godawful layouts and absolutely no sign of any design sensibility whatsoever, I sat him down and explained that what I was about to do might fuck him up or it might work out spectacularly. I said, "Joe, you are not an art director. I think you should be a writer." He could have reacted any number of ways, but, fortunately, he embraced the idea. And it worked out spectacularly.

I guess the point is: sometimes, what's in your junior book has little bearing on what you end up doing. As long as the thinking is great, it doesn't matter in what form it's expressed. Joe's curiosity, his incredible logic, and his intelligence were apparent right from the start. Even though he'd never written an ad in his life before, I hired him. BI

To see Michael Simons's work, please visit http://breaking.in

JON BUNNING
ART DIRECTOR &
PHOTOGRAPHER
NEW YORK

What do you look for in a student book? And what impresses you?

Big thinking. Simple execution. And anything that doesn't look like an "ad." The average consumer is barraged with communication overload much like the average creative director is barraged with portfolio overload. You gotta stand out in the clutter.

How important is finish? If ideas are the most important thing, can sketches be enough? Do you look at physical books anymore, or is it all websites?

A great idea is a great idea no matter what it looks like. But in this day and age, with all the resources available, bringing an idea to life is much more possible. So it's hard to be impressed by anything that doesn't look polished. You probably should have a book and a website. Everyone is looking for some kind of digital/interactive ability, so you can't ignore it. Some creative directors still like to hold a tangible book in their hands. Whatever you do, make your work easy to look at.

How important is writing? Do you need to see long copy?

Whether you're a writer or not, you need to be able to write well. We're in the business of communicating. It doesn't matter how you show it, just show that you can write.

What do you think of showing work that is not advertising? Things like art, journal writing, photography, hobbies, etc.

If it's interesting and relevant, show it. Personally, I think a book of ads is boring. Some creative directors would disagree. Treat your book like it's an experience. There should be treats and surprises

along the way. It should blow minds in some parts and crack smiles in others.

> *"TREAT YOUR BOOK LIKE IT'S AN EXPERIENCE. THERE SHOULD BE TREATS AND SURPRISES ALONG THE WAY. IT SHOULD BLOW MINDS IN SOME PARTS AND CRACK SMILES IN OTHERS."*

Do you have any other advice for a student or junior trying to get into the business, either in putting together a book or how to actually start looking for jobs?

Don't overthink your book. Make something that excites you—it will make you more passionate when you share it. It's your body of work. If you don't love it, don't show it. Don't tailor your book to what you think people will like. You're trying to find a place that will let you make the work that you want to make. If someone doesn't like your work, you probably don't want to work there. BI

To see Jon Bunning's work, please visit http://breaking.in

KIM PAPWORTH
CREATIVE DIRECTOR
WIEDEN+KENNEDY
LONDON

What do you look for in a student book? And what impresses you?

It's a weird thing: you look for the signs that there is someone there. If it's a team, it's how that team works as a team; and if it's an individual, that individual. But because you will be asking that person to come into a professional environment where they will be working with clients, I think you're also looking for an ability for that person to adapt to the clients that you have or the clients that you might have in the future. A good way of thinking about it is if you think about actors, you get your Robert De Niros, who tip up in every film, and it's Robert De Niro. And then you get your Dustin Hoffmans, who tip up and you're way surprised...bloody hell! "He's like this this time and he's like that that time." And I think, in some ways, both have their places. I think I'm a bit more of a Dustin Hoffman. I like to see the individual but I like to see the individual change and show themselves in different ways.

So would another way to say that be, you want to see a variety of voices...?

Yes. But it's weird because I'm contradicting myself because I also want to see and feel: "Oh, hang on. There's someone behind all this that I want to get to know and who feels like they've got a slightly different vision." They're not just following what everyone else is doing. So, I have to be careful there, because it's not just like, "I pretend to be this and I pretend to be that and I pretend to be that." But you still want to feel the person behind it.

Yeah. The Coen Brothers make pretty different films but they all feel like they are coming from the same place.

Yes, and Alan Parker I think is quite like that as well. They're not one-trick ponies. They don't go, "Oh, I'm good at this, I'll just carry on doing this." You know, they want to go off and do different things.

Do you like to see finished work or do you like to see sketches or do you care?

I suppose I would start by saying I don't particularly care. I'm looking for all those other things. However, I've learnt through...especially when you're working on Pan-European pieces of work— the word "texture" is very important. Because things can get lost in translation and quite often having too much language is a nightmare so you're

better off keeping things very simple and creating strong textures that make people feel things. And some understanding of, again, that ability to show different tones is important, I think. So years ago, yes, you could go around with just little drawings in your book and it didn't matter how bad or good they were. I think it just shows a level of understanding if you have got some stuff. But I wouldn't say that I want a book where everything is finished to a very high standard. I'm quite happy to see some campaigns that are very sketchy and loose and maybe just a couple that are finished up or even one that's finished up. I think I'd rather have that. Because sometimes, you know, books should be "working books." And if something's too finished up, it's like, well, what you're telling me is that that's the finished thing. Whereas if it's in a sketchy stage, it feels a bit more malleable and I think people talk about it in the more creative way. Because if it's too finished, it's like, "Well, yes, I do like that one," "Well no, I don't like that one." Whereas if it's a bit loose you go, "Oh, that's interesting! Have you thought about this?" You know, you have a different conversation.

"CREATIVE DIRECTORS...WILL PROBABLY ONLY HAVE, IF YOU'RE LUCKY, THREE MINUTES TO LOOK AT YOUR BOOK."

How do you feel about long copy in a student book? Is it important?

That's a difficult question. The hard thing is this: creative directors or the people who are in position to actually give you a job, the conundrum is, they will probably only have, if you're lucky, three minutes to look at your book. You have to realize that: that they are not sitting around all day going, "Oh, I've got an area in my diary today to look at books." I looked at some books today, that is the first time in about two months and I've had half an hour to look at five books. Now, what's difficult about that is I know I've got to get through five books in half an hour. And that means that you have to go at a certain pace, and that certain pace isn't conducive to long copy, and that's my concern. And, in a funny way, that's why a lot of people will encourage students to keep things shorter and simpler, because that's the nature of how these things work. I mean maybe, if you've got a bit of long copy that you're particularly proud of, you need to think of an entertaining way of getting a creative director to read it. And don't do it all the time, just do it once and think of an idea that goes, "I know you're busy, but please take a couple of minutes to read this," you know, and do it that way.

So if it's there and you don't have time to read it then is that okay?

Well, it's okay but I won't read it. That's the problem. I don't think there was any long copy today but if there had been long copy in there, I probably would have gone, "No, I haven't got time to read it.

And so that ends up just being a question mark for you because you don't know if it's good or bad?

Yeah.

What do you think about putting "non-ads" in the book or having a separate book of just other creative stuff?

That's fantastic. I think it's really important. It's something that Tony and I have always…if people come in and we see people with a book which we don't do so much of now but we used to do a lot of it. We want to spend half the time talking to people about what they do outside of their books, and if they've got evidence then that's even better. Because, I think, especially the way that media is going, I think the broader your thinking is, the better chance you've got of your ideas happening, and if they're not right here, well you'll be able to get them to work somewhere else. So I think it's massively important. I mean, I'm disappointed now if I just see a book and it hasn't got anything else in it. I'm more the other way now.

Do you have any other advice on how to improve or how to make a great portfolio?

It's tricky, that. Because it's one thing if you're going along with your book and it's another thing if you're just leaving a book. I remember when I was a student, I kind of did both. I had some relationships with some people where I used to just drop it off and pick it up again. And I never used to get any feedback. And then I'd go back three months later and drop it off again and then pick it up again. I never knew whether they were looking at it or not. But then there were other people where I was seeing them and then go back in three months and see them again. You know, that's a different thing. If you're going to see people, I think…Tony and I always want to talk to people about what else they do. And a lot of people just sort of go, "Oh, go get drunk" or whatever, and Hemant [copywriter who creates drawings and art constantly] does lots of other things.

So then maybe your advice is to be interested in things and to be interesting?

Maybe. You need to be interested in everything, in a funny way. And show that you're inquisitive in all things. It's the inquisitive mind, I think, that gets on well…it's weird. It's like you got to be inquisitive about everything and then incredibly focused about the one—the discipline you're trying to get good at. ⬚

To see Kim Papworth's work, please visit http://breaking.in

MATT VESCOVO ARTIST & ART DIRECTOR LOS ANGELES

What impresses you in a student book?

I think an interesting thing is a balance of voices. They have a voice to their work—there's a tone of voice—but at the same time, that doesn't override what's appropriate for the assignment or the product. Every campaign needs to feel different and have a distinct point of view.

And that they're saying something that's not ambiguous. They're really making a statement that's clear. And I think that's something that helps you empathize, and connects with you, that's relatable. That kind of touches you and hits you that way. And obviously something that's unique, which is hard. Something that has a unique voice and unique ideas, but at the same time, isn't so out there that it's not relatable. And that's a tough balance to get because you don't want to create poetry. You have to create something that people are going to respond to, and that people are going to understand.

"...CREATIVE DIRECTORS LOOK AT STUDENT BOOKS THE WAY CONSUMERS LOOK AT ADVERTISING. THEY DON'T HAVE A LOT OF TIME, THEY'RE BEING HIT WITH A WHOLE LOT OF THINGS, SO YOU REALLY HAVE TO CAPTURE THEM AND GET THEIR ATTENTION AND BREAK THROUGH."

Do you think—and it might be different for writers or art directors—but do you think work needs to be finished, or could it be sketches?

Unfortunately, yeah, I think it does need to be finished. It's so easy to make things look real now. I come from the camp that the idea is the most important thing. And I've found that sometimes in books people rely too much on the looks—making it look slick to make up for the fact that there aren't great ideas. But, even though I feel that way, I think that, if you have a great idea, and it's not done up and executed correctly, that doesn't look real, you're doing it a disservice. It's just that everybody's book is so finished-looking now, people don't do a lot of marker comps. The ideas would have to be really amazing for them to be sketched. You want them to look real and you want them to look polished, but you can't use that as a crutch. The idea has to be great to begin with.

Do you think you need long copy in a book, either as a writer to show you can write or for an art director to show you can lay it out?

It's funny, what's really appropriate about the whole thing, is creative directors look at student books the way consumers look at advertising. They don't have a lot of time, they're being hit with a whole lot of things, so you really have to capture them and get their attention and break through. So it's a very similar kind of obstacle you're confronted with, with the two different groups. It's a very subjective thing. Some people really feel you need that. For writers, you probably want to show you can write copy. I don't know if people are going to read the whole thing. You might want to have some of that in there, but it has to be appropriate for the product. It's got to be for a car, or something that's a big purchase, or something where you want to get more information to the person. You can't just write it because, "Oh geez, I need a long-copy ad. I'll write it for toothpaste." You probably don't need that much information about toothpaste.

What do you think about putting things in the book that are not ads?

Yeah. I'm a fan of doing stuff that isn't advertising, but I always think that should be secondary. But, with that said, when I had a portfolio, I stuck a copy of my "Instructo-art" [see instructoart.com] book in there because I was proud of it, and to me, those were concepts, and it took the form of advertising and animation. So, it seemed relevant to people. And I think it elevated my portfolio. And on my website now—my ad website—I have a link to my Instructo-art website. But for a student book, I think ads need to take precedent. If you have something really great that you've done, that's cool, I would find some way to include it. But again, they need to see a practical application of your talents that can benefit them. You can still say, "Look at this fun stuff." I remember we were interviewing a guy, a friend of mine who does a lot of stuff on the side. He had a pretty good book, but he had a lot of really funny things that he did on the side. Like pranks he was doing, and really crazy, really funny stuff. And it was all very conceptual. That's good. But, if you're showing like, "Here's a painting of my grandma I did," then no. But if it shows, "Hey this guy's a great conceptual thinker," and maybe it's not an ad—then that would benefit you.

Do you have any tips on how to get into the industry, or tips on how to improve as an art director or a writer?

I went to a university where I took a lot of different kinds of classes. I was practically a music minor at Syracuse. And I use music so much in advertising. I also took a lot of philosophy classes. I took all these different classes, and I think what I would say to students is, you can't create advertising in a bubble. What's going to make you great at writing ads is your life experience and relating to people and how they relate to things. So that only comes from doing a lot of different stuff. So you can't just write ads. I mean, that's part of it, but you should take a class in a language, or travel, or do things like side projects just for the hell of it. Because ultimately, that's what you're going to use when you're in your head, when you're concepting, you're going to draw from all these different things. BI

To see Matt Vescovo's work, please visit http://breaking.in

ERIC BALDWIN
CREATIVE DIRECTOR
WIEDEN+KENNEDY
PORTLAND

What do you look for in a student book? And what impresses you?

I look for thinking that is surprising and fresh. I look for things I wish I would have thought of. Since I am an art director with a graphic design background, I place a lot of importance on an art director's design skills. Not only does the idea have to be surprising when it comes to an art director's book, the design and layout are judged under the same lens.

How important is finish? If ideas are the most important thing, can sketches be enough? Do you look at physical books anymore, or is it all websites?

It depends on what I'm looking at and what discipline it's coming from. If it's an art director, the finish better be solid, be it a sketch or layout.

How important is writing? Do you need to see long copy?

If you're a writer, it's really important. If you're an art director, as long as the ideas are great, and the execution is fresh, surprising, and beautiful, I can let the writing slide. That said, I feel really good art directors should be able to write. Personally, I don't really need to see long copy in an ad book. But if you wrote a novel, you might want to mention that.

What do you think of showing work that is not advertising? Things like art, journal writing, photography, hobbies, etc.?

I like to see what creatives do outside of the office. Be it a blog or whatever art you do in your spare time. You can learn a lot about an individual's sensibilities that way. Sometimes that work is more interesting and can land you a job.

"I LIKE TO SEE WHAT CREATIVES DO OUTSIDE OF THE OFFICE… SOMETIMES THAT WORK IS MORE INTERESTING AND CAN LAND YOU A JOB."

Do you have any other advice for a student or junior trying to get into the business?

Work hard and be persistent. Take advice but don't lose your voice.Learn to have a thick skin. And don't put anything in your book that you wouldn't be excited to make at a full-time job. BI

To see Eric Baldwin's work, please visit http://breaking.in

What do you look for in a student book? And what impresses you?

Ideas that want to stand out, that are original, rather than just emulating what's already out there at the moment. And intelligence. Stuff that doesn't just tell you a gag vaguely connected with a product, but gives you some reason to be more interested in the product than you were before, and more likely to want to buy it.

Do you like to see finished work, or do you think sketches are just as good?

No, not at all. I think if we're talking about recent graduates, people trying to get into the industry, definitely just scamps. It's the thinking that you're interested in. The craft skills of design and art direction are entirely different, unless you're looking for a designer.

But art directors?

Art directors as well. I think you will learn more about art direction once you're working than you can possibly learn in a college environment over a couple of years. Art directors still need to be all about the ideas and the thinking behind things, than the visual styles.

Do you think writers need to have a long-copy ad in their books to show they can write, and do you think art directors should have long copy in their books to show they can lay it out?

I don't think it's essential, no. I don't think many people will take the time to read long copy in a portfolio anyway, because time is tight. The copywriting skills of a junior copywriter—to be able to write long copy—is something that you can tackle once you're in the job. But you must show that you are capable of writing headlines. You need to show a good enough command of the language to be able to express what you need to in a concise, persuasive way.

What do you think about including things in a book that aren't ads?

If I'm absolutely honest, I'm not that interested in it. But I know it's fashionable at the moment to hire creatives from all sorts of different areas, possibly not related to advertising at all. Some people think it makes them more interesting. But does it make them better able to produce good advertising? I'm personally not sure. I think the job itself is focused enough. You have to prove, first and foremost, that you can do the job you're there to do. If you've got an advertising problem to solve, then whether any interest in something unrelated is going to help you solve that problem is debatable.

"YOU HAVE TO PROVE, FIRST AND FOREMOST, THAT YOU CAN DO THE JOB YOU'RE THERE TO DO."

What do you think is the best way to improve?

Just never stop. Never be satisfied with anything you've done, really. There is no such thing as the perfect solution to any brief. And that's where research screws us over, because research tries to find the perfect solution. But there isn't the perfect solution. The best you can get is something that's pretty good and will do the job and persuade more people to buy your product or service, than just sticking a bit of branding in front of them or whatever. So you should never think you've done the perfect ad yourself, you should never feel satisfied with it. Always know that if you keep going you'll do something better. Just never be satisfied. If you are too easily satisfied, you become lazy, and possibly arrogant. It is easy to criticize advertising. If you've got it objectively right, then it's down to subjective opinion. If you are your own harshest critic, then you can be more confident in the work you eventually do present.

There is nothing worse than seeing a student portfolio that is too easy to criticize, and seeing that the team has heard it before. If you know something isn't right, change it. Otherwise you've wasted the other person's time and, more importantly, your opportunity. You only get one chance to make a first impression. ▣

To see Nigel Roberts's work, please visit http://breaking.in

NEIL D'SOUZA
CREATIVE DIRECTOR
BLUE APPLE
DUBAI

What do you look for in a student book? And what impresses you?

Understanding. Knowledge. Intelligence. If these are there, I know that wisdom will come with experience.

How important is finish? If ideas are the most important thing, can sketches be enough? Do you look at actual books anymore, or is it all websites?

Sketches are good enough. If you are mailing your book, a brief note, if required, on how you see the finished ad would help. Avoid words like "beautiful," "dramatic lighting," and the like to describe the visual. They might end up making the idea sound cheesy.

With books, make it personal. Websites allow you to show the viewer that you are tech savvy. It also saves time and travel money. I still like to meet people face-to-face with a physical book and a nice cup of coffee. But if you want specific people to view your website, add a personal touch, like mailing your target a creative invitation to view your website.

How important is copy? Do you need to see long-copy ads?

This has become a debating point for the sake of debate. So I'll answer that by asking: "How important is communication?" And, "What do we communicate with?" Words. I can't, even in the very distant future, imagine us waving pictures at each other to communicate. We might some day be able to communicate purely by thought, but it would still be words. The Eskimos have 40 different words to describe the color white. It's words that put things into context. End of debate.

I would love to see long-copy ads. But there is one rule about long-copy ads: they must be engagingly well written. Five hundred words of product information strung together does not count as a long-copy ad. It would show diligence, but won't flag you as a good copywriter.

What do you think of showing work that is not advertising?

Everything that makes you creative is relevant. And a good creative director will recognize your "multifaceted-ness" for what it is: the ability to see creative ideas everywhere. It's a prized gift. You just have to look at the non-advertising interests of the best creative people and you'll realize that they all have this gift for seeing creativity in everything. And it shows in their work.

Do you have any other advice for a student or junior trying to get into the business, either in putting together a book or how to actually start looking for jobs?

Besides having the qualifications, I do believe one of the best ways to break into advertising is through networking. And I don't mean just professional networking. The "six-degrees theory" really does work. Just tell everyone you know that you are very interested in landing a job as a copywriter with an agency. It helps if you're not terribly picky about which agency when you're starting out. Tell your parents, your uncles, aunts, cousins, friends, just tell anyone and everyone you know to keep an ear and an eye out for you. Your family and loved ones are your best networkers. I kid you not, but while I was working in New Delhi, I once landed a job with an agency in New York, totally out of the blue. All because my mum happened to mention me to a friend of hers who was visiting from New York who happened to have a friend in the New York agency.

Call it coincidence, luck, whatever, but the fact is connections happen all the time. But, while waiting for these connections to happen, do your bit by doing the rounds and sticking your foot into doors. Any door. You never know where it will lead. ⒷⒾ

To see Neil D'Souza's work, please visit http://breaking.in

IAN COHEN
OWNER & CREATIVE DIRECTOR
WEXLEY SCHOOL FOR GIRLS
SEATTLE

How do you like to see portfolios?

Links are great. I have zero time in my day, so the easier the better. In person, I like seeing work on a laptop or iPad. But I am fine seeing it in paper form too. For art directors it's nice to see how much care they put into the details of the presentation itself.

As far as getting in touch with me, if you send things to headmaster@wexley.com, it will get to the right person. And that person might not be me.

What do you look for in a student book?

I look for different qualities depending on whether or not I am looking at an art director or writer book. But in general I like seeing a variety of clients and voices, attention to detail, and unique approaches to solving problems.

For writers, I look for someone who has a unique way of approaching ideas and creating different voices for each client. But it is important that those voices and tones are right for the client, not just writing different for different's sake. I also like writing that doesn't feel too perfectly crafted. Any writer can write a nice, crafted headline. It's like any doctor can give someone a shot. So I am not a fan of a book full of headlines. Having some great headlines, so I can see how you tackle them, is great, but try other writing approaches too. I love writing that feels more like a conversation with the consumer than the company talking at the consumer. Also, I want to look at the writing and feel like it could only be for that company. Not anyone else.

One problem with student books is that the student doesn't always get into a real client's problems enough to let those problems help them create a difference. For example, Diadora Soccer is Italian. To compete with Nike and Adidas, that is their one point of difference. But in a student book, you might still see headlines about how hard the shoes can kick. It's more than that. And if you can find that true difference, it will help your concepts and writing and art direction stand out.

For art directors, I look for attention to detail, unique looks, and type choice. I look for a sense of design. A lot of books come to me where all the art director did was put a logo and small line over a big picture. I want to see the craft. I want a book where the art director challenged himself or herself. The same goes for type as I said for writers above. Choosing the right typeface and creating the right tone for the client, not just because the student wanted to try a different typeface, is critical. I also look for simple art direction. It can have a lot going on, but the message has to be crystal clear.

What are some common problems to avoid?

The trend, these days, is to have tons of integrated ideas in your book. Don't get me wrong, I love integrated ideas, we do them every day. But the problem with an entire book full of these is that we don't get to see how you can stay on brand throughout the chain of actual campaigns or client needs. So it is great to see a great iPhone app idea, but how does the art director art-direct the rest of the brand? You can't tell with a little iPhone app. It's cool, but not bigger thinking if we want to hire an art director that will be actually designing across a lot of mediums. I want to make sure you aren't just great thinkers, which you need to be, but that you can do your craft.

I see a lot of art directors that don't art direct and writers that don't write. What I mean by that is that we see tons of books with great thinking and concepts, but as I said before, the craft isn't there. There is no sense of design. No different writing techniques, lots of large pictures with a tagline. Lots of experiential creative that looks great, but is still singular in design and thought. I love these things. I truly do, but when it's the entire book, we can't tell if you love being an art director or writer or if you just like thinking of these fun things. You have to truly love your craft and skill in a small place like ours because we need everyone to be great conceptual thinkers, but we also need them to write and art-direct a ton.

"THAT EXTRA FIVE PERCENT DETAIL OR EXTRA 10 MINUTES CHANGING UP ONE WORD FOR A BETTER ONE CAN MAKE THE DIFFERENCE IN A PIECE."

Ideas are great and half the battle. When we hire juniors or interns, we put them to work on real clients right away. So we need to know they can finish. At a bigger shop you can get away with just having amazing thoughts. We would still find a place for someone with the most amazing ideas on napkins if that person existed. But for the most part I am looking for someone who we can coach, not teach. So for art directors especially we need to see some finish.

You mentioned writing; do you need to see long copy?

Writing is not just important but imperative. Just writing to write is not important though. If you are going to write, write what needs to be said, no more or no less. It's more about what you are writing than how much you are writing. I hate the phrase "long copy," because as a student you set out to write long paragraphs so you will have long copy in your book. Usually it's not because that ad needed long copy. So I like to think of it as a longer conversation.

I won't lie—it's great to see art directors art-direct lots of copy. It's fantastic to see writers who can

write a lot of copy and make it meaningful, but again, only if it makes sense and the product and ad call for it.

Do you like to see "non-ads," such as art, hobbies, personal work, etc.?

I love to see non-ad extras. We have hired people off of those pieces alone. For art directors, seeing their art and sense of design is a nice way to see what they are really into. We've hired a guy off of a video he made that had nothing to do with his school assignments. The more you can do to show your passion and your craft that separates you from the crowd, the better.

Do you have any other advice?

There are a ton of smart people out there with books that blend together. They are cookie cutter. Like in the real world, it is incredibly hard to stand out and do it intelligently. You have to put in the work to stand out. That extra five percent detail or extra 10 minutes changing up one word for a better one can make the difference in a piece. We can tell.

I love to see how passionate a person is about their skill. If you are a writer, show your passion for writing and thinking. If you are an art director or designer, show your passion for the craft and details. For your generation, there is a sense of entitlement out there. We see a lot of students who just want to get into advertising because it seems fun. That's great, but if you can prove that you understand how hard you will have to work, you will already have an advantage. [BI]

To see Ian Cohen's work, please visit http://breaking.in

RICHARD BULLOCK
DIRECTOR
HUNGRY MAN, UK &
REVOLVER, SYDNEY

Interviewed at 180, Amsterdam.

What do you look for in a student book? And what impresses you?

I think, just people's ingenuity to solve problems other than just with an ad. People who are able to demonstrate their ability to think outside putting things on a page. Do they have any sort of marketing ideas in there? Or a sense of solving a problem for a business? As well as doing an ad, which is only one way to solve a problem. So things outside that are clever.

Do you care if a book is full of sketches, or do you like to see finished, comped-up work?

Historically, a lot of people go around saying, "Oh, we should just do sketches and that should be fine," but the reality is that times have changed and if somebody has an ability to use the tools that we have now, a computer, a Mac, to do things up, if you have those skills you should demonstrate them. Because putting things down in a nice way is what clients kind of look for now. It's like saying, "Boy wasn't it nice when we could write beautifully with quill pens"; it's just not the reality anymore for clients. And if somebody has also collaborated with an art director, and you've seen that come out through the work, then the more the student can hit the ground running and have those skills, the more valuable they are to the company.

Do you think it is important to have long copy in a book?

Yes and no. I mean, I'd rather see that somebody had written an article, or had done a long-copy piece of writing that they'd submitted to a newspaper or something. That would be more interesting to me than a long-copy print ad. It vaguely tells me that they can write, but you know, a long-copy ad as a solution to an advertising problem is just a technique. It's not an idea or anything like that. But people's ability to write, even if they write the strategy, about why they did a certain project, you can see through that writing. So if they write a strategic piece, you can see how intelligent they are, and how they are able to get their thoughts down on paper. It doesn't necessarily have to be in a long-copy print ad.

"THE BEST CREATIVES ARE THE ONES WHO, IF THEY GET ADVERTISING TAKEN AWAY, THEN THEY'LL START FASHIONING A FREAKING BIRDHOUSE OR SOMETHING BECAUSE THEY JUST HAVE TO BE CREATIVE."

Do you think it's important to include things that aren't ads in a book?

Yeah, I think it's really, really important. I think if people have anything that they do on the side, or if they're into designing their own T-shirts, or they've written a short story, or they're into illustrations and drawings or sketchbooks or photography, anything that shows their way, that they observe the world and their interpretation of it, is valuable. It shows that the person is a natural creative. And what we look for a lot is that advertising is one way of being creative in business. But there's a lot of ways of being creative. And the best creatives are the ones who, if they get advertising taken away, then they'll start fashioning a freaking birdhouse or something because they just have to be creative. And it's not just about showing how cool you are, it's about expressing that you're a natural creative person. And we really look for that in people, to see that it just comes out of them no matter what. Because then we know that if they come into work in the agency, even if they're faced with knock-back after knock-back, or it's hard for the client, or the client is being really tough, the naturally creative person will just keep going, because that's inside them—they just have it. But the person who's in it because it's cool to be in advertising, or they want to win awards or something, will fall by the wayside, compared to the natural person. And the natural creative will also look for solutions that aren't just around them in the world of advertising.

Do you have any tips for someone who is just starting out?

The best way to improve is to be around an agency at any cost. To try and get in and work, and find somebody who's an advisor and listen and get in, just get in somewhere to get work experience, I think. Even if you can't get an actual job, just get in and work for free, and visit agencies all the time and show your book, and get your book looked at and commented on by different people. And you'll soon realize that, first, there are a lot of different opinions, but you'll also find people that you really like and respect. And one or two mentors may well be the difference between getting into the business, or not. You know, finding that person that wants to help you and push you along. [BI]

To see Richard Bullock's work, please visit http://breaking.in

Do you think it's important to have finished work that looks great, or are ideas more important and sketches are okay?

I think ideas are the most important thing. And so that can certainly be sketches, at least for a writer. I think you help yourself, though, if you have great ideas and tighter comps.

Do you think long copy is important to have?

What I would say to writers is it's okay to have a lot of conceptual ads, one-liners, television maybe, that doesn't even have copy in it, but what I think you have to have in your portfolio is some long-copy stuff. Don't put a novel in a portfolio because nobody has time to read it—but if there are some great short stories a writer has done, or some long-copy ads, that at least shows the voice that a writer would have. I think that's really important. That's what I look for now, and I think there's not much of that in most portfolios. I think they're all typical "conceptual one-liners."

"STOP LOOKING AT AD BOOKS BECAUSE THEY'RE ALL THE SAME."

SUSAN HOFFMAN
EXECUTIVE CREATIVE DIRECTOR
WIEDEN+KENNEDY
PORTLAND

What do you look for when you're looking at a student book—what impresses you?

Well, I think the thing that I'm sick of in student books is that they all look alike, and they all sound alike. And so I look for new ways to communicate, whether it be from a layout standpoint or a communication standpoint. But if I just see another "good headline" or another "good visual," I'm not so impressed with it. So that's the main thing, is looking different than any other book that comes in.

For an art director, I'm not interested in a conceptual art director only; I want a conceptual art director who knows how to design. I think the craft of design has disappeared. I don't think that's being taught in the schools. I think it is primarily because the teachers aren't being hired to do that. They're hired to teach ads…I'm forgetting where [James] Selman went to school. Selman was a great art director, and that's because he came from a design background.

Did he go to Cranbrook?

Cranbrook. Thank you very much. That's what it was. So, design is super important to me. If an art director just showed me a bunch of great ideas, and they looked like shit, forget it.

And what do you think about putting things in a book that aren't ads?

Yes, I think that's absolutely fine. Show anything that's inventive. And show that you're digitally fluent. That's my rule now. I don't want a writer or an art director who is not digitally fluent. That doesn't mean you have to put a whole site together yourself, but you have to understand how to concept digitally, and an art director has to understand how to design digitally.

What do you think is the best way for a student to improve?

That's such a tricky thing. I would say don't look at ad books. Stop looking at ad books because they're all the same. I have ads in my portfolio that are the ads in those ad books now. Maybe just a different typeface. Look at editorial magazines. Look at Nylon magazine. Look at weird magazines. Look for new and inventive editorial ways to think about advertising. That's what I would say. Be very proficient on the computer. Especially art directors. I wouldn't hire an art director who didn't know how to sit down at the computer and do a layout. BI

To see Susan Hoffman's work, please visit http://breaking.in

STEVE McELLIGOTT
FREELANCE CREATIVE DIRECTOR
NEW YORK

What do you look for in a student book? And what impresses you?

It's a tough question. I think I look for—and this sounds cheesy—but I look for passion. It does sound really, really trite. But you can tell the difference between somebody who is just following the routine from their ad school and just doing assignments, and somebody who really, really, really has the hunger, and really has a deeper understanding of what they're doing and why. And I think that comes through really quickly with anyone who cares, and for the other people who are just sort of filling in the blanks.

How do you think it comes through?

Good question.

Maybe that's a hard question.

I don't know. I think it's one of those things you can't put your finger on, honestly. Like, you know it when you see it, and you don't see it very often, which is why you know it. Because I think there's so few people out there—it's really 1 in a 100. I see a lot of books. They always shuffle them to me. And this kid came in about three months ago. And his book was so clearly apart from everybody else's. And I talked to him for five minutes, and I instantly knew this guy was going to be a smash hit. And it wasn't because he was just finishing assignments for some teacher somewhere. It was because he really gave a fuck.

Do you think that sketches can be enough to get into the business, if the ideas are good enough?

I don't think they can. I don't think so anymore. I think things need to be really polished. I'd hate to say that. There's always that story about...you know who Jeff Kling is?

Yeah.

Did you ever see his book?

Yeah.

I think it's up there in one of those One Show [annuals]. Like "That's so fucking great!" that there was a time when you could do that. But I don't think you can anymore. I think it needs to be really buttoned down. There's so much competition.

Do you want to see long copy?

Yeah, I definitely do. I think there's a real dearth of people who can really write. And I think writing is so important. Not just for the ads, but if I'm going to hire somebody...people who can't write, can't communicate—they suck. And they're all over the place. There's all these writers in this business who really don't know how to write. They can't craft a sentence. And, it comes through in more than just the ads. It comes through in how they present work to the clients, and how they communicate with people, how they present work to you, and how you read their work. So, to me, it really matters. I don't care what anyone else says. People say "long copy is dead." Well, big deal. If you're not going to show me long-copy ads, show me a great piece of writing. But to me, it's fundamental and critical.

"I THINK ONE OF THE PROBLEMS WITH AD SCHOOLS TODAY IS THAT THEY'RE SUCH FACTORIES THAT A LOT OF STUDENTS REALLY LOSE THEIR VOICE. OR MAYBE THEY JUST NEVER FIND IT."

For art directors, it's not as much. I could take it or leave it, to be honest. I'd like to see long-copy ad, just to see what they can do with it. But I don't really care. But even with an art director, I'd love to see if they can write. What surprises me is that, even at this level, after being in this business for 10 years, I'm surrounded right now with people who aren't able to communicate through writing. And it just blows. And it's horrible. I would never hire anybody without knowing that they can actually… at least that they can craft an email.

You mentioned writing that's not ads—short stories. What do you think about putting things that aren't ads like that into a book?

I think it's great if it's edited wisely. I remember this kid who came to me, and he had an okay book—he was a writer—but it didn't show that he had writing skill. And so I suggested to him that he go find something, dig up something, pick something out from before, or come back with something new, or whatever. And so he went in, and he clearly just went into his computer files, and just found things that he had written, like, these random emails, and his letters to friends, and it was so messed up. Because one, I didn't

care about all this stuff, and two, they weren't well written. But I really think it's great to have anything you can to support your work…and also show what your personality is. But, that said, your personality should come through really clearly in your book. And I think, only in about one percent of books are you actually able to read somebody's personality. But when I look at a book, it should be like a dinner conversation. It should be, when I walk away half an hour later, I've got a pretty good feeling for this person.

So you want their voice to come through in the ads.

I want it to come through really clearly. I just don't want it to come through, I want it to shout through. It doesn't mean it has to be a loud voice to shout through.

But, it's a balance right, because you also want them to be able to take on different voices, appropriate to each brand…

Yeah, definitely, but I think no matter what brand you're working on, your voice will come through. I think one of the problems with ad schools today is that they're such factories that a lot of students really lose their voice. Or maybe they just never find it. But I don't feel like I see a lot of the person coming through in any books I see, ever.

And do you have any tips for anyone who's starting out, trying to get into the business?

Don't. Just kidding.

I'd say confidence. Even if you don't know what you're doing, if you say anything confidently, people will believe it. And it will get you 75 percent of the way there. This is a business full of really insecure people and insecure clients. And if you believe in what you're saying, other people will believe it. And it's amazing what can happen. And that's not always a good thing but it's amazing. It's hard to be confident when you're working in a creative field, because it's so subjective. But if you go in with a strong belief and a strong argument for anything, people will shut up and listen. And it seems like an obvious thing to say, but I don't think it is obvious. I think when people actually get into the workplace, everybody kind of falls into a…no matter where you are, even if you're at Wieden… I think people do kind of fall into their place. Everybody acts pretty meek. But the squeaky wheel really does get ahead. And it doesn't mean you have to be a little bitch, it just means, "Always have an opinion." Like you should never, never have a moment where you don't have an opinion, ever. Even if you don't have an opinion, make one up. That's what I say. How's that?

That's good. Thank you. BI

To see Steve McElligott's work, please visit http://breaking.in

**RYAN GERBER
CREATIVE DIRECTOR
WIEDEN+KENNEDY
SHANGHAI**

What do you look for in a student or junior book?

In simple terms, I'm most interested in who you are as a person. Maybe you're a bit crazy, but you see things that others don't. Or you hate advertising but you feel like you can somehow fix it by working from inside the machine. Or maybe you're neither of those things, but you've got impeccable taste and you're a bit of an asshole. At the end of the day, I'm not hiring your book; I'm hiring the brain and the guts that crafted that thing. That's what I'm after.

So your book should speak volumes on your behalf. Because before I'll want to talk to you, I'll probably want to thumb through your work, be it on your website or iPad or other clever thing I haven't yet seen. And I'll want to see the types of things that spur you on. For better or worse.

I once had a guy come in and show me a bunch of work I could tell he hated, but it had gotten produced and was shiny, so he thought I wanted to see that shit. After talking to him for a bit, I got the sense that there was more to this kid than this shiny turd he had just shown me, so I asked him

to show me the stuff he didn't put in his book. And there it was. The spark that he had snuffed out at his last shitty job, which earned him a nice paycheck and a bronze pencil. I hired him off of three sketches and a personal project that he had made while he was still in school. His personality gave me a reason to probe, but had I just looked at his website beforehand, I would never have met with him in the first place. Be confident in the work you love. Then take your lumps.

"BE CONFIDENT IN THE WORK YOU LOVE. THEN TAKE YOUR LUMPS."

In regard to the actual work, I tend to be more interested in the types of things that catch me off guard or surprise me. It's not an easy task, but you'll get a lot further with me if I see some insane thought that changes a business or a project that challenges culture in some weirdly interesting way. It's not that I might not like that funny video you made or smirk at the clever one-off print ad that you spent all semester crafting, but you need to be honest with yourself when you're putting this body of work forward. Ask yourself, "Is this a good representation of who I am and the type of work I want to be doing?" and "Is it any good?" Be honest.

I do also like to connect with the work I'm looking at, so if your work manages to grab a tear or a giggle out of me, I'll probably remember you.

Are there common problems that someone could avoid?

This is a funny question for me, as I've spent the last two years of my life living in China. So the types of problems and things I'd say to generally avoid has evolved for the region and may be a bit different than if I were back in the US or even in Europe. But there is also some common ground.

First off, don't fucking steal. Just don't do it. It's weird that you need to say that out loud, but it's amazing how common it is. I've had an art director come in with a book full of work he couldn't explain. In fact, there was one project in particular that was really smart, but poorly crafted, so I pressed him on it, seeing as he was an art director and wanted to be one here. Turned out, the reason he couldn't explain it was because it wasn't really his work. It was something his partner had done with another art director, but he made some subtle tweak to the layout after the fact. Don't do that. It's not cool.

Second, show me the stuff you're proud of. Don't ask me to sit through 20 terrible spots for McDonald's if you only really liked one of them. I probably won't care about that 15-second Chicken Nugget cut-down unless it's amazing. So spend your time with me wisely, show me the stuff you think truly represents who you are, and stand by it. I don't have to love everything I see. Again, I'm not looking to hire your book, but I do need to see who you are.

Lastly, and this is more of an Asia-Pacific thing. Try to avoid filling your book with scamp work. It's an interesting conundrum in this part of the world, as clients will actually pay to have scamp work made, but if you couldn't get them to buy it as an actual ad, then what's the point? Why would you be of any use to me? I'd rather see an ad that a client killed because it scared the shit out of them, than a scamp ad that the client paid for, but only to be used as an award-show entry. That said, if you do show me a scamp ad, it had better knock my socks off or it'll be even more of a disappointment than it already was.

How important is the level of finish? Could sketches be enough?

Really depends on the gig you're going after. I've hired people off of sketches. Mostly writers. But I've also passed on people because of them. It really depends on the person and the magic imbued in those crude little drawings. If it's an amazing idea told in two scribbles and a line of copy, that may be enough. But don't bank on it.

Some CDs might say that they don't care and then go on about how ideas are what actually matters or some bullshit like that, but that's probably not true. It's really hard not to expect some level of polish these days. I had a team send me a video demo of a fake digital app that they came up with for Nike and it blew me away. The idea was sharp, but they packaged it in a way that not only communicated the thought concisely, but it fucking looked better than a lot of the real case studies I've seen of late. The production quality was really top shelf. Now, was all of that necessary for me to get the idea? Not really. But I watched the video all the way through and replied to them almost immediately. So the polish did help.

These days, I see less sketches and more comps with varying degrees of polish. If you are an art director looking to be hired as such, I tend to be a bit more critical of that. Craft should be in your wheelhouse, so if you comp a mediocre thought into a terribly crafted photoshlop-splosion…well, I may not look at the next thing in your book. So art directors should be able to make stuff and have a fundamental grasp of design. Something that seems to be lacking these days.

A writer I might approach differently, depending on how creative they got with what they had. A friend of mine once applied for a job with a handwritten letter, ripped from a spiral notebook, and folded it like a six-year-old would. It wasn't more than two paragraphs, but it was quirky and weird, and it was one of the funniest things I've ever read. It also got him the job. You gotta work with what you've got.

I also like creatives who aren't afraid to solve things outside of their respective disciplines. I like art directors who can write and writers who have good visual sense. Creatives who don't think in terms of a media buy. Advertising as it exists now is a clusterfuck of change and distraction. I might not ask you to write me a script or make me an ad or be "digital." I might need you to design a chair or invent a sport. So if I feel like you can tackle any strange thing that I toss at you, based on the work you've put in front of me, you'll have my attention.

Having said all of that, and not to belabor the point, there is something to be said for craft. Even a book of sketches can be pulled together nicely. I grew up working with my hands, so I appreciate people who can make things, and I have a fondness for people who can make things well.

What about the craft of writing? Do you need to see long copy?

I like words, but I don't much care for advertising

copy, so if that's all you've got, then you're at a bit of a disadvantage. A writer should exist beyond a crafted headline and some long copy. Show me how you think, that's key.

I'm not looking for any particular length or format. I just want a bit of a window into all the clever little things bouncing around in your skull. I had a writer, who was also a musician, send me his album alongside his portfolio. The lyrics he wrote for that were much better than a lot of the copy he had in his book. But I could tell there was a good writer buried beneath some of the terrible ads he was showing me—he was still finding his voice.

Nowadays, there are so many places for the written and spoken word to exist, so if you can write, it really doesn't matter what it is or how long. I know a female writer who began an email exchange and fake relationship with a Russian mail-order bride and kept a blog with every love letter to and from. It was funny.

Of course, this isn't to say that I won't need to see how well you can craft an ad. If I'm hiring you as a writer, there is a good chance that I may ask you to write some ad copy, so being able to craft your words is important. It's just not my defining criteria. I'll want to see more interesting things come out of you as we begin making things together.

Being in China changes my relationship with writers a bit, as there are fundamental language issues. I've had to learn to adapt and to trust the people I work with who understand the things that I don't. But you do tend to see a lot of flowery language used in marketing here. Marketers talking to themselves. So I find that in this market, having a voice and a point of view is even more significant. Not everybody (some of the other agencies and clients) appreciates or wants that here. We do.

Do you like to see "non-ads," such as art, hobbies, personal work, etc.?

Yes and no. Mostly, it's fantastic. It's a shortcut into your being, which is the thing I'm after. "Who the hell are you, and why are you here?"

On the other hand, it can be terribly annoying if it has no point. So make sure it helps tell your story

and gives a clear path to understanding how you think and how you solve problems. If you come to me wanting to be an art director and then proceed to show me some random portfolio of Instagram photos you took of you and your cat, I might stop liking you as a human being. If you show me a book of still-life sketches you've painted of fruits and vegetables, I'll actually leave the room.

So just make sure it helps with whatever your end goal is. I recently met a creative who has an entire side business building custom motorcycles in Beijing. It's pretty amazing, and you really get a sense of who he is through the bikes that he builds and the way he puts his wares out into the world. You want to leave us with a lasting impression of who you are and how your brain works. So everything you show, whether it's an ad or some random side project, make sure it's geared toward what you ultimately want that lasting impression to be. If the impression you want to leave is "Terrible creative, but excellent use of gouache on that papaya," then bring in the still lifes.

Do you have any other advice?

Good luck. I wouldn't want to be in your shoes right now. This is a tough gig, and it gets harder by the day. This career, like any, has its perks and its pitfalls. Figure out what you want to get out of this thing and go after it.

"CHANCES ARE THAT THE PEOPLE YOU MEET AT THIS STAGE OF YOUR CAREER WILL BE THE ONES WHO GET YOU WORK LATER. SO DON'T BE AN ASSHOLE."

Getting your foot through that first door can feel insurmountable, but don't be afraid of rejection. Embrace it and move forward. Consider the places you want to work and the people you want to report to. These people will have a profound effect on how you end up doing things—don't take that for granted. You may not want to work for a guy like me, or maybe you do. You have choices. It's not as simple as all that, but in a way it is.

You're at the start of your career, so don't be afraid to experiment and explore. Try some shit out, make stuff, go play in a medium you don't fully understand, challenge yourself, travel. Be brave. Chances are that the people you meet at this stage of your career will be the ones who get you work later. So don't be an asshole. You have a lot to be grateful for and a lot more yet to still learn. Soak it up, and never be comfortable. This industry will change again and again, and you may or may not want to change with it. That's cool, it's your career; just be prepared for it. This job can be full of uncertainty, but it can also be one hell of a ride. So have fun. There are far worse jobs to be had. 🄱🄸

To see Ryan Gerber's work, please visit http://breaking.in

JON KREVOLIN
GROUP CREATIVE DIRECTOR
360I
NEW YORK

What do you look for in a student book? And what impresses you?

Different thinking. Bold ideas. Understanding of human nature and strategy. And something that makes me laugh. Or cry.

How important is finish? If ideas are the most important thing, can sketches be enough?

For a copywriter it's all about ideas. An art director needs a bit more finish, though.

How important is writing? Do you need to see long copy?

It's not essential, but it's always good to show you can do long copy. It shows you really know how to write.

What do you think of showing work that is not advertising?

Other stuff is great and encouraged. However, show you can do advertising too.

Do you have any other advice for a student or junior trying to getinto the business?

Perseverance, baby. Even when you make it, that's what's going to help you get ahead. Don't take "no" for an answer. 🄱🄸

To see Jon Krevolin's work, please visit http://breaking.in

WILLIAM GELNER
CHIEF CREATIVE OFFICER
180
LOS ANGELES

What do you look for in a student book? And what impresses you?

Fast ideas. You'd be surprised at how many books have slow ideas. Intricate flow charts, multiple steps, a confusing and tiring journey. Yes, I want ideas that are whole and 360-degrees. But tell it simply. That said, the other issue that I see with books is the flip side of that: a lot of books coming out of school that are all visual solutions. That's really tricky when you're trying to hire a writer. Maybe it shows that they can think visually and can distill things down, but what about when you need an idea that is simple, well written, and to the point? You'd be surprised at how many writer books don't have good, concise writing in them. Just verbal diarrhea. That says "lazy" to me. I don't like lazy.

That was actually one of my follow-up questions: do you think long copy is necessary? And, you sort of answered that, so let me ask it this way: do you think writers need to demonstrate writing in ads, or could it be in something else?

I think it could be something else, as long as it's not 30 pages. I don't want to—again, we're looking for people who can write well. That means simple, concise, insightful. We are in the digital age. And digital takes many forms. It's not just websites. It's more about content and conversation. And content needs to be articulated somehow. It can be mobile, for example. Or it can be on-demand content, or it could be television shows, or whatever. So there's different varying degrees of writing that is necessary to communicate those kinds of ideas. That said, no one has the time to sit down and go through a book and read multiple pages of stuff. They just don't. So, my advice to anyone who wants to demonstrate that they're a good writer would be, "Have a balanced book." That means some all-visual solutions, some old-school headline ads, that just shows you can write a headline. I mean, we still make print ads; out-of-home and online banners is the same principle. And then people who can write ideas. So, sum up an idea before any campaign that's in your book. Write that paragraph, three or four sentences, with a heading. That's enough. If you can write that setup for an idea succinctly, clearly, and well, then demonstrate the idea in various ways, to me you've demonstrated that you can write. You don't have to write three long-copy ads to demonstrate that you can write. In fact, I think long-copy ads are the easiest to write because you have a lot of opportunities to get your point across. I think it's much harder to write succinctly. It's that famous quote: "I apologize in advance for writing such a long letter. I didn't have time to write a short one."

Do you think ads in a book can be sketches, or do you think ads need to be finished on the computer?

There was a time when I felt it could be either, as I just look for ideas. But expressing the idea visually is very important. It shows craft and care. One or two sketch ideas added in there are fine. I hate to say it but you need to comp most of it.

What do you think about putting things in a book that aren't ads?

I think it's good, to a point. It gives you insight into what gets them off, what makes them tick. I do want to know if you're a good photographer or musician or artist. Just do it gingerly. Don't make this a personality contest. Because ultimately, it's about the work and the interview. I'm not hiring you for your love of camping and the great outdoors.

"YOU'D BE SURPRISED AT HOW MANY BOOKS HAVE SLOW IDEAS. INTRICATE FLOW CHARTS, MULTIPLE STEPS, A CONFUSING AND TIRING JOURNEY."

Do you have any tips for someone who's trying to get into the business?

When you're putting together your book, and you're looking for inspiration, don't look primarily to the award shows. Find inspiration from doing cool shit. Find it in life. Go out there and do things. There's a quote from John Hegarty: "Do interesting things and interesting things will happen to you." I love that quote because, to me, it says that if you're out there living life, and doing really interesting and cool things, you're going to bring that back to the work you do. There's nothing worse than when every single thing in someone's book feels like it's an ad that they saw in Archive [magazine]. And the second thing would be: Get to the point in your book…make sure that it's a quick read, that it's good, that it's more of a coffee-table book than a novel. Make it quick, make it fun, make it interesting, make it balanced. BI

To see William Gelner's work, please visit http://breaking.in

MITCHELL RATCHIK
FREELANCE CREATIVE DIRECTOR
NEW YORK

What do you look for in a student or junior book?

A student book should be a work of love. This is before you've actually "produced" anything or had clients or CDs alter your work. That being said, competition is fierce! I personally look for good thinking above all. I put on a second lens for art directors; they need to demonstrate good type and layout abilities. I'm more forgiving with writers. The best ones solve a problem using a unique perspective, and then they execute it well. A student book should be an extension of your personality and aesthetics.

Common problems and things to avoid? Examples?

The first big mistake students make is putting work in that they've actually "produced" but doesn't really reflect their best thinking. My advice is "Don't do it." I'd rather see smart thinking and the ability to come up with a visual vernacular than some lame ad that actually ran. Also: be focused! The second big mistake is books that have a little of everything, but no focus. If you're going into advertising, you need ads. It's okay to show some other stuff as well, but the focus needs to be advertising.

How important is the level of finish? Could sketches be enough?

Finish is very important. For art directors, it's essential. Nothing makes me angrier than an art director who can't design or has no understanding of type, color, and layout. I don't want to hear it; go back to school and do the work. There is just no excuse. Some might say that's harsh and art directors direct and are not responsible for designing. My response to that is: you have no idea what you're talking about. Junior art directors are in the trenches and are expected to execute! There is no excuse now that everyone has computers and can make their comps tight. And writers need to

make an effort to find an art director to help them lay out their ideas. Make a flyer and post it up.

Sketches are great when you are concepting. I personally forbid my students to use the computer during the concepting phase. Get the idea first, then execute. I always use the hallway/room metaphor. Every idea is a room. Don't just walk into one room and stay there. Walk down the hall, peek into all the rooms, and then go back and explore the ones that looked good.

Is writing important?

Writing is extremely important! It's just as much of a process as design; you can tell how much effort has been put in. Every writer has a different process; however, I find that there is no substitute for volume. Although I'm an art director, I've been writing more and more. It's just part of the job. And it's becoming more and more enjoyable. With scripts I find that it's just good to get it down on paper in bold strokes first. Then go back and craft the language.

> *"NOTHING MAKES ME ANGRIER THAN AN ART DIRECTOR WHO CAN'T DESIGN OR HAS NO UNDERSTANDING OF TYPE, COLOR, AND LAYOUT."*

It's good to know how to write long copy, but not essential. It's a good skill to have, and if you can do it well and learn how to craft your language, you'll never go hungry. It's also important for art directors to know how to set long copy.

Do you like to see "non-ads," such as art, hobbies, personal work, etc.?

I personally do. It shows that you have other interests besides advertising. It's part of our job as creatives. This is the other metaphor I use with my students. Think of a doughnut; the hole is the status quo and the normal people. And outside the doughnut are the creators and content—artists, musicians, designers, news, movies, actors, etc. It's your job as a creative to be the doughnut and observe all that content. Then translate it and feed it back to the center. You need to be the doughnut and be part of both worlds. This is what will make you valuable as a creative!

The Rolling Stones didn't imitate the Beatles; they looked back at old blues. If you're going to reference something (I was once told a good creative steals with both hands), reference the original. Don't just look at old Archive magazines or One Show annuals. Those people who eat, breathe, and poop advertising are boring, and their work is going to be boring! Congratulations, you're doing another version of someone else's creative. I'm not saying you have to be original with every idea, just realize the importance of ingesting the culture around you. Seek it out. It's part of your job (which makes it cooler than working in a bank).

Other advice about portfolios or getting into advertising?

Keep your book to about seven to eight campaigns. Only put the best thinking in. You are your best critic. Be extremely harsh on yourself. Get lots of different opinions. Show your friends; if they keep telling you how great everything is, wake up—they're not your friend! They are just blowing smoke up your tuchus. Get real criticism and never be satisfied. Your book will and should evolve with you.

As for getting your foot in the door...by any means necessary. Get an internship, work the mailroom, work as an assistant (I know several very successful creatives that came in that way). And most important: don't give up. When showing your book, look for real feedback. If you didn't get the job, follow up and ask them how you can improve your book. BI

To see Mitchell Ratchik's work, please visit http://breaking.in

JASON BAGLEY
CREATIVE DIRECTOR
WIEDEN+KENNEDY
PORTLAND

What do you look for in a student book? And what impresses you?

Hmm. Perhaps I should have reviewed these questions. I would say I want to be surprised and delighted. I don't know if I should use the word delighted, maybe just surprised. It's a surprisingly rare quality in a portfolio.

Surprise is surprisingly rare.

Yes, surprise is surprisingly rare.

Is it just breaking out of formulas?

I think it takes a while to break out of formulas, and I understand...when I was first starting out in advertising, I was guilty of the same thing. But what I don't want to see is a bunch of clever or effective solutions—communication solutions to a client's problems.

You don't want to see that?

I don't want to see just that. And that's what you see a lot of. It's like, "Yeah that's a good concept and they effectively communicated the point of what the client would have wanted." But it's cold and sterile and boring and unsurprising. And I think you've got to...for me, I want to see something where there's personality and more of a human voice coming through so it doesn't just feel like a corporation is communicating with me. It feels more like an actual personality is coming through. I also try to ask myself, "Is something good for an ad? Or it is just good?" Like, "Is it just great regardless of what it is? Is it just great entertainment and something that gets you excited or surprises you or just blows your mind?" A brief is like a math problem, and the challenge is that when we come up with a solution, there's an excitement because we have technically "solved" it. But that excitement can cloud our objectivity.

Simply coming up with an answer isn't enough—we have to come up with a beautiful, or inspiring, or funny solution that gets people to look at the problem in a new way. I like to ask myself, "If it wasn't mine, and I saw it in a magazine, or on TV, or online, would it inspire me, or make me laugh? Is it something I would see on TV and laugh out loud or talk to my friends about? Or is it just an ad, and do I only like it because it's mine?" I think the vast majority of the time, it's just an ad, and we only like things because we came up with them. So, in the very rare times I see a book that really stands out, you can tell the creator of that book has a strong voice, and they've broken out of that mold, of the standard, responsible, workmanlike ad structure.

"SIMPLY COMING UP WITH AN ANSWER ISN'T ENOUGH—WE HAVE TO COME UP WITH A BEAUTIFUL, OR INSPIRING, OR FUNNY SOLUTION THAT GETS PEOPLE TO LOOK AT THE PROBLEM IN A NEW WAY."

How important is finish? If the ideas are good enough, can sketches be enough? And also, do you just look at websites now? Or do you actually look at paper books?

It's a little bit of both on the last question. But it depends if it's a writer or an art director, or a hybrid.

Do you look at websites initially and then, you bring them in, and then, at that point you look at books or…?

At Wieden+Kennedy we have a recruiter, so often she will bring a hard book over. But I would say more and more it's a website that I see. And if it's more of a writer, then I don't care at all about the finish. If it's a strong idea and the writing's great…the most famous example of that at Wieden+Kennedy is Jeff Kling's portfolio, which I actually saw when I was interviewing here and

it was just a bunch of white pieces of paper with hand-drawn ads, and you could tell how great he was. It was everything that you would want to see from a writer and it was almost made stronger by the fact that it was so unfinished.

Okay, for an art director?

Obviously, for an art director, that's a different ball game. I think it is important that they show what they can do.

What about copy? Is it important to have a long-copy campaign? Is it important to show that writers can write? Is it important for art directors to show that they can art-direct long copy?

I think it's nice. It's a bonus. I think the writer needs to show that they can at least do whatever copy is necessary for the ads that are in their portfolio. I don't know. For me it's not a deal breaker if there's no long copy in there. Most creative directors are so busy, and are so rushed when they have to look at portfolios, that they end up skipping most of the long-copy stuff anyway. So I wouldn't say it's essential, and more and more we live in a world of sound bites and very, very short copy.

So as long as whatever copy is in there is really good…

Is really good.

What do you think about putting things in a book that aren't ads?

I think it's fine, but if you're a copywriter, I really don't care about your photography. And again, this gets back to the fact that most creative directors are so busy that…I mean I don't really have time to read your blog and look at your home movies and that kind of stuff. I think it's great to do all that stuff and to have it. And if there's just a mind-blowing blog entry and you want to feature that and not make me go to your website, not make me go to your blog, that's fine. But I would say overall, the rule should be make your book something that a creative director can consume in as short an amount of time as humanly possible. Because if you make them work, they're either just going to skip over stuff or they're just going to stop altogether and put it off for when they have more time, which will probably be never. So I would just keep it very short and not put anything that's not really necessary and…how can I say this, articulate this better? I think you should have the minimum amount in your portfolio to blow someone away and not a piece more. Not a word more than that.

And do you have any other advice that you would give to someone who's just starting out, either in terms of putting together a book or in terms of starting to go around and show your book?

In terms of putting together a book, it took me a while to figure out what I wanted to do in advertising and the type of work I wanted to do and what my voice was. And I think it's essential to figure that out because you see so many books—and I think most people's first books suffer from this—but you see so many books that could have been done by anyone. There's really nothing particularly unique about them. It can be a very good, a very solid book but there's no personality coming through in it and there's no voice. It's just a standard, solid, smart portfolio. So I think it's helpful if someone can really kind of zero in on the type of work that they love, that they want to do. And once they know that, then hold their own work to that standard and try to put together a portfolio that represents the type of work that they are really proud of and would want to do in their career. And that can be a lot of work, but I think if you can do that, you're more likely to be hired to do that type of work. If your book has a clear voice and point of view to it, then there's a greater chance you're going to be hired to use that point of view and that voice, as opposed to just be an all-purpose creative, who can do every style of advertising, but none of it is very interesting. Many people told me when I was first in the business that the creative should be invisible in the work, but I just disagree with that—it makes for mechanical, sterile work. That doesn't mean that you can only do comedy, or you can only do serious, epic work, but whatever you do should have a strong voice and point of view. What was the other part of the question?

How do you get in touch with creative directors and recruiters other than just mailing your book or trying to send your website? Do you have any tips on the actual job-hunting part?

Yes, but let me go back to the last question and illustrate the point. When I was trying to get into a good agency, I had a very solid portfolio that I would send around. And I was getting reasonably good responses from it. It was a very tight, solid book. But then I finally sent it to Tim Hanrahan who was working at Wieden+Kennedy at that time and he was the one who really encouraged me. He was the one who told me, "Yeah, this is a very solid book, but it's kind of like every other book I see. I'd like to see something that represents you more." And at that point, I stopped…I had been making a book that I thought would get me hired at an ad agency instead of making a book that I was in love with. And at that point, I threw out almost everything in my book and started over. And I stopped thinking about what any creative director, or any ad agency would think—my only criteria was: "Does this honestly represent something that I personally love and think is hilarious?" And if I couldn't answer yes to that question, it didn't go in. And so, with that standard in mind, I worked for I think about a year, and when I finished that, I sent it to Wieden+Kennedy, and I got a call from them within 24 hours. So I'm a big believer in figuring out what you love and trying to hold your book to that standard. Was that an inspiring story? I kind of imagine the music from the end of Rudy playing while I told that story and young people across the world rising to their feet and cheering. In my mind the young people in China were especially inspired by my story.

And then, as far as hitting the streets, I don't know if I have much advice for this: Don't wear a suit, brush your teeth, personal hygiene is good. Just be yourself.

Even just getting in touch with creative directors is so tough because they're always busy…

Yeah, I mean you've got to get through the gatekeepers.

Do all the books come to you through gatekeepers, or do you get people finding you directly?

It's mostly through our recruiters that I see books. Sometimes, if I see work I love, I'll seek them out and ask for their book. But it is tough because creative directors at big agencies are so bombarded with e-mails from...everything from students to production companies to...I mean hundreds of emails a day. So it's really hard for them to respond to direct emails. But usually the good shops have pretty good recruiters. So I think if you got a good book and you are persistent with them and follow up with the recruiter...and don't be afraid to say, "I would love to hear what so and so creative director thinks of my book." And I think if you're persistent, they will be likely to show it, at least to that CD and get feedback. I can't say...I'm sure there's people who have had success going directly to creative directors, but I can't really speak to that. Most of the stuff I see is through our recruiters.

Okay. Any final words of wisdom?

On the digital front, I think digital is becoming, obviously, increasingly important on people's portfolios. But that's another area where I would just encourage students to be really, really hard on their work. And just because something is on the Internet doesn't make it a good digital idea. I can't tell you how many books I look at that have websites and various digital things that...there's no real strong, coherent, funny, entertaining idea—it's just a bunch of design and words that happen to be on the Internet. So I think it's essential to have digital work but it just needs to be as strong and as entertaining and as surprising as their print and TV work.

Okay. Thanks.

Did I sound handsome?

You sounded great. BI

To see Jason Bagley's work, please visit http://breaking.in

MONICA BUCHANAN CREATIVE RECRUITER NEW YORK

Interviewed at BBDO New York.

What do you look for in a student book? And what impresses you?

Originality. With student books, I have to be a little bit more forgiving for the lack of breadth. Because it's only as great as the different projects you'd be given at school. Although some of the kids go out of their way to do stuff. Different voices are very important. If you're an art director: craftsmanship, design sense. I'd like to see someone be able to art-direct a piece of body copy. I know it sounds old fashioned, but it's good to see that someone can do this. And, likewise, a copywriter's body copy. Show me some body copy.

I think humor is helpful. I find that if you are going to rein yourself in on a student book, you're already in trouble because we need to see how far you can go out there. And I'm talking relevance though, not just "I'm crazy." How far you can go out there on a project because inevitably your creative director will rein you in, the client will rein us in. So, if you're starting conservatively then we have no clue what you're capable of.

"YOU WANT TO BE PERSISTENT, BUT YOU DON'T WANT TO PISS US OFF. IT'S A FINE LINE."

The ease with which you can go through a book is important. I don't have a lot of time. The ability to contact the person is really important. Sometimes I get books from people and I don't know how to contact them easily. A phone number and an email address are enough. I'd like to be able to see some campaigns. All the alternative media—people are already addressing those things.

Do you think that, if the ideas are good, sketches can be enough?

I would like to be able to say yes. But I think it's the responsibility of the art director or the copywriter to be able to hook up with a partner and work together to make that idea and that concept read. It's lazy otherwise. Go out of your way, believe me. There are a lot of schools, there are a lot of programs. It's not like we're talking 30 years ago, 40 years ago. There are schools addressing this. Make sure that your brilliant headline is substantiated with the art direction. And for the art director, your visual concept should be part of the headline.

So, a writer needs to hook up with an art director who needs to have design skills...

I think it's important. Now, could I take a look at a bunch of headlines and writing with sketches? Yes, I could. Of course I could. But I'm saying, given the fact that there are so many different schools available to you and so many different people who can do art direction from these schools, why not go through the whole exercise? Why not go and make sure that the portfolio you present to us is complete?

And an art director needs to have those design skills?

Yeah, an art director should have design skills, and the ability to lay out pages and be conceptual as well. You know what? I've hired people who've had a book with great headlines and copy and really bad art direction. It's really hard for me to sell that to these guys, though. So, once again, when you look at a book, it's the whole thing. And you as a writer have to make sure that if you're hooked up with a really bad art director you switch your art director. If the concept comes from the art director and they have the ability to really visualize the idea, but the headline and copy are clunky and a little off, it's up to that creative to find a copywriter who will nail it.

What do you think about putting things in a book that aren't ads?

I have no problem with that.

Do you think it's helpful? Necessary?

I think it's a separate section. I like stuff like that actually. I think what it's all about when you're recruiting is really getting to know someone. Hobbies are very interesting to me. What people do. How they grow. Where they're going to pull from. Now, if you're going to come in with a fine-arts book and tell me you want to be an art director, that's not going to happen. If you write novels and you come in and you tell me you want a job and you're really interested in writing 30-second radio spots, that's going to be hard. It doesn't mean you can't. But I'm going to need to see radio spots. I'm going to need to see ads.

Do you have any tips for a student who's trying to get into the business?

You want to be persistent, but you don't want to piss us off. It's a fine line. A sense of humor is always great. Because, as you can see from sitting here, there are books everywhere, my whole office is loaded up with books, plus I have all of these links. And, I could show you another whole place on my desktop that is full of books. So, how are you going to be noticed? One way to do it is be really amazing. So your school calls up and says, "This is an amazing student." Or if a fantastic creative asks me to check out someone's book, you bet I will. They have already gone through a tough filter. If that is not happening, then take a job at a different shop that isn't as competitive as BBDO, Wieden, Goodby, or Chiat, and do some award-winning work. Believe me, we'll notice you.

Thank you.

You're welcome. Did I curse?

I don't think so. ⊞

NICK STRADA
GROUP CREATIVE DIRECTOR
AKQA
SAN FRANCISCO

Interviewed at Glue, London.

What do you look for in a student book? And what impresses you?

I want to see your personality in your work and the way you look at the world. Smart thinking. Just a new eye—a way of seeing things that I wouldn't have seen and that I haven't seen before. I think with American books and English books, there's a real difference you see, mostly in terms of execution and craftsmanship, particularly for art directors. The best books from either end tend to be full of good ideas and sideways thinking and really creative insights—real truisms. But there isn't as much of an emphasis on execution and craftsmanship in England and they tend to be trained more on the job in that end of things, whereas places like the Ad Center [now VCU Brand Center] and School of Visual Arts [New York] and Circus [The Creative Circus] and all those places, Miami Ad School, tend to add an emphasis on execution and craftsmanship that I think is lacking over here. So, when you look at a book from a student who's from England, you have to take that into consideration that they just haven't been taught it, generally. A lot of people over here think, "To hell with all that stuff, we get taught to think," and that is true, they do get taught to think. But I think a lot of students in America get taught to think and they get taught to execute, and I think both are useful.

That was actually my second question: sketches versus finished work.

A good idea in a sketch is better than a finished idea that isn't very good. There's no question. And I think that people who go to formal advertising programs probably come out with more polished books but there's a lot of people who do this sort of placement circuit [UK internships] and build their book as they go around, and for them it's more about the volume than taking it to the nth degree of finish. And so I think sketches for them are quite useful because you don't want to sit there, crafting the ass off of an idea that isn't very good. I think that they both have their purpose. I mean, you remember the first year at VCU [Brand Center], we didn't really take stuff to Mac level too often. It was more about learning to think. I think that just jumping on to the computer too quickly is as much of an error, or worse of an error, than never learning to execute any of it at all.

Do you think long copy is important?

I think writing is important. Just being long for the sake of being long, I think is stupid. But sometimes there's a time and a place to write more, particularly when you get into new interactive spaces and you're not limited to the dimensions of a piece of paper.

If you're selling the BMW 5 series, copy is probably important on a website, whereas if you're selling potato chips, maybe it's not. And I think that there's a time and a place for most things and that goes for copy as well. I think that ads with 500 or 1000 words of copy on it just to show that you can do it aren't so important for me in a young person's portfolio. But if you're working on a subject that requires a bit of explanation and it feels that the writing is being done for the benefit of the reader rather than the benefit of the writer—in other words, just showing that they can do it—I think then it's fine.

What do you think about putting stuff in book that is not advertising?

That's great. Oh that's fantastic. There was a young woman who came and saw me, gosh, probably about nine years ago when I was at BBH. Her name is Mira…

Kaddoura?

Yeah.

Yeah, she works at Wieden.

She had the most bizarre book I've ever seen. It was this little square, riveted-in-the-corner thing, full of self-portraits and conceptual art projects and sketches and poetry and photography—all kinds of shit, and her advertising. And my partner didn't like her book and I did. She liked her advertising but she thought that—and I probably agreed at that time—that there were agencies that wouldn't want to see all that extra stuff, but that doesn't really hold true anymore. I think advertising agencies are no longer just doing advertising. The job has changed. And we're thinking of events and we're thinking of interactive installations and we're thinking of galleries and we're thinking of exhibits and sponsorships and uniforms and letterhead. And I think that the more ways you can express your talent and creativity and ability to solve problems, the better.

"FOR THE TOP 10 AGENCIES IN LONDON—TAKE YOUR TOP 10, WHICHEVER 10 THOSE ARE—THEY WILL PROBABLY, BETWEEN THEM, HIRE SEVEN TO EIGHT JUNIOR TEAMS THIS YEAR. AND THERE'S HOWEVER MANY HUNDRED JUNIOR TEAMS LOOKING FOR WORK THIS YEAR."

And, as I've said, you want to see someone's personality in a portfolio. If I see your book before I see you, I want to feel like I know you a little bit, or a little bit about you. And I think other projects are great. In fact, it's really dry when all you see is a stack of ads. I think it's not competitive because what people trying to get into business need to remember is, the business is crying out for fresh, new talent but it's still a buyer's market. There's still more demand for places than there are places. For the top 10 agencies in London—take your top 10, whichever 10 those are—they will probably, between them, hire seven to eight junior teams this year. And there's however many hundred junior teams looking for work this year. And so it's super,

super competitive and anything you can do to give yourself an edge is definitely smart, I think.

Do you have any tips for someone who's putting together a book?

I think just "do." Just get bored easily. And I bore really, really easily and I guess, if I'm bored of this thing that I'm working on, and I have an interest and a stake in it, everybody else is going to be really bored of it, you know? People on the street and creative directors in another ad agency that you might want to impress. I think boring easily is really important, and I think staying stimulated—just filling the bucket in your head with films and all sorts of things.

I think also, you can't underestimate how important it is to work hard. I mean just sheer drive is really important. Todd Lamb was one of the guys in my class, he graduated with me and he has done a lot of really nice work, but if you meet him, he seems like this kind of weirdo, sort of creative freakazoid kind of guy, but if you watch him, he works his socks off. He's just always grinding away. And he has sideline projects, magazine articles, and those kinds of things, and I think it's just a matter of talent and effort.

Also, I think that the worst thing that you can do when you're trying to improve is to try to change your portfolio for everybody you meet. I see a lot of students who have changed their books over and over again because they're trying to tailor it to what they think the agency they're going into wants to see, and it ends up not being their portfolio anymore. And, if they do get a job off of it, the book that was hired isn't really representative of what they can do or want to do, and it never ends up being [good]. Because they went into an agency that doesn't really want them but they want this sort of construct that was hired, and then the team can't really deliver it day-to-day. And they don't want to. And that's an unhappy marriage. So I think if you stay true to yourself, work really, really hard, and do interesting things, interesting things will happen to you. ⊞

To see Nick Strada's work, please visit http://breaking.in

ANDREW KELLER
CEO
CRISPIN PORTER + BOGUSKY
BOULDER

What do you look for in a student book? And what impresses you?

Attitude. Are they going for it? Or are they lazy? Are they doing all the same things everyone else is doing? Have they invented anything? Is the work interactive and engaging or is it just two-dimensional?

How important is finish? If ideas are the most important thing, can sketches be enough? Do you look at physical books anymore, or is it all websites?

If you are an art director you have to be able to design. I'm over "idea people" that don't possess manual skills of any kind. Sketches may indicate laziness or lack of passion. If you love it, why not make it? I like some sort of physicality still in a portfolio, mainly because the alternative puts the burden on me to seek out and manage the presentation, and I don't have time for that.

"I'M NOT A FAN OF PEOPLE WHO DO ADVERTISING WHILE THEY ARE WAITING TO DO THEIR REAL PASSION."

How important is writing? Do you need to see long copy?

I don't have to see it, but if I did and it was good, I would hire that person. The question is, why are you a writer if you don't write?

What do you think of showing work that is not advertising? Things like art, journal writing, photography, hobbies, etc.

It's fine and can show true skills as long as the person is truly passionate about advertising. I'm not a fan of

people who do advertising while they are waiting to do their real passion.

Do you have any other advice for a student or junior?

There is no lack of jobs, only lack of skills. Cultivate a passion for everything. Learn digital. 🄱🄸

To see Andrew Keller's work, please visit http://breaking.in

PAT MCKAY
FREELANCE CREATIVE DIRECTOR
SEATTLE

What do you look for in a portfolio? And what impresses you?

It always comes down to ideas. That's the first thing I want to see is really good ideas. And then if the ideas are there, then you can kind of go back and see what they have as far as executional skills and taste, stuff like that. But execution, even taste to a certain degree, and just some of those kinds of things are things that you can get better at with practice. But whether or not you can come up with a good idea, I think maybe that's something that has to be a little bit more naturally instilled in you. If I see good ideas, and I know there's at least potential, then I can sort of decide from there about the level of some of the craft.

So that was my next question: How important is the finish? Do you think sketches can be enough? Or do you think you have to show finished ads?

Yeah it's a funny thing. Obviously we would be able to see an idea off a sketch. But in a way, the people who get away with doing sketches are when you're in a situation where your work kind of precedes you, that people know enough about how you work and what you've done. After you've worked in an agency for a while, and they get to know you, you can sketch out an idea and they can see what the idea is, and they kind of know the process you'll go through from there. But when you're a student, your work doesn't precede you.

That is your work. That sketch is your work. So if it's a good idea, that's fine but it's just like, face it, there are just so many books out there that have good ideas and are really tight, execution-wise. So you should really try to avoid doing sketches.

But, that being said, if you have good ideas, I wouldn't be afraid. It's going to be hard to get a job on sketches—really hard—but you can get some great feedback on sketches and it can be part of the process. I wouldn't be afraid to take sketches and put them in front of smart people that you would like advice from.

But, overall, sketches are not the best idea for a final book. Maybe it could be part of the process. But as with advertising and all creative fields, I would certainly look twice if a book came in, and it was 100 sketches. And they were all really good ideas. And it was sort of like his or her way in. If someone wanted to do something completely different and said, "I'm not going to execute any of it, I'm just going to have loads of ideas, and that's going to be the thing I want to leave in that person's mind with my book." Something like that could work. Sometimes with a book it's good to have an idea. An overall idea, and sometimes that can really get you noticed.

Do you think long-copy ads are important?

Yeah. I think you should still have a piece of copy. It might feel a little bit old fashioned nowadays to have a long-copy print ad because I'm not sure that it's really a reflection of what kind of work really is floating around now. Probably the opportunity for that is somewhere nontraditional or on a website. But show an ability to write. When I look at writers' books, for me as a writer, I really want to see the craft. And I want to get a sense of their voice. I think it's really important.

"SOMETIMES WITH A BOOK IT'S GOOD TO HAVE AN IDEA. AN OVERALL IDEA, AND SOMETIMES THAT CAN REALLY GET YOU NOTICED."

And then also, even with headlines, I think it's good to have. Again, it doesn't have to be a headline campaign—a headline print campaign—but it should be some campaign with headlines because I want to see if they can spit out lines, because there's a real process to it. And I've seen good books where I see that the writer should… and I'll always tell them: "You needed to write 200 more lines, because you've only got one funny one." Or, "You've only got one that really feels like you went through a process." I guess I want to see that they have a writing process because that's what writers do—we have processes. Sometimes it's in your head, sometimes, like for me, I have to sort of write everything out and then scrunch it back down. When I was doing headline campaigns, I literally would write 200 lines to get 10 and I had to do it all by hand. Not everybody works like that, but I would like to see evidence of a writing process because you never know when you're going to really need someone to be good with that stuff. That's my take on it.

What do you think about putting things in your book that aren't ads?

It's amazing. I think it's a great idea, actually. And specifically in cases like we've talked about, if you're at a phase where you don't want your book to feel like a formula. But for me as a writer, I would never hire a writer unless I'd know that they can write because I might need that from them and so this might be an opportunity for them to show their ability without getting trapped in that, "Oh, I need A, B, C, D, E, F for someone to hire me." So I think things like journal entries, or scripts, or stuff like that can help. Even in my career, moving from place to place, those things have played a big role in where I've ended up.

Do you have any other advice?

Be really tough on yourself. I know you hear that over, and over, and over, and over. But it's so true. You just really have to be tough on yourself. And, as far as putting a book together, just be aware of what you're going up against. And the work at the places that you're trying to get into. Be tough on yourself. Not just because it's so hard to get in, but when you're tough on yourself, sometimes you find things that are a better fit. Like, "By being tough on myself, I want to really make sure my work is good for all these different agencies. So I really go in and look at what these agencies are doing so I can see where the bar is that I have to set for myself." And then through the process of doing that, maybe you find some really great places that you like even more than you would've thought. It can take you in a lot of different places. BI

To see Pat McKay's work, please visit http://breaking.in

TODD LAMB
WRITER & DIRECTOR
CHICAGO

What do you look for in a student book? And what impresses you?

I don't look at very many student books because my attention span can't really cope with it. It's a shame, but most of them aren't very surprising. I want to laugh out loud. A lot of the student books are too controlled.

Do you think you can put together a book of sketches and, if the ideas are good, that's enough, or do you think you have to finish work on a computer?

I think that sketches could be enough. I would be more intrigued by a group of sketches that were really funny than a book that looks like it's from the future, but dull. So, I think it's very possible to have a hand-done portfolio, if it's good.

Do you think you need long copy in a book?

I've noticed that many writers in advertising can't put more than three sentences together. So long copy would show that you could write. On the other hand, I wouldn't want to read ten paragraphs about men's underwear. Unless I worked in an underwear factory, then I'd read it on my lunch break.

What do you think about putting things besides ads in a book?

I think it's good because the hope for the advertising industry is that it can be more interesting, more compelling, more entertaining than the stuff that surrounds it, otherwise no one on earth is going to care. So you shouldn't limit yourself to just the form of an ad and there shouldn't be a form to an ad. There should just be a thing you made, and hopefully it's selling a product for a company and they're happy about it. So, there's no reason why it should be like what is regarded as the traditional form for an ad. No creative person should limit themselves to that.

"A LOT OF THE STUDENT BOOKS ARE TOO CONTROLLED.

But even outside of nontraditional advertising, should you put in stuff like your journal writing or your photography, or just whatever you're into, totally separate...

Yeah, put all creative things in it. Show you're a person who has other interests. For me, I'd like intermissions that show that I'd actually want to spend some time with that person.

Do you have any tips on how to get started in the industry?

Go to ad school. Make a book. Show it to someone who works at an ad agency. Compared to the space-exploration industry, it's an easy line of work to get into. Also I would say: Don't try that hard. Everyone's trying so hard, it's like they're going to crack a safe. Do what you do, stick to your guns, and do what you want to do and make things that make you happy. BI

To see Todd Lamb's work, please visit http://breaking.in

JOE STAPLES
EXECUTIVE CREATIVE DIRECTOR
WIEDEN+KENNEDY
PORTLAND

How does the portfolio review process work for you?

We look at websites in between (or sometimes during) presentations, briefings, and lunch because we haven't had 30 minutes off in a few years. Most of the time they are sent by Lauren, the agency's recruiter, but they could also be from people who know someone who knows someone.

[Mark] Fitzloff [ECD of W+K] usually says, "If you like two things on their site and don't really fucking hate anything, that's good." I think this is quite true. I'm looking for a spark of something. Someone who seems like an interesting person who has interesting takes on things. It's important to remember that you aren't hiring them for the work that they have done, but rather for the work they have the ability to do in the future.

If I like something, I'll share it with Aaron and Tabby, who I work with. We'll probably do some private-eyeing. It's a small enough industry that if someone is a complete dick, they won't have hidden it very well at the other places they have worked.

Assuming they aren't, we would either Skype with them or invite them to come to Portland to meet the group, the agency, and the weather.

Work is important. Attitude, interests, hopes, desire, dreams, and whether you would want to spend most of your waking hours with them is probably more important.

What do you look for in a student book?

In wanky terms, I look for elegant problem solving. Someone who finds new ways to look at things. A depth of thinking with a lightness of touch. A range of tone would be great, but more important is a desire to solve problems wherever they are.

I don't want to see 30 billboards, or 30 websites or apps. I would really be into someone who could tell me what they thought they were solving for and then why they chose to solve it in the way they did.

Are there common mistakes that could be avoided?

Ad conceits. It's important to remember that outside of our mainly insipid industry, people don't really talk about ads. I know it's hard to believe. Avoiding clichés should be obvious, but watching television would suggest that I should also remind people to avoid clichés.

How important is the level of finish? Could sketches be enough?

Yes. Maybe better. It's hard to hide crappy ideas on a Post-It note. But (there is always a "but") if someone is going to be a good art director, I would think they would also want to demonstrate their love of design and craft.

Is writing important? Would you like to see a long-copy ad?

Writing is important, but thinking is far more important. It's easier to teach, help, direct, or even sit and work with someone on long copy. It's harder to teach someone to think. Being dyslexic helps me think, but made writing a challenge. I've worked on it for a long time, and I hope I'm getting better at it. I think that this process has made me more analytical about how to do it, and hopefully this has given me an insight into how to teach it.

Do you like to see "non-ads," such as art, hobbies, personal work, etc.?

Non-ad things (especially with elegant thinking) are very important. I also want to know what this person is into other than "music and film." These are the influences and sensibilities that they will bring to their work. Behind every spot that takes place in an ad agency or a "research group" is a sad creative who needs a holiday and a hobby and some clothing that wasn't given to them by a production company. Everyone in a good agency should be good at advertising, right? Then what is important is what else they are.

Do you have any other advice about portfolios or job hunting?

Understanding a problem before you give a solution is very important. Saying, "You work on cars, how about this ad" is dumb. Either find out everything there is to know about this thing you are working on, or work on something you already know about. If you are selling your stereo, sell it in a better way than Craigslist. Need a new car? Think about a better way to get one. Don't like dog shit? Think of a way to fix it.

"WORK HARDER THAN ANYONE IN THE AGENCY. SCARE THEM WITH YOUR WORK ETHIC, YOUR DESIRE, AND YOUR WILLINGNESS TO PUSH YOUR THINKING INTO MORE AMAZING PLACES THAN THEY EVER THOUGHT POSSIBLE."

One last piece of advice that no one really wants to hear. To hire a junior creative is to make an investment in that person. Creative directors could probably do the work they are asking to be done in less time than it would take to brief, review, and direct a junior creative. This is horribly bubble-bursting, I know. I was told it many years ago, but it is true. To hire is to invest in someone you see something great in. Don't take this for granted. Work harder than anyone in the agency. Scare them with your work ethic, your desire, and your willingness to push your thinking into more amazing places than theyever thought possible. Do 100 of anything before you show anyone anything. Your job is to soak up everything. To listen and to learn and to grow and then hopefully to pay them back with amazing work. BI

To see Joe Staples's work, please visit http://breaking.in

**MICHAEL LEBOWITZ
FOUNDER & CEO
BIG SPACESHIP
NEW YORK**

Just in the way of background on digital agencies, what are the different creative positions here?

Well, we're pretty different. There are no positions that aren't creative. I don't believe in having a creative department. I don't believe in calling people "creatives." In fact, I absolutely hate that in every way. The line I always say is, "If you're not creative, you can't work here," regardless of what discipline you're in. And I even take it to the point of not having creative directors. We have a design director for the design discipline, but we don't have creative directors. And while that may change someday where we have somebody who's overseeing the entire output of the company, currently that's me and I don't have "creative" in my title either. It's sort of "cost of entry" for me. So, we've got four disciplines: strategy, design, production, and technology. And all of those roles are very fundamentally and essentially creative roles. Just exercising different parts of the brain and different sense of skills, different sorts of muscles. But everybody participates in everything we do all the way through everything, in every engagement, every project.

So without going into too much detail, what are those positions?

It falls within those disciplines. So we've got designers in our design discipline. The designer is a pretty all-encompassing thing, so it's design, animation, video, any visual, basically, whether it's static illustration, character animation, broadcast design, or what we would traditionally call broadcast design. If you wanted to define it by tools, it's Photoshop, Illustrator, After Effects, Flash, all of that stuff. But it's also visual language, basically, I think that's the better way of doing it. And technology are programmers and software architects. We have a post up—one of our more popular posts on our design and technology blog called "Think" that our Associate Technical Director wrote. It's about developers all getting along and that it's really not about having "a flash developer" or "a standards developer," we just have developers, and certainly some of them are more experienced with one thing or another but the goal is that they are just developers and we do what we need to do.

Then, production. We have producers—we don't call them project managers—and they're also largely responsible for the day-to-day client interaction. We don't have a huge account discipline; we have, at the executive level, a couple of key client contacts. But producers are both internal and external champions of work and expert diplomats and people who speak lots of different languages so they can rally things into existence.

And then strategy is the most multidisciplinary because it's everything from consumer insights and user experience to information architecture. We put writing inside of strategy because we think writing, for digital platforms especially, is a highly strategic activity. It is very different to write a tweet, a blog post, promotional copy, whatever it might be. And we think everything is informed by human behavior, so the whole group is charged with understanding how people work and where we have opportunities to nudge them into new behaviors. But most of the time: how do we attach to the behaviors that are already there? Because if you think you're going to create a brand-new behavior every time out, you're probably not going to win very often. So it's about sociology, fan cultures, game mechanics; it's a very broad-based group. But not a lot of traditional planning—although there is certainly similar expertise. That's kind of the lay of the land. There are a few of us who serve in sort of relationship roles and management. We're very thin, very flat.

So, focusing on writers and visual designers, what do you look for in their book, and what impresses you?

With visual designers, if you are applying for a digital design job and you send a PDF without a really good reason, we question that. A book doesn't really make sense in digital. It's a static thing.

Okay, what do you look for in a portfolio website?

In a portfolio site, we want as much information about process—not just the finished product—as possible. Especially when you see something like "IBM.com." It's like, "Okay. A team of dozens of people worked on this…" So that's not enough and it doesn't give us enough information. And especially when you're looking at people with less experience who are coming right out of school. It's really good to understand process. How did they arrive at the finished product? And some of the best portfolios I've seen aren't about the nuance and polish of the work—certainly that's great. It's important; craft is essential. But showing that that person really thinks about the work and is really thoughtful about the decision-making process [is better]. And also anything that conveys collaboration. Because what we do is constant collaboration between disciplines and it's real time. We don't have any "lone wolves" who are off doing something and then come back. We talk about pretty much everything along the way because that's the way we need to do it to get to the level of product we have at the end. It's too complex. There's too many…everything is potentially elastic in digital, so you need people who are going to be good team players. No matter how creative their work is, if they can't collaborate, they can't really fit in here.

"IN A PORTFOLIO SITE, WE WANT AS MUCH INFORMATION ABOUT PROCESS—NOT JUST THE FINISHED PRODUCT—AS POSSIBLE."

And then, it may seem sort of archaic in a way, but I believe in a great cover letter. And it's a very, very tenuous thing because some people seek to write "the great cover letter" and it's a little much, they are a little overworked. With us, people always want to play games with the name "Big Spaceship" and it gets kind of cute after a while, and not positively so. It's kind of like a joke about somebody's name, like, "Do you think I haven't heard that before?" But while I want a concise presentation, at the same time, one of the best cover letters I ever received was from a guy who works here to this day—maybe four or five years ago now. It was a four-page cover letter. He's a developer, a technology person, and when I first saw it I was like, "Oh, this guy is a nut. We're not going to hire him." And then I got to the end of it, I was like, "If he's the same in person as the way he is on paper, he's a definite hire." And we have had a few like that, where the cover letters were so good and communicated so naturally what the personality was, that they got themselves in the door at least for an interview just for that. We pay a lot of attention to the soft stuff: not just finished work but process, not just speed but the ability to work with others. How that output comes to be and also just, "Are they going to be fun to work with?"

You mentioned finish. Are ideas more important or is finish more important or does it depend on the job?

Ideas are really important, but the way that the traditional side of the business values "the big idea" is completely out of balance with the way that you actually produce work in the digital space. I say all the time, "The greatest idea in the world, unproduced, has no value whatsoever. A mediocre idea, produced, has some incremental value." So why is the value always placed on the big idea when getting things into the world is so important? The difference in thinking makes a ton of sense because, when you have to spend a tremendous amount of money to put it out into the world, because there are limited places to put it, you would have to have a huge idea, polish it for however long, and make sure it's absolutely perfect for one big blockbuster release. But in digital, we publish whenever we want, we republish and iterate whenever we want, and it doesn't cost much, or anything, to do the actual iteration in publishing. So the mindsets are so, so different.

Do you hire some more "idea people" or does everyone have to have ideas and skill to make it?

Well, I think everybody contributes in our brainstorming sessions, whether for a pitch or a new challenge from an existing client, across all of our disciplines. It's not like strategy comes in and defines everything up front. Everybody is involved

end to end. We've had amazing ideas that have been sold to clients that have come from developers, designers, from interns across all of our different disciplines. Great ideas come from everywhere, and a lot of times, if you're open to it, a lot of great ideas come from terrible ideas. Somebody says something just because they feel safe enough in their environment to throw something out that they know is crap. And somebody else grabs it, and levels it up somehow, or turns it into something really interesting, or attaches an insight to it that actually makes it relevant. So I think basically, everybody is an idea person and, again, I know that there is sort of this Hollywood-style auteur thing going on on the other side of the fence [traditional agencies]. Maybe I'm naïve but we don't believe in rock stars. It's about the team. Everybody here makes each other better and it's that way of working that makes our work good. And it's all the same people who are executing that are also coming up with the ideas for it. With traditional agencies the process is always pretty linear: "We're going to come up with the big idea and polish that idea, then we'll bring it to the production company and they'll level it up as well, but only focus on craft and final execution." And we're letting that happen in a much more cyclical, iterative way, all the way through. Even before we've actually produced anything tangible, anything crafted I should say, the people who are traditionally considered "executional" are in the process of crafting ideas and it works really well for us.

For writers, do you get people from ad schools and people that bring in print ads? And in writers what do you look for? How would you demonstrate your ability to write?

Fundamentally, if you don't have a blog then I wonder if you have something to say and I sort of feel like writers should have something to say. If you're only going to be able to say other people's messages then are you going to really have some sort of guts behind it? Not that it's an absolute "no" if someone doesn't. But it's a question mark. I certainly don't mind looking at print ads, but you know, with static copy, the whole mind-set and strategy behind print is that you have to capture everything in one moment. And so it's branding and everything gets sort of mashed into a single space. And there's no sense of evolution or process or user experience.

And also technical considerations like writing for SEO [search engine optimization]. As much as there is that, "I want my craft to be pure" mentality—and fair enough, frankly—if you want to be seen in a world where you have to earn people's attention, then you have to be able to write to get it. That, when taken too far, is a great race to the bottom, and you see that with a lot of really salacious headlines and the top-ten list of every publication online, and stuff like that.

"I WANT TO KNOW HOW PEOPLE THINK. AND IT'S NOT THAT THE FINISHED EXECUTION ISN'T IMPORTANT, IT'S JUST EQUALLY IMPORTANT TO UNDERSTAND THE "WHY" AND THE "HOW.""

But I think we look for flexibility—tonal flexibility. We'll do work for a Hollywood-featured film, and then we're doing consumer health-related stuff for GE, and then we're doing all of our work for Wrigley. And with our writers, we don't sit people on an account. People move around and do a whole bunch of different things for the most part. So you have to really be able to leap in and out, and not just tonally, but also in the form of delivery. So we're composing blog posts for some of our clients, we're writing tweets for some of our clients, we spend a lot of our time writing about ourselves, like, "What are the case studies?" and, "What's the tone of voice that we want our brand to carry out into the world?" Because that affects what business we get and how the business that we do get and execute on gets celebrated.

So, ideally, would you like to see someone who has their own online presence—they blog or they have a personal website that's really cool—and they do all these things for themselves, and also they have a portfolio site where they have done great work on the web, that's either spec work or for clients?

Ideally, yeah. Again, it's about process. I want to understand why. I think when I look at a traditional book, I think, "Well that's a clever tagline or that's a good gag." That has no relevance to me whatsoever. "Okay that's clever. That's pretty funny." But how did you get there? Why is that what it is? Clearly, these things need to be based on insights. Was the insight theirs or did they get it from a planner? And if it came from a planner, then at least show me the process of how you translated the insight, which is abstract, into something a human can actually interact with?

Do a couple sentences of setup—a paragraph—help you to do that?

Yeah. Anything about process helps. I want to know how people think. And it's not that the finished execution isn't important, it's just equally important to understand the "why" and the "how." And certainly, if what you have is 20 print ads, spec or otherwise, even if you're a great writer, it's really hard to see what space you would fill here. That's where blogging and other stuff can start to fill in some of those gaps, because a lot of schools don't really give a lot of opportunities for anything but print ads still. But I think it's this funny thing. We're launching all sorts of software applications, basically. Yes, some things are campaign oriented, but we're launching iPhone apps, just as an example. That's not traditional copywriting. It's writing about software which means explaining functionality and getting what can be fairly complex functionality distilled down to a couple of bullets because that's all you get before you have to hit the "more" button in the App Store in iTunes. And how do you orient people? How should you create a desire for that functionality? But then how do you actually explain how to do it in tiny, little bits of language? So it's a combination of technical writing, copywriting, there's long form and short form, there's tweets. I mean, it's so amazing, the ecosystem of types of writing. If I finally see one [type of writing skill], I'm always going to ask myself the question, "Is there room for the others in this person?"

If someone were interested in online and traditional, is there anything that you would say to help them decide which way to go? Because, to a large extent, both digital agencies and traditional agencies are doing more and more of the same thing.

Yeah. Well, it seems that way and I always question whether they actually are. I think the value of this place is the people here are challenged—really, really challenged—every day. And not just like, "Here's a new complicated brand that you have to figure out how to articulate." That's one vector of challenge but there's another challenge of, "Okay, for this one, we're going to create a completely different kind of system that's totally elastic and it's going to interact differently for every single person that interacts with it. So, we have to build a system of language that is adaptable enough, that it will still make sense regardless of the use-case." And then, that will be a challenge, and you'll have to sort that one out and then you'll have to move on to another one. And it's much more fragmented in a way, and it's much more around "systems thinking."

So if you want to craft perfect lines of copy, more power to you, but that's not really a full-time job here. I'm sure at other, more advertising-oriented digital agencies it could be. I can only speak for us and I have found out more and more that we're kind of a unique animal. But I think if you want to have finished, crafted things, artifacts you've sent out into the world, you're going to get a lot more satisfaction out of the traditional side. Maybe. Maybe you will. We do send artifacts out into the world but they're hard to clearly quantify or articulate. Or harder, certainly, than, "Here's a print ad I did." So I guess it's sort of what you want out of your career. I say, more important than anything, is, "have a place where you love to go to work every day." It's the most important thing. When I was talking to VCU [Brandcenter] students I told them, "Interview these people." You could be going for an internship: you're interviewing them. This is about your day-to-day happiness. You spend a third of your life sleeping, so have a great mattress. You spend at least a third of your life at work. Have a place that's going to make you feel good. Not that it will be stress-free, you're in the wrong industry for stress-free, but that's more important I think than any type of output. Are you going to learn every day? Are you going to feel challenged every day? Are you going to get the personal satisfaction you're looking for, and then you can work backwards from there into the type of work.

Do you have any other advice for either someone who's just graduated from school and wants to work here or maybe if they've been a junior for a couple of years on the traditional side and they want to come over here?

If you've been a junior on a traditional side, if they've been anywhere on the traditional side for any period of time: humility, humility, humility. Because, in a lot of ways, if you don't have the hard-core experience, you do need to start over. Not in every way. They are certainly...being a good inhaler of culture and being able to make connections, things like that, is valuable no matter what. But your InDesign skills aren't going to have any value here, just to get very practical as an example. So it's great to make the move, it's exciting, and you'll feel like there's an endless amount to learn in front of you, but it's not usually a lateral move.

And the advice to people coming out of school is to get an internship. We've got an amazing internship program. Lots of agencies do. I think we have a more substantial one for an agency of our size. It's the clearest path to a job in any discipline. We hire a lot of our interns because we already know them really intimately and we take seriously every single person that gets hired here. So getting to know us, it's a way of dipping your toe in the water for both sides. And so, while you're in school, intern as much as possible.

Looking at schools, there are programs that insist on real serious work-study. Hyper Island has six-month-long internships required to graduate. We work a lot with University of Cincinnati's digital design program. They are on a quarter system, and every other quarter they're out in a company. Even if it's just summer, throw down. Get yourself into the work and really, really learn about it. Because being able to put that experience forward is really substantially valuable to us when we're looking. [BI]

To see Michael Lebowitz's work, please visit http://breaking.in

GILLY TAYLOR
PRESIDENT
GILLY & CO.
BEVERLY HILLS

What impresses you when you're looking at a student book, and what do you think impresses creative directors?

It will always be the concept and ideas that matter first and foremost. Expanding on that, I am now looking at books with campaigns that may originate from a digital or viral medium. Every portfolio should have campaigns that include digital work, and it's a plus if the students have enough knowledge to build the site. All books now need to be viewable online and should be easy to navigate.

Do you think writers need to have long copy?

Yes. I hope to see smart headlines, but it's also great to see at least one campaign that will showcase their writing style.

Do you think art directors need to have long copy to show they can lay it out?

No. For an art director, aside from the concept, which is the most important thing, I am looking for different styles of execution. I look at type, design, and the visual details. I am not concerned if they have worked on a long-copy ad, but I am concerned that their great idea is well art-directed, and has been executed in the best medium for it.

Any thoughts on résumés?

Yes. Résumés are very important to me. It's normally what I will look at first. It is inexcusable to have a typo, so students should triple-check it before sending it out. Also, your résumé should fit on one page and it should be very easy to digest the information. Student awards and internships are important to add. Also, make sure your site is designed so that if someone wants to download or print it, it is easy to do so.

And you already mentioned some but do you have any more tips for people trying to get into the industry?

If you can, try to get a face-to-face interview with a creative director, as opposed to just emailing your work. And then make sure you follow up with a thank-you note. If you do get in to see someone in the agency, make sure you have done your homework and researched the agency and the people you will be meeting with. Come prepared with some intelligent questions. Your first job is very important—it could define your career—so stay focused on finding the right agency for you. Is there a mentor there who you can learn from? Will you have a partner? How integrated is the creative department? What's the culture like? [BI]

GRAHAM FINK
CHIEF CREATIVE OFFICER
OGILVY CHINA
SHANGHAI

Interviewed at M&C Saatchi, London.

What do you look for in a student book? And what impresses you?

Just some kind of spark, really. I'm not necessarily looking for great advertising. I'm looking for just a clue or a hint that the person showing me his book has got something a little bit different—a point of view, really. I don't want to see the brief on the page. I want to see the person on the page. They need to stamp their soul and put their soul onto the page and in a way that is interesting, in a way that is relevant, in a way that's engaging, in a way that stops me. And I want every page to look like a page I've never seen before.

When you say a point of view, do you mean an approach to ads or just a way of looking at the world or both?

If it's an ad campaign, I want them to show me something coming from a distinct angle. And remember you're selling something off the page. But there's many different ways of doing it. What tone of voice are you going to use? If you ever had an argument with your girlfriend, you might talk to her in a particular tone of voice which would be different to talking to your mom if she's very ill. It could be very different when talking to a car mechanic who fixed your car. If he's made a complete hash of it, you might talk to him a bit differently if you're expressing your anger, but then, if you want him to sort it out and fix it, you would use a different tone of voice again. There's many strands, some of them are quite subtle. You need to decide which one you're going to use to talk to your audience.

"I'M NOT NECESSARILY LOOKING FOR GREAT ADVERTISING."

And I think it's not done very often, I think it's quite rare that someone would come in and would have really thought about those things. I've seen an awful lot of students, but a lot of them look like they just start doing ads. So they don't think about who they're talking to, and most of them don't actually know their products very well. It's much easier these days to find out about products because you have got the Internet and you can find out an awful lot of stuff. People say that everything is the same these days, but I don't agree. I think if you really, really look, and you keep looking, and you look more, and you keep looking after that, you will come across stuff that is different.

In putting your point of view across, well, there are a couple of different ways of doing it. I mean by that, one is your point of view and what makes you, you. That's very important. "What makes you unique? Why should I hire you?" I've got a great department, full of very interesting people, all capable of doing [ads]. They all have their strengths and weaknesses but together they make a great squad. "Squad"…I'm using a football analogy. And I'm not really looking for someone else

who I can put on my squad who has the same qualities as someone else. I want someone who is different. I've got my strikers, I've got my fullbacks, I've got the firefighters, I've got the people who can do ads very, very quickly and always get me out of a mess. I've got the maverick striker who might be a pain in the ass, but occasionally, if he does score a goal, it's the most amazing goal you've ever seen in your life. So I want dependable people, I want maverick people, I want great strikers, I want a great midfield who can pass on ideas to other people and hopefully they will take them on into a better place. So there's lots and lots of different types of people who make up a great squad. Who make up a great creative department. I'm always looking for someone who could come in to the team but play a slightly different role. I think it's a mistake that people look at D&AD [ad annual] and try copying. Look at D&AD and be inspired and then do your own thing. You've got to stamp your own point of view. But don't look at it and copy what I've already seen before.

I don't mind people coming in with books that are full of hundreds of ideas and are all completely wrong. But if there's a kind of spark there, and there's something in there that I couldn't do myself, I know that I can train them, I can teach them. But if they're coming in with very formulaic stuff that's dull and boring and then there's no "soul in the book," then I'll kind of think, "Well, I've got to spend the first year trying to teach them to be them again," so that's no use to me.

I want people coming in with lots of different types of new media. I like seeing lots of ideas in different media—different ways of expressing it. I don't want people to just come in with a bunch of print ads in a book, or TV scripts. If you have got a great idea, show me how it can work in 30 channels. Don't do three posters and one TV commercial. That's just boring. Do a whole book on just this one idea. You could have just one portfolio with 30 to 40 different ways of doing this idea—that would be different. And when I've seen that one book, you show me five other books—that would be different.

What do you think of showing sketches or scamps versus finished work?

I really don't care. If it has a great idea, I'll spot it. It makes no difference to me.

For writers, do you want to see writing? Do you want to see evidence that they can do either long-copy ads or something else?

Not necessarily. If they have written a long piece of copy, it's a good test because you'll find out how long you'll spend reading it. It's very difficult to write a long piece of copy. You try to write a thousand words that engage people and it's very difficult. But if you think that that shows off your skill and it's something that you have, it's different and you manage to pull it off, then great.

Also I like enthusiasm. I don't like dreary people—dreary people who look bored, seem bored, or expect a job on a plate. Remember I'm also looking at people thinking, "Do I really want you in my creative department?" Interesting and interested people—that's what I'm looking for too.

What do you think about putting pieces in a book that aren't ads at all?

Yeah, fine. People might put photographs in their book all around, or it could just be a picture they've seen of something that inspires them. Because you've got to think: essentially, I would hire someone or give them a placement based on this. And so this book has to give me a good feeling of the type of person you are, how you think, what you get excited about, and how you could communicate. I think if you just sent me photographs and paintings and such, it's probably not enough. But I hired someone last year; he was an illustrator. He hadn't done any ads but I just liked his take on stuff. I liked his attitude. When I talked to him, he seemed very interested and he came in for a placement. I just said to him, "Come in and sort of hang around a bit—we'll see what we think of you, see what you think of us." He came in and he started doing all these sorts of interesting things and eventually, he just picked it up. And he started doing ads, and three months later, I hired him.

Do you have any other advice for someone who is trying to get into the industry?

Well, I think I've said it. I'm looking for their soul in a book. Their "take." Their point of view. What they stand for, in the book. The book might be selling 10 different products—but the big product it is selling is

you. So you have got to think about that. Be yourself and remember that you are totally unique and show me your uniqueness in your book. BI

To see Graham Fink's work, please visit http://breaking.in

PHILIP BONNERY
FREELANCE CREATIVE DIRECTOR
MIAMI

What do you look for in a student book? And what impresses you?

You're looking for new, fresh ideas. It sounds a bit cliché, but that's it: innovative work. Stuff you haven't seen before. Portfolios are pretty tight nowadays. I've seen students from ad schools with really good books. Most of them do internships so they get to work like any other full-time teams, some even get awards from doing a three-month internship.

Do you think just a book of sketches is okay if the ideas are good?

Perhaps as a teaser portfolio piece to get agencies' attention and stand out from the crowd. But when reviewing books, agencies will want to see finished ads as they want to know you can execute all the work, especially for art directors. Yes, in essence you need to come up with great ideas, but agencies want to see finished pieces the same way clients want to see finished pieces.

Do you think long copy is important to have in a student book?

If you've done a long-copy ad, a brochure, or a manifesto, and were able to turn that into something that stands out as clever or funny, more power to you. We should think of ourselves as entertainers. Whatever way it can be achieved: long copy, visual tricks, exploding cats, and what have you is okay—we've done our job. In general consumers aren't fond of advertising, therefore we better make it entertaining and worth people's time.

What do you think about putting things in a student book that are not ads?

Personally, I like to see people doing things other than advertising. It shows who you are, what you like to do, and all the things that interest you. I'd prefer people who are grounded in other things rather than just "ad geeks." Also, I find it interesting when people come from a non-advertising background. Advertising is a bit formulaic sometimes— perhaps people could be more receptive to seeing things from a different perspective.

"WE SHOULD THINK OF OURSELVES AS ENTERTAINERS."

Do you have any tips on how to get into the industry?

A great portfolio is all you really need. For me, being extremely handsome has helped too. BI

To see Philip Bonnery's work, please visit http://breaking.in

**BOB BARRIE
PARTNER & ECD
BARRIE D'ROZARIO MURPHY
MINNEAPOLIS**

What do you look for in a student book? And what impresses you?

I look for work that would survive in the "real world." This doesn't mean that it can't be smart, edgy, beautiful, provocative, and fresh. This just means it has to be viable, and not designed just for the pages of Archive Magazine.

Too much of student work is simply not very clear. It feels more like a MENSA test than a piece of marketing communication. And I don't know too many consumers today who have the time, patience, or attention span to work this hard. Do a test. Show the work in your book to your roommate. Your boyfriend. Your girlfriend. Your mother. Your uncle. Your dentist. Anyone but your fellow advertising students. They're your audience. They don't have to like it, but they do need to "get" it. If they don't, you perhaps have some revising and simplifying to do.

That said, your book's main goal should be a collection of brilliant, likable, differentiating ideas that are spread across a broad range of media. But then, you already knew that.

How important is finish? If ideas are the most important thing, can sketches be enough? Do you look at physical books anymore, or is it all websites?

Finish is important to me. A big part of being a great creative is "resourcefulness." If you're a brilliant thinker who happens to be crappy at executing and polishing ideas, find someone to do it for you. Maybe it's that great art direction or graphic design student you know. Make a deal with them and they can also put your new beautifully designed idea in their book as an example of their expertise. A great idea can really come alive with some lovely design behind it holding it. Or it can sit somewhat hidden in scribbles.

"A BIG PART OF BEING A GREAT CREATIVE IS 'RESOURCEFULNESS.'"

I enjoy looking at both physical books and websites. Websites are more convenient, but a book often enjoys the benefit of lying around the office for a while as a reminder of your genius.

How important is writing? Do you need to see long copy?

Long copy is not necessary, but very impressive when done well. And very rare. A lost art that is occasionally still relevant.

What do you think of showing work that is not advertising?

Fine, but keep it as an addendum to a well-thought-out advertising book. It's always nice to get a peek at one's creative pursuits beyond advertising. And many of them are, of course, ultimately relevant to your marketing skills.

Do you have any other advice for a student or junior trying to get into the business?

In putting your book together, remember that no medium is insignificant. If you're working on an airline, for example, realize that far more customers see a ticket jacket than see a TV commercial. BI

To see Bob Barrie's work, please visit http://breaking.in

HILLARY BLACK
CREATIVE RECRUITER & OWNER
KAY & BLACK
NEW YORK

What do you look for in a student book? And what impresses you?

The first thing that comes to mind is just showing that you're smart. Not necessarily the copy or the art on its own, as separate entities, but showing solid, complete ideas that display conceptual thinking. It sounds very easy to say that but it's not easy to do. I don't like to see books that are strictly all visual solutions or all copy—I like a mix. So the other answer would be that I really like to see a range. I want to see clients that are difficult, clients that you don't want to work on, and I want you to do an ad that looks like, not only would the creative director love it, but some of the clients are actually going to love it too.

And if you're a writer, show that you can do body copy, even if you don't want to have it. And as an art director, show that you know how to work around

it and still bring the reader into it, because that is difficult, I think.

So you answered a couple of my follow-up questions already.

Oops, sorry.

One was about body copy.

I think it's important. And I think that if you can write body copy, it just shows off your skill. Sometimes the best body copy is the stuff that is really smart—it's teaching somebody something that's interesting, and if it's not an exciting client and you don't want to do it, then make it fun. That's even more impressive. And the art director's job is actually just as important. The body copy, if it's read, is the result of the headline and art direction both working together. If you get me to read the body copy then you did something right and you made the client happy.

And you touched on this already, but do you think sketches can be enough anymore or do you think it should be finished on a computer?

It needs to be finished on a computer now. It's just because that's what everyone is doing and it's what creative directors want to see. I think it's also critical that you have a website. I don't even carry any physical books anymore. We just saw two people—a junior team—and some of their stuff was just sketches and I appreciated seeing it in there actually. I like when candidates will show me where they started, and where they ended—it's cool to see that. So it could be interesting as a side project within your student book, to show your sketches from beginning to end, if you're confident enough in your beginning to end. But you can't just show sketches because it's just not what creative directors usually want to see.

It goes for writers and art directors?

Yes. But I think that some people may say other things. That's a good question for creative directors. It might be fun for some of them. But, in general, that is not what they expect to see. They want to get in and get out and see right off the bat that you have what it takes to sell the clients to consumers, and then a lot of them want you to be able to win awards for it.

What do you think about things that aren't ads in a student book?

I like it. If you're a poet, give me some poetry. If you write music, give me a song. Not everyone's going to agree with that because some people may feel like they don't have enough time to view or listen. To me, my best creatives are creative—they are often artists. The best talent I have found over the years didn't get into advertising for advertising but for the ability to be creative nine to five. They're not big into selling to the consumer. They almost want to help the consumer. One of the best said to me once, "You owe it to the consumer to give them something good." And to show that you have a personality. Sometimes I see a book and I don't think that the book is that solid, but if I think they are a great writer, and they wrote a short story, or they wrote a movie, I'm not going to read the whole script, but if I could see that there's a personality there, I'm going to be intrigued. And I think it is very important for the agencies to be intrigued.

Do you have any tips on how to get into the industry for students who are just starting out?

I think the best way to get in is to be really hungry. You have to be. So start out by going to as many things as you possibly can. I don't like to "shmooze" at all, but I recommend it. Get all the trades [publications], really know the business. Just learn. And then make lists of all the agencies while you're still in school. Just start figuring out who you like and why you like them and make notes about it. If you see an ad, and you think it's great, write down that ad, even if you're not graduating for two years. Write it down, write who did it, why you loved it, and why it inspired you. And maybe when you graduate, send a letter thanking them for inspiring you and more.

I once had a candidate who did something which I think is truly conceptual with branding herself. She created a wallet and made a fake license and credit card of the creative director and dropped it in the bathroom of the agency.

Lee Clow, right?

Yes.

It was in an award show. And it had her portfolio in the wallet, right?

Yes...and he gave her a job. So, be creative. I had a woman who did music. I don't represent music producers but she came to me and asked me for help. And I said, "You know what? You're in music. And most people just send their résumé, that's it. Put it in an old eight-track case. Or just a cassette case, or CD cover, or create something." Make yourself stand out. Be different. Really, just try to be inventive, innovative, and creative in your approach to selling yourself as a brand. Give them the unexpected. ▣

**FEH TARTY
CREATIVE DIRECTOR
MOTHER
LONDON**

Interviewed at Wieden+Kennedy, London.

Okay, here we go.

Feh Tarty. F-E-H T-A-R-T-Y.

That wasn't a required part of the interview, but I like it. I like the enthusiasm. So first question is, what do you look for in a student book, and what impresses you in a student book?

A student book is like couture advertising. You know what I mean?

No. I don't.

If you look at a fashion show, it's not necessarily things that are completely ready to wear, but it's a way of thinking. Of how to break the mold of what is normally out there or what you expect people to see. I think when students try to continue to take on real projects and make it seem real, they sort of lose their sense of creativity. Because school is the last chance you have for years, until you get some experience under your belt, to create something that's just a full-on expression of how you think. Advertising should be, design should be, or whatever it is you're into, should be like that. And so, in a book, you just look for new ways of thinking and how they push ideas, because that's what it's all about before you get hit with the reality.

> *"SCHOOL IS THE LAST CHANCE YOU HAVE FOR YEARS, UNTIL YOU GET SOME EXPERIENCE UNDER YOUR BELT, TO CREATE SOMETHING THAT'S JUST A FULL-ON EXPRESSION OF HOW YOU THINK."*

So make it conceptual…don't try and make it really realistic?

Yeah, you want to get a sense of it being realistic but it's like…the ideas that a client would have to be really brave to buy. Still responsible in their thinking, but it requires a sort of bravery.

How important is the finish? Do you think sketches can be enough?

Normally I'd say sketches would be enough because that's how it was when I was in school. I hate saying this, but I don't think sketches hold up as much anymore because student books aren't just about print. And I think you have opportunity with computers now. We did sketches because that's as far as you were able to go because you didn't have

access [to computers]. You had to go to the library and search through all these books to find an image to represent what you wanted to do. You had to go and buy all these magazines, and you probably couldn't afford them, or to get as many as you wanted. But now the Internet makes it a lot easier and makes it all really possible. So you have a lot of options to choose from. So I kind of lean away from seeing sketches in there. It's like, "Yeah, okay you have ideas, but there are tons of students who have killer ideas who also understand execution."

I think when you have that option and I see someone who has a great idea with a sketch and here's a person who has a great idea and then executes it really nicely, it's like, I know that I don't have to push that person or I have to even hold them back. You always want to have way more than talent, way more than you need, and then work it down into the real world if that's necessary. As opposed to seeing someone who has "potential"…because that's what sketches look like: "You have potential." It's a guessing game at that point.

And with advertising, I think it's fair to say that we're at the head of culture. We sort of influence culture in a certain way, so you have an obligation to be current. And right now, honestly, if you start off with sketches, it's good to get your ideas down, but you have way too many options in executing. Digital cameras are everywhere. You can go shoot something that you want. There are video [capabilities] in every camera you can get. So you can make a video of something. I think you've got to utilize the resources that you have to make something cool, because I'd rather see something poorly produced, but I can get the idea and the effort. In the past, I think we were limited by what we could do before, which is why sketches were in books. But nowadays, I don't think it really holds up. It probably comes across more as lazy unless you're going to show me 100 sketches. One hundred different ideas of one thing. Then I would say, sketches are great. Because you're just generating idea, after idea, after idea. If you come in with one sketch for a thing and then that's where you stop, it's like, I don't think you really did your work yet.

What do you think about long copy? Is that something a book should have, in your opinion?

I think when someone does that they're probably going through a checklist of "Things My Book Should Have." And I think the days of checklists in books are over. Before, advertising had specific mediums, like, "You've got briefs, you've got to do a radio spot, you have to do a print ad, you have to do outdoor, and you have to do TV." Creators got lazy because they didn't have to think outside of any of those things. And I think professors knew that. Now we're going through this sort of transitional period where those channels that we've been using to get to people are different now. It's a different playing field. Back in the day, in the States, you only had a few channels back in the '80s. You know, and here [in the UK] there were four channels. Before cable, you didn't have that many options. So it's like you had to write for those mediums. Now, what that also did was it gave people short attention spans. So if you're going to write long copy and you think you have to have that, it better be dang interesting because we're trained to: click, click, click, click, click the remote. And on the Internet: click, click, click, click. So thinking that you have to have a long-copy ad in your book to prove that you can write, that means you're not thinking hard enough, because if you have an idea, you should think of how it can be blown out in many different ways. There are so many ways to come at that now, whereas before your ad had to do everything. Good writing is good writing. And if it's good, you enjoy it, you read it, you don't stop. But if it's just for the sake of doing it then you probably don't have a good enough idea—which is a bigger problem.

What do you think about putting things in your book that aren't ads?

You should showcase who you are. How you think. And at some point you're going to tap into that. You're going to have to because I think at some point, when you're creating your work, there's a piece of you in it. I remember when I was in school one of my professors was like, "You can't have a style. Because you have to make sure it's for the brand." Yeah, true, but I think you can end up with a style in the way you do things. You evolve your style. You evolve the way you think all the time. But I think that there's a certain thing that people do well and that's because they have certain

resources, or certain talents, from other things that they pull in. There are writers who will never be able to write the way Pat [Feh's copywriter] writes. And there's some writers he can never write like. You know what I mean?

And then the style: the agency can have a brand, but you have all these people to pull from. Like, "Oh this person's really great at that, and they used to do this." So you kind of need to know that when you get assignments because it's like you get to channel other things. So it just makes the job more exciting and more fun when you can do something that you're passionate about. An assignment might call for writing a book, and if you love doing that, then do it.

Do you have any other advice?

Really, make sure you're having fun right now, because if you're not having fun now, you probably won't have fun when you start working. BI

To see Feh Tarty's work, please visit http://breaking.in

V SUNIL
EXECUTIVE CREATIVE DIRECTOR
WIEDEN+KENNEDY
DELHI

What do you look for in a student portfolio? And what impresses you?

I think it would be a cliché, but we look for fresh ideas—new ideas that we have not seen before. Because typically, what happens is that most students are trying to do work they've seen before. They're trying to do work that maybe will impress you. They're trying to do work like what has won awards. But actually, what we're looking for is new talent, new ideas, a new kind of craft which we never get to see.

Do you like to see finished work—work that's been finished on a computer—or are sketches enough?

Actually it depends. Sometimes, for an art director, we'd like to see some kind of craftsmanship, of course based on an idea. But I don't think the final finishing is that important, if the idea is strong. And from a writer, of course not—it's just the concept. But as an art director, yes. Because that kind of shows you whether they will actually pull it off. A lot of art directors are very good at ideas, but if they can't art-direct the page then I don't know. As an art director, I think there's a problem. Art directors need to know a lot of technical things because that's what will make you a very good art director. Like from idea to executing in the most fresh possible way.

And for a writer, do you want to see long copy or some evidence of writing?

Yeah. First, you want headlines. There are some writers who can just write one line and you can kind of imagine the ad on the page. Some writers can't do that, but ideally what you look for is idea-based headlines and also the ability to write long copy beautifully.

And what do you think about putting pieces of work in a book that aren't ads at all?

I think the other things are more important, actually. It kind of projects the person. If you're half creative—I think anyone can do an ad. But if you are really clever, that's when you use your ideas to do better, new things. So I think that will really help to see what other things they can do. But it also shows what kind of character they are. And very often we ask people things like, "What do you do in the evenings?" and, "Where do your parents stay?" Normally, we ask all kinds of funny questions to get what kind of person they are. So this might just answer that—by putting interesting other things on the page. That's something you'll get really excited about rather than a regular ad because that's the kind of thing that we like to do: new things. I think we are looking for the kids with new sensibilities without actually losing the ground of reality. With a lot of kids, that's the problem now. They have no "concept knowledge" of their country or where they live or generally about the world. Maybe they know more about other designers and art directors, but they may not know the culture, the history. So I think this "other work" kind of helps with that.

And what would be one piece of advice that you would give to someone who's about to graduate from school and wants to get into advertising?

I think for me, especially if you are a good creative, and especially in a country like India, right now, creative people need to be capable of being really professional. Because our world, like everything else, is about value for money and time and things like that. Somehow creative people don't understand that until the time they become very senior. When a creative director becomes a creative director, then he is very conscious about time and he gets more professional. But when you're young, that is something missing in most people. And the guys who have that, they are the ones who actually grow much faster within the system. I think that helps.

Professionalism.

Professionalism, I think. [BI]

To see V Sunil's work, please visit http://breaking.in

ROSANN CALISI
RECRUITING CONSULTANT
RAZORFISH
SAN FRANCISCO

Interviewed at Deutsch, Los Angeles.

What do you look for in a student book? And what impresses you?

I look for variety and unique projects. Variety in the kinds of campaigns they work on. Not the typical student clients: Snowboards, movie festivals, etc. Somebody who has taken a fairly unique product or service and done something kind of cool with it. And, on top of it, something that's not your traditional three-spread ads, three-spread ads, three-spread ads, because that's really completely unrealistic. I mean, even our most senior teams here never work on three-spread ads. It's very unusual. What have they done with some interesting fractionals, newspaper, guerrilla postings, websites, anything like that, that's just a little different that approaches advertising in a unique manner other than the super-traditional print. Because, if you can come up with something really unique, I'm assuming, you can probably do a great print ad too.

What do you think about sketches versus finished work?

Well, unfortunately, I think the bar has been raised. I think that part of the reality of working in an ad agency these days is that art directors and copywriters know their way around Photoshop, Illustrator, In-Design, and I think it tends to come across a little bit unfinished and lazy, to be honest with you, if somebody hasn't taken the time to put together a decent layout with maybe stock art or somewhat finished art and a finished layout. Some thought about typography. It's too amateur coming in to an agency with just sketch books. It's about the idea but it's actually also the execution.

What do you think about long copy? Is it necessary for a writer to have that?

Well, I personally think it is. I think that one of the most difficult things to find is a copywriter who can do radio, for instance. If I find a radio writer, that to me is like gold because that's writing in its most pure form. It's usually uninterrupted by a lot of different production hands, and directors, and producers, and creative directors, and so if somebody can do radio that's always terrific in my mind.

I think that visually oriented campaigns are really important and strong, but at the end of the day, sometimes you're going to have to write for the agency and maybe it involves long copy. If you look at the Saturn ads that we've done recently, it's an entire paragraph or two of nothing but copy and you might have to do something like that at an agency as a copywriter. So I personally like to see a couple of examples of long copy in a book.

What do you think about including things that aren't ads?

That is something that I'm really big on because, even if they've gone to portfolio schools, sometimes student books are a little generic and they don't really tell me much about the person.

Also, I think students make the mistake of not making their résumé part of the whole package. Sometimes people have a really corporate-looking résumé even though they are a creative person who has been in the business zero years. And I always tell them, "I don't like to see a big, corporate résumé. Use this opportunity to do something cool and tell me about you." And then, when I pull that out of them, they say, "Well, I am an artist" or, "I'm a photographer and I've got a website too." Put that in your presentation somehow. You don't have to show me everything that you've done, but I think sprinkling a traditional creative portfolio for advertising with your passion, whether it's photography, or copywriting, or poetry, or painting, I think it makes you a more well-rounded human being and sort of a student of art and culture and not just some robot that does nothing but advertising.

Do you have any tips for someone who wants to get into the industry?

I would say the days of the big, giant portfolio are literally gone. I mean, in the last six months, it's gone from, "Yeah, we're going to cut somebody a break because they are just starting out" to "You kind of seem old fashioned if you present a portfolio that is in like a big, zipper kind of portfolio case." So I would encourage people to find your way of doing a version of a mini-book, a mini-book that could be sent to somebody like me, which is easy to get through, has all the information that I need, and is very clear and legible, and nice and neat, because I might want to keep that.

Another big thing is that a lot of students who will come here in person and show me their book feel like their campaigns have to be explained. They say, "Well, let me tell you what the setup here is." I always tell them: "You're here today but when you send your book out, it has to be able to speak for itself and it's got to have to be self-explanatory." So don't write the big intro paragraph page about what I was trying to say on this ad. If it doesn't work and if it requires explanation, it's not going to work for people who aren't meeting you in person. BI

What do you look for in a student book? And what impresses you?

I'll tell you what doesn't impress me, which might be easier, is super-finished ads. Because that's now the price of entry. Before, when you'd see a super-finished ad, it'd be like, "Wow this is really cool." But then you see so much of that now that it's like people dress up bad ideas. I'd rather see a really unpolished great idea than something fully blown out that shouldn't have been. So what do I look for?

Yeah, what do you look for?

I look for a big idea because anyone can do one little joke. Anyone can write a headline, but if there's a thought that changes the way I feel about something, then, to me, that is bigger. It seems like a lot of ads you see in student books are just one-off little jokey things. And maybe they're all tied together because they have the same sort of punch-line setup. But if you can do something that really positions the way you think about something completely differently, like, "Wow. I never thought of it that way. But I should have." That's what I look for.

You mentioned too much finish. Do you think a book of sketches is enough?

I think that'd be really fresh, yeah. As long as the ideas come across. With some ideas you have to execute a little bit just because they won't be clear in sketches. But I think it'd be a fresh approach if their idea was good enough, and it just stood on its own without having to shoot it and do all those things.

You see a lot of visual ideas these days. And you just have to execute a lot of those. But I've seen so many writers' books without any words in it. It's like, "That's cool, that it's all about the idea," but show me you can write too, because you're going to have to do that.

That was actually my next question: do you think it's necessary to have long copy in your book?

I do. If you're a writer, I think you should be able to write. There's been a lot of times I've dealt with people who can do good TV spots, they can come up with good guerrilla ideas, but when they really have to just write like a writer, and put a thought down on paper, they can't. It depends on what kind of work you want to do too. But I think it's just a basic skill that you should be able to write because it shows how you think. Writing is thinking. And if you can put that together in a cool way, then it says a lot about the way you think.

What do you think about putting things in a book that aren't ads at all? Like other writing, or art, or photography?

I think it's a good idea as long as you have the other stuff covered. As long as you can say, "I can take this creativity, this wild way of looking at something, and apply it to your problem that you're going to hand me over your desk." Because, if you come back with just cool art projects that have nothing to do with the problem we're trying to solve, it's going to be no help to anybody. But I would love to see how people think. I just like to peek inside someone's mind. And I want to do stuff that doesn't feel like advertising. So if you have experience that isn't in advertising, then that's helpful.

"WRITING IS THINKING. AND IF YOU CAN PUT THAT TOGETHER IN A COOL WAY, THEN IT SAYS A LOT ABOUT THE WAY YOU THINK."

How did you get into the business initially?

I snuck in right before these polished ads came out. I had no art-direction training whatsoever. So I just did ideas that were super rough and handwritten, and I went to Kinko's and sort of Xeroxed it up. And it was during the grunge years. So I Xeroxed it up big so people could read it. And it got all distressed and cool.

I'd show it around, and they'd say, "Wow, who did your art direction? It's really cool!" And I said, "No, it's just so you could read it." It looked like I did some effect on it, and made it look like some sort of cool, grungy '90s art direction. But it was really just because I went to Kinko's, and cut and pasted my headlines from my dot-matrix printer and just put it down.

But again, now I think every book I see is so polished. Everyone is coming out of Portfolio Center and Creative Circus [ad schools]. I don't know if I could've gotten a job with my little book [nowadays]. I'd almost have to go to school. Then again, if someone came in to me with an idea that was that rough but just had fresh ideas, I think it would stand out.

Do you have any tips for someone who's just starting out? Either on how to get into the business or how to improve?

To get into the business...a lot of people call me all the time and ask if they can just come in and meet, and just show me their book. Sometimes people are super busy and it's hard to. But if you can get in and just meet people, you'd be surprised how you'll come back in a year. You'll be working at the same places. This industry is so small that it's two degrees of separation. So, if you meet one person, they can introduce you to someone else. I think that's the biggest thing: When your book is at a place where you want to hear some feedback, just get out there. And talk to people you respect, and if you've developed and grown, then come back to them. I think that's probably the best way to do it. Just build relationships with people. Not to be a pest, but to just get to know someone who can help you. Find a mentor.

Is there anything else?

Let me see if there's any other wisdom I can impart. I was trying to think what I would want to know when I was getting into it because I was completely clueless. I didn't know you had to have a book. I came out of journalism school with a bunch of writing I'd done for articles and stuff. And then I met an art director. And he said, "Well, do you have a book?" I'm like, "What do you mean?" He told me, "You have to have a portfolio with fake ads." I had no idea. So I just went on

my own and just started looking at good ads, and did it myself.

One thing is, when you start interviewing and showing your book around, you're not done. To a lot of people, it's like, "This is the book." You'll look back in a year and go, "What was I thinking, putting that in my book?" Because you've got to keep continually improving. And looking at a book, it's hard, as a creative director, but you do it. You're not supposed to but you'll grade on the worst ad that you see in there. So if you're not sure about something, don't put it in your book. Put in only the stuff you're sure about. Even if other people have said it's great, and you have that sneaking suspicion that it's not, then I wouldn't put it in. You should be the highest bar. And if someone says that they don't like something that you've done but you really like it, I'd keep that in too because you don't want to work for someone who doesn't get you. BI

To see Greg Hahn's work, please visit http://breaking.in

GUSTAVO LAURIA
CCO & MANAGING PARTNER
THE VIDAL PARTNERSHIP
NEW YORK

Interviewed at La Comunidad, Miami.

What do you look for in a student book? And what impresses you?

I like students who explore and have fresh ideas even if those ideas don't work perfectly. I'd rather see a book with good, but not quite polished, thoughts than one with safe ideas or ideas that follow a typical advertising formula. The majority of the books that we receive are pretty similar. They are full of two things: Visual solutions that maybe could win a student award but lack anything new, and excessive use of interactivity and technology just to show that they know about them, but lacking a strong concept. I don't care if a student has won awards, and I don't care in what media they developed their work. The only thing that is important is whether they are really thinking—it doesn't matter what—as long as they think, try, and show potential. Then, a CD can always help them make those crazy ideas work.

"THE MAJORITY OF THE BOOKS THAT WE RECEIVE ARE PRETTY SIMILAR. THEY ARE FULL OF TWO THINGS: VISUAL SOLUTIONS THAT MAYBE COULD WIN A STUDENT AWARD BUT LACK ANYTHING NEW, AND EXCESSIVE USE OF INTERACTIVITY AND TECHNOLOGY JUST TO SHOW THAT THEY KNOW ABOUT THEM, BUT LACKING A STRONG CONCEPT."

So you would rather see something bold and daring even if it doesn't totally work?

Yes. To me, it's better when an intern or junior creative gives you 20 different ideas that show different thoughts than only three ideas with visual solutions and really nice retouching. It's not about knowing Photoshop or Illustrator—it's more about coming up with ideas. When you are a student is the time to make mistakes, and by doing so, you can end up with something very unique.

Do you think just a book of sketches is okay if the ideas are good?

Well, for a copywriter, yes, it is. Obviously, an art director should be good not only at thinking but also designing and art directing. Because for art directors, that's part of the exploration that I was explaining before.

Do you think long copy is important to have in a student book?

Yes, it's not common to see books with good writing. And a good line can really make an ad or a campaign much better. In my opinion, that's key, and I love to see books from kids who really spend time thinking and coming up with smart lines and copy.

What do you think about putting things in a student book that are not ads?

As I said before, it is about coming up with good ideas. It doesn't matter if it is a classic long-copy ad, a social-media thing, or an artistic installation. It is great if they have other stuff because it shows that they love to think and create things. It shows passion and creative exploration.

Now anyone can come up with an idea and spread that idea with almost nothing. That's why the challenge and the opportunity is even greater for everyone. And it's nice when kids take advantage of that and create something with that freshness that only students have.

Do you have any tips on how to get into the industry?

Show passion. It is the most important thing. If you really have it, sooner or later you will get what you want. But I'm not taking about passion for the sake of it. I'm taking about that passion that pushes you to always be better. The best, top creatives will recognize it. ⊞

To see Gustavo Lauria's work, please visit http://breaking.in

KEITH WHITE
TALENT DIRECTOR
MEDIA ARTS LAB
LOS ANGELES

Interviewed at Wieden+Kennedy, Amsterdam.

**What do you look for in a student book?
And what impresses you?**

First I look for clarity of thought and simplicity in the presentation of that thought. So for instance, I like to see an idea and sometimes it could be set up with, "This is what the idea is, and this is the execution of it." I don't need to see a thousand things in a book. If I see three to five strong ideas, contained, then that gets my attention. And if I want to see more, then I'll ask for more. But I'd rather have less than more.

The ideas should be clear and expressed clearly. Also identify the media and how it would work, in print, online, TV, or radio because it's not enough to have an idea, I want to know how it lives. And it should feel real. So it doesn't matter to me if something is spec or hasn't run because the idea, once it's produced, it's produced. It's born. And that's what I like to see.

"IT DOESN'T MATTER TO ME IF SOMETHING IS SPEC OR HASN'T RUN BECAUSE THE IDEA, ONCE IT'S PRODUCED, IT'S PRODUCED. IT'S BORN. AND THAT'S WHAT I LIKE TO SEE."

And I personally like things that do not feel "ad-y." And you see a lot of that in student books. But that's also probably a symptom of how they're taught. And I think the whole approach has to be revisited. And I think that needs to start at the teaching level. The teachers need to be more in tune with what's happening outside of school, and how agencies are producing work, and the challenges that they're facing as well. And the new buzzword I suppose is "integrated." But for me, that's still just multimedia.

**Do you care if the ads or ideas are finished?
Or just sketched?**

I would say if it's a really strong idea [a sketch would be okay]. I do like the notion that it's a sketch because, if you don't have the budget to execute…sometimes execution is the death knell for an idea. And if I'm looking at work, I like to see what someone's capable of. And if it's a sketch, or if it's just a piece of copy that shows your skill as a writer for instance, for me that's fine. And then if you don't have the budget or you don't have the right skill set to execute it, I would just say leave it rough. Because people get stuck if it's too finished. And they start judging you based on the look of it and on little details.

Does that apply to art directors as well?

Yeah. I would say more so as an art director. If you can't execute it well and you're an art director, don't finish it. Because you'll be judged as an art director for poor art direction.

Do you think it's important to have long copy in a book?

I like to see some long copy, especially if you're a writer. I think it shows off your writing skill, and that you can do it. Because sometimes an ad won't have any copy. But if we're interviewing you, we want to know what you can do, what you're capable of, what your range is. And sometimes the writing is not even for the final ad. It's actually to set up a manifesto for a client. And to help articulate what the idea is, what the strategy is. Or how it's going to look when we get to the execution phase, or how other people will work with this idea that we may not execute for other mediums. So it's basically a blueprint. And I think that is very important. To be able to write, almost instructions: "This is the idea. This is how it lives." And also to help sell the concept. Because, if it's a big company, the marketing director has to take this back to their people, to their board, to sell through. They may have the direct contact with us. And unless they're great orators, they're going to need the support. And that document becomes their support. So the writing has to also do another job—it's not just for a final ad.

What do you think about including things that aren't ads?

Absolutely important. I would say, if you're a writer, include writing. And it could be a short piece of fiction, long fiction, something that shows your way of thinking, your imagination, your tone of voice. And that, for me, is very important. I'm not necessarily that interested in seeing ads, because for me, ads are what you're going to be asked to do. And for me it's always retrospective anyway—what someone has done. It's more about what they will do that decides whether or not we will work with someone, because we don't want another ad. We have to keep evolving, pushing things forward. Our work in the future may be a TV show. And it may be a short film in addition to a headline. I think, particularly with writers, we want to see writing. And again, I would say be very edited, very clear, very focused. Less is more. And for art directors, I absolutely want to see personal work. I want to see what your sensibility is as a designer, as an art director. What your taste level is. How you put things together. So personal work is important.

And what do you think is the best way to improve if you're just starting out?

Well I would say look at work that moves you. Look at work that you admire and just study it. And think about, "How was this done?" I mean, writers do this all the time. If they're reading a book, they think, "How did they do it? How was this done?" Because as you're reading it, you're just experiencing the narrative. But if you're actually a writer yourself and you're developing your craft, you want to know, "How did they do that?" And you should study work that you really like.

It's the same with movies. Tarantino, he was a cinephile. And that helps him, I think, in his own work. So it's developing a point of view and, again, keeping it really, really simple. And not derivative either. Try to be as original as you can in your expression. And I think by knowing what's out there, you can develop your own point of view so that it feels fresh. Because a creative director is looking for someone who will not only solve a creative problem, but also build the reputation of the agency and also their reputation as a creative director. Because, at the end of the day, they're being judged on the output of the creative department. And if the work is not great, it's a bad reflection on them. So they want to hire someone that's going to make them look good and also make their lives easier as a creative director. So those are the kind of parameters I'm looking for when I see a book.

It's also potential. You just feel it if someone can do it. And someone who can interact with people at all levels. And be collaborative, and creative, and a pleasure to work with as well. And somebody you want to partner with and you feel comfortable with. And I would also say people starting out should also develop their presentation skills and be good persuaders. But you first have to believe in your work. And then I think the persuasion part comes naturally if you really believe in it. And just be inspired and stay inspired. Look at stuff outside of advertising. Because ads, let's face it, are just a small part of what is out there. And actually advertising's not that interesting anymore. I mean, it's all about communication and creating things that people want to spend time with and seek out. So we have to be clever, I think, and relevant.

And then one other thing about the presentation of a book: I would strongly recommend putting everything together in a website. I think it's the perfect format for showing your work. And then, if there's interest, maybe follow up with a printed piece as a leave-behind. But to be honest with you, I'm trying to get rid of clutter. So for me, it's great to just have a link to a website. It's an efficient way to get your work seen by as many people as possible. ▣

SCOTT VITRONE & IAN REICHENTHAL
EXEC CREATIVE DIRECTORS
BARTON F. GRAF 9000
NEW YORK

What do you look for in a student book? And what impresses you?

SV: I think one of the better junior books that we remember, Ian and I both said the same thing when we saw it: that we felt like we just met the person. You could feel his personality coming through it—through the work. And it was just subtle things. You could kind of get an idea of who this guy was and what his voice was like. And a lot of times you don't see that. More often, you see books that try to reflect what people think a great book is supposed to look like.

IR: We're not talking about a book where all the campaigns were alike, or that they all seemed like they were coming from the exact same voice. It wasn't that. It was just…

SV: It was skewed a little bit.

IR: Yeah. It was just that this person had a point of view on each assignment that was different. If you gave the same assignments to 1,000 people, I bet nobody would have come up with the same idea for any of them.

What do you think about sketches? If the idea is strong enough does the presentation matter?

SV: I think it's been made to matter. If you combine a great idea with great execution, it's going to resonate a little more than a great idea… the same great idea just in a comp form. It's just the same in an agency. You have a great idea on paper, then production hopefully enhances that.

IR: If we had our choice…if we had to choose between two books, one that was really polished but filled with bad ideas and a book that was filled with really great ideas but not so polished, obviously we'd pick the one with the great ideas in it. But it's probably true that, if you have great ideas and you know how to produce them well, that would be more valuable than just the book full of great ideas in sketch form. It's part of what we're going to ask of a new team…a lot of their job is putting ideas together.

What about copy for writers? Do you need to see evidence of writing ability? Or is long copy just not as important anymore?

IR: I think it is. Yes, I definitely want to see evidence that the person can write. It's important in digital. It's important in film…

You mean in digital ideas?

IR: Yes. In long-format digital ideas, in film, in all different forms of branded content…so yes, we want to see it. But an equally important skill—and something that we definitely also want to see—is that you know how to be succinct. So to answer your question: yes, long copy. But also yes, short copy.

What do you think about putting things that aren't ads in a book?

SV: I think it's good. But if you're going to put personal stuff in, it needs to be really interesting. It can't just be, "Hey, I paint sometimes," and then there's a bunch of shitty paintings in there. I think if you're going to put your personal work in, your personal work needs to be as conceptual and as innovative as the other stuff.

"MORE OFTEN, YOU SEE BOOKS THAT TRY TO REFLECT WHAT PEOPLE THINK A GREAT BOOK IS SUPPOSED TO LOOK LIKE."

IR: I think it needs to be more interesting, because you don't have to also sell a cholesterol drug at the same time. You can do whatever you want. So I think it needs to be at least as interesting, or more interesting, than what you have in your book if you're going to include it.

If you were to give someone who was just starting out advice on how to put together a book, or how to get into the industry, what would you say?

SV: Give it the proper amount of time. About two years. You have to commit to it. When I started, I tried to half-ass it. I was working full-time and was trying to do it at night, and do it by myself. And it showed. It wasn't until I fully committed, and surrounded myself with people who wanted to do the same thing, that I got traction. So you've got to give yourself enough time and fully, fully commit.

IR: I don't know if I have any single pearl of wisdom for that question. But I would say, be honest about the stuff in your book. You have to be able to look at your own work and kill it if it honestly isn't up to par. And that's hard to do. Especially at first, your honesty about what's in the book is fighting your urge to be done with the whole process. They're fighting each other. You really, really want to be done with it and get out there and get a job. So you want to believe that the book is finished. But really, you have to—even with all of that going on—you have to really look at it and be painfully honest with yourself and say, "That ad's not ready, that's not ready to go in yet."

SV: Also don't put a number on it. I wouldn't say you have to have a certain number of pieces in your book. I know that was something that always came up. How many pieces should I have in my book?

IR: Oh yeah. That's in all of these kinds of put-your-book-together type books. People always say, "Oh, you should have exactly this many."

SV: I just think you have to look at all of the pieces together, and when it feels good, and if they all work well together, then that's your book. BI

To see work from Scott Vitrone & Ian Reichenthal, please visit http://breaking.in

**ROB REILLY
GLOBAL CREATIVE CHAIRMAN
MCCANN WORLDGROUP
NEW YORK**

What do you look for in a student book? And what impresses you?

It's hard these days. And I'm sure students are trying to figure out the secret formula. There really isn't one. In the end, a good idea is what landed you a job 20 years ago and it is most likely the thing that will land you a job today.

How important is finish? If ideas are the most important thing, can sketches be enough? Do you look at actual books anymore, or is it all websites?

I personally like paper books. Though I will look at a website if it loads fast and it is easy to navigate. If you can't go to finish on stuff and just have sketches, you better be damn sure you have the greatest idea ever.

How important is copy? Do you need to see long-copy ads?

The ability for a copywriter to write is incredibly important. More and more, brands are asking agencies to write their stories. Writing a narrative is difficult. But if you are good at it you will have a long career.

What do you think of showing work that is not advertising?

It is always helpful to have more than less.

Do you have any other advice for a student or junior trying to get into the business, either in putting together a book or how to actually start looking for jobs?

Internships are very important. You learn a lot and you actually get to talk to people who have successfully done the very thing you are trying to do. BI

To see Rob Reilly's work, please visit http://breaking.in

What do you look for in a student book? And what impresses you?

To say I look for something original wouldn't be very original at all. What I like most is just people who aren't afraid. A lot of books are cookie cutter. A lot of them are the same. I don't think that means what they have isn't good work. But I like to see stuff that's different. Someone who took a risk. Not for shock value. It has to be good, obviously. Otherwise you end up looking bad.

I like writers who can art-direct and art directors who can write. That's impressive and important. What you'll sometimes get in real-world advertising is, "Let's come up with the idea and then I'll take care of the art direction and you take care of the copy" or vice versa. I enjoy working with people who won't draw a line. I'm a writer but I'm very passionate about design, too. And I love working with art directors who can sit down and say, "Let's write it like this." They'll be just as involved with the writing as I will be in the art direction. And nowadays, with new media and, more than ever, lines should be blurred, or even not there at all in some cases.

Are sketches enough or do things need to be comped up? And do you ever look at hard-copy books or just websites?

I guess it would be correct to say, "Yes, sketches are fine." But you know what? I think it's kind of lazy if you don't go the distance and try to impress. When I started out as an aspiring copywriter without a job, I could have just done sketches. I didn't know how to use Photoshop and Quark—what we used back in the day—but I taught myself. It's important to show it how you want it to look. And if you don't know how to do it then teach yourself. Get a friend to help. Pay someone. Barter your services. That's not only getting creative. That's showing passion.

I'm a bit of a hybrid. I've always delivered in every medium, and I think it shows in how I present my work. Or, at least, how I started presenting it. I was one of the first creatives I know, in my circle at least, to have an online portfolio. Just because I wanted people to see what I'm doing no matter where they were. And since everyone I know lives all over the world, it was, and still is, the best way. Obviously, it's better to have both a website and a hard-copy portfolio, or just something people can download and print out.

I prefer websites though. Take a banner ad, for example. It's motion. And showing it in motion is better. In a book, showing a banner is like showing a TV spot in storyboard. It works, but not the way it ran. In this day and age, you have to have a website. They're simple enough to create. And for the site, don't get fancy. Just get to the work. And let it do the talking.

What do you think about long copy? Is it important to have in a book?

As a writer, you should know you'll be faced with writing brochures, websites, email newsletters, and more. You might have to do little mini-booklets for that cool guerrilla idea or an insert for magazines. So, yes, absolutely. I think long body-copy is important to show. But only if it's great. I wouldn't include something just for the sake of having it in there. Writing long body-copy isn't easy. But when you have it down, it's a brilliant feeling. And when someone reading it reacts with, "Damn, this kid can write!" then so much the better.

"JUST GET TO THE WORK. AND LET IT DO THE TALKING."

At some point, I included in my book the first page of a Volkswagen New Beetle brochure I'd written. It was in there because I was proud of the writing. It was two or three paragraphs long. I remember spending hours and weeks tweaking and finessing the copy for all the brochures to make sure all the copy was airtight and bulletproof. I'd made countless revisions and had endless debates with my creative director about this comma and that word before the brochures went to print. I'm not ashamed of the obsessive thinking, care, and endless hours that went into them. Quite the contrary. For me, a love for writing isn't optional. It's a mandate.

What do you think about putting things in a book that aren't ads?

Interesting question. There are loads of people in advertising who are, if you ask me, true artists. People who happened to take on advertising as a career. But they could have been painters, playwrights, musicians. Then there are people like me. I work in advertising. But I'm not an artist. For me, the book is all about showcasing work. Work that would help clients move their products. Not art. Unless art works for the work. The work should be artistic. But I don't think it's art. Personally, I'd save artistic work for your art portfolio, or prose for your novel, play, or blog. But whatever floats your boat. You should include whatever you want. If what's in there is related to this industry in a real and tangible way and you can prove it, then go for it. If not, don't.

Do you have any tips for someone who's just starting out on how to get into the industry?

Put yourself out there. Stay current, look at work, read articles and publications. See what's going on and immerse yourself in it—just so you know what's going on. And write to people. Say what you liked. Or didn't.

If and when you get in front of people for interviews or meetings, then be professional, be passionate, and be courteous. And listen. I think that's huge because, if you can get in front of some top brass, then it's safe to say they're extremely busy and their time will be limited. Their words will count. They've been through a lot and will give you some great advice in the little time they have. So I think that's pretty crucial. That's important in life, too. To just listen. Be respectful, be sure to ask questions, and make an impression, too. It also goes without saying, follow up. Stay in touch and appreciate the connection. Touch base once in a while and share what you're doing. Networking is also a skill. All these things, combined with raw talent, will help you to go the distance. BI

To see Eitan Chitayat's work, please visit http://breaking.in

ALAN BUCHANAN
ASSOCIATE CREATIVE DIRECTOR
APPLE
CUPERTINO

Interviewed at Wieden+Kennedy, New York.

What do you look for in a student book? And what impresses you?

I look for a clean, simple thought that is communicated quickly and without unnecessary, unrelated frills or decoration. I see a lot of books where it seems like there is so much effort put into trying to make the ad funny, or surprising, or different, that the point of the ad is lost.

In particular, I seem to see a lot of long-copy ads that are guilty of being somewhat self-indulgent in this way. The copy can be really funny, but if you have to read through a whole page to actually get an inkling of the point—or if the copy takes on a voice that is inconsistent with the brand—you may have lost the interest of the audience, wasted a lot of time, and/or actually damaged the product you're trying to build.

Do you think long copy is important in a student book?

Yeah, definitely. It's a chance for the writer to show his ability to capture the brand voice. And it gives the art director a chance to demonstrate how he would design something when there is more to consider than finding a place to put the logo.

But when you're making a book, you should think very carefully about how those long-copy ads play off the rest of your work and how they influence the pacing of the book. I just saw a great book today and the last ad campaign was just a simple visual solution. By then I had already looked through a variety of ads, some that demanded more attention than others, and I was ready for something quick and easy. That was nice; he paced it really well.

Do you like to see things that aren't ads?

Definitely, yeah. I think Kevin [Proudfoot, ECD of W+K NY at the time] once hired a writer here and he had great work, but the most interesting parts of the book, he told me, were the scans from a sketchbook of his which were just doodles and miscellaneous ideas and random thoughts. One of the thoughts was the concept for branding Republican peanut butter.

"VARIETY OF TONE AND VARIETY OF SUBJECT MATTER."

And if you're an art director, bringing examples of design that you've done shows your breadth there; or if you dabbled in photography. Or, there's a guy who came in today, and he was in a band, and just the fact that he was in a band at one point, and he played in Athens, Georgia, and hung out with Mike Mills from REM, gave him an interesting story, other than just being a guy whose focus was solely on advertising. So it's sort of nice to see that other stuff. You have to have advertising in there, obviously, but it's the other stuff that sets you apart from everyone else.

Do you think you can get a job with just sketches, or do you think the work has to be finished and comped up?

For an art director, no. But for a writer, I think maybe you could.

Do you have any tips or guidance that you would give someone who's just starting to put together a book or trying to get a job?

I'm thinking back on what I did when I got a job, and I think if there was anything in the way I did my book that helped me out, it was that it didn't look like other books that I had seen. I didn't design it to be different just to be different; the design came out of the specific demands of the work. I had a campaign where the copy was organically placed within the environment of the ad—the headlines were on a newspaper someone was holding—and the ads looked better and were more legible when printed at full size. Also, when you looked at the ads together as a campaign, their colors complemented each other and made the campaign look more cohesive. So instead of simply placing one ad on each page, to maximize their size, or putting them all on one page, to show how they worked together, I did

both. I designed a book where each page folded out into an extra-large accordion page so you could see the ads together in their entirety, yet the book wasn't obscenely cumbersome either. The design of the book was unique and stood out, but it was designed in a way that served the demands of the campaign.

But in general, the thing I like to see in a student book is smart, maybe dense, but still elegantly simple ads. Ads where it doesn't seem like you have to wade through so much information to get the point.

It needs to be quicker.

Yeah, I saw another book once that was—and these are things not to do, I guess—the whole book was just sarcastic, frat humor. Every single ad was the same thing. So, it goes without saying, but it's a good idea to try to get a variety of voices within the ads. Like something sort of serious and smart, and something that's just sort of pleasurably ridiculous. Variety of tone and variety of subject matter.

Cool. Thank you.

Are you going to send me a transcript so I can sign off on it?

No. 🄱🄸

To see Alan Buchanan's work, please visit http://breaking.in

DAVID OAKLEY
CO-FOUNDER &
CHIEF CREATIVE OFFICER
BOONEOAKLEY
CHARLOTTE

What do you look for in a student book? And what impresses you?

Looking at a student's book is kind of like porn. It's hard to describe what you like, but you know it when you see it. I look for ideas. Also I look for unique ways of looking at things. Approaching a problem from a different angle. And one thing that I don't seem to see anymore is long, well-crafted copy. I'm really getting tired of visual solution executions.

How important is finish? If ideas are the most important thing, can sketches be enough? Do you look at physical books anymore, or is it all websites?

Mostly I look at students' websites or the occasional PDF that is sent. Finish is nice, but I think it's a waste of time to make a half-baked idea look nice.

How important is writing? Do you need to see long copy?

As a writer myself, I think that the craft of copywriting is falling by the wayside. I hardly ever see well-written long-copy ads in student work. I've heard it said that nobody reads copy. That's not true. I do.

"I HARDLY EVER SEE WELL-WRITTEN LONG-COPY ADS IN STUDENT WORK."

What do you think of showing work that is not advertising?

I love seeing photography from art directors. I like seeing things that aren't advertising. Sometimes seeing something completely different that has nothing at all to do with an ad shows a level of creativity that you don't see in their work. I don't want to look at a whole portfolio of their art, or read their whole journal, but a little look at their real personality is sometimes helpful. It could be the tiebreaker that says hire this guy over the other guy.

Do you have any other advice for a student or junior trying to get into the business?

Talk to as many people in the business as possible. Go on lots of interviews. Even if there is no job available. You'll meet people who will tell you about other people to meet. This is a very small business.

Keep trying. Keep knocking on doors. If you want a job bad enough, you'll get one. [BI]

To see David Oakley's work, please visit http://breaking.in

**GERRY GRAF
FOUNDER
BARTON F. GRAF 9000
NEW YORK**

What do you look for in a student book? And what impresses you?

The first thing I look for is campaign ideas. It's like the first filter. Not just a lot of one-shot-y things, or guerrilla tactics, or this and that. Just a bigger idea. And then I look for people who don't think the way I think. I like to look at an ad and not really be able to figure out how the person came up with it. I mean, a lot of times, you still see the same crap… like you see a lot of toothpaste ads with a lot of white people because it makes things really white. I love seeing ads that I like but not understanding what wavelength that person is on. So, odd thinking, I guess.

"I LOVE SEEING ADS THAT I LIKE BUT NOT UNDERSTANDING WHAT WAVELENGTH THAT PERSON IS ON."

Do you think that the book needs to be comped up, or if the ideas are good enough, then are sketches enough?

Well, if the ideas are awesome, it doesn't matter. I've never seen one with every single ad that's just like pure gold, you know? [Jeff] Kling's book is famous, you can just tell like you want to work with that type of person, but there's got to be a certain level of finish and, today, there's no real excuse for not putting something together, as opposed to some drawings and scribbles. But I have a problem with books that are finished too much. I've gone to portfolio nights and people have books and their ads look better than some finished ads here. Like they spent five thousand dollars to make them look great. It seems that they should have put more time into their ideas rather than trying to get by on good looks and stuff.

Do you think long copy is important for a writer and even for an art director to show that they can lay it out?

I am more interested in the bigger conceptual idea, but when I am hiring a writer I read long copy and I need to know that they're writers and not just, I guess, copywriters. I worked with Josh Denberg at Goodby and he's the greatest copywriter I've ever met. He would write 1000-word blocks of copy and I would want to read it. And if you can approach it like that and you're a writer...I just need to know you're a writer, not just an ad guy.

Or [Jeff] Kling's manifesto for Miller High Life. It's fantastic, you know? So, I mean, those are high standards but…

What do you think about seeing things in a student book that aren't ads? Like art or other writing or photography, or just things that aren't ads?

If it's good, I'd like to see it. It shows that you're talented, especially if you're hiring a junior, just trying to see some creative talent, even if they go to school for two years or no years, or whatever, it's like you're trying to see some spark of talent in the mush that is usually a student book. So I don't mind it. I don't like if it's crap. So if it's just extra crap, on top of crappy ads...but if it's good, smart stuff like good writing, or good design from an art director, or a student film, something like that. It shows that you have talent. It works.

How did you get into the industry initially?

I was a stock broker when I graduated from college. I wrote for a comedy review at Notre Dame. I went to the University of Notre Dame and I loved doing

that. So I kind of had a sit-down with myself and I wanted to wake up each morning and want to do what my job was. And I thought back to what my favorite thing to do was and it was writing for that review. So I screwed around with pilots and all that kind of stuff, and it didn't go anywhere and somebody said, "You should try advertising." So I took a class in LA, some night class with some guy who used to work at Chiat, and I put a horrible portfolio together. It was horrible, and I showed it to everybody in Los Angeles where I was living and couldn't get a job. And then one guy liked one ad out of the twelve that I had and he pushed me a little and then he had a friend in New York who was hiring at Saatchi and they hired me. And I've told the story before, but I found my first book when I was moving a couple of years ago, and it's just dreadful, but that's why I don't...I never look for a perfect book because they rarely come by. You just try to see something, some kind of talent in there.

Do you have any tips for someone who's just starting out on how to put together a book or how to improve?

How to put together a book? Well, nowadays, you need a website. That's the easiest way to get somebody to look at your work. That's not the best way. To present your work, it would be great to sit down with the creative director and have the actual ads and be there to talk through everything. But I think the big thing about getting a job isn't how your book looks, or how you put together the book, or do you have a website or a disk, or whatever. The hard thing is getting somebody to look at it. I mean look around us—see this? All of this stuff, except for my kids' pictures, are people's books— people's lives, right? My advice is to keep calling, and calling, and calling, and calling, and don't ever worry if you're bothering somebody because I have a guy who works for me now, who hounded me once a week for about a year and a half. And he kept working on his book, and working on his book, and working on his book, and then I hired him. So, I would say, put something together to show your ideas, but be relentless when it comes to getting your work in front of somebody because that's the biggest thing—is to get somebody to stop and look at your work. And if it's really good, if there's a couple of things in there, then I'd take the book off the ground and I bring it over to my creative manager and I say, "Call this person in." So it's a bitch. It sucks. It's really hard. BI

To see Gerry Graf's work, please visit http://breaking.in

MIRA KADDOURA
FOUNDER/CREATIVE DIRECTOR
RED+CO
PORTLAND

Interviewed at Wieden+Kennedy Portland.

What do you look for in a student book? And what impresses you?

A voice. Someone with a point of view I haven't seen before. And craft. Someone who pays attention to crafting their work. It so obvious when a person loves what they do. They pay attention to detail, to type, to words, to proportions, to how things come together, and so on. You know, old school.

How important is finish? Can sketches be enough?

Initially, sketches are fine, but to really sell an idea you have to bring it to life as best you can. A great idea, poorly executed, is a total miss.

Do you mostly just look at websites now or paper books?

Mostly websites. I have to say though, when I do get a book and it's beautifully crafted and where I can see the art direction and read the copy at the size it was printed, I get pretty excited.

What do you think about long copy? Do writers need it?

You have to have long copy. You see so many writers nowadays that just don't write anymore. Writing and campaigns show me thinking. And that, more than anything, is what I'm looking for.

What do you think about showing work that isn't advertising?

Yes, please. So many books look alike. Show me what you're passionate about. Show me what you're going to bring to the table. Show me what gets you excited and, most importantly, how you think.

"…DON'T TRY TO COPY WHAT EVERY OTHER STUDENT IS DOING."

Do you have any other advice?

Put yourself out there. Meet people. As many as you can. Take them to coffee. Pick their brains. Try to learn what you can from them. Who knows, maybe if they like who you are or what you've got they'll either hire you, hook you up with people they think might hire you, or just keep you in mind for later if nothing's open right now. I think the biggest piece of advice is don't try to copy what every other student is doing. Do your own thing. And show me how passionate you are about whatever it is you do. People are attracted to people who inspire them. Remember that and you'll be fine. BI

To see Mira Kaddoura's work, please visit http://breaking.in

TED ROYER
CHIEF CREATIVE OFFICER
DROGA5
NEW YORK

What do you look for in a student book? And what impresses you?

What impresses me most are smart business ideas, not just funny ads. If a student can show that he or she has thought about the real business needs of that company, then I'll know they have the kind of brain that can do exciting work. It's one thing to be clever and communicate something well, it's entirely another to show me you can push a client to change the way they do business or to truly change a consumer's behavior.

What I don't look for is work that has already been produced, unless it's great. No CD gives a crap that you got something made unless it's exactly the type of work you want to make. I want to see where you want to go, not where you've been.

In the best interview with students I ever had, two guys walked in and put their book in front of me. I opened it. The first idea was a huge, business-changing idea. The second was almost as good. I closed the book and offered them a job right then and there.

How important is finish? If ideas are the most important thing, can sketches be enough? Do you look at physical books anymore, or is it all websites?

Depends on what job you're going for, but again, I want to see thinking and intention. Having said that, the polish I see now in books is really high. And I almost never see physical books. It's all websites and iPads. But sketches can definitely be enough. I hired one team because they had a website to which they added one idea a day that they would crudely sketch up. Sometimes the ideas were crap, sometimes great, sometimes just ridiculous. But the whole thing was charming, and again, showed me their passion.

How important is writing? Do you need to see long copy?

I don't need to see anything except great thinking. Too many students think they need to put in long copy to show they can do it, and that usually results in a mediocre long-copy campaign. "Ticked that box!" Yeah, ticked it with mediocrity that brings down your whole book. Just put forth the best ideas and don't worry about the range of execution styles. A creative director who wants that "range" is no different from a client who wants to see a lot of ideas just for the sake of seeing a lot of ideas.

What do you think of showing work that is not advertising?

Perfectly fine, and in some cases fantastic. Again, I want to know you and what kind of work you're dying to do. I pick directors not just on the basis of what they've done but on what they are dying to do—that way you know you'll get passion. Where's your passion?

"I WANT TO KNOW YOU AND WHAT KIND OF WORK YOU'RE DYING TO DO."

One guy I hired had a technical blueprint of Noah's Ark in his book. He tried to fit in every animal. It was the size of a monster cruise ship. Had nothing to do with advertising, but the thinking was hilarious. Another showed me a book he had made for his mom on her 65th birthday. Made me feel like a bad son, it was so good. The point is, I got to see what these guys were capable of when they were truly passionate.

Do you have any other advice for a student or junior trying to get into the business?

It's tough, I know. Cold calling or writing isn't effective. Making some attention-getting mailer may be funny but also may just be annoying. Persistence and focus on your goal—there's no substitute for that.

Keep your head up. Just because you don't have a job and the guy next to you just got one doesn't mean you suck, it just means he got a job. I stressed so much in school my last quarter because other people were getting jobs that I would wake up at 5 a.m. and go running. I don't run. I hate running. But I thought someone's gain was my loss. And looking back, I should have realized what they were doing didn't matter—all I really had to do was stay focused on my goal. BI

To see Ted Royer's work, please visit http://breaking.in

MARK SCHRUNTEK
FREELANCE CREATIVE DIRECTOR
NEW YORK

What do you look for in a student book? And what impresses you?

I think it's always going to come down to good ideas. And the biggest challenge is to differentiate a good idea from a great one. Sometimes it's the smallest details that somebody actually took the time to figure out to get to the best way to really communicate something. A great idea has to have everything: a good strategy and a great execution that really nails it. So you have to have it all.

What do you think about finish? Can sketches be enough?

If you're an art director, it's probably wise to finish things. There are a lot of mediocre books out there, and if you have great ideas, those will shine, and people will notice them, but if you can show your craft, you're going to be much more valuable.

And, for a writer, what about copy? Is that important to have?

Yes. I wouldn't suggest that you make a whole book out of long-copy ads. But, eventually, it will be important. You're going to get stuck with a radio assignment. Whether or not you want to do it, that is going to happen. You're not always going to be able to use visuals when you're in the real world. I don't think long copy is a mandatory, but it is important and it is a good skill to have. You just better make sure that the copy is really, really good, if you're going to put something like that in your book. Creative directors tend to look through things quickly. They will click through the website or flip through the pages extremely quickly, and they may not even read that copy, so you've got to make them want to read it, and once they do, you don't want them to be angry that they did.

What do you think about showing work that isn't advertising?

I think it is important on some level for a creative person to have multiple outlets. I think you shouldn't be completely married to the world of advertising. And if you have other interests, I think that is part of what you are bringing to the table as a creative person. To know that you have all those things and that you can take those experiences and you can apply that to your advertising work as well is good. The people who lead more interesting lives may have the better portfolio. That's not scientifically proven.

"A GREAT IDEA HAS TO HAVE EVERYTHING..."

The first thing I'm going to look through is your advertising work, and if you have some really interesting hobbies, and other things that you're doing, I want to know about them. That's the good thing about creative people too is they have so many interests, and you find musicians and artists, and people doing all sorts of things that are related to advertising. For me, that extra work is secondary. But, some agencies are all about hiring people who aren't in advertising. And don't have any ads in their book. I'm just not from that school.

Do you have any tips for someone on how to put together a book or get into the business?

Putting together a portfolio now is very different to when I was doing it. It's not just about print. They do want to see a lot more digital and, let's just call it, "360" thinking. And the way that you go about approaching a brand or a client is bigger now. Showing that you can do more than just a print ad is helpful. That said, I still think that you need to show that single thought: the campaign idea. And, if you can show me that in print, and then how it blows out from there, then you have big thinking there.

As far as getting into the business, I think it's about connections. You never know who can open up a door. You can start with headhunters. Find out who the in-house recruiters are at the different agencies and contact them directly. Be aggressive and interested at the same time. Let a place know that you want to work there. I walked into Mother one time. It was raining and I walked in soaking wet and said, "I love the work you guys are doing and I want a job here," and they said, "We're not hiring, but we are looking for freelance," and they ended up asking me to come in for a couple of weeks.

Knowing who you are talking to, the people, the agency, and the work that they do, and why you want to work at a particular agency, are all really important. BI

To see Mark Schruntek's work, please visit http://breaking.in

CRAIG ALLEN
CREATIVE DIRECTOR
WIEDEN+KENNEDY
PORTLAND

What do you look for in a student book? And what impresses you?

It sounds generic, but I just look for good ads. I've heard about people getting hired for all kinds of odd reasons like writing a word on a rock, or baking cookies with notes on them, but all I look for is ads. I think it's good to add a little personality to a book for sure, but if the book relies on a gimmick, that's probably not a good sign.

How important is finish? If ideas are the most important thing, can sketches be enough? Do you look at physical books anymore, or is it all websites?

Before I understood advertising I didn't understand advertising. Two summers before I graduated, I took my book and went to California. My book was 100 percent hand drawn with colored pencil. I was told, "If the idea is great it doesn't matter." The recruiters I met with looked at me with an expression that was equal parts confused and embarrassed. They thought it was cute and didn't take me seriously. I'm not saying I had great ads at the time by any means, in fact I think I was far

from it, but I doubt it would have mattered. The sad fact is that you have to have good ideas and present them in a somewhat polished manner so people will take them seriously. I think you can have some ideas in sketch form, but you should also be able to show you know how to use a computer in some capacity.

"FIND OUT WHICH AGENCIES ARE DOING THE ADS YOU LOVE AND START THERE."

I prefer physical books, but I also know that most creative directors and recruiters don't have a lot of time. I think it's good to have both. Maybe send a link to your website and offer up the option to ship them a book. The one great thing about a physical book is that it sits on a desk as a reminder that I need to look at it. A link can easily be lost in the email shuffle.

How important is writing? Do you need to see long copy?

I think if you're good at writing long copy then yes, you should include it. Whatever makes you look the best. I don't think it's a mandatory by any means. I was always told you had to have long copy in your book. I put in one campaign and everyone told me it was boring and I should take it out. Lesson learned.

What do you think of showing work that is not advertising?

I think that's fine to put in a book to help you stand out, but ads have to be the hero. If you have 95 percent awesome photography or artwork and five percent ads then maybe you should go be a photographer or artist. You have to show you can do ads. Then you can do whatever you want.

Do you have any other advice for a student or junior trying to get into the business?

Obviously, a lot of getting into advertising is luck. I was so stressed out putting my final book together that I forgot the most important ingredient: my name. The fact that I got a job at all is mind-blowingly amazingly lucky to say the least. I would start there and say first things first, put your name on your book. I would also say that you should look at what ads you respond to. Which ads you wished you did. Find out who did those ads and write directly to them. Find out which agencies are doing the ads you love and start there. Work every angle. Someone will be willing to talk to you. I promise. BI

To see Craig Allen's work, please visit http://breaking.in

ANDY FACKRELL
EXECUTIVE CREATIVE DIRECTOR
DDB NEW ZEALAND
AUCKLAND

What do you look for in a student book? And what impresses you?

Firstly, it shouldn't look like a student book. Not meaning to sound derogatory, but the schools are always about making someone hire-able. Of course, that's the aim in all this, but I think you won't stand a chance if ten kids from the same course rock in with slight variations on a theme. You've got to go with what shows your personality, not your school's.

How important is finish? If ideas are the most important thing, can sketches be enough? Do you look at physical books anymore, or is it all websites?

Mostly it's websites, and I haven't seen a physical book for a year. And really, that has to be the case these days. Some kind of leave-behinds are always useful. A young Dutch team we hired left funny little paper sculptures that sat on my desk for a few months, before actually hiring them. So '80s of them.

As always, it's the ideas that will be remembered, not the slickness of a blog, or the shininess of the portfolio. Creating a blog is a trend for juniors up to creative directors. And dangerous for employers. I mistrust them, as they are disposable in a way, and loose in their truth. People can post their colleague's work that they admire, somehow implying it's their own. I've seen it happen on all levels. As my friend says, you're a creative, not a curator. Show me your ideas.

How important is writing? Do you need to see long copy?

Definitely, you can see how disciplined young people are by actually working through the process of writing an ad or website. Writers are more important now than ever before. But it's a bit different than the tortured prose of the golden era of '80s D&AD. These days, agencies are more multifaceted, meaning less pretension in this particular craft. You will find a lot more nuts-and-bolts writing is needed, as well as poetry. But traditional long copy? A rarity.

"…IT SHOULDN'T LOOK LIKE A STUDENT BOOK."

What do you think of showing work that is not advertising?

It can [provoke a] wince—having peoples' souls displayed—so you have to be super careful showing personal work. It depends who you're talking to. I remember Kash Sree and I being interviewed through video conference by Dan Wieden and all his creative directors. He asked that very question. Kash had a very obscure book project that made him, and by association, me, look pretty smart. The obscure always worked with Dan.

Do you have any other advice for a student or junior trying to getinto the business?

By all means be out there and original, but also be professional. Find out everything you can about the people you meet. The worst thing, and it has happened a lot here at 180, is when they have only a vague idea of your agency's work. I'm not saying they need to list all the work on my personal reel, and reread scripts back at you, but a little flattery never hurts. BI

To see Andy Fackrell's work, please visit http://breaking.in

TOYGAR BAZARKAYA
EXECUTIVE CREATIVE DIRECTOR
BBDO
NEW YORK

What do you look for in a student portfolio? And what impresses you?

What impresses me is when you take on tough problems and solve them. If a student came and showed me great work on Gillette, that would impress me much more than great work on Nike. Great work on a tattoo shop is not as impressive as a washing detergent. They are harder problems to solve. Oftentimes you get hung up on the brand that you love and you get yourself in trouble because you're not as good as the actual work that is out there. So you do yourself a favor if you take things on that are wrong in advertising, rather than trying to improve on things that are already good.

How important is finish in a student book? Could sketches be enough?

It depends if you are an art director or copywriter. And for art directors it doesn't change if you're a student or you've been in the business for 20 years. Attention to detail, good art direction, typography, layout is just as important for a student as it is if you've been in the business for a long time. I have a strong point of view there. I don't like art directors who are not art directors. They have great ideas but they shouldn't call themselves art directors. It's a craft. And that's the tough thing: you have to be as good at creating ideas as you have to be in your craft. As hard as it is for copywriters to write an awesome long-copy ad, art directors have to be good at their craft. Not everyone has that skill.

So, for writers' books, polish is less important?

Yes.

Sketches could be enough?

Absolutely.

And do you look at paper books anymore, or is it all websites?

You don't really have a choice anymore. I'm looking at a lot of online books. It's actually pretty convenient. The one thing is: I still like being able to touch and hold the physical book but you don't get that much and it's fine.

For a writer, how important is copy? Do you need to see a long-copy campaign?

Not necessarily long copy but the writing has to be great. There is a craft to writing, and even if it's not long copy, you see if someone can write just from headlines. Just to see visual solutions in a writer's book is not satisfying. Although he might have come up with the visuals and the ideas, I want to see writing in a writer's book. But it doesn't need to be long copy. It's a weird feeling looking at a writer's book with almost no copy at all, and I have seen that.

What do you think about putting work in a book that is not advertising at all?

I love it. There was someone I hired because I saw some ideas that I thought could change the whole business. They were groundbreaking ideas that didn't have anything to do with ads as we know them. And, oftentimes, you can see their thinking better. With print and TV, a lot of the time, we're talking about executions, and they are great ideas but within that format. And when you go beyond that, you're talking about bigger ideas.

And what about personal work that isn't advertising. Like art, photography, journal writing, short stories, personal projects...

I think that's really important to know if they do that stuff. If you're capable of keeping that up, it says a lot about you as a person and how passionate you are about creative things. What we're doing is hard enough, and so when I see art directors painting or writers who are writing books or plays that's the most impressive thing for me because I have a hard time finding time to even play soccer or golf.

Do you have any other advice for someone who is trying to break into the business?

One thing I notice: sometimes people put something in their book just to prove that they can do it. I see books with a mediocre website. And the person puts it in to say, "I've got online work too." But it's not good and it hurts them.

With the book, not only are the pieces themselves important, but when you take a step back, it says a lot about their creative judgment in evaluating what is a good and a bad idea. So I'm going through a lot of books right now, and it makes me nervous to see 10 good pieces and five mediocre ones. I know we've all done it [mediocre work]—not everything you do is going to be brilliant. But then to put it in your book says something about your judgment. Never make the mistake of putting something in your book just to prove that you can do it. It doesn't prove anything. Other than that, make it easy to go through. Sometimes it can be really difficult to go through books—especially the online books. Don't try to be clever; make it easy to go through. Don't waste our time. BI

To see Toygar Bazarkaya's work, please visit http://breaking.in

**TONY GRANGER
GLOBAL CCO
YOUNG & RUBICAM
NEW YORK**

How can students prepare to get into the industry? How can they improve?

It used to be that you had to look to the past to do well in this business. But now, you not only have to have this historical foundation, you have to have an eye on the future. A view of it. The people who succeed are naturally inquisitive. They hang onto their childlike enthusiasm about the business. They have an instinctive feel for innovation and an innate comfort with technology.

"SOME OF THE BEST MENTORS YOU'LL HAVE ARE PEOPLE YOU'LL NEVER MEET."

I think it's also important, if you're a student, to thoroughly dissect the media landscape today and know what's happening—who's doing what, which agencies are the best, what kind of work is getting the accolades, what people are buzzing about on blogs. Schools can teach you a lot, but you've got to have a natural passion for the work and lots of motivation.

Some people say the idea is the most important thing. That's the only thing they care about. Where does craft fit in? Are they both important? Is it enough to have the big ideas, or do you also have to have the craft as well?

Both are important, absolutely. But you have to be careful about what you think craft means. People often think craft means "beauty." But it's really about having the talent to create something completely appropriate to the idea. Is it right to use 16mm film, or more appropriate to shoot with a hand-held? Does the work call for elaborate typography, or are you going to spray words on a wall? So you have to have both lots of knowledge and great instincts. Craft is the window to an idea, not the wallpaper around it.

It seems like it is getting harder and harder to get into the business. What does it take to stand out at that level?

You need to be enthusiastic. Passionate. Your work needs to be brilliant. But maybe the most important thing, really, is to have a wide-eyed enthusiasm about our business. That's what's going to make the difference.

Is it important to have a mentor, and if so, how can a student hook up with someone who's already in the business?

The easy answer is that you need to find people you want to learn from. It's important for people to have many mentors throughout their careers. But then, there's a second piece to it. Some of the best mentors you'll have are people you'll never meet. They may not even be alive anymore. I've always drawn my best inspiration from popular culture. My mentors have always been artists and musicians and filmmakers and writers—some of whom were long gone before I was born. The thing is, great creatives know great advertising, but they don't stop there. They reach beyond the industry and immerse themselves in all kinds of ideas and ways of achieving your craft. If you're only looking at advertising, the work gets too insular and self-referential. I'm telling you, that's a deadly formula. Learn what you can from your cultural heroes.

What do you think of putting things in the portfolio that aren't ads?

A must. Our business is about content today, and it has many forms and faces. It's digital to the core. So, your portfolio has to reflect the industry. That might mean you'll want to put in ideas for movies, or new products, or a concert tour, or video game. But not gratuitously. You want to show that you have a wide and varied creative palette, but the important thing is to show ideas that are so strong, they seem inevitable for the brand.

I just want to ask you a little more about that because it's interesting. What do you see as the future of advertising? Is it content and entertainment, or a wide range of things?

Absolutely. Technology has empowered people to engage with the content they want to, on their own time, and in formats of their choosing. So to get noticed and to engage, you need to have ideas that can move across channels. Our job is to create work that is irresistible and draws people to it, because then they will become the most powerful advocates for the work or brand.

Do you think it's a good idea for a student or a junior to put those kinds of new ideas—non-interruptive ideas—in a portfolio?

Yes, yes, and yes. If your portfolio doesn't have these new forms of content, with a digital underpinning, you won't be able to function in the industry today. It's that plain and simple.

But do you think it's also important to have the basic print ads...?

Of course! Print is still relevant. Television is still relevant. The 30-second spot is still thriving. Magazine, newspaper, radio ads are still produced every day. New media hasn't killed the old at all. We are just lucky today to have so many other ways of connecting to consumers. This has to be the most exciting time in our business since that box called TV was invented. [BI]

To see Tony Granger's work, please visit http://breaking.in

**RICK BOYKO
FOUNDING MEMBER
SPARKSTARTERS
PHILADELPHIA**

Interviewed at VCU Brandcenter while Rick was director.

What do you look for in a student book? And what impresses you?

What I have always looked for in any book are consistent conceptual and strategic solutions to legitimate business problems. No longer can books be filled with fun, little, easy-to-do, local-business print executions. We challenge Brandcenter students to take on real brands with difficult problems as assignments. Then they have to build out communications across whatever mediums best come in contact with the target, which in almost all cases include or begin with a digital, social component. Any book that does not demonstrate the ability to think about real brands strategically across multiple mediums will most likely not even get a viewing by most agencies today.

How important is finish? If ideas are the most important thing, can sketches be enough? Do you look at actual books anymore, or is it all websites?

Execution is still very important because craft still matters. You have to be able to demonstrate that you are not just someone who can think strategically and conceptually but you can also execute. So, while ideas are king, being able to bring them to life is just as important. While most books today are first viewed on a website, I still believe having a tangible one is valuable to bring the thinking to life and helpful in judging craft.

How important is copy? Do you need to see long-copy ads?

Given that most executions are found in many different mediums today, it is imperative to be able to demonstrate that you can engage and entertain an audience with smart communications that tell and build on a brand story. In fact, for some time now I have been a proponent of us not calling ourselves advertising people, or copywriters, or art directors, all of which are arcane terms that minimize and marginalize what we do. Instead I propose we begin to call ourselves "storytellers" in the service of brands. [This is] a much bigger and more descriptive term for what we do for brands across so many different mediums today.

What do you think of showing work that is not advertising?

Anything that helps bring who you are to life is worth including. In the end, no one hires a portfolio—they want to know how the person they are looking at thinks. So what other ways you express yourself and how diverse you and your interests are is important to demonstrate.

Do you have any other advice for a student or junior trying to get into the business?

This is an exciting time to enter the business because of the pace and speed which opportunities to help build and tell a brand story are changing. Yet most people looking for a job do so in a very pedestrian fashion. So when seeking a job, think about and approach it just as you would an assignment you'd be given. How do you make yourself stand out and stop someone who is inundated with people just like you trying to get their attention? You can demonstrate that you think in new ways by what you do to get a potential employer's attention. BI

VALDEAN KLUMP
COPYWRITER/PRODUCER
GOOGLE
SAN FRANCISCO

What do you look for in a student book? And what impresses you?

I look for a book that has a lot of good, realistic ideas. Pretty obvious, right?

"Good" is a given, of course, and fortunately advertising offers a million and one ways to make a good book. You can create clever print ads, shoot funny videos, build mind-bending websites, comp ridiculous outdoor billboards, record your own radio spots, or anything else you can think of—a mix of media is advisable, but good ideas are good ideas, period. So fill 'er up with goodness. And remove anything you're not into 100 percent. They say your book is only as good as the worst ad in it—it's a tired truism, but there's something to it.

Realism is a personal pet peeve of mine. Student books will often be filled with ideas that the client would never buy or that feel totally wrong for the brand. Be smart; go crazy, but be smart. And make extra sure that your digital ideas are realistic. Working at Google makes me especially sensitive to this one. Think about the constraints of the

Internet and work inside them. You can't click a button on "Snickers.com" and have a Snickers bar eject itself out of your optical drive—that would be a great idea if it were possible, but it's not. This is especially true for any idea relating to Facebook, which is a very locked-down platform. Maybe I'm being crotchety here, so please don't limit yourself...just be intelligent about it.

Finally, show a lot of work. A lot. Early in my advertising career, a creative director told me that he wouldn't hire anyone who had less than 10 campaigns of three ads each, meaning you should have 30 ads in your portfolio, minimum. Upon hearing this, my art director and I spent six weeks, 12 hours a day, doing nothing but Photoshopping print ads for every product we could think of. We finished with 15 to 16 campaigns we thought were good. We then showed these ads to everyone who would pay attention and asked them to pick their favorites—inevitably, everyone picked the same ads as the best—and we ended up with a pretty big book of over 30 ads. Creative directors love to see this kind of output. Quality in volume is a very attractive thing in a junior creative, because you can't spend all your time crafting one idea in this business. When you first get a brief, ideas should leap from your head onto the wall until it's covered.

As for what impresses me most—it's the ability to make things. More and more these days, young people are coming into the business able to shoot their own commercials, create websites, program games, take photos, make animations, build Facebook apps, and generally act as one-person ad agencies. This not only serves to intimidate the senior creatives, it makes the CDs salivate, because getting ideas off paper is at least as hard as getting them on paper in the first place, especially at smaller shops. Making stuff for little or no money is also useful for presentations, which, as you will learn, often feels like half the job. If you can make things, and make them well, you will never be unemployed.

How important is finish? If ideas are the most important thing, can sketches be enough? Do you look at actual books anymore, or is it all websites?

My temptation is to say "not very," but I think finish is becoming more important than it used to be. Software makes putting together ads easier than ever. Creating nice-looking type is no longer much of a chore. Quality photos are easy to take. This is the YouTube generation, after all.

"STUDENT BOOKS WILL OFTEN BE FILLED WITH IDEAS THAT THE CLIENT WOULD NEVER BUY OR THAT FEEL TOTALLY WRONG FOR THE BRAND."

That said, sketches are enough to get a job if they're good enough. That's what so great about the ad business—in theory you could spend two hours sketching nonstop on a pad of paper, walk into any agency in the world, and walk out with a job. In fact, if you put your ideas on a website, you might not even have to get out of your chair—the world will beat a path to your door. What other industry has this level of egalitarianism? It's not about experience, in the creative world it's about talent. For all its politics, advertising is a meritocracy, which explains a lot of its appeal to young people.

As for paper books versus websites, it's no competition: websites all the way. And the easier they are to find and the faster they get straight to your work, the better. Creative directors are busy and impatient people who don't want to spend any time thinking about what to click. My advice is to skip the fancy website and make your site one big cascade of work—easy to navigate, large images, videos that play on click, and the option to download one big PDF file that holds everything. Make viewing your brilliance effortless.

How important is copy? Do you need to see long-copy ads?

The ability to write a good headline will never go without a paycheck. Obviously this is true for copywriters but the same is true for art directors too—

ultimately, if you want to progress in your career, you'll have to be good at all parts of the ad-making process. So if you're an art director, you should be a passable writer, or at least unafraid of trying—the best art directors I've worked with have all been decent writers who occasionally blurt out something brilliant. It's like a good marriage—each partner has their responsibilities, but in a pinch, you have to be able to do everything. In the same vein, writers should also be good art directors. Creative advertising is a single skill set, and those who master all aspects of it are the only ones who get to become creative directors.

As for long copy: absolutely, yes. Long-copy print ads are the single easiest way for a copywriter to show that he or she can write. Art directors love long-copy ads too because laying them out in an appealing way is a fun exercise and makes a portfolio instantly look more respectable. It's win-win for everyone. If I have one piece of advice for budding copywriters, it's always to have multiple long-copy ads as the foundation for your portfolio.

What do you think of showing work that is not advertising? Things like art, journal writing, photography, hobbies, etc.?

By all means, yes. Although it's important, again, not to let anything slow down a creative director who is looking for your ad portfolio. But if you made a short film on YouTube or wrote a short story you're proud of, show it. Ultimately, very few of us in this business dream only of making ads. We want to create other things too, and there is zero danger in expressing that fact—in fact, it's a positive.

One word of advice, however; if you want a job as a copywriter, for example, I would advise you to call yourself a copywriter on your website, and not a filmmaker or a "creative genius" or anything other than a copywriter. Show dedication to the craft. It also helps to have a little information about yourself—some photographs, a short bio; agencies want to hire human beings.

Do you have any other advice for a student or junior trying to get into the business?

Remember that the advertising industry seeks out a specific skill set—the ability to make ads—and your

success and failure in this industry is not indicative of your creative talent as a whole. Do not be discouraged if you struggle to land a dream job. Do your best and keep your eyes open for any new opportunities that happen to come along. Every agency is different. And don't be afraid of taking risks with your career—your résumé is more resilient than you think.

Also, consider working overseas. Advertising is a global business, and working outside your home country is exciting. If you're fortunate enough to travel abroad, look up some local creative directors and send them a link to your portfolio before you arrive. You never know what might happen. I spent two years working in New Zealand because I shopped my portfolio around while traveling there. Career-wise, it was the best thing that ever happened to me.

Last but not least, practice presenting your work. This is especially true after you're hired. The ability to speak eloquently and confidently in support of your ideas is perhaps the most valuable skill in the entire business after the ideas themselves.

Good luck. BI

To see Valdean Klump's work, please visit http://breaking.in

DAN WIEDEN FOUNDER & CEO WIEDEN+KENNEDY PORTLAND

So, first question is—

Yes! First question.

—what do you look for in a student book? And what impresses you?

Well, I always like to see anybody's book, student or old-timer. I like to see the book before I meet the people because I'm too easily swayed by the personality. But what I look for in the book is that personality. I want to see if there's a voice there that's unique or an eye that sees the world a little bit differently, and has a unique sense of taste, and color, and all that kind of stuff. Or a way of talking to people that is unique to them. I think those traits make for much more interesting advertising or art. I really want to know more about who they are and what they've done, almost to get a sense of what their life experiences are.

So the personality and the voice are really important?

Right.

So a lot of people would say, "But don't you want a variety of voices, so that you can write for anything, or art-direct for anything?" How does that fit with what you just said?

I want a very specific voice and that's our job to make sure we can find some place that that works. When you take Nike, Nike has [many different voices]— primarily because they're appealing to so many subsets of an athletic audience. Tennis players are far different from runners, or basketball players. And all brands have some similar sort of latitude. Times when they're funny and times when they're more serious. So my passion is for the individual talent, and we'll find that place to plug it into.

How important is the finish of a book?

Well, for a writer, not at all. I mean, Jeff Kling can tell you, the book he sent me was a joke. It was all [sketches]—although he's a pretty damn good cartoonist—and it was extremely rough, but you could just feel the idea there. But I think when you look at the art side of the equation, you expect a little bit more of a sense of, "What are you capable of, and what's your aesthetic range, and what kind of finish do you feel more comfortable in?"

So for an art director you probably want to see some design sense?

Right.

And a good sense of finish?

Right. I still want to see the conceptual way you handle it visually. But also a range of finish would be really interesting.

But for a writer, not really important?

Not so much.

For a writer, how important is copy? A lot of people say, "I don't need to see long copy, I don't even have time to read it. So don't show me that." And other people say, "If you're a writer, I need to see that you can write." What do you think?

I think they're both right. I love people who can take me along and keep my attention over a long period of time, and that's a whole different kind of personality, but an important skill. Because we're not always doing print ads around here. We're also doing films and a bunch of other stuff. But you also have to be [concise]. There's something about that ability to boil it down into a few words that you can't get out of your brain—that stick with you and somehow resonate. That's incredibly important as well. So if you find both of those talents in one person, that's really great. But you don't, always. They both have a place.

So the quality is most important, and if they can keep you interested for some quantity then that's a bonus, is that about right?

Well there's so many different ways of saying what's in a fortune cookie, you know? And if you're going to write short, it better be powerful and memorable. And if you're going to write long, it better be holding your attention. And however you do that is fine with me as long as you keep my attention. Say something I tend to remember.

What do you think about putting things in a book that aren't ads at all?

I think that's fine. I think you need to realize that in a majority of cases, these things aren't going to get looked at in depth. So you'd better have some things that are more potent, and quick, and well edited. And then if you want to add a layer underneath that, I think that's really great. If you want to show me poetry, I'm fine with that. If you want to show me an oil painting, I'd love to see that. But odds are, what I'm going to be using that talent for won't be quite that wide ranging, but I love to see the background.